VOYAGES
IN ENGLISH
GRAMMAR AND WRITING

7

Patricia Healey, I.H.M.
B.A., Immaculata University
M.A., Temple University
20 years teaching; 20 years in administration

Irene Kervick, I.H.M.
B.A., Immaculata University
M.A., Villanova University
46 years teaching

Anne B. McGuire, I.H.M.
B.A., Immaculata University
M.A., Villanova University
M.A., Immaculata University
*16 years teaching; 14 years as elementary
principal; 10 years staff development*

Adrienne Saybolt, I.H.M.
B.A., Immaculata University
Pennsylvania State Board of Education,
professional certification
M.A., St. John's University
40 years teaching

LOYOLA PRESS.

Loyola Press has made every effort to locate the copyright holders for the cited works used in this publication and to make full acknowledgment for their use. In the case of any omissions, the publisher will be pleased to make suitable acknowledgments in future editions.
Continued on page 567.

Cover Design: Think Book Works   Cover Artist: Pablo Bernasconi
Interior Design: Kathy Greenholdt/Loyola Press
Art Director: Judine O'Shea/Loyola Press
Editor: Catherine T. Marcic Joyce/Loyola Press

ISBN-13: 978-0-8294-2821-6
ISBN-10: 0-8294-2821-6

LOYOLA PRESS.
3441 N. Ashland Avenue
Chicago, Illinois 60657
(800) 621-1008
www.loyolapress.com

16 17 18 Webcrafters 10 9 8 7 6 5 4

Contents

PART 1 Grammar

PART 2 Written and Oral Communication

How many ways can you write the same sentence?

PART 1 GRAMMAR

SECTION ONE
Nouns

1.1 Singular and Plural Nouns

A **noun** is a name word. A singular noun names one person, place, thing, or idea. A plural noun names more than one person, place, thing, or idea.

Add -*s* to most nouns to form the plurals.

SINGULAR	PLURAL
writer	writers
canyon	canyons

SINGULAR	PLURAL
brick	bricks
hope	hopes

Add -*es* to form the plurals of nouns ending in *s, x, z, ch,* and *sh.*

SINGULAR	PLURAL
dress	dresses
church	churches
princess	princesses

SINGULAR	PLURAL
box	boxes
flash	flashes
march	marches

Form the plurals of nouns ending in *y* preceded by a vowel by adding -*s.*

SINGULAR	PLURAL
toy	toys
birthday	birthdays

SINGULAR	PLURAL
attorney	attorneys
guy	guys

Form the plurals of nouns ending in *y* preceded by a consonant by changing the *y* to *i* and adding -*es.*

SINGULAR	PLURAL
lily	lilies
colony	colonies

SINGULAR	PLURAL
baby	babies
party	parties

Some plural nouns are not formed by adding -*s* or -*es.* Check a dictionary to find the correct plural form.

SINGULAR	PLURAL
woman	women
ox	oxen
tooth	teeth
mouse	mice
congressman	congressmen

SINGULAR	PLURAL
trout	trout
swine	swine
Chinese	Chinese
corps	corps
moose	moose

EXERCISE 1 Identify each noun. Tell whether it is singular or plural.

1. Soccer is a popular sport in many countries.
2. Soccer is called football outside of the United States.
3. The sport was invented in England.
4. The World Cup is enjoyed by many all over the world.
5. There are 11 players on a team.
6. To play the sport, teams need two nets and a ball.
7. The goalkeeper tries to keep the ball from entering the net.
8. A player moves the ball primarily with his or her legs or head.
9. Many children play soccer at their schools or in parks.
10. Many young enthusiasts practice with just a ball in a yard.

EXERCISE 2 Complete each sentence with the plural form of the noun or nouns in parentheses.

1. Our school has _____ (team) in several _____ (sport).
2. Every year _____ (child) sign up for their favorite sporting _____ (activity).
3. Many _____ (boy) and _____ (girl) play on the teams.
4. _____ (Teammate) become _____ (friend) in and out of school.
5. The _____ (coach) are _____ (teacher) and parents.
6. The school's soccer team practices on _____ (Wednesday) and _____ (Friday) for 50 _____ (minute).
7. The team has won several local _____ (championship), and it doesn't have any _____ (loss) so far this year.
8. _____ (Bus) take _____ (adult) and _____ (child) to games at other schools.
9. Several _____ (series) of important _____ (match) are starting next week.
10. All our _____ (hope) and _____ (wish) are for many _____ (victory) for the team.

APPLY IT NOW

Write a three-sentence note to a friend, describing a recent school activity. Include a singular noun in the first sentence and a plural noun in the second sentence. Use both singular and plural nouns in the third sentence.

Tech Tip You can send this note as an e-mail.

1.2 More Singular and Plural Nouns

If a noun ends in *o* preceded by a vowel, form the plural by adding *-s*.

SINGULAR	PLURAL
trio	trios

SINGULAR	PLURAL
rodeo	rodeos

If a noun ends in *o* preceded by a consonant, form the plural by adding *-es*. There are exceptions to this rule. Check a dictionary.

SINGULAR	PLURAL
tomato	tomatoes

SINGULAR	PLURAL
echo	echoes

EXCEPTIONS:	
piano	pianos
zero	zeros or zeroes
alto	altos

EXCEPTIONS:	
burro	burros
solo	solos
soprano	sopranos

For most nouns ending in *f* or *fe*, form the plurals by adding *-s*. For some nouns, however, you must change the *f* or *fe* to *ves*. Always check a dictionary.

SINGULAR	PLURAL
roof	roofs
safe	safes

SINGULAR	PLURAL
calf	calves
leaf	leaves

Form the plurals of most compound nouns by adding *-s*.

SINGULAR	PLURAL
forget-me-not	forget-me-nots
merry-go-round	merry-go-rounds

Form the plurals of some compounds by adding *-s* to the principal word. Use a dictionary to be sure.

SINGULAR	PLURAL
mother-in-law	mothers-in-law
attorney-at-law	attorneys-at-law

Form the plural of compounds ending in *ful* by adding *-s*.

SINGULAR	PLURAL		SINGULAR	PLURAL
handful	handfuls		armful	armfuls

Some nouns are used only in the plural form.

pajamas   **binoculars**   **scissors**   **slacks**

Some nouns are plural in form but singular in meaning and use.

civics   **mathematics**   **news**   **physics**

EXERCISE 1 **Write the plural of each item listed below. Use a dictionary when necessary.**

1. bicycle
2. spoonful
3. deer
4. moose
5. soprano
6. tree
7. point of view
8. mousetrap
9. candy
10. knife
11. Portuguese
12. trumpet
13. gentleman
14. baby
15. chief
16. corps
17. trout
18. oasis
19. kimono
20. eyetooth

EXERCISE 2 **Put the following singular nouns in one column and the plural nouns in another column. Some words will go in both columns. Use a dictionary when necessary.**

shelf
echoes
duo
pulleys
cuff
series
bison
sister-in-law
gulf
tax

Iroquois
volcano
drive-ins
salmon
analyses
clothes
classes
tomatoes
hoof
physics

goose
bucketful
teeth
measles
species
swine
zoos
congresswoman
victories
treasure
crises
Chinese

APPLY IT NOW

Find the mistakes in the use of plural nouns in the paragraph below and rewrite them correctly. It was a cold winter night, and my dad was getting ready to build a fire. He needed help hauling in lumber from the woodes behind our house. First, we inspected the wood for tickes, since the deers that roam our yard often carry them. We found none, so we each carried several log into the house. Then my Dad put the wood in the fireplace and took out a book of matchs to light the fire. In no time, sparkes flew and heat from the fire warmed the room.

Grammar in Action. Find three plural nouns used in the p. 222 excerpt.

1.3 Nouns as Subjects and Subject Complements

A noun can be the **subject** of a sentence. The subject tells what the sentence is about. In this sentence *Canada* is the subject.

Canada borders the United States on the north.

A noun can be a **subject complement.** A subject complement renames the subject; it refers to the same person, place, thing, or idea. A subject complement follows a linking verb such as the forms of *be* (*am, is, are, was,* and so on).

In this sentence *capital* is the subject, and *Ottawa* is the subject complement.

The capital of Canada is *Ottawa*.

What are the subject and subject complement of this sentence?

Toronto is Canada's most populous city.

To find the subject, ask yourself *who* or *what* the sentence is about *(Toronto)*. Then see if there is a linking verb such as *am, is, are, was,* or *were.* Is the linking verb followed by a noun that renames the subject? That noun is the subject complement *(city)*.

EXERCISE 1 Identify the subject of each sentence.

1. Quebec is a province in Canada.
2. Many Canadians speak French.
3. The largest French-speaking city in Canada is Montreal.
4. The Great Lakes form part of the border between the United States and Canada.
5. The tallest freestanding structure in the world is the CN Tower in Toronto.
6. Vancouver has been a popular location for filming movies and television shows.
7. Canada's geographic coordinates are 60° 00" N 95° 00" W.
8. The Canadian forests are home to a variety of wildlife.
9. Niagara Falls can be explored on both the Canadian and New York sides of the falls.
10. The weather in Vancouver is often mild as in nearby Seattle, Washington.

EXERCISE 2 Identify the subject of each sentence. Name the subject complement if there is one.

1. Newfoundland is a province in Canada.
2. This province is an island off the east coast of Canada.
3. The island has miles of rugged coastline with high cliffs.
4. Cape St. Mary's, on the island's south coast, is home to a seabird sanctuary.
5. Countless seabirds build their nests along the shoreline.
6. No person may legally harm the birds or take their eggs.
7. This place has been a sanctuary for wildlife for decades.
8. The cold wind off the Atlantic carries the birds' shrill cries.
9. Wheeling above the rocky cliffs, the birds are an amazing sight.
10. The cliffs are an attraction for bird-watchers.
11. Summer is the best time for bird-watching.
12. Masses of birds cover the cliffs then.

EXERCISE 3 Complete each sentence. Then tell whether the word you added is a subject or a subject complement.

1. One of the most beautiful sights I have ever seen was _____.
2. _____ is a typical neighborhood in my area.
3. An interesting thing to see in this locale is _____.
4. If I could visit any park, _____ is the park I would choose.
5. A place I didn't like was _____.
6. The _____ is the perfect place for camping.
7. When we take our vacation, _____ is the first sight I want to explore.
8. An animal often seen in that national park is _____.
9. The _____ is the most exciting place to visit.
10. The body of water that I would most like to sail on is _____.

APPLY IT NOW

In Exercise 3 you completed some sentences that tell about places you have visited or would like to visit. Choose one place and write five or six sentences about it. Include subjects and subject complements in at least two of your sentences. When you have finished writing, identify the subject complements.

Tech Tip With an adult, research a tourist attraction online.

1.4 Nouns as Objects and Object Complements

A noun can be used as a **direct object.** The direct object tells *whom* or *what* after the verb. In this sentence the direct object is *club.* It answers the question *What did the students join?*

Many students joined the drama *club*.

A noun can be used as an **indirect object.** An indirect object tells *to whom* or *for whom,* or *to what* or *for what,* the action is done. In this sentence the indirect object is *students.* It answers the question *To whom did the drama teacher teach acting basics?*

The drama teacher taught the *students* **acting basics.**

A noun can be the **object of a preposition** such as *in, into, on, to, by, for, from, with,* or *without.* In this sentence the object of the preposition *about* is *play.* It answers the question *What were the students talking about?*

The students were talking about their next *play*.

A noun can be an **object complement.** Just as a subject complement renames the subject, an object complement renames the direct object. In this sentence *Brigitte* is the direct object. The noun *designer* is an object complement that renames *Brigitte.*

The drama teacher appointed Brigitte costume *designer*.

EXERCISE 1 Identify the direct object in each sentence.

1. The drama club performed a play at the local theater.
2. The group chose a comedy.
3. Before deciding, the actors read and studied several scripts.
4. The wardrobe designers chose appropriate period costumes.

EXERCISE 2 Identify the indirect object in each sentence.

1. A local actress gave the cast free coaching.
2. Ms. Stanton offered the actors costumes.
3. A local shop loaned the stagehands saws, hammers, and nails.
4. The casting director assigned Claire the lead role.

EXERCISE 3 Identify the objects of prepositions in these sentences. A sentence may have more than one preposition and one object.

1. The play was the best thing I've ever seen on a stage.
2. It was excellent from beginning to end.
3. All of the students acted with enthusiasm.
4. There was a huge round of applause for the actors.
5. All the people in the audience were on their feet at the end.
6. Stage acting combines imagination with hard work and confidence.

EXERCISE 4 Identify the object complement in each sentence.

1. The town paper named Emma the best actress of the year.
2. The school newspaper declared the play a great success.
3. Ms. Stanton appointed Charles director of the next play.
4. We chose Pilar president of the drama club.
5. We made Mickey Mouse our unofficial mascot.
6. We practiced the play *Our Town.*

EXERCISE 5 Tell whether each underlined noun is a direct object, an indirect object, an object of a preposition, or an object complement.

1. People still consider ancient Greek <u>plays</u> masterpieces.
2. Greek dramas are performed on <u>stages</u> around the <u>world</u> today.
3. The actors in ancient Greek <u>drama</u> wore <u>masks</u>.
4. The masks expressed the <u>nature</u> of their <u>characters</u>.
5. A festival in <u>Athens</u> offered <u>winners</u> prizes for acting.
6. In my <u>opinion</u>, we should perform more Shakespearean <u>plays</u>.
7. The theater committee pronounced <u>Hamlet</u> the next <u>performance</u>.
8. The director first read the <u>actors</u> the unabridged <u>version</u>.
9. We are planning a <u>trip</u> to the <u>theater</u>.
10. Our teacher gave <u>us</u> a <u>play</u> to read.

APPLY IT NOW

Write five or six sentences about a movie you have recently seen. In your sentences use each of the following at least once: direct object, indirect object, and object of a preposition.

Tech Tip   With an adult, send an opinion to a movie Web site.

1.5 Appositives

An **appositive** is a word that follows a noun and helps identify it or adds more information about it. An appositive names the same person, place, thing, or idea as the noun it explains. An **appositive phrase** is an appositive and its modifiers.

In the sentence below, the noun *Louis Armstrong* is an appositive that explains the noun *musician.* It is not set off by commas because it is **restrictive.** The restrictive appositive is necessary in order to know which musician is meant. The phrase *a jazz band* is an appositive phrase that explains the noun *Hot Fives.* The appositive phrase is set off by a comma because it is **nonrestrictive.** The nonrestrictive appositive is not necessary in order to understand the sentence; it just gives extra information.

> **The famous musician *Louis Armstrong* was the leader of the Hot Fives, a *jazz band*.**

An appositive that follows a common noun can be restrictive or nonrestrictive, depending on the circumstances. An appositive that directly follows a proper noun is almost always nonrestrictive. In the first example below, the appositive *David* is nonrestrictive because Carl has only one brother. In the second example, the appositive *Miguel* is restrictive because it is necessary in order to know which of Maria's brothers is meant.

> **Carl's brother, *David*, is a good trumpet player.**
> (Carl has one brother whose name is David.)
> **Maria's brother *Miguel* is an excellent violinist.**
> (Maria has three brothers—Julio, Miguel, and Roberto.)

EXERCISE 1 Identify the appositive in each sentence. Tell which noun it explains.

1. Jazz, an American invention, is a popular type of music today.
2. One important quality of jazz is improvisation, the creation of new music on the spot.
3. Syncopation, changes in regular musical patterns, is an important quality.
4. Often jazz is performed by a combo, a small group of musicians.
5. The trumpet, a brass instrument, is associated with jazz.
6. Saxophones and clarinets, the traditional reed instruments of jazz, help give the music its particular quality.

Louis Armstrong

7. Blues, music with sad sounds, had an important influence on jazz.

8. Another influence on jazz was ragtime, an energetic musical form popular in the 1890s.

9. The trumpet player Louis Armstrong was important in the development and popularization of jazz.

10. New Orleans, the home of jazz, holds an annual jazz festival.

11. Bebop, an art form of jazz, has an unpredictable style.

12. Herbie Hancock, a well-known jazz fusion performer, uses electric instruments and complex harmonies.

EXERCISE 2 **Identify the appositive in each sentence and decide if it is restrictive or nonrestrictive. Rewrite those sentences with nonrestrictive appositives, adding commas where necessary.**

1. The jazz musician Wynton Marsalis was born in New Orleans.

2. New Orleans a city in Louisiana is known for its jazz music.

3. He attended Juilliard a prestigious music school in New York City.

4. Marsalis a member of a large family has several brothers in the music profession.

5. In 1982 Wynton started a jazz combo with his brother Branford.

6. The record producer Delfeayo Marsalis is their brother.

7. Their father Ellis Marsalis is a noted jazz pianist and teacher.

8. The trumpet Wynton's primary instrument is featured on many of his jazz recordings.

9. The bass trumpet the type of trombone most often used by trombone players is played with a special mouthpiece.

10. Wynton has also won Grammy Awards the most prestigious prizes given to musicians.

11. Wynton's musical composition *Blood in the Fields* deals with slavery and race relations.

12. His classical album *Trumpet Concertos* won a Grammy Award in 1983 the same year that his jazz album *Think of One* won.

Wynton Marsalis

APPLY IT NOW

What kind of music do you like to listen to? What are your favorite singers and songs? Write five or six sentences about this topic and use appositives to explain some of the nouns in your paragraph.

1.6 Possessive Nouns

A **possessive noun** expresses possession or ownership.

> That *girl's* skill at drawing is impressive.
> (The girl possesses skill.)
> The *Wilsons'* home has many paintings on the walls.
> (The Wilsons own the home.)

To form the singular possessive, add -'s to the singular form of the noun.

student	**student's**
Madeline	**Madeline's**

To form the possessive of plural nouns ending in *s*, add the apostrophe only. If the plural form of a noun does not end in *s*, add -'s.

cowboys	**cowboys'**
children	**children's**

The singular possessive of proper names ending in *s* is usually formed by adding -'s.

James	**James's**
Mrs. Williams	**Mrs. Williams's**

The plural possessive of a proper name is formed by adding an apostrophe to the plural of the name.

the Joyces	**the Joyces'**
the Adamses	**the Adamses'**

The possessive of compound nouns is formed by adding -'s to the end of the word.

commander in chief	**commander in chief's**
sister-in-law	**sister-in-law's**

If two or more nouns are used together to indicate **separate possession**—that is, that each person owns something independently—the -'s is used after each noun. If two or more nouns are used together to indicate **joint possession**—that is, to show that one thing is owned together—the -'s is used only after the last noun.

> *Owen's and Charlotte's* murals are colorful. (separate possession)
> *Finn and Otto's* mural is colorful. (joint possession)

EXERCISE 1 **Complete each sentence, using the singular possessive or plural possessive form of the noun in parentheses.**

1. My _____ (family) vacation included a stop at a museum in Chicago.

2. The Art Institute is one of that _____ (city) treasures.

3. _____ (Georges Seurat) *Sunday Afternoon on the Island of the Grand Jatte* is one of the most famous paintings in the museum.

4. Tiny dots of paint cover the _____ (painting) surface.

5. My sister _____ (Iris) favorite painting is *American Gothic*, which shows a man and a woman outside a farmhouse.

6. The _____ (man) and the _____ (woman) expressions are somber and stern.

7. The old suits of armor in a large gallery were my _____ (brother) favorite objects, and they took many pictures of them.

8. At the special exhibit of miniature homes, we felt like giants looking through the _____ (miniature) windows.

A man views Georges Seurat's famous painting at The Art Institute of Chicago.

EXERCISE 2 **Use the information in the items below to write sentences showing either separate or joint possession.**

1. Anna and Charles started an art club together. It meets monthly.

2. Mr. Saunders offered to help. Mrs. Jackson also offered to help. The members accepted both offers.

3. David and Jenna worked together on the first project. Their first art project was a colorful mural.

4. Lilly and Brandon each did a painting for their first project. Their paintings were in watercolors.

5. Jason and Sophia worked together on a sculpture. Their sculpture won first prize at the local fair.

6. Miguel and Connor had ideas about what to paint. Their ideas were different.

7. Experienced artists exhibit their work at this gallery. Novice artists exhibit their work at this gallery too.

APPLY IT NOW

What are your family's favorite museums or attractions that you enjoy visiting? Do some of your family members enjoy different ones? Write one sentence using joint possession and one sentence using separate possession.

Grammar in Action

Find the three possessive nouns on p. 223.

Noun Review

1.1 **Write the correct plural of the nouns in parentheses.**

1. (Attorney) by day, my mom and dad pursue different (hobby) after work.

2. Mom fishes for all kinds of (trout).

3. In our basement there are (box) of (fly) she has tied.

4. She also collects old (reel) and (tackle box).

5. Dad likes to eat (fish), but he would rather tend to his (lily) than fish.

6. He posts (story) and (essay) on his gardening blog.

7. Many (woman) and (man) work.

8. My (parent) share their (vocation), but not their (hobby).

1.2 **Change each sentence by making the underlined word plural. Write the new sentence, adjusting any additional words so that it is grammatically correct. Some sentences are correct.**

9. We will celebrate his <u>birthday</u>.

10. The cowboy helped the <u>calf</u> out of the water.

11. The policewoman guarded the <u>safe</u>.

12. The tourist wanted to climb the <u>volcano</u>.

13. My mom put a <u>potato</u> into the soup.

14. I need water for the <u>lily of the valley</u> in my vase.

15. I had an <u>armful</u> of newspapers that had to be delivered.

16. Hannah brought her <u>portfolio</u> to the meeting.

17. My dad adjusted the <u>shelf</u> in my bedroom.

18. Mrs. Vicente put the <u>scissors</u> away.

19. The hikers saw the <u>fox</u> in the woods.

20. The <u>deer</u> ate all the pumpkins in the garden.

1.3 **Identify each underlined word as a subject or subject complement.**

21. One of the most exciting sports is <u>soccer</u>.

22. Soccer <u>players</u> are treated as royalty in some countries.

23. My <u>uncle</u> belongs to a soccer club in this country.

24. The men are all accomplished <u>athletes</u>.

25. If I could meet any soccer player in the world, <u>Beckham</u> is the one I would choose.

26. Although I practice every day during the week, Saturday is game <u>day</u>.

1.4 Identify each of the underlined words as a direct object, an indirect object, an object of a preposition, or an object complement.

27. The seventh grade performed _Our Town_ last spring.

28. High school actors gave the <u>cast</u> helpful <u>tips</u>.

29. Parents, teachers, and friends filled the theater for every <u>performance</u>.

30. The cast voted <u>Marny</u> best <u>actress</u>.

31. Ms. Scott appointed me <u>director</u>.

32. She named Carl <u>manager</u>.

33. The award winners received new <u>trophies</u> for their <u>efforts</u>.

34. Tears of <u>happiness</u> rolled down their <u>faces</u>.

1.5 Identify the appositives and punctuate them if needed.

35. Ten to fifteen thousand sea otters cuddly and playful mammals once lived in Prince William Sound.

36. A tragic event occurred in Valdez a small Alaskan town on the Sound.

37. The supertanker _Exxon Valdez_ left port.

38. Supertankers huge ocean-going vessels are hard to steer.

39. The supertanker hit Bligh Reef a mass of rock.

40. An oil slick a large gooey puddle of oil spread across the water.

41. George Crain a marine biologist will be arriving in Valdez to explore and search for any remains.

42. He is asking for help from volunteers people who can donate their time.

43. His daughter Elizabeth can come, but his daughter Lilly cannot leave her job.

1.6 Correct the possessive nouns.

44. The teens projects failed. (plural)

45. The sisters-in-law potluck was a success. (plural)

46. The men book clubs were postponed. (plural)

47. Carlos dog ran home. (singular)

48. My brother scout group had a fair. (singular)

49. Mr. Saunders car was stuck in the snow. (singular)

50. The puppies food is in the basement. (plural)

51. The children job is to shovel the snow. (plural)

52. Put it on the desk in the boss office. (singular)

Tech Tip Go to www.voyagesinenglish.com for more activities.

Noun Challenge

EXERCISE 1 Read the selection and then answer the questions.

1. Paris, the capital of France, is regarded by many travelers as the most beautiful city in the world. 2. Its tree-lined boulevards and gracious buildings attract many visitors each year. 3. Some of the internationally famous monuments of Paris are the Arc de Triomphe, the Cathedral of Notre Dame, and the Eiffel Tower. 4. The beauty of this capital offers tourists a delight for the eyes. 5. Paris is a chic city, and many fashion designers call Paris home. 6. If the opportunity to visit France's most elegant city presents itself, be sure to go.

1. What is the subject of sentence 1?
2. What is the direct object of sentence 2?
3. What are the subjects of sentence 2?
4. What is the indirect object of sentence 4?
5. Name the appositive in sentence 1.
6. Name the subject complements in sentence 3.
7. Name the two subjects in sentence 5.
8. Name the objects of prepositions in sentence 4.
9. What is the object complement in sentence 5?
10. Name a possessive noun in sentence 6.

EXERCISE 2 Read the following and respond.

Paris is home to many tourist attractions. Besides the monuments mentioned in the above paragraph, other attractions include the Louvre, the largest and most famous museum, and Disneyland Paris.

1. Write a paragraph identifying one tourist attraction near your home and why it is a tourist attraction. Answer the following questions in your paragraph: Have you read about it, or have you been there yourself? If your family had out-of-town guests, would you recommend that they visit this attraction, or would you suggest to skip the attraction?

2. In your paragraph, use one of each of the following: a direct object or an indirect object, a subject complement or an object complement, an object of a preposition, a possessive noun, and an appositive.

Adjectives

2.1 Descriptive Adjectives, Position of Adjectives

A **descriptive adjective** gives information about a noun or a pronoun. It tells about number, color, size, or another quality.

In this sentence the adjectives *two, large,* and *black* give information about number, size, and color of the noun *vases.*

> Two large, black **vases were on display.**

Most adjectives go before the words they describe. In this sentence the adjective *Mexican* describes the noun *pottery.*

> Mexican **pottery comes in many shapes.**

Adjectives may also directly follow nouns. In this sentence the adjectives *ancient* and *cracked* describe the noun *vase.*

> The vase, *ancient* and *cracked,* **was found nearby.**

An adjective can act as a **subject complement,** a word that follows a linking verb and describes the subject. It can also act as an **object complement,** a word that follows a direct object and describes it.

In this sentence *green* is a subject complement that describes the subject, *vase.*

> The vase is *green.*

In this sentence *green* is an object complement that describes the direct object, *vase.*

> The artist painted the vase *green.*

EXERCISE 1 **Name the descriptive adjectives in the following sentences.**

1. The Native American peoples of the Pacific Northwest have created some beautiful works of art.
2. Tall pillars, called totem poles, tell the stories of families.
3. The poles are carved from the wood of giant cedars.
4. Cedars, strong and majestic, grow throughout the forests.
5. Colorful figures are stacked one on top of the other.
6. These carved figures of animals are abstract and strange.

EXERCISE 2 **Identify the noun modified by each italicized adjective. Then tell whether the adjective comes before the noun, after the noun, or is a subject complement or an object complement.**

1. People consider Alaska's climate *cold* and *icy*.

2. Indeed, its winters are *harsh*.

3. The tundra, *frozen* and *bleak*, covers much of the land.

4. This *treeless* area springs to life only in the summer.

5. Summers there bring *lovely* wildflowers and *pleasant* days.

6. The warm summer days, *long* and *sunny*, seem *endless*.

7. The summer is actually *short*, however.

8. In contrast some areas of Alaska are *fertile* farmlands.

9. In some places the temperatures are fairly *moderate* because of the nearness of the ocean.

10. Alaska, in fact, has a *great* variety of climates.

11. The climate of the interior of Alaska is *extreme*.

12. Alaska's *hottest* and *coldest* temperatures have occurred there.

13. The Alaskan weather can get *hotter* than Florida.

EXERCISE 3

1. Use the following adjectives in sentences of your own.

ancient	powerful	sincere	historic
Greek	majestic	energetic	modern
careful	weary	Chinese	colorful
young	orange	foggy	tiny

2. Use an appropriate adjective with each of these nouns.

story	leaves	grandmother
breeze	ocean	brook
squirrel	sidewalk	cherries
dog	stairs	stage
motorcycle	jewels	homework

APPLY IT NOW

Write a short advertisement for an interesting object in your bedroom. Be creative and do your best to convince the audience to purchase it. Use adjectives in a variety of positions in your sentences.

With an adult, use an online thesaurus to find adjectives.

2.2 Demonstrative, Interrogative, and Indefinite Adjectives

Demonstrative adjectives point out definite persons, places, things, or ideas. The demonstrative adjectives are *this, that, these,* and *those*.

> *This* box is heavy.
> *Those* bags are light.

> *That* house is my house.
> *These* houses are new.

Interrogative adjectives are used in questions. The interrogative adjectives are *what, which,* and *whose. Which* is usually used to ask about one or more of a specific set of items.

> *What* equipment do you need to play tennis?
> *Which* tennis racket on the table is yours?
> *Whose* tennis racket is this?

Indefinite adjectives refer to any or all of a group. Indefinite adjectives include *both, few, every, several, all, another, some, many, most, each, either,* and *neither*. Note that *another, each, every, either,* and *neither* are singular and that the others are plural.

> *Each* student receives special attention. (singular)
> *Neither* boy is to blame for the accident. (singular)
> *Few* friends are as loyal as you are. (plural)
> They have walked this path *many* times. (plural)

EXERCISE 1 Tell whether each italicized adjective is demonstrative, interrogative, or indefinite.

1. *Which* students have joined the photography club?
2. *This* club meets twice a month and sponsors events, and the big event for *this* year is a photography show.
3. *Every* club member can enter *several* photos in the competition.
4. *Each* student can decide on the subject for *those* photos.
5. *Most* club members plan to enter the contest.
6. A new digital camera is the top prize, and a subscription to a photography magazine is *another* prize.
7. I'd like to win *either* prize.
8. *All* entrants must fill out one of *these* applications.

9. *Whose* application for the show is on the floor?

10. *What* subject should I choose for my photos?

11. *Many* photos contain animals, but *which* picture is the most interesting?

12. *Neither* of the lion photos came out clear.

EXERCISE 2 Complete the following sentences with a demonstrative, an interrogative, or an indefinite adjective.

1. _____ object are you trying to photograph?

2. I like _____ photo in the album.

3. We will have to wait _____ day before we develop them.

4. It looks as if _____ picture is slightly blurry.

5. _____ cameras got wet in the sudden downpour.

EXERCISE 3 Identify the demonstrative, interrogative, and indefinite adjectives in these sentences.

1. I decided to take pictures of my neighborhood for this project.

2. I wanted to show both good and bad points of the neighborhood.

3. All places can be viewed in two ways.

4. Some rundown buildings are shown in that picture.

5. See how all the windows are broken, and several homes do not have doors.

6. A colorful mural in the neighborhood is shown in these pictures.

7. Whose work is it?

8. It was created by many young artists.

9. Each person added original details.

10. What aspects of the neighborhood does the mural show?

11. It shows those aspects of the neighborhood in which every resident can take pride.

12. Several community workers are installing new playground equipment at this park.

APPLY IT NOW

Write five or six sentences about a place that you think has both good and bad points. Create a Venn diagram to help you get started. In your sentences circle all the demonstrative, interrogative, and indefinite adjectives that you use.

Grammar in Action. Find the indefinite adjectives in the p. 222 excerpt.

2.3 Comparative and Superlative Adjectives

Most adjectives have three degrees of comparison: positive, comparative, and superlative. The **positive** degree of an adjective shows a quality of a noun or pronoun.

My grandmother is *tall*.

The **comparative** degree is used to compare two items or two sets of items. This form is often followed by *than*.

My grandfather is *taller* **than my grandmother.**

The **superlative** degree is used to compare three or more items.

My uncle Jack is the *tallest* **member of the family.**

For adjectives of one syllable and some adjectives of two syllables (generally those ending in *y*), the comparative is formed by adding *-er* to the positive form, and the superlative is formed by adding *-est.* Note the spelling change in some words when endings are added.

POSITIVE	COMPARATIVE	SUPERLATIVE
smart	smarter	smartest
wise	wiser	wisest
funny	funnier	funniest
hot	hotter	hottest

For adjectives of three or more syllables and many adjectives of two syllables, the comparative is formed by using *more* or *less,* and the superlative is formed by using *most* or *least.*

POSITIVE	COMPARATIVE	SUPERLATIVE
courteous	more courteous	most courteous
famous	less famous	least famous

Certain adjectives have irregular comparisons. If you are uncertain what comparative and superlative forms an adjective has, check the word in a dictionary.

POSITIVE	COMPARATIVE	SUPERLATIVE
good	better	best
bad	worse	worst
little	less	least

EXERCISE 1 Complete each sentence with the comparative or superlative form of the adjective in parentheses.

1. Of my relatives in my grandparents' generation, my great-uncle William is the _____ (old) person.

2. My grandmother is several years _____ (young) than he is.

3. When I decided to do a family history, Great-Aunt Sofia was the _____ (cooperative) of all my relatives.

4. It was from her that I received the _____ (good) research materials of all—two family photo albums.

5. Most of her pictures were in _____ (bad) condition, however, than the pictures I got from Uncle John.

6. Uncle John's photos were in generally _____ (good) condition than hers.

7. My mom found the _____ (beautiful) photo in the attic.

8. It was of the _____ (tall), _____ (ornate) ship my grandfather ever sailed.

9. Which picture is _____ (old), this one or that?

10. When we discovered a box in my grandmother's attic filled with old photos, it was _____ (exciting) than opening a birthday present.

EXERCISE 2 Write the comparative and superlative degrees of each of these adjectives. Check a dictionary if needed.

1. difficult
2. sunny
3. long
4. amusing
5. generous
6. cheap
7. popular
8. lucky
9. strange
10. dependable
11. studious
12. narrow
13. happy
14. far
15. late

Grammar in Action. Find the comparative adjective in the p. 232 excerpt.

APPLY IT NOW

Find an advertisement in a magazine or a newspaper and list all the comparative and superlative adjectives you see.

2.4 *Few* and *Little*

Concrete nouns name things that can be seen, touched, or counted: *table, artist, Ohio River*. **Abstract nouns** name things that cannot be seen, touched, or counted. They express qualities or conditions: *morality, sadness, duration*.

Use the adjectives *few, fewer,* and *fewest* to compare concrete nouns that can be counted. Note that the nouns are plural in form.

> **Lorna made *few* free throws.**
> **Gail made *fewer* free throws than Lorna.**
> **Mary Pat made the *fewest* free throws of all.**

Use the adjectives *little, less,* and *least* to compare abstract nouns that cannot be counted. Note that the nouns are singular in form.

> **I have *little* time to practice free throws.**
> **My brother has *less* time to practice free throws than I do.**
> **Of us all, my sister has the *least* time to practice free throws.**

For some nouns, you can use either *less* or *fewer,* depending on the noun's usage in the sentence. With the whole class or a partner, discuss the different circumstances in which you would use *less* and *fewer* for the following nouns: *soda, belief, joy, talent*.

EXERCISE 1 Place these words in two columns, *Concrete Nouns* and *Abstract Nouns*.

dime	governor	log	wood
love	happiness	lump	compassion
courage	drop	ballad	gallon
honesty	jewelry	necklace	paper
story	advice	pear	fruit
sheep	forest	truth	time

EXERCISE 2 Tell whether the nouns being modified are abstract or concrete. Then choose the correct word to complete the sentence.

1. (Fewer Less) cranes return to the marsh every year.

2. Sadly, (few little) attention is paid to the dwindling number.

3. This year there are (fewer less) nests than last year.

4. This means, of course, that there will be (fewer less) young birds next year.

5. (Fewer Less) concern with conservation means that more marshland may be taken over for commercial and residential use.

6. (Fewer Less) land in which animals can nest is available.

7. (Fewer Less) citizens seem to be interested in environmental issues.

8. (Fewer Less) funds are set aside for conservation.

9. The average citizen seems to have (little few) basic knowledge about the issue of the cranes.

10. Even the (fewest least) effort can have significant results on saving land for these endangered creatures.

EXERCISE 3 **Rewrite any sentences that use the incorrect form of *few* and *less*. Some sentences are correct.**

1. Less participants attended this year's wilderness cleanup.

2. This probably was because there was less publicity for it.

3. There were less ads for it in the newspapers.

4. There was fewer time for the cleanup because rain fell in the afternoon.

5. Perhaps fewer people participated because of the rain.

6. I was able to fill fewer bags with garbage than I did last year.

7. These plants require fewer attention than those.

8. Luckily, we had less trouble with the recycling trucks than we had last year.

9. Some of us had fewer motivation because of the low turnout in participants.

10. As a result, everyone is less enthusiastic about this year's cleanup.

EXERCISE 4 **Complete the sentences with the correct adjective *fewer* or *less*.**

1. There are _____ trees in the world's rain forest every year.

2. Despite the efforts of environmentalists, rain forests cover much _____ area every year.

3. The loss of trees actually results in _____ rain for an area.

4. There is _____ rich soil on the floor of the rain forest than in other places.

APPLY IT NOW

For several days write down examples of friends or someone on TV using few/ fewer/fewest and little/less/ least. Are the adjectives used correctly? Share your findings with classmates.

2.5 Adjective Phrases and Clauses

A **prepositional phrase** is made up of a preposition, the object of the preposition, and any modifiers of the object. A prepositional phrase can be used as an adjective. In this sentence the prepositional phrase *of the mission* modifies the noun *ruins*. It is an **adjective phrase.**

Did they see the ruins *of the mission*?

A **clause** is a group of words that has a subject and a predicate. A dependent clause does not express a complete thought. Some dependent clauses are used as adjectives. They describe nouns. In this sentence the dependent clause is *which was once part of the Spanish empire.* It modifies *California.* It is an **adjective clause.**

California, *which was once part of the Spanish empire,* **has many historic sites.**

An **adjective clause** usually begins with a relative pronoun *(who, whom, whose, which, that)* or a subordinate conjunction *(where, when).* These words connect the clause to the noun it modifies.

A **restrictive** adjective clause is necessary to the meaning of a sentence. A **nonrestrictive** clause is not necessary to the meaning. Nonrestrictive clauses are set off with commas. As a general rule, use the relative pronoun *that* with restrictive clauses and *which* with nonrestrictive clauses.

I learned about the mission *that is famous for its swallows.* (restrictive—necessary in order to know which mission is being discussed)

San Juan Capistrano, *which is a town on the Pacific coast,* **dates back to the 1700s.** (nonrestrictive—not necessary in order to identify the exact town.)

EXERCISE 1 **Identify each adjective phrase and name the noun it modifies.**

1. Our class did research about Oakwood's history.
2. We read newspapers from the past.
3. Our neighborhood was once a home for African American workers.
4. During World War II, African Americans from the South came here to work.
5. Their role in the community's history was important.
6. They built the school at the corner.

EXERCISE 2 In each sentence identify the adjective clause and the noun that it modifies. Then tell whether each clause is restrictive or nonrestrictive.

1. San Juan Capistrano, which is near Los Angeles, is one of California's historic missions.

2. It was one of the many missions that was founded by the Spanish priest Junipero Serra in the 1700s.

3. The mission was named for Saint John Capistrano, who was an Italian theologian of the 1400s.

4. The mission's large stone church, which was called the Great Stone Church, was once the largest stone structure west of the Mississippi River.

5. The church, which stood five stories high and was topped by domes and a bell tower, collapsed in an earthquake in 1812.

6. Today the ruins are a picturesque site that attracts many tourists.

7. However, it is another event that has made the mission famous.

8. San Juan Capistrano is the place where swallows return to nest every spring from their winter homes in Argentina.

9. March 19, the feast of Saint Joseph, is the day when thousands of swallows return to the mission.

10. The people of San Juan Capistrano celebrate the return with a parade that features horses and dancing.

EXERCISE 3 Tell whether the italicized words in each sentence are an adjective clause or an adjective phrase.

1. San Juan Capistrano is called the jewel *of California missions* because of its beauty.

2. The original mission church, *which is still standing,* was built in 1782.

3. This church is the oldest building *in California,* according to some historians.

4. The swallows came to Capistrano as an escape from an innkeeper *who had destroyed their nests,* according to legend.

5. The swallows build mud nests *that hang under the eaves of the mission buildings.*

6. The mission, *which had fallen into ruins,* was restored in the 20th century.

Mission San Juan Capistrano

APPLY IT NOW

Think about a current news event that you heard about. Write a sentence about it, and be sure to include an adjective clause. Underline that clause.

Tech Tip With an adult, read about your topic on the Web.

Adjective Review

2.1 List the nouns modified by the underlined adjectives. Write whether the adjective comes before the noun or after the noun, or is a subject complement or an object complement.

1. Moviemakers create <u>magical</u> worlds.
2. Steven Spielberg is <u>famous</u> for his films.
3. His <u>adventure</u> films are always exciting.
4. <u>Computer-generated</u> images fool and amaze us.
5. Technology, <u>modern</u> and <u>ever-changing</u>, has affected movies.
6. Animators create worlds both <u>ancient</u> and <u>futuristic</u>.
7. Actors' voices make cartoons <u>fun</u>.
8. Movies can be <u>expensive</u>.
9. It's still my <u>favorite</u> entertainment.

2.2 Write whether each underlined adjective is demonstrative, interrogative, or indefinite.

10. <u>Which</u> books on the list have you read?
11. I've read <u>several</u> mysteries.
12. <u>These</u> biographies are great.
13. <u>Which</u> author wrote <u>that</u> series?
14. I've read <u>this</u> one <u>many</u> times.
15. <u>Neither</u> author is familiar.
16. <u>That</u> science fiction story is my favorite.

17. Have you read <u>those</u> myths and legends?
18. <u>Most</u> readers like ghost stories.
19. I generally like scary stories, but <u>some</u> ghost stories are too scary for me.
20. When you return the book, <u>either</u> she or I will borrow <u>it</u> next.

2.3 Write the comparative and superlative degrees of each of these adjectives.

21. green
22. bad
23. sunny
24. good
25. little
26. beautiful
27. evil
28. big
29. round
30. windy
31. hot
32. expensive

2.4 Complete the sentences with the correct form of *few* or *little*. Write whether the underlined noun is concrete or abstract.

33. _____ people can resist our new baby.

34. My mom has _____ time now than ever before.

35. Dad has the _____ patience.

36. I have _____ advice for siblings.

37. Eventually, there will be _____ diapers.

38. You may lose a _____ hours of sleep.

39. _____ small babies sleep through the night.

40. You will have _____ trouble if you have your own room.

41. My brother made the _____ bottles.

42. He has also done the _____ babysitting.

2.5 Punctuate the sentences if needed and write whether the underlined words are adjective phrases or adjective clauses.

43. We did research about cowboys.

44. Roundups which took place twice a year were hard work.

45. A cowboy threw a lariat that he kept at his side at an angry longhorn.

46. The trail drive to town was long.

47. Cowboys and their cattle which don't walk very fast could be traveling for months.

48. Cowboys' contribution to history is important.

49. Life on horseback was difficult and dangerous.

50. The songs that the cowboys sang kept the cattle quiet during the night.

51. Bacon, beans, and corn bread were staples of cowboys' diets.

52. Cowboys' meals which were cooked over an open fire were very simple.

53. The bandana around his neck could be used to keep dust out of his nose and mouth.

54. Sturdy boots had heels that helped him keep his feet in the stirrups.

Go to www.voyagesinenglish.com for more activities.

Tech Tip

Adjective Challenge

Read the selection and answer the questions.

Samuel Clemens

1. The humorous writings of Samuel Clemens, who is known to the world as Mark Twain, have made countless readers happy for more than a century. 2. This great American writer was raised in Hannibal, Missouri, a small town on the Mississippi River. 3. As a boy, young Clemens was enchanted with life on the sprawling Mississippi; in fact, many of his later books would feature the Mississippi and the remarkable people who called it home.

4. Clemens's most famous books, *The Adventures of Tom Sawyer* and *The Adventures of Huckleberry Finn,* relate the story of two Mississippi youths and their lively escapades. 5. Each boy longs for excitement and discovers it in the haunted graveyards and dark caves that surround his town. 6. Although these characters lived in another century, their experiences and adventures still amuse today's readers throughout the world.

1. Name three descriptive adjectives in sentence 1.
2. Which adjective in sentence 1 is an object complement?
3. Find an adjective clause in sentence 1.
4. Find an adjective phrase in sentence 2.
5. Name three descriptive adjectives in sentence 2.
6. How is the adjective *enchanted* used in sentence 3?
7. Name a comparative adjective in sentence 3.
8. Name a superlative adjective in sentence 4.
9. Name the adjective clause in sentence 5. Tell whether it is restrictive or nonrestrictive.
10. Name an indefinite adjective in sentence 5.
11. Name a demonstrative adjective in sentence 6. Is it singular or plural?
12. Find an indefinite adjective in sentence 6.

Pronouns

3.1 Person, Number, and Gender of Pronouns

A **pronoun** is a word used in place of a noun.

> **The textbook has a poem by Emily Dickinson.**
> *She* **wrote inspiring poems.**

Pronouns help avoid repetition. In the second sentence, the pronoun *she* refers to *Emily Dickinson.* The word that a pronoun refers to is called its **antecedent.** *Emily Dickinson* is the antecedent of the pronoun *she.*

Emily Dickinson

Learning how pronouns work will help you use them correctly. Look at the personal pronouns in the chart below.

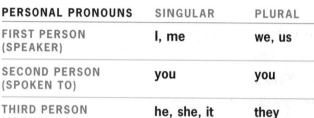

PERSONAL PRONOUNS	SINGULAR	PLURAL
FIRST PERSON (SPEAKER)	I, me	we, us
SECOND PERSON (SPOKEN TO)	you	you
THIRD PERSON (SPOKEN OF)	he, she, it him, her, it	they them

Study the chart. First, you can see that pronouns change form depending on **person**—who is speaking. Second, you can see that pronouns also change form depending on **number**—whether they refer to one or more.

Pronouns in the third person singular also change form depending on **gender**—whether the antecedent is feminine, masculine, or neuter. The third person singular pronouns are *he, him*—masculine; *she, her*—feminine; and *it*—neuter.

Pronouns also change form according to how they are used in a sentence. *I, we, you, he, she, it,* and *they* are used as subjects and subject complements; *me, us, you, him, her, it,* and *them* are used as objects.

> *I* **must write a report on Dickinson tonight.** (first person singular)
>
> **Ms. Scott gave** *us* **the assignment last week.** (first person plural)
>
> **Dickinson was very creative;** *she* **wrote some 1,800 poems.** (third person singular feminine)
>
> *We* **studied several in class.** (first person plural)
>
> **Please check out the book—***it* **is on the top shelf—before you leave.** (third person singular neuter)
>
> **Jorge said** *he* **will help with the report.** (third person singular masculine)

Note that only the third person singular pronouns have gender.

EXERCISE 1 **Give the person and number of each italicized pronoun.**

1. Did *you* know that Lincoln was born in Kentucky?
2. Lincoln met Mary Todd in Illinois and married *her* in 1842.
3. *He* delivered the Gettysburg Address in 1863.
4. *It* honored the soldiers who died in the Civil War.
5. *We* should honor *them* for their great sacrifice.

EXERCISE 2 **Identify the pronoun or pronouns in each sentence. Tell if each is first person, second person, or third person and if it is singular or plural. Tell the gender of the third person singular pronouns.**

1. What are you reading, Deborah?
2. We don't want to bother you.
3. I was reading a poem by Carl Sandburg.
4. It is called "Grass."
5. He mourns the death of young people killed in wars.
6. Deborah, will you read the poem aloud for us?
7. Maybe we could use the poem in tomorrow's English assignment.
8. If we look for more poems by Sandburg, we will find them.
9. I am sure that other poems by him would be just as powerful.
10. The three of us could do a reading of them.

EXERCISE 3 **Complete each sentence with the correct pronoun. Use the directions in parentheses.**

1. Have _____ read the poem "The Highwayman" by Alfred Noyes? (second person singular)
2. _____ enjoyed that poem. (first person singular)
3. _____ tells of a dashing young man and his true love. (third person singular neuter)
4. Noyes creates unforgettable characters, and _____ carries the reader to another time and place. (third person singular masculine)
5. Our teacher read the poem to _____. (first person plural)

Carl Sandburg

APPLY IT NOW

Find a newspaper or magazine article. Using only the first two paragraphs, list all the pronouns that appear. Then write the person, number, and gender of each pronoun.

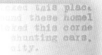

Tech Tip With an adult, find the article at right online.

3.2 Subject Pronouns

A **subject pronoun** can be the subject or subject complement of a sentence. The subject pronouns are *I, we, you, he, she, it,* and *they.*

> **We went on vacation.** (subject)
> **The ones who got lost were my brother and I.**
> (subject complement—part of a compound subject complement)

Be sure to use the subject pronouns for subjects and subject complements. To identify a pronoun subject complement, check whether the verb is a form of the verb *be* (or some other linking verb) and whether the pronoun renames the subject.

One frequent error is not using the subject form of a pronoun when the pronoun is part of a compound subject or subject complement. How would you edit these sentences?

> **My cousins and me like to shop.**
> **The ones talking on the phone were Vivian and her.**

You are correct if you changed *me* to *I* in the first sentence. The pronoun is part of a compound subject. For the second sentence, you should change *her* to *she.* The pronoun is part of a compound subject complement.

Note that a pronoun referring to the speaker should come last in a pair or series. How would you improve this sentence?

> **I and Audrey got good marks on the test.**

You are correct if you changed the subject to *Audrey and I.*

EXERCISE 1 Choose the correct pronoun to complete each sentence.

1. My family and (I me) went on a trip to New York City.
2. (We Us) went to visit our aunt, uncle, and cousins there.
3. My cousins and (me I) hadn't seen one another in several years.
4. My sister Madeline is a very good friend of one cousin. My cousin Julia and (her she) exchange e-mails often.
5. My cousins expected us to arrive much earlier, but (they them) still waited up for us.
6. Only (we us) knew the shortcut to SoHo.
7. Did Madeline and (her she) make it to the Broadway play on time?
8. (Them They) went to Central Park to get hot dogs with sauerkraut.

EXERCISE 2 **Complete each sentence with a subject pronoun. It should refer to the underlined antecedent.**

1. My <u>family and I</u> wanted to see many tourist attractions, so _____ did a lot on the first day.

2. My <u>cousins</u> know the city well, and _____ took us to some interesting places in Central Park, including the zoo.

3. My <u>sister</u> loves to shop, so the leader of our shopping trip was _____.

4. My <u>father and mother</u> wanted to see the Statue of Liberty instead of shopping, so _____ went by boat without us.

5. Although my <u>brother</u> convinced us to go to the wax museum, the person most bored by it was _____.

EXERCISE 3 **Rewrite the sentences to correct the use of pronouns. Not all sentences have errors.**

1. Me and my older brother wanted to go to the top of the Empire State Building.

2. So him and me went off on our own.

3. On the way back, I and my brother got lost.

4. We stopped a friendly-looking woman on the crowded street, and the person who helped us find our way back was her.

5. My mother was worried, and she told us we couldn't go off on our own again.

EXERCISE 4 **Choose the correct personal pronouns in the following sentences. Tell whether each pronoun is used as a subject or a subject complement.**

1. My relatives and (I me) enjoyed being among the crowds in the city.

2. My sister and (I me) usually do things together, but she wanted to go to the theater with my parents.

3. (She Her) and (they them) went to a Broadway musical show.

4. Neither my cousin Jake nor (I me) wanted to see the show.

5. Instead, (we us) walked around Times Square.

6. The one who suggested we watch the live TV show in the square was (he him).

7. The person waving at the camera was (I me), so I'll be on TV.

8. (We Us) and the other tourists watched the TV show.

APPLY IT NOW

Think about a trip you took with your family or friends. Pretend you are writing a postcard to someone, describing the trip. After you finish, circle the subject pronouns and check whether they are used correctly.

3.3 Object Pronouns

An **object pronoun** can be used as the object of a verb or a preposition. The object pronouns are *me, us, you, him, her, it,* and *them.*

> **My uncle took** *us* **to the museum.** (direct object)
>
> **He showed** *me* **ancient Greek vases.** (indirect object)
>
> **The guide explained the meaning of the images painted on** *them*. (object of a preposition)

One of the sentences below shows a common error in object pronoun usage. Which sentence is correct?

> **These presents are from Jerry and I.**
>
> **These presents are from Jerry and me.**

If you chose the second sentence, you are correct. The object pronoun *me* is correct since the pronoun is the object of the preposition *from.* It is part of a compound object.

EXERCISE 1 **Identify the object pronoun in each sentence. Tell how each is used.**

1. My uncle showed my family and me pictures of his trip to Greece.
2. Most were pictures of tourist sites, but a few were pictures of him.
3. My mother collects dolls, so my uncle brought my sister and her dolls dressed in native Greek costumes.
4. His presents to my brother and me were books of Greek myths.
5. We enjoyed them very much.
6. We all thanked him for the gifts.

EXERCISE 2 **Choose the correct pronoun or pronouns to complete each sentence.**

1. Atalanta was a beautiful, athletic young woman, and many men fell in love with (she her).
2. Her father wanted his daughter to choose a husband and marry, so an agreement was made between Atalanta and (he him).
3. Any suitor who could outrun Atalanta in a race would marry (her she), but if any suitor lost, he would be killed.
4. Many suitors challenged her, but she outran (they them) all.
5. Finally, a young man named Hippomenes arrived, and Atalanta's beauty and strength impressed (him he) immediately.
6. He knew that he wasn't a swift runner, so he waited until a plan of attack came to (he him).

7. He went to the goddess of love, Aphrodite, and a strategy was planned by (him he) and (she her).

8. She gave (he him) three golden apples.

9. Hippomenes then challenged Atalanta, and the race between (him he) and (she her) was set.

10. At first, Atalanta was in the lead, but at intervals Hippomenes threw one of the three golden apples in front of (she her).

11. Atalanta lost time stopping to grab each of (them they).

Atalanta

12. Hippomenes was able to win the race, and Atalanta's father married his daughter and (he him) on the spot.

EXERCISE 3 Rewrite the sentences to correct the use of pronouns. Not all sentences have errors.

1. In another version of Atalanta's story, the marriage between Hippomenes and she does not end happily.

2. It seems that Hippomenes forgot to thank Aphrodite, and she became angry with Atalanta and he.

3. The goddess gave Atalanta and he a severe punishment.

4. Hippomenes and Atalanta were turned into lions by her.

5. Between you and I, I prefer the happy ending.

EXERCISE 4 Choose the correct personal pronouns in the following sentences. Tell whether each is used as a direct object, an indirect object, or an object of a preposition.

1. My parents often read my sister and (I me) tales of the Greek gods.

2. It was fun to read the stories with (they them).

3. The tales of the amazing Greek gods always fascinated (I me).

4. Zeus was the king of the gods, and the other gods lived with (he him) on Mount Olympus.

5. Between you and (I me), my favorite Greek hero is Hercules.

6. A mean king gave (he him) impossible tasks to do.

7. My sister likes tales, too, and I share my favorites with (she her).

8. Myths from all countries interest (she her) and (I me).

9. Finding similarities among myths from different places is fun for (we us).

10. Can you tell (we us) the story of your favorite myth?

APPLY IT NOW

Write two or three sentences about a mythological character with which you are familiar. Use at least two pronouns in the sentences. Identify how they are used— as a direct object, an indirect object, or an object of a preposition.

3.4 Pronouns After *Than* or *As*

The words *than* and *as* are used in comparisons. These conjunctions join two clauses; sometimes part of the second clause is omitted. You may need to add the missing parts mentally to determine whether to use a subject pronoun or an object pronoun after *than* or *as*.

> **Michelle is better at science than *I*.**
> **This week's big science test worried her as much as *me*.**

Study these examples. The words that might be omitted from the clauses are in brackets. In the second and third sentences, Elena is being compared to Sarah.

> **Elena is on the basketball team.**
> **Sarah is faster than *she* [is fast].**
> **The coach gives Sarah more playing time than [he gives] *her*.**

In the second sentence, the pronoun after *than* is the subject of the clause introduced by *than*. So the correct pronoun is *she*, a subject pronoun. In the third sentence, the pronoun after *than* is the direct object of the verb *gives*. So the correct pronoun is *her*, an object pronoun.

Sometimes either a subject or an object pronoun may be used, depending on the meaning of the sentence.

> **I've known Lisa longer than *she* [has known Lisa].**
> **I've known Lisa longer than [I've known] *her*.**

In sentences with *than* or *as,* remember to supply the missing words mentally to check for correct pronoun usage.

EXERCISE 1 Rewrite these sentences. For each underlined pronoun, add in brackets the missing information that helps determine correct pronoun use.

EXAMPLE   **I am further along with my social studies project than she [is with her social studies project].**

1. She has not spent as much time on her project as <u>I</u>.
2. I think that I have chosen a more difficult topic than <u>she</u>.
3. Social studies interests me more than <u>her</u>.
4. Jim is as interested in social studies as <u>I</u>.
5. I wish Ms. Hanks were as helpful to me as <u>him</u>.
6. I wish Ms. Hanks were as helpful to me as <u>he</u>.

EXERCISE 2 **Complete each sentence with the correct pronoun.**

1. The subject of our science project, to build a xeriscape garden, interests my two partners as much as (I me).

2. I was as excited about building a garden with plants that require less water as (they them).

3. Mia and Sophie, my partners, spent as much time learning about plants such as cactus and jade as (I me).

4. Digging up the ground for the garden outside the school was easier for Mr. Danforth, our sponsor, than (we us).

5. He dug much faster than (I me).

6. Sophie was better at taking care of the plants than Mia and (I me).

7. Because our project involved cultivating plants over a period of time, most other groups finished earlier than (we us).

8. This fact bothered my partners, Mia and Sophie, more than (I me).

9. Mia and I got along, but I enjoyed working with Sophie more than with (she her).

10. Mr. Danforth said he learned as much about these gardens as (we us).

EXERCISE 3 **Choose the correct pronoun to complete each sentence. Then tell the words that were omitted from each sentence. For some sentences both pronouns may be correct.**

1. No one was as happy about the neighborhood garden as (I me).

2. My sister wasn't as eager as (I me) about the project.

3. The garden project interested me more than (she her).

4. Our neighbors were more experienced than (we us) at gardening.

5. More land for plants was given to them than (we us).

6. The project organizer was as helpful to us as (they them).

7. My sister worked more in the garden than (I me).

8. No one was as surprised at the large size of our tomatoes than (she her).

9. My neighbors grew more tomatoes than (we us).

10. We harvested our tomatoes earlier than (they them).

11. They planted their crops later than (we us).

12. We harvested more beans than (they them).

13. Our neighbors were as surprised at our success as (we us).

APPLY IT NOW

Choose two celebrities that interest you. Use a Venn diagram to help you compare their qualities. Write four sentences in which *you* compare the two people. Use *than* and *as* followed by personal pronouns.

 Tech Tip Use a computer tool to help you create your diagram.

3.5 Possessive Pronouns and Adjectives

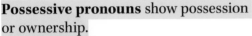

Possessive pronouns show possession or ownership.
They take the place of possessive nouns.

> **These shoes are** *Liz's.* (possessive noun)
> **These shoes are** *hers.* (possessive pronoun)

The possessive pronouns change in form to indicate person, number, and gender. Be careful of the spelling of the forms. Unlike possessive nouns, possessive pronouns do not contain apostrophes.

POSSESSIVE PRONOUNS	SINGULAR	PLURAL
FIRST PERSON	mine	ours
SECOND PERSON	yours	yours
THIRD PERSON	his, hers, its	theirs

Possessive pronouns work in sentences as possessive nouns do.

> *Theirs* **are hanging in the closet.** (subject)
> **That costume is** *his.* (subject complement)
> **Have you seen** *mine*? (direct object)

Words similar to possessive pronouns are **possessive adjectives.** The possessive adjectives are *my, our, your, his, her, its,* and *their.* Possessive pronouns can be confused with possessive adjectives. Possessive pronouns stand alone. Possessive adjectives precede nouns. Remember that *it's,* with an apostrophe, is the contraction for *it is* and should not be confused with *its,* the possessive adjective.

POSSESSIVE PRONOUNS	POSSESSIVE ADJECTIVES
Mine is new.	*My* bike is new.
His is broken	*His* skateboard is broken.
That is *hers.*	That is *her* car.
Ours is painted gray.	*Our* house is painted gray.
Did you see *theirs*?	Did you see *their* camera?

EXERCISE 1 **Identify each possessive pronoun or possessive adjective in these sentences. Then identify the noun each possessive adjective modifies.**

1. The choice of the play for the drama club to perform was ours.

2. The suggestion to do *Beauty and the Beast* was mine.

3. One of our teachers was chosen to direct the play.

4. It is now her task to assign jobs to the students.

5. Since Andrew knows a lot about theater, the important job of stage manager will naturally be his.

6. Their script is on top of ours on Andrew's desk.

Beauty and the Beast illustration by Jennie Harbour

EXERCISE 2 **Complete each sentence with a possessive pronoun. The pronoun should refer to the underlined antecedent.**

1. Edward is playing the Beast, and that ugly animal mask is _____.

2. Allison is making some of the sets for the play. The painted backdrop of the castle is _____.

3. Lewis and Elaine are practicing their lines over there, so I think that the script on that table is _____.

4. You misplaced your copy? Is that one on the bench _____?

5. The actors needed additional makeup, so I brought _____.

6. The extra costumes in that box are _____.

EXERCISE 3 **Rewrite the sentences so that the use of possessive pronouns and possessive adjectives is correct. Not all sentences have errors.**

1. Yvette had the biggest role, and it's language was the most difficult.

2. The teacher praised Edward's acting, and she also praised yours'.

3. The teacher recognized Lynne's work with the lighting, and she also recognized mine's with the costumes.

4. After the last performance, all who worked behind the scenes were called onstage. Much of the credit was really theirs.

5. We all received theater trophies. Mine was for costumes and yours was for sound effects, but hers was for lighting.

6. We called the teacher onstage to show ours appreciation for her help.

APPLY IT NOW

Imagine that you and your friends are dressed nearly alike for a costume party, but there are some differences in your costumes and makeup. Write five sentences comparing your costume with theirs. Use possessive pronouns and adjectives in your writing.

3.6 Intensive and Reflexive Pronouns

Intensive and reflexive pronouns end in *self* or *selves*. An **intensive pronoun** is used to emphasize a preceding noun or pronoun.

> **My mother paid for her education as a veterinarian** *herself***.**
> **I** *myself* **want to be a veterinarian.**

A **reflexive pronoun** is used as the direct or indirect object of a verb or as the object of a preposition. The reflexive pronoun refers back to the subject of the sentence.

> **We consider** *ourselves* **responsible enough to have a pet.** (direct object)
> **They bought** *themselves* **a book on pet care.** (indirect object)
> **Henry takes care of his pets by** *himself***.** (object of a preposition)

The chart shows forms of intensive and reflexive pronouns. These pronouns should agree with their antecedents (the word to which a pronoun refers) in person, number, and gender.

INTENSIVE AND REFLEXIVE PRONOUNS	SINGULAR	PLURAL
FIRST PERSON	myself	ourselves
SECOND PERSON	yourself	yourselves
THIRD PERSON	himself herself itself	themselves

Note that *hisself* and *theirselves* are not good usage. What words would you use instead? You are correct if you said *himself* and *themselves*. It is also incorrect to use an intensive or a reflexive form instead of a subject or an object personal pronoun.

> **Joseph and I** (*not* myself) **have gerbils as pets.**
> **The project was done by Chloe and** *me* (*not* myself)**.**

EXERCISE 1 Identify the intensive or reflexive pronoun in each sentence.

1. You yourself are responsible for your pet.
2. He fed his bearded dragon live crickets himself.
3. Eleanor taught herself how to be comfortable with new dogs.

4. I myself gave medicine to the injured raccoon.

5. Owen fed every one of the chicks himself.

6. Having followed the rabbit, Ann found herself surrounded by bunnies.

7. I gave myself a reward for rescuing the squirrel—a piece of chocolate cake.

8. You are going to fix the injured wing by yourself.

EXERCISE 2 Identify the intensive or reflexive pronoun in each sentence. Then identify its antecedent.

1. Early in her career, British naturalist Jane Goodall found herself fascinated with chimpanzees.

2. From the time she was four years old, Jane immersed herself in animal behavior.

3. At that age she hid herself in a chicken coop for hours to see how a hen lays an egg.

4. Rather than attending college, Goodall got herself a job, saving the money to go to Africa.

5. Once there, she met the famous Professor Louis Leakey himself, and she asked him for a job.

6. Dr. Leakey and his family were themselves in Africa to study fossils.

7. Their work did not itself involve living animals.

8. With their help, however, Jane Goodall stayed in Africa, and she was able to be near the chimps themselves and to study them.

9. Gradually, they began to put themselves in her path, no longer afraid of her.

10. Her work itself became a model of how to study animals in their natural environments.

Jane Goodall with a chimpanzee

EXERCISE 3 Rewrite the sentences so the use of intensive and reflexive pronouns is correct. Not all sentences have errors.

1. My older brother, Michael, and I studied the ape and how it entertained itself in its new environment.

2. We ourselves have observed animals—our pets of course.

3. My brother hisself has worked as a volunteer in the local zoo.

4. He has even fed the big elephants theirselves.

5. I hope that in the future I can volunteer at the zoo myself.

APPLY IT NOW

Look through magazine or newspaper articles for intensive and reflexive pronouns. Using the first three paragraphs, list the pronouns and their antecedents.

Grammar in Action. Find the intensive pronoun in the p. 260 excerpt.

3.7 Agreement of Pronouns and Antecedents

The word to which a pronoun refers is called its **antecedent.** Pronouns must agree with their antecedents in person, number, and, when appropriate, gender.

My brother is an archaeologist, and *he* spends a lot of time on digs.

The antecedent of the pronoun *he* is *brother.* Because *brother,* the person spoken of, refers to a male and is singular, the third person singular masculine pronoun is the correct choice.

In the following, what is the antecedent of *her*?

Megan, a friend of mine, is interested in archaeology, so my brother frequently talks to her about his work.

You are correct if you answered *Megan.* So the object pronoun *her* is third person singular feminine to agree with its antecedent.

In the following sentence, can you find the pronoun and antecedent and explain the agreement?

Heinrich Schliemann

My brother and I enjoy history programs on TV, and we sometimes watch these programs together.

The antecedent of the subject pronoun *we* is *brother and I.* Because the antecedent is in the first person and is plural, the subject pronoun must also be first person and plural.

EXERCISE 1 **Identify the antecedent for each underlined pronoun.**

1. My sister and I love stories from the *Iliad* and the *Odyssey,* and <u>we</u> own copies of both books.
2. You <u>yourselves</u> may have read them.
3. When I read the book, I read some parts of <u>it</u> aloud to my sister.
4. One man was so fascinated by the stories that <u>he</u> did something that no one had done before.
5. Heinrich Schliemann tried to locate the site of the fabled city <u>itself</u>.
6. The people of Troy had fought the ancient Greeks in a war. <u>It</u> was the conflict that Homer described in the *Iliad.*
7. The travelers found <u>themselves</u> in a modern commercialized city of Troy.
8. The archaeological site <u>itself</u> has been excavated too many times.

Sophia
Schliemann

EXERCISE 2 Identify the pronoun that goes with each underlined antecedent.

1. To search for ancient Troy, Schliemann used stories for <u>information</u> to help. It took him to a site in Turkey.

2. <u>Turkey</u> has a unique culture because it is bordered by eight countries. It has many Eastern and Western influences.

3. <u>Sophia</u>, Schliemann's wife, was Greek, and she supervised the assistants who worked on the excavation.

4. Although the <u>Schliemanns</u> were unsuccessful initially in finding the ruins, they did not give up hope.

5. In May 1873, <u>Schliemann</u> found the ruins of a large building behind two gates. He declared it the palace of King Priam.

6. In Greek <u>mythology</u>, King Priam was the king of Troy during the Trojan War. It says that Priam's youngest son was the cause of the war.

EXERCISE 3 Complete these sentences with a pronoun, making sure it agrees with the underlined antecedent.

1. <u>Heinrich Schliemann</u> made some important discoveries, but people have criticized _____ on several counts.

2. <u>Heinrich and his assistants</u> had not uncovered the ruins of Homeric Troy, but, in fact, _____ had dug right through them.

3. Also, Heinrich had agreements with several <u>countries</u> to share discoveries with _____.

4. <u>Heinrich</u> kept many objects for _____, however.

5. A photo of <u>Sophia</u> shows _____ wearing jewelry from the digs.

6. A <u>country</u> with a site would want to keep ancient objects for _____.

7. Some say that Schliemann's <u>accounts</u> of his exploits were not always true and that _____ cannot be relied on for accuracy.

8. His <u>work</u> was important, because _____ popularized archaeology.

9. What do <u>you</u> _____ think of the Schliemanns?

10. <u>We</u> _____ want to read more about them.

APPLY IT NOW

Which inventor would you like to learn more about? Find information on this person and write a short paragraph about him or her. Replace each pronoun with the antecedent and reread your paragraph. How does it sound? Why is it important to use pronouns to replace antecedents?

Grammar in Action Find the first pronoun and antecedent in p. 261 excerpt.

Pronouns • 45

3.8 Interrogative and Demonstrative Pronouns

An **interrogative pronoun** is used to ask a question. The interrogative pronouns are *who, whom, whose, which,* and *what.*

Who refers to persons. It is often the subject in a question.

> **Who is reading** *A Wrinkle in Time*? (subject)

Whom refers to persons. It is the object of a verb or a preposition.

> **Whom did you see in the library?** (direct object)
> **To whom did you recommend the book?** (object of a preposition)

Whose is used when asking about possession. *Which* is used when asking about a group or class. *What* is used for asking about things and seeking information.

> **Whose is this book?**
> **Which of the books on the list are you going to read?**
> **What did you borrow from the library?**
> **What is the book about?**

What is the error in the use of an interrogative pronoun in this sentence?

> **Who did you ask for a copy of the book?**

The interrogative pronoun *whom* should be used because it is the direct object of the sentence.

The **demonstrative pronouns** are *this, that, these,* and *those.* They point out a particular person, place, or thing.

SINGULAR	PLURAL
This is a good mystery.	*These* are all nonfiction books.
That is an exciting adventure story.	*Those* are novels by contemporary writers.

Use *this* and *these* to point out what is near. Use *that* and *those* to point out what is far.

EXERCISE 1 Identify the interrogative or demonstrative pronoun used in each sentence. Then tell what type of pronoun it is.

1. I think these are your wet towels.
2. Whose are the swimming fins near the pool?
3. Which of the swim caps are yours?
4. Is this Ben's beach ball?
5. Mom asked, "What is under the beach umbrella?"
6. Those are your swimming fins, aren't they?
7. Who used my life vest?
8. Ann yelled, "Don't take that. It's my water noodle."

EXERCISE 2 Complete each question with an interrogative pronoun.

1. _____ wrote the novel *The Pool Party*?
2. With _____ does the main character live?
3. _____ is one of his favorite pastimes?
4. _____ are his friends?
5. _____ is the name of the book you are reading?
6. _____ do you like best about it?
7. To _____ will you lend it when you have finished?
8. _____ did you think of the ending?
9. _____ told you the ending and spoiled the surprise?
10. _____ do you like better—true-to-life stories or science fiction?

EXERCISE 3 Complete each sentence by adding the correct demonstrative pronoun. Use the directions in parentheses.

1. Is _____ (near) the swimsuit you wanted?
2. No, _____ (far) is my old one.
3. Are _____ (near) the pool towels?
4. Yes, _____ (far) are the gray ones for the pool.
5. _____ (near) are white and are for the shower.
6. Are _____ (near) your flip-flops?
7. Yes, _____ (far) are mine.
8. Is _____ (near) the swim cap I can use?

APPLY IT NOW

Write five fun trivia questions. Use an interrogative pronoun in each. Trade papers with a classmate and see if you can answer his or her questions. Circle the interrogative pronouns and any demonstrative pronouns you may have used in your answers.

3.9 Relative Pronouns

Le Petit Journal

A LOUIS PASTEUR

A **relative pronoun** is used to join a dependent clause to its antecedent in the independent clause. The relative pronouns are *who, whom, which, that,* and *whose.*

> **The student who earned first place received a scholarship.**
>> **Independent clause: The student received a scholarship.**
>> **Dependent clause: who earned first place**

The relative pronouns *who* and *whom* refer to people. The relative pronoun *which* refers to animals, places, or things.

Portrait of
Louis Pasteur

> **Louis Pasteur, who discovered bacteria as the cause of many diseases, was a French scientist.**
> **Vaccines, which help people fight off disease, were his work.**

The relative pronoun *that* refers to people, animals, places, or things. The relative pronoun *whose* often refers to people but can also refer to animals, places, or things.

> **Bacteria are simple organisms that have one cell.**
> **Pasteur, whose vaccines saved many lives, understood that.**

When choosing between *who* and *whom,* use *who* when the relative pronoun is the subject in a dependent clause.

> **Louis Pasteur, who was a chemistry teacher, studied bacteria.**

Use *whom* when the relative pronoun is the object in a dependent clause.

> **Louis Pasteur, whom the French honor as a hero, is famous around the world.** (object of a dependent clause)
> **I read a book about Pasteur, about whom we had studied in class.** (object of a preposition in a dependent clause)

EXERCISE 1 Identify the relative pronoun or pronouns in each sentence. Then identify its antecedent.

1. The strain of influenza that hit after World War I was deadly.
2. This outbreak, which took place in 1918, killed half a million people in the United States alone.
3. Many soldiers who survived the war battles were killed by the influenza.
4. The virus that caused the disease apparently originated in China but spread rapidly around the world.

5. The disease, which was especially hard on people in their 20s and 30s, was over by the spring of 1919.

6. Particularly alarming was the high death rate among 20- and 30-year-olds who were otherwise healthy.

7. Usually, the old and the young, whose health is generally weaker, make up the majority of deaths in flu epidemics.

8. In some places, it was decided to quarantine people whom the disease had struck.

9. *Quarantine* means "to isolate those who are already ill as well as others who have been in contact with them."

10. Medicine, which was quite different then than it is today, was not much help in treating this flu.

EXERCISE 2 **Rewrite the sentences to correct the use of relative pronouns. Not all sentences have errors.**

1. Edward Jenner, to who credit is given for inventing the first vaccine, sought to stop the spread of smallpox in the 1700s.

2. Jenner, who I did a report on, was an English physician.

3. Smallpox was a deadly disease to people who it claimed as victims.

4. Louis Pasteur, by who many health discoveries were made, used Jenner's term *vaccine* for immunization against any disease.

5. Jenner, who was a country doctor, made his discovery by close observation.

EXERCISE 3 **Complete each sentence with an appropriate relative pronoun. More than one answer may be correct.**

1. Scientists have long known about a chemical _____ helps clot blood.

2. Bats, _____ seem scary to many people, produce this amazing chemical in their saliva.

3. Scientists _____ develop new medicines are investigating bat saliva.

4. A drug company _____ sells chemicals is researching this.

5. The company hopes to produce a medicine for people _____ are victims of strokes.

6. The bats _____ saliva was studied for the medicine are blood-sucking ones.

APPLY IT NOW

Look in magazines and newspapers for sentences with relative pronouns. Cut out five sentences and glue them on a sheet of paper. Underline dependent clauses, circle relative pronouns, and draw arrows to their antecedents.

Tech Tip With an adult, look at news Web sites.

3.10 Indefinite Pronouns

Old West cowboy
Nat Love

An **indefinite pronoun** refers to any or all of a group of people, places, or things.

SINGULAR		PLURAL	SINGULAR AND PLURAL
another	neither	both	all
anybody	nobody	few	any
anyone	no one	many	more
anything	nothing	others	most
each	one	several	none
either	other		some
everybody	somebody		
everyone	someone		
everything	something		
much			

Like nouns, indefinite pronouns act as subjects and as objects.

> *Much* **about the cowboy is myth.** (subject)
>
> **This book about cowboys was given to me by** *someone*—**I can't remember whom I got it from.** (object of a preposition)

Negative indefinite pronouns, such as *no one*, *nobody*, *none*, and *nothing*, should not be combined with other negative words, such as *no*, *not*, or *never*.

EXERCISE 1 Identify the indefinite pronouns in these sentences. Not every sentence contains an indefinite pronoun.

1. Is there anyone not interested in the Old West?

2. Many have read books or seen movies set back then.

3. Nothing appeals more than the romantic figure of the cowboy.

4. Few in my class knew that the classic era of the cowboys was short—only about 20 years, from 1865 to about 1885.

5. The life of cowboys was hard and dangerous, according to each of the books I read.

6. All rode horses and drove cattle.

7. Many were African Americans and Mexicans.

8. They spent much of their day in the saddle.

9. Cowboys drove cattle hundreds of miles over trails to railroads, where the cattle were sent to market.

10. Several of the famous cattle trails were the Shawnee Trail, the Chisholm Trail, and the Western Trail.

11. A few on a cattle drive had special roles, particularly the wrangler (who took care of the horses), the cook, and the trail boss.

12. Singing by campfires at night was something that cowboys did do.

13. Everyone likes cowboy hats, but few realize that the broad brims were to help protect their wearers from sun and rain.

14. Cowboy boots had tapered toes so that a rider could pull his foot easily from the stirrup if he fell from a horse.

EXERCISE 2 Identify the indefinite pronoun in each sentence. Tell its function in the sentence.

1. Anything about outlaws of the Old West interests us.

2. True or not, these tales were told to anyone who would listen.

3. Few seem to really care if the tales are true or not.

4. No one seems to mind as long as the story is good.

5. Many of the outlaws have colorful names—such as the Sundance Kid, who robbed banks with Butch Cassidy.

6. Their exploits brought both a certain amount of fame.

7. Neither used his own name: Butch Cassidy was Robert Leroy Parker, and Sundance Kid was Henry Longabaugh.

8. Another of these outlaws was the train robber Sam Bass.

9. Bass was supposedly somebody who robbed from the rich and gave to the poor.

10. This view is challenged by others, who say he was an outlaw who liked to rob for the thrill of it.

EXERCISE 3 Rewrite each sentence so that the indefinite pronoun is used correctly. Not all sentences have errors.

1. The students didn't know nothing about Annie Oakley.

2. Doesn't nobody know feats of this famous Old West figure?

3. No one was as good a sharp shooter as she was.

4. Everybody wanted to see her shoot in Wild West shows.

5. She never missed no target during her performances in the show.

6. She didn't disappoint nobody at her shows.

APPLY IT NOW

In small groups, create a visual graph of four of your group's favorite foods. Without using specific names, numbers, or percentages, write an explanation of your group's graph, using as many indefinite pronouns as you can. What do you notice about the accuracy of your report?

Tech Tip Create the graph in a PowerPoint presentation.

3.11 Agreement with Indefinite Pronouns

Most indefinite pronouns are singular, but some are plural. When an indefinite pronoun acts as the subject of a sentence, the verb needs to agree with it in number.

Singular indefinite pronouns include *another, anybody, anyone, anything, each, either, everybody, everyone, everything, much, neither, nobody, no one, nothing, one, other, somebody, someone,* and *something.* They take singular verbs. In this sentence *everyone* is followed by *is,* the third person singular form of the verb *be.*

> *Everyone* **is busy working on a project.**

Which verb correctly completes the following sentence?

> **Everyone** (want wants) **to contribute to the community.**

The correct answer is *wants.* It is a third person singular verb, to agree with the singular indefinite pronoun.

Plural indefinite pronouns include *both, few, many, others,* and *several.* They take plural verbs.

> *Both* **are good ideas for projects.**
> *Several* **want to work at a community center.**

Some indefinite pronouns can be either singular or plural, depending on how they are used in a sentence. They include *all, any, more, most, none,* and *some.* These pronouns are singular and take a singular verb when they are followed by a phrase with a singular noun or an abstract noun. They are plural and take a plural verb when they are followed by a phrase with a plural noun.

SINGULAR	PLURAL
All **the pie was eaten.**	*All* **the pies were eaten.**
Most **of the work is done.**	*Most* **of the projects are done.**

EXERCISE 1 **Choose the correct verb or verbs to complete each sentence. Make sure the verb agrees with its subject.**

1. At our school everyone (is are) expected to take part in a project.

2. All the students (is are) encouraged to pick projects that suit their talents and interests.

3. No one (has have) to pick any particular project.

4. Everybody (works work) with an adult or an older student.

5. Many of the projects (is are) extremely rewarding.

6. Several (involves, involve) working with seniors.

7. Some of the students (goes go) to a nursing home.

8. A few (is are) allowed to take their pets.

9. Helen and Sam can take their dogs; both (has have) dogs that are specially trained.

10. Nothing (lights light) up people's eyes more than a dog.

11. Helen and Sam are very helpful; either (is are) always happy to explain how to train a dog as a visiting dog.

12. Somebody in the organization (helps help) you train your dog.

13. A few of the students (works work) at a soup kitchen.

14. Some (serves serve) food; others (cleans clean) tables.

EXERCISE 2 **Rewrite the sentences so that the verbs agree with the indefinite pronouns. Not all sentences have errors.**

1. This school term somebody are organizing a local food pantry.

2. Some are going to visit businesses to ask for donations.

3. A few has already collected boxes of food.

4. Neither of the cans were soup.

5. All the food are going to the local food pantry.

6. When the trucks were loaded, each were filled to capacity with food.

7. Everyone involved want to make the project a success.

8. Many worked through the night to finish the job.

9. Of the pantries, either were available at any hour to accept donations.

10. All the students find most people to be generous.

APPLY IT NOW

Write five sentences about a class or school project you have participated in. Underline all the indefinite pronouns in your writing. If they are the subjects of sentences, check to see that they agree with their verbs.

Pronoun Review

3.1 Identify the pronoun in each sentence. Tell whether it is first, second, or third person; whether it is singular or plural; and, if it is third person singular, whether it is masculine, feminine, or neuter.

1. We grew up reading Shel Silverstein's poetry.

2. Did you boys like the funny poems or drawings better?

3. It was my best friend's birthday present.

4. Andrea knew about the book, and she gave a recommendation.

3.2 Rewrite the sentences to correct the pronouns.

5. Me and my cousin wanted to take surfing lessons.

6. Her and I went to find the telephone book.

7. Mom and me looked everywhere for it, but it was her who found it.

8. The people discussing the cost were Dad, Mom, and her.

3.3 Rewrite the sentences to correct the use of pronouns.

9. Most of the pictures were of he and the frisky puppy named Flash.

10. Mrs. Avila raises pugs, and John gave she and her daughter pictures.

11. He said he would give Flash to Mrs. Avila and she.

12. Flash's mother was a gift from Ernesto and I.

3.4 Complete each sentence with the correct pronoun.

13. David Beckham is better at soccer than (I me).

14. I have not spent as much time practicing as (he him).

15. Finding information about soccer was easier for the librarian than (we us).

16. I learned as much about the Internet as (they them).

3.5 Complete each sentence with the correct possessive form. Tell whether it is a possessive pronoun or a possessive adjective.

17. The lunch in the old-fashioned pail is (her hers).

18. (Our Ours) lunches are always the same on Friday.

19. Marie and Sylvia bought (their theirs) at the concession stand.

20. (His Its) pizza was ready when he got there.

21. (Yours Your) ice cream will not be delivered on time.

3.6 Identify the underlined pronouns as intensive or reflexive. Tell the antecedent for each pronoun.

22. Eugenie Clark <u>herself</u> was fascinated with creatures of the deep.

23. We allowed <u>ourselves</u> several visits to observe the sharks at her laboratory.

24. Our work <u>itself</u> did not involve swimming with the sharks.

25. I got <u>myself</u> a job there as an intern.

26. After I met the director <u>herself</u>, we discussed sharks.

3.7 **Identify the antecedent for each underlined pronoun.**

27. Sarah and I went out for dinner, and <u>we</u> both ordered hamburgers.

28. The server asked if we wanted anything to drink, and <u>she</u> recommended the chocolate shakes.

29. Sarah told me about <u>her</u> brother, who just got a kitten.

30. Jessica has two cats, and <u>they</u> like to go outside when it's snowing.

31. William likes snow, and <u>he</u> has a great throwing arm for snowball fights.

3.8 **Complete the first two sentences with the correct interrogative pronouns and the last two sentences with the correct demonstrative pronouns.**

32. _____ do you think dropped it?

33. To _____ did you give the card?

34. Is _____ your dirty laundry?

35. _____ are full laundry bags I'm carrying.

3.9 **Rewrite the sentences to correct the use of relative pronouns.**

36. The giant *T. Rex* named Sue, who is the largest known

T. Rex specimen, was found by Susan Hendrickson.

37. After the bones were unearthed, they were sold to the Field Museum in Chicago, that paid $8.36 million for them.

38. The scientists studied the head and learned that the part of the brain which helps smell was huge.

3.10 **Identify the indefinite pronouns.**

39. How many of your friends really like to eat?

40. Everyone I know likes to eat, though he or she may have different likes and dislikes.

41. Some prefer Italian food, while others prefer Chinese.

42. My favorite meal is one that I don't have to cook.

3.11 **Identify the indefinite pronouns. Tell whether they are singular or plural.**

43. After drinking one root beer, James asked Joe to bring another to the table.

44. Of the 10 people at the adjoining table, several asked Joe the same thing.

45. Some, who didn't like root beer, wanted lemonade.

46. Chocolate cake and carrot cake were the desserts, and guests could choose either or both.

47. However, all the chocolate cake was eaten.

Tech Tip Go to www.voyagesinenglish.com for more activities.

Pronoun Challenge

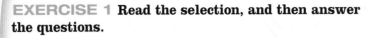

EXERCISE 1 **Read the selection, and then answer the questions.**

1. Do you know how to make a collage? 2. It is a craft that anyone can do. 3. What exactly is a collage? 4. It is a picture made by attaching paper, fabric, or any other material onto a background. 5. The materials are arranged to form a picture or other pleasing pattern. 6. *Collage* comes from the French word for "glue," but that in itself is not enough to produce one—creativity is needed. 7. A plentiful and inexpensive material that a beginning collage artist can use is newspaper. 8. Tear out a page and rub a soft white candle over its back. 9. Once this is done, flip it over and cut out the shapes you want for the collage—triangles, squares, or circles. 10. Arrange the pieces onto a black poster board with the sticky, waxed side down. 11. Once you learn this technique, experiment with textured fabrics, bright materials, and different glues. 12. When you are able to plan your collages and get your creativity to come across in each, you yourself will be a budding collage artist.

1. What is the personal pronoun in sentence 1? What is its person?
2. What is the relative pronoun in sentence 2? What is the antecedent?
3. Which sentence—1, 2, or 3—contains an indefinite pronoun? What is it?
4. What is the reflexive pronoun in sentence 6? Identify its person, number, and gender.
5. What is the relative pronoun in sentence 7? What is its antecedent?
6. What is the possessive form in sentence 8? Is it a possessive pronoun or a possessive adjective?
7. Find the demonstrative pronoun in sentence 9.
8. Find an indefinite pronoun in sentence 12. Is it singular or plural?
9. What is the intensive pronoun in sentence 12? Identify its person and number.
10. Which sentence has an interrogative pronoun? What is it?

EXERCISE 2 **Write a short paragraph explaining how you do a hobby or craft, including information such as the history of the craft.**

1. Use an interrogative pronoun, a subject pronoun, and an object pronoun.
2. Identify the subject pronoun as either a subject or a subject complement and the object pronoun as a direct object, an indirect object, or an object of a preposition.
3. Use either *who* or *whom* at least once in your paragraph.

Verbs

4.1 Principal Parts of Verbs

Verbs show action or state of being.

Lance Armstrong *won* **the Tour de France many times.** (action)
Greg LeMond *was* **the first American cyclist to win that competition.** (state of being)

The three principal parts of a verb are the **base form,** the **past,** and the **past participle.** A fourth part, the **present participle,** is formed by adding *-ing* to the base form. Participles have three functions in sentences. They can be part of a verb phrase or act as an adjective or a noun.

Regular verbs form the past and past participle by adding *-d* or *-ed* to the base form.

BASE	PAST	PAST PARTICIPLE	PRESENT PARTICIPLE
play	played	played	playing
wade	waded	waded	wading

Use a dictionary to find the principal parts of **irregular verbs.**

BASE	PAST	PAST PARTICIPLE	PRESENT PARTICIPLE
do	did	done	doing
eat	ate	eaten	eating

A **verb phrase** is two or more verbs that work together as a unit. A verb phrase may have one or more **auxiliary verbs** and a main verb. In this sentence *have* is an auxiliary verb; *watched* is the main verb, and it is in the past participle form. Note that the past participle is often used with auxiliary verbs, while the past form stands alone.

Ten million people *have watched* **the Tour de France each year.**

Can you find the auxiliary and main verb in this sentence?

Have you begun your report on the Tour de France?

You are correct if you said that *have* is the auxiliary verb in the sentence and that *begun* is the main verb.

Common auxiliary verbs are *be* and *have* and their various forms, as well as *do, did, can, may, might, should, could,* and *will.*

EXERCISE 1 **Identify the verb or verb phrase in each sentence.**

1. What do you know about the Iroquois Indians?
2. The Iroquois inhabited the northeastern United States.
3. Native Americans from this area are called Woodland Indians.
4. The Iroquois lived around the Great Lakes in Ohio, Pennsylvania, New York, and lower Canada.
5. The League of the Iroquois was a confederation of six tribes.
6. The league included the Cayuga, Mohawk, Oneida, Onondaga, Seneca, and Tuscarora nations.
7. Travelers today will recognize many of these as place names.

Iroquois
Indian Chief
Pau-Puk-Keewis

EXERCISE 2 **Complete each sentence with the past or past participle form of the verb in parentheses.**

1. At one time the Iroquois _____ (use) deerskins for clothing.
2. Hunting _____ (be) also a major source for food.
3. Cleared areas of the forest were _____ (farm) by the Iroquois.
4. They _____ (grow) varieties of squash, corn, and beans.
5. Longhouses were _____ (build) by the Iroquois.
6. These structures _____ (hold) many families.
7. Iroquois villages _____ (contain) a number of longhouses.
8. They _____ (fortify) the villages with trenches.
9. Words from the Iroquois, such as *wampum,* are _____ (use) in English today.

EXERCISE 3 **Identify the verb or verb phrases in each sentence. Identify the auxiliary verb in each verb phrase.**

1. Iroquois longhouses have disappeared over time.
2. Some museums feature reconstructions of Iroquois villages.
3. The reconstructions are visited by the public.
4. You can get a feel for the daily life of Iroquois.
5. The longhouses were divided into smaller areas.
6. One or two families would live off the main corridor.
7. Visitors may walk through the reconstructed longhouses.

APPLY IT NOW

Write six sentences about what you did this past weekend, using different verbs. Use the past form in three sentences and the past participle form in the other three sentences.

Grammar in Action. Find the first verb phrase on p. 299.

4.2 Transitive and Intransitive Verbs

A **transitive verb** expresses an action that passes from a doer to a receiver. The receiver of the action is the direct object. In this sentence the verb *saw* is transitive. Its direct object is *musical*. To determine if there is a direct object, ask *whom* or *what* after the verb.

Andres *saw* **the new musical.**

Some transitive verbs are phrasal verbs. A **phrasal verb** is a combination of the main verb and a preposition or an adverb, such as *burn down, drag out, hand down, look after, put on,* and *set up.* Although the main verb may appear to be followed by a prepositional phrase, the noun or pronoun that follows the preposition or adverb is a direct object. In the following sentence, *on your coat* is not a prepositional phrase.

Put on **your coat.** (*Put on* is the phrasal verb; *coat* is the direct object.)

An **intransitive verb** does not have a receiver for its action. It does not have a direct object.

Andres *went* **to the Fremont Theater.**

Can you tell whether the verb in this sentence is transitive or intransitive? How can you tell?

Andres enjoyed the show.

The verb *enjoyed* is transitive. Its direct object is *show,* which answers the question *Andres enjoyed what?*

Some verbs may be either transitive or intransitive, depending on their use in the sentence.

Juan *practices* **the guitar every day.** (transitive)
Juan *practices* **after school.** (intransitive)

EXERCISE 1 **The verbs in the following sentences can be both transitive and intransitive. Identify the verb in each sentence and tell whether it is transitive or intransitive.**

1. James Herriot writes about his work as a country veterinarian.
2. James Herriot wrote the book *All Creatures Great and Small.*
3. The winner dropped to the ground at the end of the race.
4. Grace, the winner, dropped the medal on the grass.

5. Olga practices her routine in the gym.

6. Olga, a dedicated gymnast, practices regularly.

EXERCISE 2 **Identify the verb or verb phrase in each sentence. Then tell whether the verb is transitive or intransitive.**

1. Placido Domingo has sung on stages around the world.

2. He sings opera primarily.

3. He gives his time and energy to support young artists.

4. He has contributed to the popularity of operatic and Spanish music.

5. He performs a wide variety of roles.

Placido Domingo

EXERCISE 3 **Identify the verb, verb phrase, or phrasal verb in each sentence. Tell whether it is transitive or intransitive. If the verb is transitive, identify the direct object.**

1. Placido Domingo originally came from Spain.

2. As a boy, he lived in Mexico.

3. His parents worked as performers of Spanish songs.

4. From an early age, Domingo often joined his parents on stage.

5. His family's group achieved success after much hard work.

6. Domingo benefited from this early stage experience.

7. As a young boy, Domingo also had a passion for soccer.

8. According to Domingo, soccer and opera speak the same language of emotion.

9. Domingo joined the National Opera of Mexico at the age of 18.

10. Domingo took on at least 120 different operatic roles—the largest number of any singer yet.

11. In 1985 a major earthquake struck Mexico.

12. Domingo flew to the site of the disaster.

13. He helped out with the rescue work.

14. Later, his efforts raised two million dollars for the earthquake victims.

15. The Mexican government awarded Domingo its highest honor for his work.

16. He has received tributes for both his singing and his humanitarian work.

APPLY IT NOW

Write five or six sentences about a person you admire. Include special things the person has done. Circle the verbs in your writing. Tell if each is transitive or intransitive.

Tech Tip   With an adult, research this person online.

4.3 Troublesome Verbs

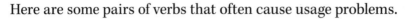

Here are some pairs of verbs that often cause usage problems.

lie, lay
The verb *lie (lay, lain)* means "to rest or recline." It is intransitive; it does not take a direct object. The verb *lay (laid, laid)* means "to put or place in position." It is transitive; it takes a direct object.

> **Those gloves have *lain* in my drawer since last winter.**
> **I *laid* my book somewhere, and now I can't find it.**

sit, set
The verb *sit (sat, sat)* means "to have or keep a seat." It is intransitive; it does not take a direct object. The verb *set (set, set)* means "to put or place." It is transitive; it takes a direct object.

> **I *sat* quietly throughout the concert.**
> **Lori *set* the salad bowl on the table.**

rise, raise
The verb *rise (rose, risen)* means "to ascend or move up." It is intransitive; it does not take a direct object. The verb *raise (raised, raised)* means "to lift up, put up, or elevate," or "to care for to maturity." It is transitive; it takes a direct object.

> **They *rise* at dawn and swim in cold water.**
> **We *raise* the flag each morning.**

let, leave
The verb *let (let, let)* means "to permit." The verb *leave (left, left)* means "to abandon," "to depart from," or "to allow to be."

> **My parents *let* me attend the movie.**
> **Amber *left* her jacket at school.**

teach, learn
The verb *teach (taught, taught)* means "to give instruction." The verb *learn (learned, learned)* means "to receive instruction."

> **Mom *taught* us how to correctly hammer a nail in the board.**
> **I've already *learned* how to do algebra.**

borrow, lend
The verb *borrow (borrowed, borrowed)* means "to obtain the use of something from another person." The verb *lend (lent, lent)* means "to give another person something to use for a time."

> **I *borrowed* a funny costume from Spencer.**
> **Spencer *lent* me his funny hat to go with the costume.**

EXERCISE 1 **Choose the correct verb to complete each sentence.**

1. My friend's family (rises raises) dogs to sell.
2. In the past they (raised rose) many champion border collies.
3. That dog (laying lying) over there belongs to them.
4. (Leave Let) him be; he should not get excited before the competition.
5. Let's go (set sit) in the audience and watch.
6. Will you (lend borrow) me your binoculars?
7. The woman who is (raising rising) now will show the dog.
8. She will (leave let) him run around the ring three times.
9. Of course, she will (leave let) his leash on him.
10. When he is told to (set sit), he quickly obeys.
11. (Learn Teach) us how to show our dog.
12. My cousin (learned taught) his dog that difficult trick.
13. That Newfoundland, the one that is (setting sitting) over there, won the top prize.
14. Annie (borrowed lent) Dan the extra leash and harness.

EXERCISE 2 **Rewrite the sentences to correct the use of troublesome verbs. Not all sentences have errors.**

1. Did you lay the puppy in the basket with its brothers and sisters?
2. Madeline, borrow me your copy of the puppy guide.
3. The puppies have laid in that basket all afternoon.
4. Amelia borrowed a larger basket from our neighbor.
5. The puppies are so tiny that they can scarcely raise their heads.
6. Rise the blanket so we can see them.
7. Their mother is setting out on the porch.
8. She usually lays there in the sun.
9. You should leave her come into the house now.
10. Sit her food bowl near the basket.
11. I'll leave you have him, but not until he is older.
12. Come set down until Mom comes home, and we'll ask for her permission.
13. James has already taught me to measure the dog food.
14. Learn the puppies to stay in the kitchen.

Woof!

APPLY IT NOW

Write your own sentences with the following verb forms:

lay (*past of lie*)	laid	lain
let (*past of let*)	leave	left
raised	rose	risen

4.4 Linking Verbs

Not all verbs express action. A **linking verb** joins a subject with a **subject complement.** The subject complement is a noun, a pronoun, or an adjective that renames or describes the subject.

SUBJECT	LINKING VERB	SUBJECT COMPLEMENT
Margaret	**is**	**our spokesperson.** (noun)
It	**was**	**she who got the prize.** (pronoun)
The grounds	**look**	**beautiful.** (adjective)

The verb *be* in its various forms (*am, is, are, was, were, will be, has been, had been,* and so on) is the most common linking verb. Other common linking verbs are *appear, become, feel, grow, look, remain, seem, smell, sound, stay, taste,* and *turn.* Some of these verbs can act as either action verbs or linking verbs.

> **She *felt* tired after hours of working in the garden.** (linking verb)
> **She *felt* the heat of the sun during her work in the garden.** (action verb—a transitive verb with the direct object *heat*)

When these words are used as linking verbs, a form of the verb *be* can be substituted for the original verb.

> **She *felt* tired after hours of working in the garden.**
> **She *was* tired after hours of working in the garden.**

EXERCISE 1 Complete each sentence with the part of speech indicated.

1. The weather seemed _____. (adjective)
2. We became _____. (noun)
3. Skating in the park is _____. (noun)
4. It was _____ who found the lost cat. (pronoun)
5. The flowers smelled _____. (adjective)
6. I felt _____ last night. (adjective)
7. He appeared _____ by the event. (adjective)
8. She remained _____. (adjective)
9. We stayed _____ through it all. (adjective)
10. That is _____ by the bus stop. (pronoun)
11. The potato chips tasted _____. (adjective)
12. Our neighbor is a(n) _____. (noun)

EXERCISE 2 Identify the linking verbs and the subject complements in the sentences. Not every sentence contains a linking verb.

1. The little park appeared overgrown and littered.
2. It was Nora who suggested we clean it up.
3. Our alderman became enthusiastic about our plan.
4. It was he who lent us gardening tools and bags for the litter.
5. To him, our ideas sounded worthwhile.
6. We decided to work at the park all day Saturday.
7. At first we felt overwhelmed by the job ahead of us.
8. Bit by bit we picked up the litter, and we trimmed the bushes.
9. The bench by the pond was dirty.
10. The new paint color looks better.
11. By the end of the day, the park was again a welcoming place.
12. We are a very helpful group.

Frederick Law Olmsted

EXERCISE 3 Identify the verb or verb phrase in each sentence. Then tell whether that verb is transitive, intransitive, or linking.

1. Many American cities have public parks near their center.
2. Frederick Law Olmsted was the designer of many such parks, including Central Park in New York City.
3. He lived in the 1800s.
4. Cities were growing quickly at the time.
5. Because of people like Olmsted, cities became hospitable places.
6. People needed green places for relaxation and amusement.
7. For Central Park, Olmsted designed winding paths, scenic views, and open spaces.
8. In the middle of Central Park, the world seems quiet and peaceful.
9. The traffic and bustle of the surrounding city disappear.
10. The overworked carriage horses deserve a long rest in the shade.
11. The park looks beautiful and interesting.
12. We still benefit from the work of these urban pioneers.

APPLY IT NOW

Write six sentences about yourself, using the words below. For ideas, write about your favorite things. Identify if the word is used as a linking verb or an action verb.

| feel | remain | smell |
| sound | taste | turn |

Tech Tip Post sentences for peer review.

4.5 Active and Passive Voices

When a transitive verb is in the **active voice,** the subject is the doer of the action. In the **passive voice,** the subject is the receiver of the action. Compare these sentences.

> **The Chinese *invented* paper.**
> **Paper *was invented* by the Chinese.**

In the first sentence, *Chinese,* the subject, is the doer of the action, *invent.* The verb, therefore, is in the active voice. In the second sentence, the subject, *paper,* is the receiver of the action, *was invented.* The verb, therefore, is in the passive voice.

A verb in the passive voice is formed by combining some form of *be* with the past participle of the main verb. Which of the following sentences is in the passive voice?

> **Gwen writes the editorials for the newspaper.**
> **The editorials for the newspaper are written by Gwen.**

You are correct if you said the second sentence is in the passive voice. The subject, *editorials,* is the receiver of the action, and the verb consists of a form of *be (are)* and the past participle of the verb *write.*

In your own writing, keep in mind that sentences in the active voice are generally more alive, exciting, and direct.

> **I watered the plants.**
> **The plants were watered by me.**

Sometimes, however, passive voice is the better choice, for example, when the doer of the action is unknown or unimportant.

> **All our athletic equipment was stolen over the weekend.**
> **Many railroads were built in the 19th century.**

EXERCISE 1 Identify the verb or verb phrase in each sentence and tell whether it is in the active voice or the passive voice.

1. What do you know about inventors and inventions?
2. The Chinese are credited with many inventions.
3. During the Song Dynasty (960–1279), many significant things were invented.
4. A complex water clock was designed by Su Song, an expert on calendars, in 1088.
5. The finished clock tower rose five levels.

6. Its ornate surface was decorated by carvers and other craftsmen.

7. Other useful Chinese inventions included paper money.

8. Interchangeable type for printing was developed.

9. Techniques for making porcelain were improved.

10. The Chinese abacus of the time is still used for mathematical calculations.

EXERCISE 2 **Rewrite each sentence in the voice indicated.**

1. A dynasty is formed by a succession of rulers from the same family. (active)

2. China was ruled by a succession of families. (active)

3. In the 10th century, the various Chinese states fought wars. (passive)

4. Old emperors were replaced by new emperors frequently. (active)

5. Finally, in 960 Zhao Kuangyin won control of the country. (passive)

6. The Chinese people appreciated the subsequent period of peace. (passive)

7. The Song emperors developed a strong central government. (passive)

8. The Song Dynasty built many cities. (passive)

9. The cities nurtured economic growth and social change. (passive)

10. Literacy and education were fueled by this growth. (active)

EXERCISE 3 **Identify the subject and verb or verb phrase in each sentence. Then tell whether the verb is in the active voice or the passive voice and whether it is transitive or intransitive.**

1. The Song Dynasty ended with the rise of Kublai Khan.

2. The Chinese were conquered by the Mongol ruler, the grandson of Genghis Khan.

3. Kublai Khan reigned in China from 1271 to 1294.

4. A new dynasty was started by Emperor Kublai Khan.

5. It is called the Yuan dynasty.

6. You may know Khan because of Marco Polo.

7. Polo's book about his experiences in China is still widely read in the West.

8. The culture and trappings of the Chinese were adapted by Kublai Khan.

9. He built a lavish summer palace with the name of Xanadu.

10. The Great Wall was rebuilt during his reign.

Emperor
Kublai
Khan

APPLY IT NOW

Look in textbooks and magazines for examples of sentences in the passive voice. Write down five such sentences. Change the sentences from the passive voice to the active voice.

Tech Tip With an adult, find the sentences online.

4.6 Simple, Progressive, and Perfect Tenses

Verb forms indicate **tense**, or the time of the action.

Simple tenses are the **present tense,** the **past tense,** and the **future tense.** They indicate whether the action is repeated or always true or takes place in the past or in the future.

Present tense:	Willis *reads* poetry often.
Past tense:	Willis *read* several poems yesterday.
Future tense:	Willis *will read* poetry again tomorrow. He *is going to read* a book by Robert Frost.

Progressive tenses are made up of a form of the auxiliary verb *be* and the present participle (the form ending in *ing*) of the main verb. These tenses show continuing, or ongoing, action.

Present progressive:	Natalie *is studying* Spanish.
Past progressive:	Natalie *was studying* Spanish last term.
Future progressive:	Natalie *will be studying* Spanish for years to come.

Perfect tenses consist of a form of the auxiliary verb have and the past participle of the main verb. The present perfect tells about an action that took place at an indefinite time in the past or that started in the past and continues into the present. The past perfect tells about an action that was completed before another action was begun or was completed. The future perfect tells about an action that will be completed before a specific time in the future.

Present perfect active:	I *have read* the book you mentioned.
Past perfect active:	I *had read* the book before the start of school.
Future perfect active:	I *will have read* the book by the end of this term.

In the perfect tenses, the passive voice is formed by inserting *been* between the auxiliary verb *have* and the main verb.

Present perfect passive:	The cat *has been groomed* already.
Past perfect passive:	The cat *had been groomed* only yesterday.
Future perfect passive:	The cat *will have been groomed* when I pick it up.

EXERCISE 1 **Identify the tense of each italicized verb and whether it is in the active or passive voice.**

1. Mr. Lee *has told* us to make a list of our favorite poems.
2. I wish we *had been asked* about favorite movies instead.
3. I still *am working* on my list.
4. My first list *contains* only one item.
5. I *had seen* the play *Cats* before I knew about T. S. Eliot's book of poetry.
6. Then I *read* this book with his poems.
7. The musical *had been inspired* by these poems.
8. I *will be looking* for my favorite poem in his book.

A character from the musical *Cats*

EXERCISE 2 **Identify the verbs in the following sentences. Tell the tense and the voice if perfect tense is used.**

1. The poetry assignment had been made last week.
2. Some students have completed their lists of poems already.
3. My list will have been completed by next Monday, before the due date.
4. The date for the reading of the poems has been set.
5. The class will be voting on the best poems.

EXERCISE 3 **Complete each sentence with the verb in parentheses. Use the tense and voice indicated.**

1. I _____ (*think*—present perfect, active) of several poems I like.
2. I _____ (*remember*—simple past, active) that I _____ (*memorize*—past perfect, active) a poem by Maya Angelou last year.
3. Many funny poems _____ (*write*—present perfect, passive) by Shel Silverstein.
4. I _____ (*choose*—simple future, active) one of those for sure.
5. Tennyson's "The Charge of the Light Brigade" _____ (*pick*—present perfect, passive) for its rhythm and action.
6. I _____ (*try*—present progressive, active) to think of others.
7. When I _____ (*think*—past progressive, active) about the assignment, I _____ (*get*—simple, past, active) the idea to read my literature textbook.
8. I am sure that I _____ (*find*—future perfect, active) a few old favorites in it.

APPLY IT NOW

Write three sentences about a favorite sport or a hobby that you enjoy. Include one sentence about your past involvement with the sport or hobby and another sentence about your plans for future involvement. Circle the verbs and identify their tenses.

4.7 Indicative, Imperative, and Emphatic Moods

Verb forms also indicate **mood.** There are four moods in English: **indicative, imperative, emphatic,** and **subjunctive.** You will examine the first three in this section and the fourth in the next one.

The **indicative mood** is the form of a verb that is used to state a fact or ask a question.

> I *took* a kayaking class.
> *Have* you ever *tried* kayaking?

Note that all the tenses studied in Section 4.6—the simple tenses, progressive tenses, and perfect tenses—are forms of the indicative mood.

The **imperative mood** is the form of a verb that is used to give commands. The subject of a verb in the imperative mood is almost always in the second person, either singular or plural. The subject *you* usually is not expressed. To form the imperative mood, use the base form of the verb.

> *Follow* all the safety rules.
> *Do* not *forget* your water bottle.

In the above sentences, the subject *you* is understood. Even when a person's name is mentioned in direct address, the subject is *you.*

> Maria, read the instructions.
> Maria, (you) read the instructions.

To form a command using the first person, use *let's (let us)* before the base form of the verb.

> *Let's sign up* for kayaking classes.

The **emphatic mood** is the form of a verb that gives special force to a simple present or past tense verb. For the present tense, use *do* or *does* before the base form of the verb. For the past tense, use *did* before the base form of the verb. Do not confuse this use with *do, does,* and *did* used as auxiliary verbs in questions or negative sentences.

> The Great Barrier Reef *does interest* me.
> I *did take* the dog for a walk.

EXERCISE 1 Identify the verb or verb phrase in each sentence. Then tell whether the sentence is in the indicative, imperative, or emphatic mood.

1. Tina, try the sport of kayaking.
2. Kayaking is becoming a more popular sport—even among kids.
3. Here are some tips on kayaking.
4. At first, go on the water only with an experienced kayaker.
5. Do not submerge the entire paddle in the water.
6. One danger of kayaking is the boat's tipping over.
7. In lakes and rivers, do be careful of boat traffic.
8. Kayaking can tire you out quickly.
9. Take a bottle of drinking water with you.
10. Most of all, do have fun!

EXERCISE 2 Rewrite the sentences in the imperative mood.

1. Each kayaker should wear a life jacket for safety.
2. It is a good idea to stay close to shore at first.
3. It is best not to elevate your hand with the paddle above your head.
4. You should rotate your upper body as you paddle.
5. You shouldn't move your head during your stroke.
6. You should know the advantages and disadvantages of hardshell kayaks.
7. No person should kayak alone.

EXERCISE 3 Identify the verbs or verb phrases in the following sentences. Tell whether each is in the indicative or imperative mood. If the verb is in the emphatic mood, tell its tense.

1. Did you find the origin of the word *kayak*?
2. I did know about its Inuit origin.
3. How does a kayak differ from a canoe?
4. Let's take a kayak ride on our next holiday.
5. People do kayak in many expected places.
6. Do you know about the kayakers on the Hudson River in New York City?
7. Many places do rent kayaks for a few hours.
8. Find the kayak rental place in your local area.

APPLY IT NOW

Write a short set of instructions for something you can do well. It might be making a food or something related to a sport or hobby. Use imperative sentences for the instructions. Consider using indicative sentences to add more information or tips to your instructions.

Grammar in Action.

What is the primary mood used in the verbs on p. 298?

4.8 Subjunctive Mood

The **subjunctive mood** of a verb can express a wish or desire or a condition that is contrary to fact. The past tense is used to state present wishes or desires or contrary-to-fact conditions. *Were* is used instead of *was,* and *would* is used instead of *will.*

Wish or desire:	I wish summer *were* here.
	I wish we *had* a band at school.
Contrary-to-fact condition:	If I *were* a better soccer player, I'd join the team.
	If I *practiced* more, I would be a better trumpet player.

The subjunctive mood is also used to express a demand or recommendation after *that* or to express an uncertainty after *if* or *whether.* The base form of the verb is used in the clause after *that, if,* or *whether.*

Demand after *that*:	I must insist that Victor *be* at the meeting.
Recommendation after *that*:	I recommended that Audrey *report* our group's conclusion.
Uncertainty:	Whether he *be* right or wrong, Paul is always coming up with ideas.
	Whether she *make* a pie or a cake, my mother will do her best.
	Patrick Henry said, "If this *be* treason, make the most of it."

EXERCISE 1 In each sentence identify the verb in the subjunctive mood. Then tell whether it expresses a wish or desire, a condition contrary to fact, a recommendation or demand following the word *that,* or an uncertainty.

1. Some of us wish that we had a chess club at school.
2. Marian suggested that Jason speak to Mrs. Price, the student advisor.
3. Mrs. Price recommended that our group send out a questionnaire.
4. If there were at least 15 students, we could form a club.
5. Jason suggested that we each submit questions for the questionnaire.
6. If we were to receive a good response to the questionnaire, we had to get it out early.

7. Many students wrote "I wish that I knew how to play chess."

8. Marian said to Jason, "If I were you, I would have sections in the club—for learners, beginners, and advanced players."

9. As if he were able to read her mind, Jason had already decided to organize the club that way.

10. Whether the club be a success or not, at least we are starting one.

EXERCISE 2 **Choose the correct form to complete each sentence.**

1. When I read about the past, I wish I (was were) living at the time.

2. Whether it (be was) America during the Revolution or ancient Rome under Julius Caesar, I'm ready to go there after only a couple of pages.

3. If I (was were) not such an avid reader, I wouldn't think about things like this.

4. I don't recommend that anyone (stop stops) reading, however, to avoid this problem.

5. When I told Mother about my wanting to go into the past, she laughed aloud and then insisted that I (am be) back in time for dinner.

EXERCISE 3 **Tell whether the italicized verb in each sentence is in the subjunctive, indicative, emphatic, or imperative mood.**

1. *Start* a photography club or class.

2. Many students wish that they *did know* more about photography.

3. In a club they *learn* about camera settings for focus, speed, and exposure.

4. *Take* photos with different camera settings.

5. Many advisors recommend that a learner *test* different settings on his or her digital camera.

6. Some advisors suggest that everyone *do get* a high-quality film camera.

7. *Compare* the features of different cameras.

8. *Discuss* the qualities of a good photo.

9. Subject matter, lighting, and framing *are* important elements in a good photo.

10. *Do* you and others *agree* on the best photos?

11. Experts recommend that a photographer *test* different printers and paper.

APPLY IT NOW

Write three sentences using the following phrases. Write about things that relate to your school and community. When you have finished, circle all the verbs that are in the subjunctive mood.

I wish that . . .

If I were . . .

I recommend that . . .

4.9 Modal Auxiliaries

Auxiliary verbs may be common auxiliaries, such as forms of *be (am, is, are, was, were)* and *have (has, had),* or modal auxiliaries.

Modal auxiliaries are used to express permission, possibility, ability, necessity, obligation, and intention. They are used with main verbs that are in the base form. The common modal auxiliaries are *may, might, can, could, must, should, will,* and *would.* Study the verb phrases in each of these sentences.

Permission:	**Anyone who helps** *may attend* **the party for volunteers.**
Possibility:	**We** *might need* **more help collecting clothes.**
Ability:	**June** *can mend* **just about anything.**
Necessity:	**You** *must clean* **everything in the hall after the sale.**
Obligation:	**We** *should help* **at the clothing sale.**
Intention:	**I** *will finish* **the posters for the sale.**

EXERCISE 1 Identify the verb phrase with a modal auxiliary in each sentence. Tell whether the phrase expresses permission, possibility, ability, necessity, obligation, or intention.

1. I could show you the latest addition to my wardrobe—from a used-clothing sale.

2. If you want, you may go with my mom and me to the used-clothing sale next weekend.

3. We might get some good bargains.

4. One must arrive early for the best selection.

5. You should be ready by 6:30 in the morning.

6. The clothing is packed in big bundles, called bindles, and only an employee may cut open the wire that holds a bindle together.

7. I believe that I can spot a three-dollar bindle, the cheapest, a mile off.

8. You will look for a leather jacket at the sale.

9. The boiled wool Austrian jacket could fit you.

10. It's my Dad's birthday soon, and I should buy him a present.

11. Natasha may purchase one for him if I can't find what I'm looking for.

12. Here is the piece we must find for him: a 1950s bowling shirt with names embroidered on it.

EXERCISE 2 Complete each sentence with a verb phrase containing a modal auxiliary. Use the verb in parentheses with the meaning indicated after the sentence. More than one modal auxiliary may be correct for some sentences.

1. Our class _____ (raise) money. (necessity)

2. We _____ (start) our fundraising efforts now. (obligation)

3. The teachers say that our class _____ (organize) a fundraising event. (permission)

4. We _____ (hold) a secondhand clothing sale. (possibility)

5. Would that bring in the money we _____ (have) for our class trip? (necessity)

6. Everyone in class _____ (collect) old clothing. (possibility)

7. What one person no longer wants _____ (be) someone else's treasure. (possibility)

8. Actually everyone in class _____ (participate) in the sale in some way. (obligation)

9. People have different talents, and they _____ (do) different things well. (ability)

10. Students in other grades and even their families _____ (show) interest in such a sale. (possibility)

11. According to the principal, other classes _____ (attend) our event during lunch period. (permission)

12. We _____ (have) after-school hours too. (obligation)

13. That way families and people in the neighborhood _____ (come). (possibility)

14. We _____ (advertise) our sale so that other people know about it. (necessity)

15. I _____ (design) some attractive signs. (ability)

16. I _____ (leave) now to go to the bank. (necessity)

17. Yes, you _____ (borrow) my bike to go there. (permission)

18. Hailey _____ not (find) her bike lock. (ability)

19. We _____ (work) to make the fundraiser a success. (obligation)

20. I _____ (get) the information you need from the principal. (ability)

21. Someone _____ (fold) these clothes. (obligation)

APPLY IT NOW

Write a short paragraph about your plans for the upcoming weekend or school break. Tell about what you might do and with whom. Circle all the modal auxiliaries in your writing.

4.10 Agreement of Subject and Verb—Part I

A verb agrees with its subject in person and number. Remember that the present tense verbs for third person singular subjects end in *s* or *es*.

> **Several holidays** *occur* **in February.** (base form with a plural subject)
> **Valentine's Day** *occurs* **in February.** (base form plus *s* with a singular subject)

Use *doesn't* when the subject is third person singular. Use *don't* in other cases.

> **Arbor Day** *doesn't* **occur in March.**
> **I** *don't* **know the history of Arbor Day.**

Use *are* and *were* with *you* whether the subject is singular or plural. Do not use *is* or *was* with the subject *you*.

> *Were* **you at the Saint Patrick's Day parade?**

When *there is* or *there are* introduces a sentence, the subject follows the verb. Use *there is (was, has been)* with singular subjects. Use *there are (were, have been)* with plural subjects.

> *There is* **a national holiday in September.** (singular subject)
> *There are* **several holidays in February.** (plural subject)

When there is an **intervening phrase** between the subject and the verb, the verb still must agree with the subject (not the noun or pronoun in the intervening phrase).

> **A parade with marching bands** *is* **part of the celebration.**

EXERCISE 1 Choose the correct forms of the verbs to complete the sentences.

1. What (was were) you doing on Earth Day?
2. Actually there (is are) two Earth Days—one of them (is are) celebrated in March and the other on April 22.
3. The purpose of the celebrations (is are) to think about environmental issues.
4. Our school (doesn't don't) celebrate the day in March; its celebration (takes take) place in April.
5. There (is are) many special projects in conjunction with Earth Day.
6. A project (don't doesn't) have to be elaborate.

7. Children in our school (is are) decorating garbage bags with slogans.

8. A card with slogans (has have) been designed by seventh-grade students for distribution, and there (is are) a pledge on the back to protect the earth.

9. There (is are) Earth Day posters in the corridors.

10. You (was were) at the Earth Day Circle of Hands ceremony last year, (wasn't weren't) you?

EXERCISE 2 **Complete each sentence with *doesn't, don't, is,* or *are.***

1. Thanksgiving Day _____ occur on the same day in Canada as it does in the United States.

2. There _____ floats in the Tournament of Roses Parade.

3. _____ you remember where it takes place?

4. There _____ also many marching bands.

5. A parade with large figures _____ happen every day.

6. Michael _____ want to watch the parade on TV.

7. _____ you aware that each float is covered with fresh flower blossoms?

8. Unfortunately there _____ only one Rose Parade every year—on New Year's Day.

9. The biggest Thanksgiving Day parade in the United States _____ take place in California.

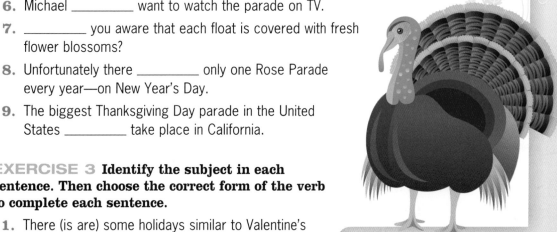

EXERCISE 3 **Identify the subject in each sentence. Then choose the correct form of the verb to complete each sentence.**

1. There (is are) some holidays similar to Valentine's Day around the world.

2. An important holiday for people in Japan and Korea (is are) White Day on March 14.

3. On that day candy, often white chocolates, (is are) given by men to their girlfriends.

4. Chocolates (is are) given by women to men on February 14, Valentine's Day.

5. There (is are) also a new holiday for people without a boyfriend or girlfriend.

6. Young people without a boyfriend or a girlfriend (get gets) together, and black noodles (is are) eaten.

7. The name of this holiday (is are) Black Day.

APPLY IT NOW

Choose a holiday that you celebrate or one that you are curious about. Use the words below in sentences in which you explain what you know or do not know about the holiday. Include what people typically do on that day.

don't/doesn't

you are/you were

there is/there are

4.11 Agreement of Subject and Verb—Part II

Compound subjects with *and* usually take a plural verb. If the subjects connected by *and* refer to the same person, place, or thing or express a single idea, however, the verb is singular.

> <u>Soccer and basketball</u> *are* **popular team sports.**
> <u>Macaroni and cheese</u> *is* **easy to make.**

When *each, every, many a,* or *no* precedes singular subjects connected by *and* or *or,* use a singular verb.

> <u>Every adult and child</u> *benefits* **from exercise.**

When compound subjects are connected by *or* or *nor,* the verb agrees with the subject closer to it.

> <u>Neither the pitcher nor the umpires</u> *are* **on the field yet.**
> <u>Neither the umpires nor the pitcher</u> *is* **on the field yet.**

A **collective noun** names a group of people or things considered as a unit. Examples are *audience, band, herd,* and *public.* A collective noun usually requires a singular verb. When the meaning suggests that the members are being considered as separate individuals, however, use a plural verb.

> **The baseball team uses a field in the park.**
> **The team have all finished their warm-ups.**

A **noun that shows amount** takes a singular verb; that same noun used to show number requires a plural verb.

> **Three cups is a lot of sugar.** (amount)
> **Three cups are on the shelf.** (number)

> **Indefinite pronouns** such as *another, anyone, anybody, anything, each, everyone, everybody, everything, either, neither, no one, nobody, nothing, one, somebody, someone,* and *something* are singular and take singular verbs.

> <u>Everyone</u> *wants* **a ticket to the swim meet.**

Some special nouns are **plural in form but singular in meaning.** These include *civics, mathematics, measles, news,* and *physics.* They take singular verbs.

EXERCISE 1 **Choose the correct form of the verbs to complete the sentences.**

1. The swim team (is are) scheduled to compete next week.
2. Every teacher and student (is are) supporting the team.
3. The news about the team (seems seem) bad.
4. Measles (seems seem) to have broken out.
5. Someone (has have) said that this is just a rumor.
6. Nobody (knows know) what is going on.
7. Dorothy and Karen (says say) the problem is the flu.
8. Either Bob or Kevin (maintains maintain) that measles (is are) the problem.
9. Neither the coach nor the players (has have) talked about the problem so far.
10. The principal and the athletic director (has have) just spoken and told us what they know.
11. The team (has have) undergone physical examinations.
12. No one on the team (has have) the measles, but stomachaches have been common.
13. The stress and strain about the upcoming event always (has have) an effect on team members.
14. A doctor and a nurse (is are) monitoring the swimmers for signs of illness.
15. Everyone on the team (is are) recovering.

EXERCISE 2 **Complete each of the following sentences with the correct form of the verb on the left. Use the present tense of the verbs.**

attract 1. Athletics _____ many young people.

spread 2. News _____ rapidly.

be 3. _____ those scissors sharp?

need 4. The large pliers _____ tightening.

be 5. Aeronautics _____ the science of flight.

cause 6. Chicken pox used to _____ many absences from school.

deal 7. Physics _____ with matter and energy.

go 8. The proceeds from the concerts _____ to charity.

APPLY IT NOW

Write original sentences for each of the following subjects:
- neither art nor music
- either you or your friend
- everyone in our class
- tennis and soccer
- news
- boys and girls

Verb Review

4.1 Identify the verb or verb phrase. Then tell the principal part of each main verb—base form, past, or past participle.

1. What do you know about the Native Americans of the western Great Lakes?

2. Native people have lived in this region for at least 12,000 years.

3. Historians call three of the western Great Lakes tribes The Three Fires.

4. The Three Fires were the Anishinabe, the Potawatomi, and the Odawa.

5. These groups intermarried and traded goods with one another.

4.2 Identify the verb or verb phrase. Tell whether the verb is transitive or intransitive.

6. Connor auditioned for the Chicago Symphony Orchestra.

7. He had studied the cello for 15 years.

8. Many hopeful musicians arrived for the auditions.

9. None of the players saw the judges behind a curtain.

10. Players performed passages from symphonic works.

4.3 Choose the correct verb to complete each sentence.

11. Our gym teacher (rises raises) herbs.

12. Jessica came home from work and (lay lie) down on the sofa.

13. Will you please (leave let) the cover on the soup?

14. Each child (sat set) still for the class portrait.

15. By last night we had carefully (laid lain) the remaining bricks.

4.4 Identify the linking verbs and the subject complements. Tell whether each is an adjective, a noun, or a pronoun.

16. I felt sorry for her.

17. My dad had been her acting coach in college.

18. It was he who encouraged her.

19. Learning lines was always easy for her.

4.5 Identify each verb or verb phrase. Tell if it is in the active voice or the passive voice.

20. What do you know about community-supported farms?

21. Shares are bought by individuals and families.

22. The money is used to buy seeds and to pay workers.

23. Fresh produce is delivered once a week for 20 weeks.

24. Shareholders must collect their own produce.

4.6 Identify the tense of each underlined verb.

25. My grandmother has told each of us to pick out a gift.

26. I will have chosen mine by tonight.

27. Rebecca is trying to think of something she'll do later.

28. His choice <u>had inspired</u> Dad.

29. Each of us <u>will be selecting</u> something for Grandma.

4.7 Identify each verb or verb phrase. Tell whether the sentence is in the indicative, imperative, or emphatic mood.

30. Let's make our own wrapping paper this year.

31. Get some potatoes, a knife, stamping ink, and paper.

32. First, use the knife to cut out a shape in relief on a potato half.

33. We did make two stamps from each potato.

34. Practice stamping on scrap paper.

4.8 Choose the correct subjunctive form to complete each sentence.

35. If every school (was were) to compete in the Battle of the Bands, it would be amazing!

36. Winning required that each band member (practice practices) faithfully.

37. I wish the band's playing time (was were) later.

38. The band members requested that playing times (were be) posted a week beforehand.

4.9 Complete each sentence with a verb phrase containing a modal auxiliary. Use the verb in parentheses with the meaning indicated after the sentence.

39. The seedlings _____ (require) more sunlight. (possibility)

40. We _____ (transfer) the flats into the kitchen. (necessity)

41. The family _____ (prepare) their meals around them. (ability)

42. We _____ (take) care of them. (obligation)

4.10 Rewrite the sentences to correct subject-verb agreement. Not all sentences have errors.

43. What is you doing for Arbor Day?

44. That holiday don't get much attention.

45. There is several other holidays we celebrate.

46. The truck with all the trees is here already.

47. There is lots of children ready to plant the trees.

4.11 Choose the correct form of the verb to complete each sentence.

48. Cake and ice cream (is are) traditional at our family birthdays.

49. Every adult and child (chooses choose) chocolate cake.

50. Either a layer cake or cupcakes (is are) my choice.

51. That way, everyone (gets get) the most possible frosting.

52. Our family (disagrees disagree) on the best ice-cream flavor.

53. Vanilla and fudge swirl (is are) popular choices.

Tech Tip

Go to www.voyagesinenglish.com for more activities.

Verb Challenge

EXERCISE 1 **Read the selection and then answer the questions.**

1. On that eventful day when the Wright brothers successfully flew their heavier-than-air machine, an ages-long ambition of the human race became a reality. 2. For hundreds of years, humans had dreamed of flight. 3. Long ago the artist Leonardo da Vinci designed an "artificial bird." 4. He had even tested wings and propellers. 5. During the 18th and 19th centuries, extensive experiments were conducted with balloons and dirigibles. 6. Gliders were developed and improved. 7. Aviation, however, took a giant step forward when Orville and Wilbur Wright powered their vehicle with a gasoline engine and demonstrated the practicality of such a machine. 8. If we were to choose only one event that marked the birth of aviation, we would choose the Wright brothers' flight. 9. Their ingenuity and perseverance led to the achievements that aeronautics has made and will make in the future.

Leonardo da Vinci's flying machine

1. In sentence 1, is the verb *flew* regular or irregular? What is the present tense form of *flew*?
2. Identify the linking verb in sentence 1. Is the subject complement a noun or an adjective?
3. Find the verb in sentence 2. Is it transitive or intransitive?
4. Find the verb in sentence 3. Is it transitive or intransitive?
5. What is the tense of the verb in sentence 4?
6. Is the verb phrase in sentence 5 in the active or the passive voice?
7. Find an example of a verb in the subjunctive mood in the passage.
8. Find the verb phrase in sentence 8 that contains a modal auxiliary.
9. Find all the verbs and verb phrases in sentence 9.
10. Name the tenses of the verbs and verb phrases in sentence 9.

EXERCISE 2 **Rewrite the paragraph below, using the active voice.**

The jungle floor is covered with many plants and small trees. This region is inhabited by such animals as armadillos, anteaters, snakes, and wild pigs. The roof of the jungle is formed by the tops of tall trees and vines. The tops of these vines are covered with many beautiful flowers and fruits. This area is inhibited mostly by jungle birds. The roof of the jungle is called the "high jungle" by scientists. Every day, more and more is being learned by scientists about this fascinating world.

Verbals

5.1 Participles

Verbals are words made from verbs to function as another part of speech. There are three kinds of verbals: participles, gerunds, and infinitives.

A **participle** is a verb form that is used as an adjective. It describes a noun or a pronoun. A present participle ends in *-ing,* and a past participle generally ends in *-ed.*

A **participial adjective** stands alone before or after the word it modifies or after a linking verb.

> The *sobbing* **child nodded her head.** (before the noun)
> **The child,** *sobbing,* **clung to her mother.** (after the noun)

A **participial phrase** consists of the participle, an object or a complement, and any modifiers.

> *Kissing the child gently,* **the mother cuddled the little girl.** (participle with a direct object and an adverb)
> **The child,** *sobbing loudly in the silent theater,* **refused to quiet down.** (participle with an adverb and an adverb phrase)

Like a regular verb, a participial adjective can be active or passive, and it can show tense.

> *Starting,* **I checked the instructions carefully.** (active)
> **The other project** *being started* **is to end today.** (passive)
> **Our team discussed the plans,** *starting* **with construction of the model.** (present)
> *Started* **yesterday, our project was ahead of schedule.** (past)
> **Their group,** *having started* **late, rushed to finish.** (present perfect)

The present participle shows a relationship between the time of the action of the participle and that of the main verb. Past and perfect forms show action that was completed at some time before the action indicated by the main verb.

A participle that is essential to the meaning of a sentence is restrictive and is not set off by commas. A participle that is not essential to the meaning of the sentence is nonrestrictive and is set off by commas.

> **The project** *started on Monday* **ran into terrible snags.** (restrictive)
> **The other one,** *started a day later,* **finished first.** (nonrestrictive)

EXERCISE 1 Identify the participle and the main verb in each sentence. Then tell which noun or pronoun the participle describes.

1. After the death of Robert Frost's father, the family moved to the East, settling in Lawrence, Massachusetts.
2. Frost, aspiring to write poetry, began writing at age 16.
3. His grandfather, concerned about Frost's economic future, bought his grandson a farm.
4. The grandfather, knowing Frost's love for writing, questioned the would-be farmer.
5. Unknown as a poet at age 38, he left for England.

EXERCISE 2 Identify the participle and the participial phrase in each sentence. Tell the noun or pronoun that the phrase describes.

1. Jasmine, having volunteered for community service, works at the local animal shelter on Saturday.
2. Wearing a T-shirt with the shelter logo, she goes to work for two hours every Saturday morning.
3. Answering phones, she gives information about the shelter.
4. People looking for pets often call the shelter.
5. Last Saturday Jasmine fed some puppies found in an empty car near the fire station.
6. She watched while a vet treated a cat frightened by its new surroundings.
7. Having cleaned the animal cages, she then did photocopying in the office.
8. Having heard Jasmine's stories, Tania volunteered to help out at the shelter as well.

EXERCISE 3 Identify the participial phrase in each sentence and tell the noun or pronoun that it describes. Then identify the participle and tell whether it is present, past, or perfect.

1. Looking at the City Animal Shelter Web site, I found its application form for volunteer work.
2. I filled out an application downloaded from the Internet.
3. Having completed the application, I mailed it in.
4. Having received a call back, I visited the shelter.
5. Starting next Saturday, I am an official volunteer.

APPLY IT NOW

Write five sentences, using one of these participles in a participial phrase in each sentence: *wearing, walking, bored by, having worked,* and *waking up late.*

Grammar in Action Find the past participle in the excerpt on p. 338.

5.2 Placement of Participles

A **participial adjective** after a linking verb should not be confused with a participle that is part of a verb phrase.

> **The outlook was** *promising*. (participial adjective modifying *outlook*)
>
> **The day was** *promising* **to be a complete delight.** (part of the verb phrase *was promising*)
>
> **The man was** *honored* **for his bravery.** (part of the verb phrase *was honored*)
>
> **The man was** *honored* **to be part of the team.** (participial adjective modifying *man*)

To determine whether a participle is a participial adjective, ask these questions:

- Can the participle be used in front of the noun *(honored man)*?
- Can it be compared *(least honored)*?
- Can it be modified *(very honored)*?

If the answer is yes to these questions, the participle is a participial adjective.

Because a participial phrase acts as an adjective, there must be a noun or pronoun in the sentence for it to describe. A participial phrase in a sentence that does not contain this related noun or pronoun is called a **dangling participle.** Watch out for dangling participles and correct any that creep into your writing.

Can you find the dangling participles in these examples?

> **Feeling ill, the room began to sway.**
>
> **Having eaten a big dinner, dessert was not appealing.**

You are correct if you said *feeling ill* and *having eaten a big dinner*. There is no word in either sentence to tell who performed the action.

EXERCISE 1 **Write phrases with these participles. Use each as an adjective before a noun.**

1. freezing
2. swaying
3. frozen
4. aching
5. forgotten
6. known
7. retired
8. annoying
9. uneaten
10. running
11. wailing
12. frazzled

EXERCISE 2 **Identify the participial adjective in each sentence.**

1. Nicolaus Copernicus, a Polish astronomer of the early 1500s, was a dedicated scientist.
2. He studied information on the changing locations of heavenly bodies.
3. He made detailed notes on their movements.
4. He offered the disturbing theory that all the planets moved around the sun.
5. The shared belief of the time was that Earth was the center of the universe.
6. Copernicus's views were shocking to people.
7. Others became convinced of their correctness.
8. They proved that Earth was indeed a moving planet.

Nicolaus Copernicus

EXERCISE 3 **Identify the participial adjective and the noun it modifies in each sentence.**

1. Ptolemy's ideas about the movement of the sun around Earth long remained unchallenged.
2. His sketch of the universe was the accepted map for centuries.
3. Copernicus's startling theory was confirmed by later scientists.
4. Galileo made an improved telescope in the 1600s.
5. Galileo's observations of the revolving moons of Jupiter proved Copernicus's ideas.

EXERCISE 4 **Choose the sentence in each pair that contains a dangling participle.**

1. a. Having read about Copernicus, he unlocked secrets of the universe.
   b. Having read about Copernicus, I knew he unlocked secrets of the universe.
2. a. Having worked for years, Copernicus published his theory about the solar system.
   b. Having worked for years, the theory about the solar system was finally published.
3. a. Using large telescopes, new discoveries about the stars are still being made.
   b. Using large telescopes, scientists are making new discoveries about the stars.
4. a. Studying the sky, the stars shone brightly.
   b. Studying the sky, I saw the shining stars.

APPLY IT NOW

Write a short review of a movie, book, or TV program. Use some of the following words as participial adjectives: *amazing, annoying, confusing, disappointed, surprised.*

Tech Tip With an adult, post your review on a Web site.

5.3 Gerunds as Subjects and Subject Complements

A **gerund** is a verb form ending in *-ing* that is used as a noun. Because it acts as a noun, a gerund can be used in a sentence as a subject, a subject complement, an object of a verb, an object of a preposition, or an appositive.

Running is his main form of exercise. (subject)

Currently my favorite pastime is *dancing*. (subject complement)

A gerund may have an object or a complement, and may be modified by an adverb or an adverbial phrase. The entire **gerund phrase**—made up of the gerund and any other parts—acts as a noun. In these sentences the gerund phrase is in red and the gerund is underlined.

Reading mysteries **is Mom's favorite form of recreation.**

Andrea's favorite pastime is *writing* poetry about nature.

How does the gerund function in the first sentence? in the second? You are right if you said the gerund acts as the subject of the first sentence and as a subject complement in the second. In the first sentence, *mysteries* is the object of the gerund *reading*. In the second sentence, the phrase *poetry about nature* acts as an adverbial phrase describing the gerund *writing*.

EXERCISE 1 **Identify the gerund phrase in each sentence. Tell whether it is a subject or a subject complement.**

1. One of my least favorite chores is cutting the lawn.
2. Getting help with the task is my top priority.
3. One option is switching chores with my sister.
4. Babysitting my little brother usually isn't much fun either.
5. Playing a game or a sport with him does make the task easier.
6. Relaxing with him for even a minute isn't possible.
7. His idea of fun is getting into a mess of one sort or another.
8. Chasing him around can be entertaining.
9. Cleaning up after him is just plain work.
10. Afterward my favorite way to relax is reading novels.

EXERCISE 2 Identify the gerund phrase in each sentence. Tell whether it is a subject or a subject complement. Identify any direct objects in the gerund phrases.

1. In a recent survey of middle school students, one of the most popular physical activities was riding bikes.

2. Playing basketball is also a popular activity.

3. The kids' favorite activity with their parents was going to the movies, according to another survey.

4. Attending a sport event with parents also ranked high as a popular family activity.

5. In many surveys a popular free-time activity with teens is hanging out with friends.

6. Watching TV ranks as a popular activity with most age groups.

7. Collecting things—such as coins, comics, and lunch boxes—is a popular hobby with both kids and adults.

8. For me, collecting old lunch boxes seems a most unusual hobby.

9. Apparently getting lunch boxes decorated with early comic book characters is a great achievement.

10. One way to find items for many collections is attending garage sales.

EXERCISE 3 Complete each sentence with a gerund used as a subject or a subject complement.

1. _____ is my favorite free-time activity.

2. _____ is my oldest hobby.

3. My favorite activity with my friends is _____.

4. My least favorite chore is _____.

5. _____ is fun for me.

6. When my family and I go on vacation, the hardest part is _____.

7. _____ is dangerous work.

8. _____ are good health habits.

9. Courage is _____.

10. _____ was not my idea of a good time.

APPLY IT NOW

Do a survey of activities with students your age. Ask five students about their favorite and least favorite free-time activities. Use gerunds to write a short paragraph explaining the results.

Tech Tip Post results on a class blog for peer review.

5.4 Gerunds as Objects and Appositives

A gerund can be used as a direct object.

> **People around the world enjoy** watching **firework displays.**

The gerund phrase *watching firework displays* is the object of the verb *enjoy.* Within the phrase, *displays* is the direct object of *watching.*

A gerund can function as the object of a preposition.

> **Americans celebrate the Fourth of July by** attending **firework shows.**

The gerund phrase *attending firework shows* is the object of the preposition *by.* The gerund is *attending,* and *firework shows* is its direct object.

A gerund can be used as an appositive. Remember that an appositive is a word or group of words used immediately after a noun to rename it and give more information about it.

> **The Grucci's business,** organizing firework shows, **sounds exciting.**

The gerund phrase *organizing firework shows* explains the noun *business.*

What are the gerund phrases in these sentences? Can you identify their functions in the sentences?

> **Dad's promise, getting us last-minute tickets to the firework show, proved impossible to keep.**
> **We regretted missing the show.**

In the first sentence, the gerund phrase *getting us last-minute tickets to the firework show* is used as an appositive. It explains the noun *promise.* In the second sentence, the gerund phrase *missing the show* is the direct object of the verb *regretted.*

EXERCISE 1 **Identify the gerund in each sentence. Tell whether it is used as a direct object, an object of a preposition, or an appositive.**

1. The Chinese began making fireworks centuries ago.
2. The Chinese also once used them for frightening enemies in battle.
3. Another use, fighting evil spirits, has made fireworks a traditional part of New Year's celebrations.
4. Some experts, however, credit people in India or Arabia with inventing fireworks.

5. By the 1400s the city of Florence was the center for manufacturing fireworks in Europe.

6. Fireworks became part of celebrating special holidays.

7. Kings and queens started using them in elaborate royal festivities.

8. A new practice, adding chemicals for brilliantly colored fireworks, began in the 1800s.

9. A modern development, incorporating a musical soundtrack into the firework display, started in France.

10. Because fireworks contain explosives, experts recommend leaving firework displays to professionals.

11. The most important part of fireworks, keeping safe, involves careful thought.

12. By keeping your distance, fewer injuries will occur.

EXERCISE 2 Complete the sentences with gerunds. Then tell whether each is used as a direct object, an object of a preposition, or an appositive.

1. My favorite recreation, _____, is something I do often.

2. I excel in _____.

3. I really hate _____.

4. My chores include _____.

5. As a career I have considered _____.

6. My task in the project, _____, is an important one.

7. The latest trend, _____, is something I might try.

8. I have always avoided _____.

9. My goal of _____ is a difficult one.

10. What is the most effective way of _____?

11. My summer activities, _____, take up much of my time.

12. I got the birthday party started by _____.

APPLY IT NOW

Choose five photos in this textbook and write a sentence about each. Include the page number on which each photo appears. In each sentence use a gerund as a direct object, an object of a preposition, or an appositive.

5.5 Possessives with Gerunds, Using -ing Verb Forms

Gerunds may be preceded by a possessive form—either a possessive noun or a possessive adjective. These possessives describe the doer of the action of the gerund.

> *Our losing the game* **was heartbreaking.** (not *Us losing the game*)
> **The worst moment was** *John's missing that pass.* (not *John missing that pass*)

What is the correct choice of word in these sentences?

> **Because you were so terribly busy,** (you your) **offering to help is much appreciated.**
> **Due to the time-zone difference, I was surprised by** (Jorge Jorge's) **calling me last evening.**

If you chose *your* and *Jorge's,* you are correct. These are the possessive forms, the form to use before a gerund.

Whether an *-ing* form of a verb is a participle or a gerund depends on the emphasis in the sentence. When the emphasis is on the doer, the form is a participle; when it is on the action, the word is a gerund.

> **We heard the** *boys singing.* (The boys—the doers—are our main interest; therefore, *singing* is a participle modifying *boys.*)
> **We heard the** *boys' singing.* (The singing of the boys—the action—is what we are interested in; therefore, *singing* is a gerund and *boys* must be possessive.)

Notice the difference:

> **The student** *winning the award* **was I.** (participle describing *student*)
> *My winning the award* **was a surprise.** (gerund acting as a subject)

EXERCISE 1 Choose the correct word to complete each sentence, using the *-ing* form indicated.

1. (Us Our) putting together the jigsaw puzzle proved to be a long-term task. (gerund)

2. (Mom Mom's) buying a 1,500-piece puzzle surprised us. (gerund)

3. (Dad Dad's), agreeing to work on the puzzle, surprised us all. (participle)

4. (Me My) organizing all the blue pieces for the sky was a big help. (gerund)

5. (Mom Mom's) putting the puzzle on a folding table in the living room meant we could work on it over time. (gerund)

6. The (cat cat's) jumping on the puzzle is trouble. (participle)

7. (Us Our) working little by little meant our progress was slow but sure. (gerund)

8. Grandma was proud of (us, our) working so diligently on the puzzle. (participle)

EXERCISE 2 **Rewrite the sentences so that they correctly use the possessive form. Not all sentences have errors.**

1. My playing the drums in the morning upsets my neighbors.

2. The music teacher approved Ferdinand attending the symphony with the school band.

3. There is no doubt about she being the best pianist in our family.

4. Him being transferred to another office made us upset.

5. She was upset by him looking at Julia's diary.

6. There was some question about Alex's being able to pass the test.

7. Grandma was afraid of the garage being robbed.

8. Mom noticed Claire's caring for our neighbors' plants while they were out.

9. The cat purring soothed my little sister.

10. Dad's being offered the job was cause for celebration.

EXERCISE 3 **For each sentence tell whether the word ending in *-ing* is a gerund, a participial adjective, or a verb. Then, where it is appropriate, name the gerund phrase, the participial phrase, or the verb phrase.**

1. Making pancakes is a Sunday-morning ritual in my family.

2. Arising early, we all make our way to the kitchen.

3. Assembling the ingredients, I start the process.

4. Mom's job, mixing the batter from scratch, is the most important task.

5. Mom pours the batter onto the sizzling griddle.

6. Dad's flipping over the pancakes is a real art.

7. When Dad is flipping them, we gather around.

8. Holding our breaths, we all watch for one to fall on the floor, but this seldom happens.

9. Our finishing all the pancakes is never a problem.

10. Cleaning up the kitchen is not my chore.

APPLY IT NOW

Use the word *hammering* in three sentences—as a gerund, a participial adjective, and a verb in a verb phrase. Exchange papers with a partner and see whether that person can tell how the word is used in each sentence.

An **infinitive** is a verb form, usually preceded by *to,* that is used as a noun, an adjective, or an adverb. Like participles and gerunds, infinitives can appear alone or in phrases. An infinitive phrase consists of the infinitive, its object, and any modifiers.

> *To study* **is your job.** (infinitive used as a noun)
>
> **I have a history report** *to do.* (infinitive used as an adjective)
>
> **I went** *to get a history book at the library.* (infinitive phrase used as an adverb)

Also like participles and gerunds, infinitives may have objects and be accompanied by adverbs and adverbial phrases. In the examples above, *to study* and *to do* are examples of infinitives used alone. *To get* is the infinitive in the phrase *to get a history book at the library.*

A French castle in the Middle Ages

When an infinitive or infinitive phrase is used as a noun, it can function as a subject, a complement, an object, or an appositive.

> *To finish the report* **was my goal.** (subject)
>
> **My task was** *to describe society during the Middle Ages.* (subject complement)

Are the infinitive phrases used below subjects or subject complements?

> **My hope is to find information in these books.**
>
> **To look through the books took a great deal of time.**

The infinitive phrase in the first sentence, *to find information in these books,* is a subject complement. The infinitive phrase in the second sentence, *To look through the books,* is a subject.

EXERCISE 1 Identify the infinitive or infinitive phrase in each sentence. Tell whether it is used as a subject or a subject complement.

1. During the Middle Ages, the lord's duty was to protect the people.
2. To do this job required fighting skills.
3. To defend a territory often required a large castle.

4. The peasants' task was to farm the land.

5. To grow crops meant hard work from dawn to dusk.

6. The job of the clergy was to teach people about God.

7. To pray was an important duty for them.

8. To honor God was the primary focus of many people's lives.

9. One expression of this desire was to build a soaring cathedral.

10. To construct it required many people and much ingenuity.

11. To build a cathedral sometimes took centuries.

12. The goal of each town was to have the tallest church.

13. The purpose of the pictures in stained-glass windows was to show biblical stories to people who could not read.

14. The purpose of the exterior buttresses was to help support the heavy stone walls with their huge glass windows.

15. To visit a medieval cathedral is an unforgettable experience.

The Sainte-Chapelle in Paris, France

EXERCISE 2 Complete each sentence with an appropriate infinitive or infinitive phrase.

1. _____ is one goal of mine.

2. _____ is a scary feeling.

3. _____ can be exciting.

4. _____ requires a lot of practice.

5. _____ takes a great deal of money.

EXERCISE 3 Complete each sentence with an infinitive or infinitive phrase. Then tell whether it is used as a subject or a subject complement.

1. _____ is a useful skill.

2. _____ is a real accomplishment.

3. _____ would be very exciting.

4. My plans for the summer are _____.

5. _____ is a pointless task.

6. One way to get good grades is _____.

7. _____ requires many years of school.

8. A fun hobby is _____.

APPLY IT NOW

Many proverbs have infinitives. Invent new proverbs by completing the following with infinitive phrases.

_____ is the best way to keep a friend.

The best way to make a friend is _____.

_____ is the easiest way to make an enemy.

The way to know who your friends are is _____.

Grammar in Action. Find infinitives used as subjects in the p. 356 excerpt.

Verbals • 95

5.7 Infinitives as Objects

When an infinitive functions as a noun, it can be used as a direct object in a sentence.

> **In the 1800s suffragists wanted** *to obtain the vote for women*.
> **Many women also hoped** *to gain equal rights for women*.
> **They tried** *to make the public aware of the issues*.

An infinitive used as a direct object may be preceded by a noun or pronoun. This noun or pronoun, the subject of the infinitive, tells the doer of the action of the infinitive. The infinitive and its subject form an **infinitive clause.** This construction always follows the main verb of the sentence, and a pronoun used as its subject is always in the object form.

> **Susan B. Anthony asked** <u>women</u> *to work for the suffragist cause*.
> **She urged** <u>them</u> *to work in an organized fashion*.

In the second sentence, *them to work* is an infinitive clause, and *them*, the object form of *they*, is its subject.

Susan B. Anthony

EXERCISE 1 Identify the infinitive used as a direct object in each sentence.

1. Some women managed to vote in colonial America and in the early days of the United States.
2. Some states and local governments allowed women to have the vote.
3. By the early 1800s, all states decided to deny women that right.
4. In the 1840s women began to organize for their voting rights.
5. They decided to fight for women's suffrage at the Seneca Falls Convention in 1848.
6. Women hoped to gain their voting rights back.

EXERCISE 2 Identify the infinitive, infinitive phrase, or infinitive clause in each sentence. Identify the verb of which each is the direct object.

1. Susan B. Anthony hoped to secure equal rights for women.
2. She had begun to work as a teacher in the 1830s.
3. She decided to demand equal pay for women teachers.
4. Local governments refused to give the same pay to women teachers as to men teachers.
5. Her protests eventually caused her to lose her job.

6. She managed to find another position as a teacher.

7. She intended to pursue a career in teaching.

8. Anthony continued to work for social reform, however.

9. She and other workers for women's rights needed to get attention and support from the public and the government.

10. With Elizabeth Cady Stanton, she hoped to form an effective organization by establishing the National Woman Suffrage Association in 1869.

11. The pair continued to collaborate for many years.

12. They persuaded others to join them in the struggle for women's rights.

EXERCISE 3 **Identify the infinitive phrase or clause used as a noun in each sentence. Tell whether it is used as a subject, a subject complement, or a direct object.**

1. To gain rights for women was Susan B. Anthony's goal.

2. Anthony dared to vote in the election of 1872.

3. At her trial for this action, the court did not even allow her to speak.

4. The court ordered Anthony to pay a fine.

5. Anthony failed to see the attainment of the women's vote in her lifetime.

6. She did manage to win worldwide respect for her work and determination.

7. The outcome of the suffragists' work was to achieve the passage of the Nineteenth Amendment in 1920.

8. The purpose of the Nineteenth Amendment was to grant women the vote.

9. To vote in elections is a right that is unchallenged for women.

10. The U.S. government began to mint a dollar coin in 1979.

11. The government decided to put the image of Susan B. Anthony on the coin.

12. The reason for the choice was to honor Anthony's work.

13. The coin, however, failed to gain popularity.

14. Merchants did not want to have both paper dollars and coins of the same value.

APPLY IT NOW

Write a short paragraph about one of your parents or another important person in your life. Include infinitives as direct objects in your work. Here are some verbs for which you could use infinitives as direct objects: *ask, begin, encourage, expect, decide, try, hope, learn, manage, plan, want, wish.*

5.8 Infinitives as Appositives

An infinitive functioning as a noun can be used as an appositive. An appositive is a word or group of words used after a noun or pronoun to rename it and give more information about it.

> **My suggestion,** *to do a project on Greek myths*, **was accepted.**

The infinitive phrase in red is an appositive. It renames and tells something about the noun *suggestion*.

Infinitive appositives can be used in various positions.

> **My good deed,** *to help them with the packing*, **meant giving up a free day.** (subject)
>
> **The challenge was this—***us to fit all the camping gear into one car and them to get up at three in the morning*. (subject complement)
>
> **I didn't anticipate the problem,** *to get two flat tires at the same time*. (direct object)
>
> **I decided I must give the task,** *to fix the flat tires*, **my immediate attention.** (indirect object)

Venus

In these sentences the pronoun used as the direct object *(them)* and as the subject *(us and them)* of the infinitives is in the object form. A pronoun used as the subject, direct object, or subject complement of an infinitive is always in the object form, including those following *to be*.

> **We didn't expect the driver to be** *him*.
>
> **Penelope wanted it to be** *her* or *me*.

EXERCISE 1 Identify the infinitive phrase used as an appositive in each sentence.

1. The ancient Greeks' strategy for victory against the Trojans, to hide soldiers in a large wooden horse, was a success.

2. Odysseus's fate, to travel for years before his return home after the Trojan War, forms the story of Homer's *Odyssey*.

3. Orpheus's impossible quest, to free his wife, Eurydice, from the Underworld, ended in tragedy.

4. Venus, the goddess of love, made possible Hippomenes's tactic in a life-or-death race, to throw golden apples in Atalanta's path.

5. Hercules's amazing feat, to complete a series of 12 impossible tasks, proved his extraordinary strength.

6. Ancient art often shows one of Hercules's tasks, to kill a fierce lion with his bare hands.

7. Persephone's fate, to live six months every year in the Underworld, is the reason seasons change in ancient Greek myth.

8. War, pain, and illness in the world resulted from Pandora's mistake, to open the forbidden box.

EXERCISE 2 Identify the infinitive phrase used as an appositive in each sentence. Then tell what word the appositive explains.

1. King Midas's fault, to be greedy, got him into trouble.
2. His wish, to turn things into gold with his touch, was a curse.
3. Prometheus's action, to give fire as a gift to humans, angered Zeus.
4. It was Prometheus's punishment to stay tied to a rock eternally.
5. It was Daedalus's idea to invent wings for flying.
6. Icarus's mistake, to fly too close to the sun, led to his death.

EXERCISE 3 Identify the infinitive phrase used as a noun in each sentence. Tell whether it is used as a subject, a subject complement, a direct object, or an appositive.

1. Echo, a wood nymph, liked to talk.
2. She managed to anger the goddess Juno with her talk.
3. It was Echo's punishment to lose her speaking ability.
4. The wordless Echo managed to meet the handsome youth Narcissus.
5. Narcissus's fault, to be vain, meant he could show no love.
6. Echo desired to tell of her love—but made only echoes.
7. Narcissus refused to bother with the creature with no words of her own.
8. Narcissus forbade Echo to come close to him.
9. Echo's wish was now to get revenge on Narcissus.
10. One day Narcissus wanted to take a drink at a pond.
11. Narcissus's fate, to fall in love with his own image in the water, was a terrible one.
12. His only desire was to stay near the image.
13. In love with his own image, he forgot to eat anything.
14. His final destiny was to turn into a flower.
15. Echo's body began to fade away because of her grief over Narcissus.
16. To produce the sound of an echo is her only remaining trace.

Narcissus

APPLY IT NOW

Whom do you consider to be a modern-day hero? Write three or four sentences about someone you read or heard about. Incorporate infinitives used as nouns in your writing and identify them.

5.9 Infinitives as Adjectives

Infinitives can be used as adjectives to describe nouns and pronouns. These infinitives follow the words they describe.

> I got a **chance** *to take a helicopter ride*.
> The ride is a great **way** *to see the city*.
> The ride was **something** *to anticipate*.

The words that the infinitives describe are underlined. Notice that the word described in the third sentence is the indefinite pronoun *something*.

Can you find the infinitive phrases used as adjectives and the nouns they describe in the sentences below?

> **The helicopter met the need for an aircraft to hover in the air.**
> **The helicopter's use to rescue people remains important.**

In the first sentence, the infinitive phrase *to hover in the air* acts as an adjective describing *aircraft*. In the second sentence, *to rescue people* acts as an adjective describing the noun *use*.

EXERCISE 1 Identify the infinitive phrase used as an adjective in each sentence. Then tell the noun it describes.

1. Igor Sikorsky, a Russian-born American, was not the first person to invent a helicopter.

2. The first person to design a working helicopter was a Frenchman named Paul Cornu in 1907.

3. The first helicopter to fly for a significant distance was a German model.

4. Sikorsky, however, was the designer to receive credit for the first practical helicopter.

5. The idea to use a single rotor for the helicopter top and a small vertical one at the tail was his.

6. The single rotor increased the helicopter's ability to remain stable in the air.

7. Others saw Sikorksy's design as something to imitate.

8. He was recognized for his design to develop helicopters efficiently.

Igor Sikorsky

EXERCISE 2 Identify the infinitive phrases in each sentence. Tell whether each is used as an adjective or a noun. For those used as adjectives, tell the word that the infinitive phrase describes.

1. As a schoolboy in Russia, Igor Sikorsky developed the ability to build model airplanes and helicopters.

2. He pursued a path to be an aircraft designer.

3. In the early days, people wanted to build multimotor planes.

4. They expected such aircraft to fly longer distances more safely.

5. Sikorsky managed to design the first successful plane of this type.

6. In the face of political unrest in Russia, Sikorsky decided to move to the United States.

7. He was given the challenge to build better aircraft.

8. He perfected an airplane to land, maneuver, and take off on water.

9. The possibility of a helicopter continued to intrigue him.

10. His work to design one continued.

11. In 1938 a company agreed to build a helicopter from his designs.

12. Sikorsky finally had a chance to see his invention in operation.

13. Sikorsky decided to fly the test plane himself.

14. When he discovered problems in the helicopter's operation, Sikorsky tried to improve the design.

15. He needed to reduce the aircraft's vibration.

16. Soon he found ways to solve the problems.

EXERCISE 3 Complete each sentence with an infinitive used as an adjective.

1. I have had the desire _____ in a helicopter for a long time.

2. I finally had a chance _____ a helicopter ride last week.

3. Some friends offered me the opportunity _____ them on a brief ride.

4. A helicopter ride is a great way _____ the expanse of the landscape below.

5. I'm not the only person _____ that a helicopter ride is an amazing experience.

APPLY IT NOW

Tell about a difficult task that you or someone you know once had to do. Use three of the phrases below in sentences. Complete the infinitives. Use them as adjectives to describe the nouns and pronouns.

a chance to . . .
one way to . . .
something to . . .
the person to . . .
the plan to . . .
time to . . .

Verbals • 101

5.10 Infinitives as Adverbs

CLIPPER SHIP "FLYING CLOUD"

An infinitive can be used as an adverb—to describe a verb, an adjective, or another adverb. Study the infinitives used as adverbs in these sentences.

Butch went *to see the old sailing ship in the harbor*. (describing the verb *went*)

He was disappointed *to learn of its departure the day before*. (describing the adjective *disappointed*)

He arrived too late *to see it*. (describing the adverb *late*)

Identify the infinitives used as adverbs in these sentences. What does each infinitive phrase describe?

> I didn't know enough to explain the history of the clipper ship.
> I visited the library to get a book on clipper ships.
> I was determined to learn more about them.

In the first sentence, the infinitive phrase *to explain the history of the clipper ship* describes the adverb *enough*. In the second sentence, *to get a book on clipper ships* explains the verb *visited*. In the third sentence, the infinitive phrase *to learn more about them* describes the adjective *determined*. Notice that an infinitive that describes a verb often answers the questions *why* or *how*.

EXERCISE 1 Identify the infinitive phrase used as an adverb that describes each underlined word. Tell the part of speech of the underlined word: adjective, adverb, or verb.

1. We were <u>excited</u> to see the tall ships in the harbor.
2. We <u>came</u> to sail on one of them.
3. We were <u>lucky</u> to win a trip on a clipper ship.
4. The crew <u>used</u> the motor to take us out to sea.
5. Then we <u>gathered</u> to raise the sails.
6. In groups we <u>strained</u> to pull the ropes.
7. The task wasn't too <u>difficult</u> to manage as a team.
8. Together we were strong <u>enough</u> to complete the task.
9. We <u>looked</u> up to see the sails billowing in the wind.
10. We <u>cheered</u> to show our delight in our successful effort.

EXERCISE 2 Identify each infinitive phrase used as an adverb. Then tell the word it describes and that word's part of speech.

1. We sat on the deck to listen to the crew member.
2. We were happy to learn the history of the clipper ship.
3. We were eager to learn sea chanteys.
4. Sailors in the past sang these songs to accompany their work.
5. There was time enough to learn a couple of chanteys.
6. I took the ship's wheel for a minute to steer the ship.
7. Some of the smaller children were not big enough to do so.
8. They were disappointed to miss the opportunity.
9. Some of us went to the ship's side to watch for sea lions.
10. Others walked around the ship to take photographs.
11. The crew members were relieved to see us leave.
12. They sang us the chanty to send us off.

EXERCISE 3 Identify the infinitive phrase in each sentence. Tell whether it is used as a noun, an adjective, or an adverb.

1. Replicas of ships give us a chance to experience life at sea.
2. Merchants used clipper ships to take goods long distances.
3. Such ships were necessary to move goods before the widespread use of ships with engines.
4. Clipper ships were designed to move quickly on the water.
5. Replicas are a way to relive the history of sailing.
6. My grandfather's hobby was to make these replicas.
7. Some tourists want to take a trip in these magnificent ships.
8. It is quite an experience to sail on them.
9. Our goal was to learn about sailing in the past.
10. We were pleased to observe marine life in the process.
11. We were sad to return to shore after only a few hours.
12. To return for a longer trip on the ship is now our goal.

Bark!

(Did you know that sea lions bark?)

APPLY IT NOW

Pretend you are entering a writing contest to win a sailboat. Write a short paragraph in which you tell why you would like to take a trip with your friends or family on that boat. Use three infinitives in your writing and identify how they are used.

5.11 Hidden and Split Infinitives

The word *to* is called the sign of the infinitive, but sometimes infinitives appear in sentences without the *to*. Such infinitives are called **hidden infinitives.**

After verbs of perceptions such as *hear, see, know,* and *feel,* the infinitive is used without a *to*. This is also the case for the verbs *let, make, dare, need,* and *help.*

> I <u>heard</u> the crickets *chirp* at night.
> I wouldn't <u>dare</u> *take* anyone else's beach towel.

The *to* is also omitted after the prepositions *but* and *except* and the conjunction *than.*

> After finals I will do nothing <u>but</u> *sleep* for an entire day.
> I'd rather fish <u>than</u> *bait* hooks.

An adverb placed between *to* and the verb results in a **split infinitive.** Good writers avoid split infinitives.

> Split infinitive: We were asked to *quickly* leave the boat.
> Improved: We were asked to leave the boat quickly.

Where to place the adverb you remove from the middle of the infinitive depends on the meaning of the sentence.

> Split infinitive: I began to *optimistically* check my e-mail.
> Correction: I began optimistically to check my e-mail.
>   *or* Optimistically I began to check my e-mail.

EXERCISE 1 Identify the hidden infinitive or infinitives in each sentence.

1. My parents let me go to camp last summer.
2. I did little but think about camp for weeks before.
3. Mom made me pack lots of sweaters and medicines.
4. I watched the sun rise many mornings at camp.
5. At night I heard the water lap against boats in the lake.
6. We once saw a bear approach our camp.
7. We sometimes heard raccoons move through the camp.
8. I dared not forget my daily call home.

9. We made one another laugh with jokes over the campfire.

10. A counselor helped me learn new swimming strokes.

11. I did nothing but swim one day.

12. I would rather canoe than kayak.

13. I once felt my kayak tip to one side.

14. I dared not show my moment of fear.

15. I told myself I need not panic.

16. The counselors always make us wear life jackets.

EXERCISE 2 **Rewrite the sentences so that they do not contain split infinitives.**

1. I learned to efficiently paddle a canoe.

2. I managed to not tip over on my first trip in a canoe.

3. I hope to eventually learn to kayak better.

4. Once I failed to completely extinguish the campfire.

5. The embers began to slowly rekindle.

6. The counselor helped me to totally extinguish it.

7. I managed to deftly bait hooks with squirming worms.

8. I also managed to foolishly lose my binoculars while I was bird-watching.

9. I struggled to tightly fit everything back into my suitcase.

10. I don't expect to quickly forget the camping experience.

EXERCISE 3 **Indicate where in the sentence the adverb in parentheses belongs.**

1. The lost puppy seemed to eat the hamburger but not the dog food. (hungrily)

2. Andre studied his notes all night so that he would be able to pass the exam. (finally)

3. He grabbed his backpack and jacket so that he was ready to leave when the bus arrived. (immediately)

4. Miguel learned how to set up a tent. (quickly)

5. Chloe was hoping to fail her lifeguard certification test. (not)

APPLY IT NOW

Picture a place you like to visit and relax. Write four sentences about it, using your senses and emotions to describe it. Use phrases with hidden infinitives in a format like the following:

I *hear* the children shout in play.

Verbal Review

5.1 Identify each participial phrase, each participle, and the noun or the pronoun it describes.

1. Looking out the window, John expected rain.
2. A man carrying a briefcase stepped out of the house.
3. The worker used the concrete mixed in the wheelbarrow.
4. Amazed by the mason's work, the homeowner thanked him.

5.2 Identify the participial adjectives used as subject complements. Correct sentences that have dangling participles.

5. The crowd remained hushed as they watched the golfers.
6. Studying the green, the ball rolled to the hole.
7. Sinking the putt, the crowd cheered.
8. Having won the tournament, the victory party began.
9. The golfer seemed pleased with the tournament.

5.3 Identify the gerunds and gerund phrases. Tell if each is a subject or a subject complement.

10. Reading a newspaper is important for most people.
11. Seeing the headlines can be alarming.
12. A good habit is reading a newspaper at least once a week.
13. Discussing current events improves one's critical thinking skills.

5.4 Identify the gerund phrases. Tell whether it is used as a direct object, an object of a preposition, or an appositive.

14. In democracies people enjoy choosing their leaders.
15. Romans tried another method, using beans, to vote.
16. At meetings settlers voted by shouting their choices.
17. My job, counting ballots, is challenging.
18. Today most voters will try voting by computer.

5.5 Identify the words ending in *-ing*. Tell whether each is used as a gerund, participial adjective, or part of a verb phrase.

19. Swimming at the pool is enjoyable.
20. My winning the race was exciting.
21. Yvonne was competing in her first race.
22. From the starting block, the swimmer quickly took the lead.
23. His practicing twice a day is hard work.

5.6 Identify the infinitives and tell whether each is used as a subject or a subject complement.

24. To land on the moon was one of President Kennedy's goals.
25. The main purpose of the mission was to advance the space program.
26. Neil Armstrong's intention was to walk on the moon.

27. Michael Collins's task was to orbit the moon.

28. To be an astronaut requires courage.

5.7 Identify the infinitive phrases. Write the verb of which each is a direct object.

29. On Saturday we went to hear poetry.

30. The award-winning poet began to read softly from a piece of paper.

31. Many of us strained to hear the poem.

32. His quiet words, however, managed to affect most of the audience.

33. People persuaded him to read a second poem.

5.8 Identify the infinitive phrases used as appositives.

34. My goal, to finish my homework, was accomplished.

35. A phone call put an end to my plan—to complete all the reading by five o'clock.

36. The assignment, to read Chapter 12, was time-consuming.

37. Mr. Hidalgo told us his goal, to demonstrate photosynthesis.

5.9 Identify the infinitive phrases used as adjectives. Name the noun or pronoun each describes.

38. Before the game Michael had the opportunity to meet Ron Santo.

39. Santo was one of the first known people with diabetes to play major league baseball.

40. Despite having the disease, he displayed great ability to play the game.

41. He is a person to respect as a role model.

5.10 Identify the infinitive phrases used as adverbs. Name the word each describes and that word's part of speech.

42. The class was fascinated to learn about Ben Franklin.

43. Franklin worked to achieve a productive life.

44. As a scientist, Franklin was interested to learn about electricity.

45. He lived long enough to assist in writing the Declaration of Independence.

5.11 Identify any hidden infinitives. If a sentence contains a split infinitive, rewrite the sentence.

46. Ignacio's parents let him plan the trip to France.

47. Sonia helped Ignacio carry his suitcase to the car.

48. He tried to not admit homesickness.

49. The plane began to quickly descend.

50. The passengers were told to securely fasten their seatbelts.

Tech Tip Go to www.voyagesinenglish.com for more activities.

Verbal Challenge

Read the selection and then answer the questions.

1. To find the lost city of the Incas occupied the dreams of explorers for centuries. 2. Some adventurers hoped to find Incan gold. 3. However, it was not until 1911 that outside explorers, moving through the mountainous jungle forest, discovered the ruins of Machu Picchu. 4. Its stone terraces, looking like giant steps cut into the mountainside, held the foundations and walls of a royal city. 5. The city's amazing stone masonry, which was not held together by mortar, made the explorers stare in wonder. 6. Some of the city's terraces had been used to farm, and others held temples to worship the gods. 7. The dream of finding riches was not realized, however.

8. Recently researchers have continued looking for another lost city of the Incas. 9. They believe that Inca soldiers took refuge in the mountains to hide from the Spanish conquerors. 10. Some researchers, having claimed the discovery of the ruins of such a city, continue their excavation work at a yet unnamed site near Machu Picchu.

1. Find the infinitive phrase in sentence 1. How is it used?
2. What is the participial adjective in sentence 1?
3. Find the infinitive phrase in sentence 2. How is it used?
4. What is the participial phrase in sentence 3? What noun does it describe?
5. How does the phrase *looking like giant steps cut into the mountainside* function in sentence 4?
6. Identify the hidden infinitive in sentence 5.
7. How is the word *amazing* used in sentence 5?
8. Which infinitive phrase in sentence 6 describes a verb? Which describes a noun?
9. Find the gerund phrase in sentence 7. How does it function?
10. How does the phrase *looking for another lost city of the Incas* function in sentence 8?
11. Find the infinitive phrase in sentence 9. How does it function?
12. Find the participial phrase in sentence 10. What tense is it in?

Adverbs

6.1 Types of Adverbs

An **adverb** is a word that describes a verb, an adjective, or another adverb.

Social reformers have worked *tirelessly* against injustice. (describes the verb *have worked*)

Social reformers are *fervently* dedicated people. (describes the adjective *dedicated*)

Social reformers work *extremely* hard to help others. (describes the adverb *hard*)

Adverbs of time tell *when* or *how often*. These adverbs include *again, daily, early, now, soon, then, today,* and *usually*.

Children *sometimes* worked long hours in factories.

Adverbs of place tell *where*. These adverbs include *away, down, far, here, inside,* and *up*.

Boys working in a textile mill, photographed by activist photographer Lewis Hine

The conditions for workers were unsafe *there*.

Adverbs of manner tell *how* or *in what manner*. These include *carefully, quickly, sincerely,* and *steadily*.

Many reformers *determinedly* informed the public of the terrible conditions in factories.

Adverbs of degree tell *how much* or *how little*. These include *almost, extremely, much, quite, rather, too,* and *very*.

The conditions for workers could be *quite* appalling.

An **adverb of affirmation** tells whether a statement is positive or expresses consent or approval. The adverbs of affirmation include *allegedly, indeed, positively, undoubtedly,* and *yes*.

The reformers *undoubtedly* had a positive effect.

An **adverb of negation** expresses a negative condition or refusal. Among the adverbs of negation are *no, not,* and *never*.

Laws did *not* allow child labor any longer.

EXERCISE 1 Give the type of each italicized adverb. Then name the word it describes and the part of speech of that word.

1. At the beginning of the 20th century, various reform groups worked *diligently* for the cause of workers.

2. At that point in history, child labor was *fairly* common.

3. Children were considered *highly* desirable employees.

4. Because of their small size, they could *easily* perform some tasks adults were unable to do.

5. The children could *often* be hired for less money.

6. They also complained *less*.

7. Poor families *usually* had no choice but to have the children work.

EXERCISE 2 Identify the adverb or adverbs in each sentence. Then tell the word the adverb describes.

1. In mines "breaker boys" carefully sorted the coal, removing rocks.

2. The coal dust completely covered the boys.

3. Many later died of lung ailments.

4. Children in the textile industry commonly worked 14-hour days.

5. The machinery was an extremely dangerous hazard to workers.

6. Efforts to change these rather awful conditions soon found an eloquent champion in photographer Lewis Hine.

7. Hine frequently took his camera to the sweatshops.

8. His photos accurately portrayed real-life conditions.

9. Hine's photos woke a nation to the human cost of the goods and services it often used without thinking.

10. Some of the first child-labor laws can be traced directly to the effects of Hine's photos.

EXERCISE 3 Complete each sentence with an adverb of the type indicated in parentheses.

1. Alonzo looked _____ at the photos. (manner)

2. I will put the photos _____. (place)

3. He _____ takes photos after it rains. (time)

4. _____, I have received the zoom lens I ordered. (affirmation)

APPLY IT NOW

What did you do this past weekend? Write five sentences about it. Each sentence should use an adverb of time, place, degree, affirmation or negation, or manner. Identify each adverb.

Grammar in Action. Find the last adverb of manner in the p. 377 excerpt.

6.2 Interrogative Adverbs and Adverbial Nouns

An **interrogative adverb** is an adverb used to ask a question. The interrogative adverbs are *how, when, where,* and *why.*

> *Why* did you choose the gold rush as a topic?
> *When* did the California gold rush start?
> *Where* did people go on the gold rushes of the 19th century?
> *How* did people find out about discoveries of gold?

An **adverbial noun** is a noun that acts as an adverb by describing a verb. Adverbial nouns usually express *time, distance, measure, value,* or *direction.*

Time: The California gold rush lasted only a few *years.*
Distance: People traveled many *miles* on gold rushes.
Measure: During the trek over desert areas, temperatures could reach 100 *degrees* or more. One gold nugget weighed 150 *pounds.*
Value: An ounce of gold can cost 400 *dollars.*
Direction: People have voyaged *north, south, east,* and *west* in search of gold.

EXERCISE 1 Identify the interrogative adverbs and adverbial nouns in these sentences.

1. When did the gold rush in Alaska begin?
2. It began approximately a century ago.
3. How did people get to Alaska?
4. Many traveled north by boat from the West Coast of the United States to Skagway, Alaska.
5. Was the trip they took inland easy?
6. The gold rushers crossed over many mountain passes to the Yukon River and then sailed some 500 miles to Dawson City.
7. One steep mountain pass rose more than 1,000 feet in less than a half mile.
8. The trip on the Yukon River took three weeks.
9. Why did people go to the Klondike?
10. According to early reports in newspapers, some miners were worth more than 10,000 dollars due to their discoveries.

EXERCISE 2 Identify each adverbial noun. Tell whether it expresses time, distance, measure, value, or direction.

1. Gold seekers survived months of travel and hardships to get to the Klondike.
2. Most had covered many treacherous miles to seek their fortunes.
3. They went north to find gold.
4. Gold rushers' supplies weighed nearly a ton because Canada required these people to have a year's supply of goods.
5. Most of the gold lay 10 feet or more underground.
6. It was impossible to dig in the winter when temperatures hit –60 degrees Fahrenheit.
7. A few claims did produce one million dollars in gold.
8. The Klondike gold rush lasted only one year.

EXERCISE 3 Complete each sentence with an interrogative adverb.

1. _____ was the age of the gold rushes?
2. _____ did so many people take part in gold rushes?
3. _____ did people go to look for gold in 1849?
4. _____ did the gold rushers travel to California?
5. _____ did miners separate gold from other metals?
6. _____ did people go in California to look for gold?
7. _____ were many gold rushers disappointed with their efforts?

EXERCISE 4 Complete each sentence with an adverbial noun that expresses the quality indicated in parentheses.

1. The gold rush exhibit lasted _____. (time)
2. The discount tickets cost only _____. (value).
3. We turned _____ at the entrance to reach the exhibit. (direction)
4. To see the gold-rush photos, we walked _____. (distance)
5. We saw gold nuggets that weighed several _____. (measure)
6. We spent _____ in the exhibit. (time)
7. The fake nuggets cost five _____, and my friend bought one. (value)

APPLY IT NOW

Imagine submitting historical information about your city or town (or another nearby place) to a local history museum. Write three sentences that give interesting facts about the history of your city or town. Use adverbial nouns in your writing.

 With an adult, research your city or town online.

6.3 Comparative and Superlative Adverbs

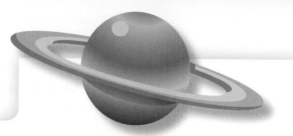

Some adverbs can be compared. Like adjectives, they have **comparative** and **superlative** forms.

Positive: Saturn rotates *quickly*.
Comparative: Jupiter rotates *more quickly* than Saturn.
Superlative: Jupiter rotates *most quickly* of all the planets.

The comparative and superlative forms of most adverbs that end in *ly* are formed by adding *more* or *most* (or *less* or *least*) before the positive form of the adverb. The comparative and superlative forms of many adverbs that don't end in *ly* are formed by adding *-er* or *-est*.

POSITIVE	COMPARATIVE	SUPERLATIVE
carefully	more carefully	most carefully
hastily	less hastily	least hastily
fast	faster	fastest
long	longer	longest
late	later	latest

Using *more* or *most* with adverbs that end in *er* or *est*—such as *more faster* or *most fastest*—is incorrect.

Some adverbs have irregular forms of comparison.

ADVERB	COMPARATIVE	SUPERLATIVE
well	better	best
badly	worse	worst
far	farther	farthest
little	less	least
much	more	most

EXERCISE 1 **Write the comparative and superlative form of each adverb.**

1. sharply
2. bravely
3. fiercely
4. hard
5. gracefully

6. clearly
7. well
8. willingly
9. early
10. boastfully

11. positively
12. closely
13. quietly
14. attentively
15. soon

EXERCISE 2 **Choose the correct word or words to complete each sentence.**

1. A year on Mercury lasts (fewer fewest) than two days.
2. Mercury orbits the sun (faster fastest) of all the planets.
3. Of all the planets, Venus shines (more brightly most brightly).
4. Looking with the unaided eye, a person can see Venus (more easily most easily) than the other planets.
5. Of all the planets, Venus turns (more slowly most slowly)—one turn on its axis takes about 243 Earth days.
6. Jupiter turns (more quickly most quickly) of all the planets.
7. Winds on Jupiter blow (more weakly most weakly) than winds on Earth.
8. Compared with the other large planets, Neptune orbits the sun (more slowly most slowly); it takes approximately 165 Earth years.
9. Neptune travels (farther farthest) of all the planets to orbit the sun.
10. Earth travels around the sun (more quickly most quickly) than Neptune.

EXERCISE 3 **Rewrite the sentences with adverbs that use incorrect forms of comparison. Not all sentences have errors.**

1. The Soviet Union sent a probe into space earliest than any other country.
2. The *Voyager* spacecraft traveled farthest of any space probes—beyond the planets.
3. As the *Voyager* travels more farther into space, its messages reach Earth most slowly, taking more than 10 hours.
4. The *Voyager* missions traveled more nearer to the outer planets than other space probes did.
5. Of all recent space missions, the *Voyager* missions were followed more attentively by the public and the press.
6. In 2004 U.S. land rovers photographed the surface of Mars most clearly than had been done previously.
7. These amazing rovers sent back data more longer than scientists expected.
8. The rovers traveled along on Mars more slowly than many tortoises.
9. Their missions succeeded more better than scientists had hoped.
10. Some scientists now talk most confidently than before about the existence of water on Mars.

APPLY IT NOW

Write sentences with the following adverbs. Use the form of comparison indicated in parentheses.

attentively (comparative)
quickly (superlative)
near (superlative)
well (comparative)
patiently (positive)
generously (superlative)

6.4 Troublesome Words

Study these sets of words that are commonly confused.

Well and good
Good is an adjective and is used to describe a noun or a pronoun but never a verb. The word *well* is an adverb that describes a verb except when it describes health.

> **Leo's poetry is good.** (describes the noun *poetry* as a subject complement)
> **Leo writes poetry well.** (describes the verb *write*)
> **Incorrect: Leo writes really good.**
> **Correct: Leo writes really well.**

Farther and further
Farther refers to distance. *Further* means "in addition."

> **I walked farther down the aisle to find poetry books.**
> **We should discuss the topic further.**

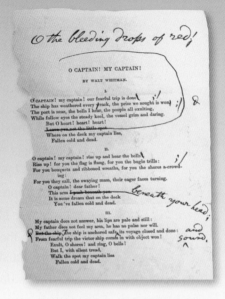

Draft of "O Captain! My Captain" by poet Walt Whitman

There, their, and they're
Although the words *there, their,* and *they're* are pronounced the same, they are used differently. *There* is an adverb of place. *Their* is a possessive adjective. *They're* is a contraction for *they are.*

> **Walt Whitman lived in Brooklyn for a long time, and he wrote much of his poetry there.** (adverb of place)
> **Some of his poems had as their theme the death of Abraham Lincoln.** (possessive adjective)
> **They're powerful poems.** (contraction for *they are*)

There can also be used as an introductory word in a sentence. In sentences like these, the subject follows the verb.

> **There might be no better poet than Whitman.**
> **There are a few poems by Whitman in our textbook.**

Bad and badly
Bad is an adjective; *badly* is an adverb. When the predicate of a sentence is a linking verb, it must be followed by *bad*, not *badly*.

> **I felt bad after I read "O Captain! My Captain!"** (subject complement)
> **Several books of his poetry in the library are badly worn.** (adverb modifying *worn*)

EXERCISE 1 **Choose the correct word to complete each sentence.**

1. Most people know Walt Whitman only as a poet, and (they're there) often surprised to learn of his volunteer hospital work.

2. He wanted (badly bad) to help humanity.

3. He moved to Washington, D.C., during the Civil War and worked in hospitals (there their).

4. Many soldiers lay wounded in hospitals; (their there) plight was unenviable.

5. The conditions in hospitals were often poor, and (farther further), medical treatments were less advanced than they are today.

Walt Whitman

6. Whitman talked to the patients, wrote letters for them, and generally helped raise (their there) spirits.

7. Many soldiers felt (badly bad) because they were homesick.

8. Some soldiers were (farther further) from home than they had ever been before.

9. Whitman aided in lifting (their they're) moods.

10. (Farther Further), Whitman used the little money he had to buy small presents for the sick or wounded soldiers.

11. He earned (their there) gratitude for all his kindness.

12. Whitman got along (good well) with the hospital patients.

13. He also interacted (good well) with the staff and doctors.

14. He was well known at the hospital, and the people respected him (there their).

15. (There They're) was a strong sense of compassion in Whitman's character.

EXERCISE 2 **Rewrite the sentences to correct errors in the use of adverbs. Not all sentences have errors.**

1. They're many famous poems by Walt Whitman.

2. There available in many editions.

3. Their message was usually one of celebration.

4. I decided I wanted to study his poems farther.

5. I can now recite "O Captain, My Captain!" fairly good.

6. Americans felt bad after President Lincoln's death.

7. Some of Whitman's poems captured Americans' feelings good.

APPLY IT NOW

Write sentences using each of these words: *good, well, farther, further, there, their, they're, bad, badly.*

Post your sentences on a classroom blog for peer review.

6.5 Adverb Phrases and Clauses

Prepositional phrases can be used as adverbs to describe verbs, adjectives, or other adverbs. Prepositional phrases used in this way are called **adverb phrases.** Like adverbs, adverb phrases answer the questions *how, when, where, why, to what extent,* or *under what conditions.*

> **My family travels** *in the summer*.

The adverb phrase *in the summer* describes the verb *travels*. It tells *when*.

What are the adverb phrases in these sentences? What does each describe?

> **Last year we went to Florida.**
> **We were eager for our trip.**
> **We arrived late in the evening.**

You are right if you answered the following way: In the first sentence, the adverb phrase *to Florida* describes the verb *went*. In the second sentence, the adverb phrase *for our trip* describes the adjective *eager*. In the third sentence, the adverb phrase *in the evening* describes the adverb *late*.

A clause is a group of words containing a subject and a predicate. A dependent clause does not express a complete thought and cannot stand alone. A dependent clause that acts as an adverb is called an **adverb clause.** Adverb clauses answer the same questions as adverbs and adverb phrases.

> **It rained** *when we least expected it*. (The adverb clause tells when it rained. It describes the verb *rained* in the main clause.)
> *Because the weather was hot*, **we spent a lot of time on the beach or in the water.** (The adverb clause tells *why*. It describes the verb *spent* in the main clause.)

Some common conjunctions used to introduce adverb clauses are *although, after, as, because, before, if, in order that, provided that, since, so that, unless, until, when, whenever, where, wherever, whether,* and *while*.

EXERCISE 1 Identify the adverb phrase or phrases in each sentence. Tell the word each phrase describes.

1. We visited the beach on Thursday.
2. I saw the Atlantic Ocean for the first time.
3. We stood on the sandy shore and stared in wonder.
4. A school of large fish was swimming near the shore.
5. Their dorsal fins rose above the waves.
6. Then the entire group moved into the distance.

EXERCISE 2 Identify the adverb clause in each sentence.

1. Because summers can be hot and muggy on the west coast of Florida, most people vacation there in the winter.
2. It was full summer, however, when we first visited there.
3. Since we don't mind hot weather, we enjoyed our stay.
4. We weren't happy, however, when thunderstorms threatened.
5. As we stood on the shore of the Gulf of Mexico, black and purple thunderheads rolled above us one day.
6. Although the clouds were menacing, it was somehow thrilling to see such a powerful force of nature.
7. When rain started to fall in heavy drops, we ran for shelter.
8. A small, wooden structure with an "Eat Here" sign became visible through the rain as we ran down the beach.
9. While we waited inside for the storm to blow over, we feasted on the café's freshly caught shrimp.

EXERCISE 3 Identify the adverb phrase or adverb clause in each sentence and tell whether it is a phrase or a clause.

1. Whenever we go to Marco Island, we visit our grandparents.
2. We go swimming every day, provided that we wear sunscreen.
3. My little sister puts on her floatie and swims across the pool.
4. Unless it is raining, my grandfather and my sister build sand castles every afternoon at the beach.
5. Because we visit Marco Island every year, my family has many cherished memories.

APPLY IT NOW

Write six sentences about events that happened in your school. Construct four sentences with adverb clauses and two with adverb phrases.

Grammar in Action.

Find the first adverb phrase in the p. 377 excerpt.

Adverb Review

6.1 Find the adverb in each sentence and identify its type: time, place, manner, degree, affirmation, or negation.

1. Cathy has been running daily for many years.

2. She steadily increases the distance of her runs.

3. Her shoes look very worn from all the use.

4. She did not stretch before running, though she should.

5. When it rains, she runs inside on a track.

6. Her health has undoubtedly benefited from years of regular exercise.

7. Cathy usually runs in the morning.

8. The weather is quite cool at that time.

9. When it's cool, she can run far.

10. She moves quickly in the cool morning air.

11. She never runs in the afternoon.

12. Cathy determinedly completes her run in good and bad weather.

6.2 Identify each interrogative adverb and adverbial noun. For each adverbial noun, tell whether it expresses time, distance, measure, value, or direction.

13. When did Mount St. Helens erupt?

14. The enormous eruption in 1980 lasted nine hours.

15. The eruption rose 80,000 feet into the air.

16. How did the eruption affect the surrounding area?

17. After the blast the water temperature in Spirit Lake reached 100 degrees.

18. Lava traveled five miles from the volcano.

19. Where did volcanic ash fall?

20. The damage from the eruption reached over one billion dollars.

21. When did plants and wildlife return to the area around the volcano?

22. The return of plants and animals took many years.

6.3 Rewrite the sentences that use incorrect forms of comparison. Not all sentences have errors.

23. Of all passenger aircraft, supersonic jets move more swiftly.

24. The Concorde flew more faster than a regular passenger jet.

25. It could travel many miles farther in the same amount of time.

26. A ride on the Concorde cost most than a regular airline ticket.

27. A flight from New York to London took less time on the Concorde.

28. It took about four hours least than on regular jets.

29. Because of the time difference, passengers actually arrived in London earliest than the time they left New York.

30. Of all airline passengers, the passengers on the Concorde were treated better.

31. According to scientists the supersonic jets affected the environment most negatively than regular jets.

6.4 **Complete each sentence with the correct word.**

32. Many art critics think Picasso painted (good well).

33. Do you think Picasso was a (good well) painter?

34. (There Their) is a painting by Picasso for sale in New York.

35. Many collectors want the painting (bad badly).

36. (Their They're) willing to pay $100 million for the painting.

37. (There, Their) are many people waiting for the start of the auction.

38. The Picasso painting is hanging (farther, further) down the wall.

39. Collectors can see the painting very (good, well).

40. Will the auctioneer take (farther further) bids?

41. Collectors who don't get the painting will feel (bad badly).

42. (There, Their) bids on the painting will be too low.

6.5 **Find the adverb phrase or adverb clause in each sentence and tell whether it is a phrase or a clause.**

43. I prepared my experiment for the science fair during the past year.

44. With great interest I studied pollution's effect on trees.

45. When pollution increases, trees suffer.

46. Before I started my experiment, I made a hypothesis.

47. I collected data so that I could test my hypothesis.

48. I have studied the trees for several months.

49. I measure changes in the trees with various tests.

50. After I complete all the experiments, I'll write a report.

51. After that I'll also make a display of the results.

52. If I prove my hypothesis, I may win a prize.

53. Winners go to the state science fair.

54. The fair is held in the state capital.

Tech Tip Go to www.voyagesinenglish.com for more activities.

Adverb Challenge

EXERCISE 1 Read the selection and then answer the questions.

1. Candid photography involves taking pictures on the spot. 2. Its basic methods can be learned fairly easily. 3. First rule: You can often photograph people more readily if they are doing something. 4. They may be picnicking in a park, for example, or intently watching some game. 5. In such instances and places, you can move almost invisibly among your subjects. 6. Second rule: Never take pictures wildly. 7. You may have to wait hours for a really interesting gesture or expression. 8. Third rule: Tilt your camera lens up or down. 9. The result may be a surprisingly original composition. 10. You undoubtedly will get some less-than-perfect shots with candid photography. 11. Some of the pictures that you take swiftly, however, can be quite dramatic because they have captured the spontaneous excitement of a single, unique moment.

1. In sentence 2 what kind of adverb is *fairly*? What word does it describe? What part of speech is that word?
2. Find the adverb in the comparative form in sentence 3. Give its superlative form.
3. Find the adverb clause in sentence 3.
4. Find the adverb phrase in sentence 4.
5. Find the adverb of manner in sentence 6. What word does it describe?
6. What is the adverbial noun in sentence 7? Does it tell about time, distance, or direction?
7. What are the two adverbs in sentence 8? What kind of adverbs are they?
8. What kind of adverb is *undoubtedly* in sentence 10?
9. Name the adverb clause in sentence 11.
10. In sentence 11 what word does the adverb *quite* describe? What part of speech is that word?
11. Which sentence contains an adverb of negation? What is that adverb?

EXERCISE 2 Write a paragraph describing an activity you like to do after school or on the weekend. Include the following.

1. two simple adverbs
2. a comparative adverb and a superlative adverb
3. an adverb phrase and an adverb clause

Prepositions

7.1 Single and Multiword Prepositions

A **preposition** is a word that shows the relationship between a noun or a pronoun and some other word in a sentence.

> My older brother painted the pictures *on* our wall.

On is a preposition that shows the relationship between the words *pictures* and *wall*. *On our wall* is a prepositional phrase. It consists of the preposition *on* and the noun *wall,* the object of the preposition. The word *our* is an adjective; it tells something about the object of the preposition. Within the sentence the prepositional phrase acts as an adjective describing the noun *pictures*.

Here are some common prepositions.

about	behind	for	over
above	below	from	past
across	beside	in	through
after	between	inside	throughout
against	beyond	into	to
among	by	near	toward
around	down	of	under
at	during	off	up
before	except	on	with

Some prepositions are made up of more than one word. In each sentence below, the prepositional phrase is in red and the multiword preposition is underlined.

> <u>According to</u> my mother, my brother is the best artist in the family.
> My parents sent him <u>instead of</u> me for art lessons.
> <u>Because of</u> his talent, Jeremy Jamelli has won highest-honors prizes in several shows.

Here are some common multiword prepositions.

according to	in regard to
aside from	in spite of
because of	instead of
by means of	next to
in addition to	on account of
in front of	prior to

EXERCISE 1 **Identify the prepositional phrase or phrases in each sentence. Name each preposition.**

1. People owe a debt to the painter George Catlin.
2. In the 1830s he began to paint representatives from various Native American groups in the United States.
3. Originally, he painted members of the Iroquois in New York State.
4. He used natural landscapes for the background of his paintings.
5. He placed the Iroquois against the grandeur of Niagara Falls.
6. He proposed traveling to the West.
7. He was warned about the hardships of such an undertaking.
8. In spite of these warnings, Catlin continued with his plan.
9. He painted individuals and scenes from 40 or more different Native American groups.
10. He gave an accurate portrayal of Native Americans.

EXERCISE 2 **Identify the prepositional phrase or phrases in each sentence. Name the object of the preposition.**

1. George Catlin traveled through the West on horseback and by canoe.
2. He painted Plains Indians on a hunt for buffalo.
3. In one famous picture George Catlin painted himself painting.
4. He stands in front of his easel with his brush and palette.
5. He is surrounded by a large group who watch him paint one of their leaders.

EXERCISE 3 **Choose the correct preposition to complete each sentence. Not all the prepositions will be used.**

| because of | in addition to | in spite of |
| before | of | after |

1. _____ his skill as a painter, Catlin was able to preserve for us images of a vanishing world.
2. The portraits captured the dress _____ each particular group.
3. He created realistic, detailed portraits _____ the widespread use of photography.
4. _____ beautiful art, he provided us with a record of this period.
5. _____ difficulties, he achieved his goal.

APPLY IT NOW

If you took photographs of the world today, what subject would you choose? Why? Write a short paragraph explaining your choice. Identify the prepositions in your writing.

Grammar in Action Find the third preposition in the p. 377 excerpt.

7.2 Troublesome Prepositions

Study the following examples to avoid misuse of these prepositions.

Beside and Besides

Beside refers to position; it means "next to." *Besides* means "in addition to."

Come sit down *beside* **me and let's talk.**

Who *besides* **me will be on the committee?**

Between and Among

Between is used when speaking of two people, places, or things. *Among* is used in speaking of more than two.

The debate *between* **the two candidates will be on TV.**

Choosing *among* **the five candidates was not easy.**

Differ With, Differ On, and Differ From

You *differ with* someone when you disagree. You *differ on* things. *Differ from* describes differences between people or things.

I *differed with* **Maria over the best candidate.**

The candidates *differ on* **the need for a new lab.**

This campaign banner *differs from* **that one in size.**

Like, As, and As if

Like is a preposition and is used in prepositional phrases. *As* and *as if* are conjunctions and introduce subordinate clauses.

She had a hat *like* **mine.**

Liam was late, *as* **I was, because we took the same bus.**

He acted *as if* **he had never been late before.**

Angry With and Angry At

One is *angry with* a person but *angry at* a thing.

We were *angry with* **the editor for running the editorial.**

Natalie is *angry at* **the newspaper for printing the article.**

From and Off

From can indicate removal or separation. *Off* means "away from." Use *off*, not *off of*, to indicate movement away from something.

Take the heavy box of brochures *from* **Gillian.**

Take the campaign poster *off* **(or** *from* **but not** *off of***) the wall.**

EXERCISE 1 Choose the correct preposition to complete each sentence.

1. During the student election, the three candidates for class president differed (with on) many issues.

2. Isabel and Juan discussed some issues (like as) starting a volunteer tutoring program.

3. (Beside Besides) the possibility of starting a volunteer tutoring program, there were other issues.

4. There were many other differences (among between) the three candidates.

5. All the candidates, however, are angry (at with) the decision to end the marching band.

6. Although I differ (with on) Isabel on many issues, I think I have to vote for her.

7. Because she is my friend, she behaves (like as if) she expects to get my vote.

8. (Among Between) you and me, I do know that she is a good leader.

9. The voting booths are going to be set up (beside besides) the cafeteria entrance.

10. The voting time is different (from than) last year.

EXERCISE 2 Rewrite the sentences to correct errors in preposition usage. Not all sentences have errors.

1. I sat besides Jake at the campaign rally.

2. He applauded so much that he almost fell off of his chair.

3. He differs from Isabel on the tutoring program.

4. He is angry with the amount that will be spent on the campaign.

5. Between Will and Lilly, the campaign will exceed the budget.

6. He is deciding among Will and Lilly as his choice.

7. Jake will vote for the same person as last year.

APPLY IT NOW

Choose four sets of prepositions from page 126. Write sentences to illustrate the correct use of the prepositions in each set.

Tech Tip Post your work on a classroom blog for peer review.

7.3 Words Used as Adverbs and Prepositions

Some words can be either adverbs or prepositions, depending on how they are used in sentences.

Matt and Wilson hurried *along* **the dark road.**
Matt and Wilson hurried *along.*

In the first sentence, the adverb phrase *along the dark road* contains the preposition *along* and the object of that preposition, *road*. The phrase describes the verb *hurried*. In the second sentence, the word *along* is used alone as an adverb, describing the verb *hurried*.

What parts of speech are the words in red in these sentences?

As we sat on the mountaintop, an eagle flew *below* **us.**
As we sat on the mountaintop, an eagle flew *below.*

In the first sentence, the word *below* is a preposition, part of the phrase *below us.* In the second sentence, *below* is not part of a phrase. It is an adverb describing the verb *flew.*

To distinguish between prepositions and adverbs, remember that a preposition is always part of a phrase that ends with a noun or a pronoun. A preposition must have an object.

EXERCISE 1 **The italicized word in the first sentence of each of the following sets is an adverb. Use the word as a preposition in the second sentence by adding an object.**

1. Let's walk *up.*
   Let's walk up _____.

2. Let's go to the park *after.*
   Let's go to the park after _____.

3. We can look *around.*
   We can look around _____.

4. The music store is *near.*
   The music store is near _____.

5. I had been waiting for you *outside.*
   I had been waiting for you outside _____.

EXERCISE 2 Tell whether each italicized word is an adverb or a preposition.

1. Please come *in*.
2. You can wait *inside* for Mia.
3. Come *through* the hall.
4. Sit *down* and make yourself comfortable.
5. Just move those things *off* the chair.
6. Mia just went *out*.
7. She'll be back *in* a few minutes.
8. The store is *near* our house.
9. She'll be happy you came *by*.
10. Have you been in our house *before*?
11. Look *around*.
12. Come *along* into the kitchen.
13. You can look *in* the refrigerator.
14. I think there is some yogurt *inside*.
15. Look *below* the milk.
16. Sit here *by* the window.
17. Look *out*.
18. You can see our garden *outside*.
19. Look! Mia is coming *in* the gate.
20. She's walking *down* the path.

EXERCISE 3 Choose the correct word to complete each sentence. Then tell whether each word is used as an adverb or as a preposition.

by   before   in   since   inside   after

1. We can finish this job _____ a short time by working together.
2. As I mentioned _____, we need to clean the entire basement.
3. I thought we would have removed all the old junk _____ this time, but we're still working on it.
4. Brad has been busy on the project _____ dawn.
5. Clean the cabinets outside and also remove the dirt _____.
6. We can rest _____.

APPLY IT NOW

Using your home as the topic, write two sentences for each of these words. Use the word once as an adverb and once as a preposition.

along	around
before	below
off	underneath

7.4 Prepositional Phrases as Adjectives

A prepositional phrase that describes a noun or a pronoun is called an **adjective phrase.**

> **Our class got tickets** *for a play*.
> **The name** *of the play* **appeared in bright lights.**

Both prepositional phrases in red are adjective phrases. In the first sentence, the prepositional phrase *for a play* tells something about *tickets,* a noun. In the second sentence, the prepositional phrase *of the play* describes the noun *name.*

In the sentences below, what are the adjective phrases and what do they describe?

> **The notice on the board has been taken down.**
> **We gave David the money for the tickets.**
> **We asked Mrs. Jones's opinion of the play.**

You are correct if you said that *on the board* describes the noun *notice* in the first sentence. In the second sentence, the adjective phrase *for the tickets* describes the noun *money,* and in the third sentence, *of the play* describes the noun *opinion.*

EXERCISE 1 In the following sentences, tell what word each italicized adjective phrase describes.

1. Our class saw a production *of Shakespeare's famous comedy* A Midsummer Night's Dream.
2. It was the first play *by Shakespeare* that I have seen.
3. Our teacher gave us information *about the play.*
4. A play *with live actors* is a magical experience.
5. Many *of my classmates* liked the character Titania best.
6. Titania is the queen *of the fairies.*
7. Some other students preferred the role *of Puck.*
8. Many characters *in the play* are fooled by Puck's tricks.
9. Bottom's use *of English* always receives a laugh.
10. I especially like when he wears the head *of a donkey.*
11. The laughter *at his foolish antics* was enormous.

A flower fairy costume for
A Midsummer Night's Dream

EXERCISE 2 Identify the adjective phrase and the word it describes in each sentence.

1. The production of a play interests me.
2. I ask myself, would I use a donkey's head of papier-mâché?
3. How would you create the forest with its magical beings?
4. Will you change the lighting for each scene or keep it the same?
5. What sorts of costumes would you use?
6. The decisions by the director are important.
7. I am the director of our class play.
8. The action in this one-act drama is set in the present day.
9. The cafeteria in a school is the play's setting.
10. I won't need to worry about special props for this play.

EXERCISE 3 Rewrite each group of words so that the noun is described by an adjective phrase.

1. soccer rules
2. ticket price
3. price increase
4. Canadian team
5. fresh flower bouquet
6. opera program
7. pencil holder
8. top shelf

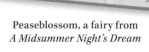

Peaseblossom, a fairy from *A Midsummer Night's Dream*

Write an adjective phrase to describe each noun.

9. costume
10. color
11. rule
12. book
13. villages
14. information
15. path
16. trees
17. popcorn
18. lake
19. car
20. house

EXERCISE 4 Write an adjective phrase using each troublesome preposition.

1. differ from
2. among
3. like
4. angry at
5. off

APPLY IT NOW

Have you ever seen a live performance? Was it a school play or a local production? Describe your experience by writing four sentences that contain adjective phrases.

7.5 Prepositional Phrases as Adverbs

Slave family in cotton field

Prepositional phrases can be used as adverbs—to describe verbs, adjectives, or other adverbs. Prepositional phrases used in this way are called **adverb phrases.**

Like single-word adverbs, adverb phrases answer the questions *how, when, where, to what extent, why,* and *under what condition.*

Adverb: The runaway slaves moved *cautiously* as they traveled north.

Adverb phrase: The runaway slaves moved *with caution* as they traveled north.

What are the adverb phrases in these sentences? What does each describe?

The slaves proceeded through the Underground Railroad.
The trip north was dangerous for the runaways.
The slaves began to move late in the night.

In the first sentence, the adverb phrase *through the Underground Railroad* describes the verb *proceeded.* In the second sentence, the adverb phrase *for the runaways* describes the adjective *dangerous.* In the third sentence, the adverb phrase *in the night* describes the adverb *late.*

EXERCISE 1 In the following sentences, tell what each italicized adverb phrase describes.

1. Many slaves owed their freedom *to the Underground Railroad.*
2. The name was applied *to a special system.*
3. The system was too risky *for some slaves.*
4. The Underground Railroad began in the colonial period and became part of a larger movement later *in the 19th century.*
5. The railroad expanded *in the 1840s.*
6. Runaway slaves escaped *from the South.*
7. Most left *for their personal freedom.*
8. They traveled *to the North.*
9. They were aided *by compassionate people.*
10. Those who helped were sympathetic *to the slaves' cause.*

Harriet Tubman

EXERCISE 2 Identify the adverb phrase or phrases in each sentence. Name the word or words the adverb phrase describes.

1. The runaways were escorted by "conductors."

2. The most famous conductor, Harriet Tubman, went south on 19 occasions.

3. She met runaways at "stations" and led them to the North.

4. She herself had been a slave earlier in her life.

5. Tubman was successful beyond measure.

6. The runaways stayed at the houses of helpful people.

7. Actually, runaways often were hidden in barns.

8. They usually stayed for only a night.

9. Most had never been far from home before.

10. Because of the danger, they received secret directions.

11. They were also guided by "the drinking gourd," the Big Dipper.

12. These stars pointed to the north.

13. Runaways usually traveled on foot.

14. They were returned to the South if they were captured.

15. Many escaped slaves settled in Canada.

16. The trip on the "railroad" was mostly taken by men.

17. Louisa May Alcott once found a runaway in her family's stove.

18. She was terribly affected by the slaves' plight.

19. When the Civil War started, she went to Washington, D.C.

20. There she worked as a nurse at various hospitals.

21. Conductors on the Underground Railroad and station owners acted bravely despite great danger.

22. They remain famous for their work.

Louisa May
Alcott

EXERCISE 3 Write a sentence replacing each adverb with an adverb phrase.

1. moved northward
2. lived peacefully
3. moved silently
4. worked courageously

APPLY IT NOW

Write four or five sentences about someone in the news who helps others. Include an adverb phrase in each sentence and identify the adverb phrases.

Tech Tip With an adult, research this person online.

7.6 Prepositional Phrases as Nouns

You may occasionally find a sentence in which a prepositional phrase is used as a noun.

In the Appalachians is where I want to be.

In the Appalachians is a **noun phrase** used as the subject of the verb *is*. A prepositional phrase can also appear as a noun in other places within a sentence.

The time we usually visit is *in the summer*.

Above, the prepositional phrase acts as a subject complement.

Which of these sentences contains a prepositional phrase used as a noun?

After school is the only time I can possibly see you.
Before class she finished the last of her homework.

In the first sentence, the phrase *after school* acts as a subject.

EXERCISE 1 Identify the prepositional phrase used as a noun in each sentence. Tell how the prepositional phrase functions in the sentence—as a subject or a subject complement.

1. A good time to visit Appalachia is in the spring or fall.
2. In the mountains is where I love to be.
3. On a mountain trail is a wonderful place to enjoy nature.
4. From a mountaintop is the best place to view scenery.
5. On foot is the surest way to travel through the mountains.
6. Before 7:00 a.m. is the best starting time for hiking.
7. At noontime is when a person might rest and have lunch.
8. Between noon and one o'clock is an advantageous time to seek shelter from the sun.
9. Under a shady tree is a perfect place to relax.
10. Another fine place is near a running stream.

EXERCISE 2 Tell whether each italicized prepositional phrase is an adjective phrase, an adverb phrase, or a noun phrase.

1. The Alps stretch *from Austria* to France.
2. The Alps were once a major barrier *to travelers.*

3. *Through the passes* was the only way to cross them.
4. The name *of the highest peak* in the chain is Mont Blanc.
5. Many people climb *to the top* of Mont Blanc.
6. The Alps are now popular *for sports*.
7. Meadows *with lovely flowers* grow above the tree line.
8. *During late spring* is the best time to visit the alpine meadows.

EXERCISE 3 **Find the prepositional phrases in these sentences. Tell whether each is an adjective phrase, an adverb phrase, or a noun phrase.**

1. The Andes Mountains stretch along the west coast of South America.
2. They begin in Panama.
3. They end at the southern tip of the continent.
4. The Spanish name for the Andes is *la Cordillera de los Andes.*
5. This name may come from a native word for copper.
6. The mountains are rich in natural resources.
7. Aconcagua, which is 22,831 feet high, is the highest peak in the Americas.
8. It rises in Argentina.
9. Some of the Andean mountains are active volcanoes.
10. Earthquakes occur often in the Andes region.
11. Many passes of the Andes are narrow and steep.
12. Roads have been built with great difficulty.
13. Some routes actually go over the mountains.
14. The Peruvian range is crossed by the highest railroad in the world.
15. A huge statue stands on the border between Chile and Argentina.
16. It was built to commemorate the settlement of a boundary dispute.
17. Llamas graze in the grasslands of the central Andes.
18. The Andean condor lives on the mountains' steep cliffs.

APPLY IT NOW

Choose two of the following phrases. Use each in a sentence as an adjective phrase, an adverb phrase, and a noun phrase. Identify the use of each phrase.

in the summer
on the beach
at camp
after the game
by the train
on foot

Grammar in Action.

Find the first prepositional phrase used as a noun in the p. 380 excerpt.

Preposition Review

7.1 Find the prepositional phrase in each sentence. Name each preposition.

1. Because of Destiny's toothache, her mother scheduled a dentist appointment.
2. Destiny had cracked her tooth on some hard candy.
3. Destiny visited the dentist with her mother.
4. The dentist looked into Destiny's mouth.
5. During the dentist's examination, the dentist explained his diagnosis.
6. According to the dentist, she also had a cavity.
7. The dentist explained the dental procedure in great detail.
8. Destiny was brave throughout the dental work.
9. Before long, the dentist had finished.
10. Instead of hard candy, Destiny now chews sugarless gum.
11. On account of her experience, Destiny brushes her teeth regularly.
12. She follows all the recommendations from the dentist.

7.2 Choose the correct preposition to complete each sentence.

13. The argument (between among) two students started suddenly.
14. Marcus differed (with from) Amelia over how to divide the group's work.
15. Amelia became angry (with at) Marcus when he wouldn't compromise.
16. Her ideas differed (from than) his.
17. The teacher asked both students to sit (beside besides) her.
18. (Between Among) the teacher and the two students, there was a serious discussion.
19. No one (besides beside) the three people knew what was discussed.
20. At the end no one was angry (with at) anyone else.
21. Afterward, everyone acted (like as if) nothing had happened.

7.3 Tell whether each underlined word is an adverb or a preposition.

22. Should we eat <u>after</u> the movie?
23. Let's eat <u>before</u>.
24. It's chilly, so I would like to dine <u>inside</u>.
25. Nora and James sat <u>near</u> the window.
26. They chose their meal <u>from</u> the menu.
27. They looked <u>around</u> as they waited for their food.
28. We saw some friends come <u>in</u> during that time.
29. We all ate <u>at</u> the same table.

7.4 Identify the adjective phrase and the word it describes in each sentence.

30. People of all ages enjoy soccer.

31. David is a player on our school soccer team.

32. The cheers before the game encouraged our team.

33. David could hear the cheers from his family and friends.

34. A player on the opposing team scored the last goal.

35. The goalie for our side couldn't block the ball.

36. The team from Brownsburg won the game.

37. The end disappointed many fans at the game.

38. All the players on both teams played well.

39. We have high hopes for victory next time.

7.5 Identify the adverb phrase in each sentence. Name the word or words the phrase describes.

40. Georgia O'Keeffe lived on a Wisconsin farm.

41. She studied at Chicago's Art Institute.

42. Many pictures of flowers were painted by Georgia O'Keeffe.

43. She moved to New Mexico.

44. She was inspired by the state's stark landscape.

45. In her work, rocks and animal bones often appear.

46. She remained creative throughout her life.

47. Because of her work, O'Keeffe gained fame.

48. Georgia O'Keeffe is recognized as a very important American artist.

49. Many of her paintings now hang in famous museums.

7.6 Identify the prepositional phrase in each sentence. Tell whether the phrase is an adjective phrase, an adverb phrase, or a noun phrase.

50. At the pool is the best place to be when it's hot.

51. Salma wore sandals with beaded straps.

52. She carried a book of mystery stories.

53. She sat under an umbrella.

54. The umbrella gave her protection from the sun.

55. She watched children play in the water.

56. In the baby pool is where toddlers swim.

57. Salma went to the snack bar.

58. Near the snack bar was the noisiest spot.

 Tech Tip Go to www.voyagesinenglish.com for more activities.

Preposition Challenge

Read the selection and then answer the questions.

1. The photographer bent low in the tall grass and watched the lion as it moved gracefully across the plain. 2. She could see the muscles of its back ripple as the great beast sauntered along. 3. Its teeth were large and slightly yellowed, and its tawny mane blew gently in the breeze. 4. As the pair crept forward, the lion seemed to notice neither the photographer nor her assistant in spite of their nearness. 5. Suddenly, the beast turned and stopped. 6. "Oh," the photographer whispered, "it has picked up our scent." 7. "In our van is the best place for us to be now," the assistant quietly replied. 8. They slowly and quietly retreated until they reached the safety of the vehicle. 9. There they watched as the lion once again bounded through the tall grass that waved across the plain.

1. Name the two prepositions in sentence 1.
2. What are the objects of the two prepositions in sentence 1?
3. Is *along* in sentence 2 an adverb or a preposition? How do you know?
4. Is *of its back* in sentence 2 an adjective phrase or an adverb phrase?
5. Is *in the breeze* in sentence 3 an adjective phrase or an adverb phrase?
6. What sentence contains a prepositional phrase used as a noun? What is that phrase?
7. In sentence 8 find a prepositional phrase used as an adjective. What does it describe?
8. Find two prepositional phrases in sentence 9. How does each one function? What word does each describe?
9. What sentence contains a multiword preposition? What is the preposition?

EXERCISE 2 **Think of a book that you've read recently or a current movie that you have seen. In one to three paragraphs, write a review of the book or movie. Follow the instructions below.**

1. Use a prepositional phrase as a noun, as an adjective, and as an adverb.
2. Label each prepositional phrase.
3. Include two troublesome prepositions discussed on page 126.

Sentences

8.1 Kinds of Sentences

Pelé, legendary soccer star

A **sentence** is a group of words that expresses a complete thought. There are four kinds of sentences. A **declarative sentence** makes a statement. It ends with a period.

> **Soccer is a popular international sport.**

An **interrogative sentence** asks a question. It ends with a question mark.

> **Do you play soccer?**

An **imperative sentence** gives a command. It usually ends with a period but may end with an exclamation point. In imperative sentences the subject is usually *you*.

> (You) **Tell me the basic rules of soccer.**

An **exclamatory sentence** expresses a strong emotion. It ends with an exclamation point.

> **What a great shot you made!**

The parts of a sentence are a subject and a predicate. The person, place, or thing that a sentence is about is the simple subject. The simple predicate, or verb, says what the subject is doing or being.

> **Our school** _team_ | _won_ **the soccer tournament.**

Find the simple subject by asking *who* or *what* before the verb. (The verb is *won*. The simple subject is *team*.) The **complete subject** is the simple subject plus all the words and phrases that describe it. The **complete predicate** is the verb with all its modifiers and complements or objects. In the sentence above, the complete subject and the complete predicate are separated by a vertical line.

EXERCISE 1 Tell whether each sentence is declarative, interrogative, imperative, or exclamatory.

1. Have you ever heard of Edson Arantes do Nascimento?
2. You may know him as Pelé.
3. He is considered the greatest soccer player of all time.
4. Read about his records.
5. Did you know that between the years 1956 and 1974 he scored 1,220 goals?

6. He averaged one goal in every international game in which he played.

7. He scored five goals per game six times; four goals, 30 times; and three goals, 90 times.

8. That's astonishing!

9. His Brazilian national team won the World Cup three times.

10. What a star he truly was!

EXERCISE 2 **Identify the complete subject and the complete predicate in each sentence. Then name the simple subject and the simple predicate, or verb.**

1. This international soccer legend was born in Tres Coracoes, Brazil, in 1940.

2. His international fame blossomed in Sweden in 1958.

3. The teenaged star led the Brazilian team to its first World Cup crown that year.

4. The end of his long and awesome career came in 1977.

5. People still remember his amazing goals from shots off his head!

6. The beloved Pelé became Brazil's Minister of Sport after his retirement.

7. His work for children through UNICEF is well known.

8. Pelé came in second to Muhammad Ali, the boxer, in voting for Sportsman of the Century in 2000.

EXERCISE 3 **Tell whether each sentence is declarative, interrogative, imperative, or exclamatory. Then name the complete subject and complete predicate.**

1. Pele's fame increased the world's awareness of soccer.

2. The United States made its debut in the Major League Soccer in 1996.

3. Have you been to a Major League Soccer game?

4. It is an amazing experience!

5. More than 92,000 fans packed the Rose Bowl stadium in 1996 to watch the Los Angeles Galaxy defeat the Tampa Bay Mutiny.

6. Imagine the roar of that crowd.

7. Besides being a professional sport, soccer is also an Olympic sport.

8. Who has heard of Mia Hamm?

9. She is an amazing athlete!

10. Hamm led her U.S. soccer team to win the gold medal in the 1996 and 2004 Olympics.

APPLY IT NOW

Write a short paragraph about a current event. Use at least one of each of the four kinds of sentences. Identify the simple subjects and simple predicates in your paragraph.

8.2 Adjective and Adverb Phrases

A **phrase** is a group of words that is used as a single part of speech. Unlike a sentence or a clause, a phrase does not contain a subject and a verb. Phrases often function as adjectives and as adverbs.

A **prepositional phrase** is made up of a preposition, an object of the preposition, and modifiers of the object.

> World's fairs started *in the 1800s.* (adverb phrase describing the verb *started*)
>
> The exhibits *at world's fairs* showed the latest inventions, discoveries, and developments. (adjective phrase describing the noun *exhibits*)

A **participial phrase** is made up of the present or past participle and any words that go with it. Participial phrases always act as adjectives.

> *Attending world's fairs,* people learned about the latest advances in technology. (participial phrase describing the noun *people*)

An **infinitive phrase** is made up of the infinitive—*to* and the base form of a verb—and all the words that go with it. Some infinitive phrases function as adjectives or adverbs. Others act as nouns.

> A good place *to see new products* was a world's fair. (infinitive phrase used as an adjective describing the noun *place*)
>
> Usually there wasn't time enough *to see all the exhibits in one day.* (infinitive phrase used as an adverb describing the adverb *enough*)
>
> People came *to see the latest technology* and *to learn about other countries.* (infinitive phrases used as adverbs describing the verb *came*)

EXERCISE 1 Tell whether each italicized phrase is prepositional, participial, or infinitive. Then tell whether it is used as an adjective or an adverb.

1. World's fairs offered people *of the 1800s* the chance to learn about other places and about other people's accomplishments.

2. A famous world's fair occurred *in 1889* in Paris.

3. The Eiffel Tower, *built for the fair,* was intended to show the industrial capabilities of France.

4. The tower was then the tallest structure *in the world.*

5. *Taking elevators up and down,* visitors enjoyed splendid views of Paris.

6. The Chicago World's Fair in 1893 was an event *to commemorate Columbus's voyages.*

7. *Knowing of the Eiffel Tower's success,* the organizers of the Chicago fair wanted a spectacular structure.

8. It was not good enough just *to build something tall*—the structure had to be special.

9. An engineer *attending a fair meeting* heard the call from the fair's organizers for a unique structure.

10. An idea formed *in the young engineer's head*.

EXERCISE 2 Find the adjective and adverb phrases in these sentences. Tell whether they are prepositional, participial, or infinitive.

1. The Ferris wheel became the symbol of the Chicago World's Fair.

2. The idea to build such a wheel came from Pittsburgh engineer George Ferris.

3. The Ferris wheel, rising 264 feet, towered over the fair buildings and provided magnificent views.

4. Crowds of people flocked to experience a ride on the new attraction.

5. Ferris wheels soon became popular attractions at other fairs and amusement parks.

6. Ferris wheels today are smaller compared to the one George Ferris built in the late 1800s.

7. Starting a new trend, George Ferris found great success in his invention.

8. The Ferris wheel reminds young engineers and inventors to follow their dreams.

EXERCISE 3 Complete each sentence with the phrase used as indicated in parentheses.

1. The Ferris wheel was constructed _____.
   (prepositional, adverb)

2. _____, engineers assembled the massive structure at the fair. (participial, adjective)

3. Visitors had _____ tickets to ride the Ferris wheel. (infinitive, adverb)

4. The crowds _____ had never seen anything like it before. (prepositional, adjective)

5. _____, people marveled at the height of the Ferris wheel. (participial, adjective)

6. George Ferris wanted _____ an amazing machine, and he surely succeeded. (infinitive, adverb)

APPLY IT NOW

Use these phrases in sentences of your own. Tell whether each phrase is used as an adjective or as an adverb.

into our room
laughing all the while
to finish
telling a sad story
making noise
to behave

8.3 Adjective Clauses

A **clause** is a group of words that contains a subject and a predicate.

An **independent clause** is one that expresses a complete thought and so can stand on its own.

My family originally came from Italy.

A **dependent clause** cannot stand alone. Notice that the dependent clauses in red below do not express complete thoughts, even though each has a subject and a verb.

The assignment *that I was given* **was very difficult.**
It wasn't about any topic *that I had studied.*

An **adjective clause,** one type of dependent clause, describes a noun or a pronoun. Almost all adjective clauses begin with *who, whom, whose, which,* or *that.* These words are called **relative pronouns** because each relates to a word in the independent clause.

My grandmother, *who is from Italy*, **is named Martina.**

The adjective clause above relates to the noun *grandmother.* The relative pronoun introducing the clause is *who.* The word in the independent clause to which a pronoun relates is its **antecedent.** The antecedent of *who* is *grandmother.*

Can you identify the adjective clause, the relative pronoun, and the antecedent of the pronoun in this sentence?

I am happy with the first name that I was given.

The adjective clause is *that I was given. That* is the relative pronoun, and *name* is the antecedent of the pronoun.

Adjective clauses can also begin with the **subordinate conjunctions** *when, where,* and *why.*

Italy is the place *where my grandmother was born.*

EXERCISE 1 Identify the adjective clause in each sentence. Name the noun or pronoun that the adjective clause describes.

1. People are fascinated with the history of surnames, which is another word for last names.

2. A large city's phone directory is a place where you can find surnames from a wide variety of ethnic groups.

3. Genealogists, whose job is to study family history, can also supply information about last names.

4. Genealogy is a study that interests me.

5. People who lived in certain places often took the place names as their own.

6. A person whose home was near a field might have gotten the last name *Field* in English or *Hara* in Japanese.

7. People might be called by the name of the job that they held.

8. The last name *Cook* in English or *Yee* in Chinese might be given to a person who worked as a chef.

9. People whom you meet with the name *Smith* actually have the most common surname in the United States.

10. The Chinese, to whom credit is given for first using surnames, have surnames 3,000 or more years old.

EXERCISE 2 Add an adjective clause to each of the following.

1. I can't find the book _____.

2. My report, _____, got a good grade.

3. The street _____ is where I live.

4. My friend, _____, is visiting me.

5. My goal _____ is not yet realized.

6. Tony received a Rhodes scholarship, _____.

EXERCISE 3 Identify the adjective clause in each sentence. Name the noun or pronoun that the adjective clause describes. Then identify the relative pronoun or subordinate conjunction.

1. Approximately 22 million people entered the United States through Ellis Island, which was the gateway for immigrants entering the United States.

2. This means that more than half the population of the United States has immigrant ancestors who entered through Ellis Island.

3. The registry room, where the people's names were recorded, often had thousands of people a day pass through it.

4. Can you imagine how excited the immigrants, who were exhausted from long journeys, were to finally be in the United States?

5. Families that came from great distances arrived with hopes of making a good life in the United States.

APPLY IT NOW

Write five sentences about your family. Include at least one of each of the following: independent clause, adjective clause, relative pronoun, antecedent, and subordinate conjunction. Identify these parts.

Grammar in Action. Find the first relative pronoun in the excerpt on p. 415.

8.4 Restrictive and Nonrestrictive Clauses

Odin, mythological Norse god

Some adjective clauses are essential to the meaning of the sentences in which they appear. Without them the sentences no longer make sense. These essential clauses are called **restrictive clauses.** An adjective clause that is not essential to the meaning of the sentence is a **nonrestrictive clause.**

> **The special goddesses** *who assisted the chief god, Odin,* **were named the Valkyries.** (restrictive clause)
>
> **The Valkyries,** *who rode horses in the sky,* **were special goddesses in Norse mythology.** (nonrestrictive clause)

The adjective clause in the second sentence is not necessary to the sentence; it just gives additional information.

Can you tell which clauses are restrictive and which are nonrestrictive in the following sentences?

> **The Valkyries,** *who wore armor,* **did not fight in battle.**
>
> **The goddess** *who led the Valkryies* **was Freyja.**
>
> **The chariot** *on which she rode* **was pulled by a boar.**

The clause in the first sentence is nonrestrictive, and those in the second and third sentences are restrictive. In the first sentence, the adjective clause merely adds information; if it is removed, the basic meaning of the sentence remains. The adjective clauses in the other sentences cannot be removed; if they are removed, the sentences are unclear.

Note the following characteristics of adjective clauses:

- A nonrestrictive clause is set off by commas.
- A restrictive clause is not set off by commas.
- A proper noun is usually followed by a nonrestrictive clause.
- The relative pronoun *that* is generally used for restrictive clauses and *which* for nonrestrictive clauses.

EXERCISE 1 Identify the adjective clause or clauses in the following sentences. Tell whether each clause is restrictive or nonrestrictive.

1. The Valkyries were goddesses who appeared in Norse myths.
2. The goddesses, whose primary role was to select the bravest warriors in battle, were important in many Norse myths.

3. They chose the slain warriors who deserved a glorious afterlife.

4. The chosen warriors were received at Valhalla, which was the grand residence hall of the gods.

5. These warriors, who would spend their afterlife fighting by day and feasting by night, had obtained the highest reward possible.

6. Valhalla had 540 suites that could each accommodate 800 such heroes.

7. The Valkyries were also caretakers of a banner that prophesied the outcomes of wars.

8. In times of peace, the banner, which was woven, shone pure white.

9. During battle, however, a raven, which appeared on the banner only during war, disclosed the outcome.

10. A raven that flapped its wings signaled victory, but a raven that stood motionless meant defeat.

EXERCISE 2 **Identify the adjective clause in each sentence and decide whether it is restrictive or nonrestrictive. Rewrite the sentences with nonrestrictive clauses, adding commas where necessary.**

1. The Valkyries who rode through the sky were Odin's messengers.

2. Their sparkling armor was supposedly the cause of the northern lights which are also known as the aurora borealis.

3. The magnificent lights that appear in the sky were explained as being the riding Valkyries.

4. War which was an important part of life to the Norse became an important part of their myths.

5. Ragnarok which was the name for a final world battle in Norse mythology was to be followed by an era of peace.

6. Brunhilde who was one of the most famous Valkyries played an important role in these battles.

7. The Valkyries who wore winged clothing flew the warriors to Valhalla.

8. Norse mythology which has inspired poets and playwrights throughout generations dates back to the 11th century.

Lucienne Bréval as Brunhilde in Richard Wagner's opera, *Die Walkure*, 1893

APPLY IT NOW

Write five sentences with adjective clauses that you find in books or magazines. Underline the adjective clauses and indicate whether each is restrictive or nonrestrictive.

8.5 Adverb Clauses

Dependent clauses may function as adverbs, describing or giving information about verbs, adjectives, or other adverbs. These clauses, called **adverb clauses,** tell *where, when, why, in what way, to what extent (degree),* or *under what condition.*

> **Because settlers took over their habitats**, **mountain lions disappeared east of the Rockies, except in Florida and Texas.**

The adverb clause tells *why* and describes the verb *disappeared.*

Adverb clauses are introduced by **subordinate conjunctions,** some of which are listed below.

after	as though	since	when
although	because	than	whenever
as if	before	though	where
as long as	if	unless	wherever
as soon as	in order that	until	while

A subordinate conjunction joins an adverb clause to an independent clause. Find the subordinate conjunctions in these sentences. What does each adverb clause tell about?

> Florida panthers became a distinct species after they were separated from their cougar relatives in the West.
> Florida panthers are smaller than their Western relatives.

In the first sentence, the subordinate conjunction *after* introduces an adverb clause that modifies the verb *became.* In the second sentence, the subordinate conjunction *than* introduces an adverb clause that modifies the adjective *smaller.*

When an adverb clause begins a sentence, it is usually followed by a comma.

> After they were separated from their cougar relatives in the West, Florida panthers became a distinct species.

EXERCISE 1 Identify the adverb clause in each sentence. Name the subordinate conjunction.

1. Although it is almost extinct, the Florida panther is the state animal of Florida.

2. The panther became endangered because its habitat was destroyed.

3. Unless drastic action is taken, according to some concerned environmentalists, the panther will surely become extinct.

4. After an initial recovery plan was prepared in 1981, efforts to save these animals increased.

5. Some panther deaths occurred when the animals were hit by cars.

6. Bridges over highways were built wherever panthers were known to cross the roads.

7. Since the structures were completed, no panthers have been killed by cars in those areas.

8. While a reduction in speed limits in other areas is possible, the results of such action are debatable.

9. Speed zones don't seem to help if panthers wander onto the highway.

10. Until more studies are done or more action is taken, the fate of the Florida panther hangs in the balance.

EXERCISE 2 Identify the dependent clause in each sentence. Tell whether it is an adjective clause or an adverb clause.

1. The Florida panther, which was once common throughout the Southeast, is now found only in Florida.

2. The animal prefers remote areas that have adequate prey.

3. Many of these cats have been fitted with radio collars in order that wildlife experts can track their movements.

4. Panthers need habitats that have good places to hide and sleep.

5. As long as its habitat keeps getting smaller, the panther seems to be on a path to extinction.

6. These animals, which vary in size, can grow to be over six feet long.

7. Although thought to be very shy animals, panthers have been known to approach humans.

8. Panthers, while part of the large cat family, are unable to roar.

9. Panthers, who have very strong legs, can leap more than 15 feet.

10. Wildlife agencies are, whenever it's possible, doing everything they can to protect the Florida panther.

APPLY IT NOW

Choose an endangered species and write four sentences using different subordinate conjunctions. Underline the adverb clauses and indicate what the clauses tell about.

Tech Tip With an adult, research online the species you choose.

8.6 Noun Clauses as Subjects

Dependent clauses can be used as nouns. These clauses, called **noun clauses,** function as subjects, complements, appositives, direct objects, indirect objects, or objects of prepositions. Although a noun clause is a basic part of the independent clause and cannot be eliminated from the sentence, it is still a dependent clause. A noun clause used as a subject generally takes the singular form of the verb. Compare these sentences.

> My *surprise* **must have been written all over my face.**
>
> *That I was surprised* **must have been written all over my face.**

In the first sentence, the noun *surprise* is the subject. In the second sentence, the clause *that I was surprised* is the subject. The clause does the work of a noun, and so it is a noun clause.

Most noun clauses begin with one of the following introductory words: *how, that, what, whatever, when, where, whether, who, whoever, whom, whomever,* and *why.*

How do these noun clauses, which are in red, function?

> *That* **our project would be a time capsule was never in doubt.**
>
> *Whoever* **is interested can participate in the project.**

In the first sentence, the noun clause is the subject of the verb *was,* and in the second sentence, it is the subject of *can participate.*

In the first sentence, *that* introduces the clause but serves no specific purpose within the dependent clause. In the second sentence, however, *whoever* acts as the subject of the dependent clause. What is the verb? You are right if you said *is.*

EXERCISE 1 Identify the noun clause used as a subject in each sentence. Name the introductory word.

1. That time capsules are popular is an undisputed fact.
2. Why these capsules are so popular isn't clear.
3. What a time capsule is designed to do is to give a glimpse of a specific moment in time.
4. What you decide to put into a capsule may require some thought and effort.
5. That people often include a favorite poem, a family tree, and current newspapers in time capsules is no secret.
6. That some companies sell sturdy containers for time capsules shows the popularity of such capsules.
7. That a time capsule was made for the 1963 World's Fair is a fact.

8. What people chose for that capsule included a ballpoint pen, contact lenses, and a credit card.

9. Whether our school grounds were once used as a site for a capsule is a question to explore.

10. Whoever has worked at the school a long time may know the answer to this question.

11. Whomever we ask should have worked here at least 20 years.

12. Why no one left instructions for locating a capsule is unknown.

EXERCISE 2 **Complete each of the following with a noun clause used as a subject.**

1. _____ is my motto.

2. _____ was long remembered.

3. _____ was soon discovered.

4. _____ is an important piece of information.

5. _____ has always interested me.

EXERCISE 3 **Identify the noun clause and the introductory word. Then name the complete subject and complete predicate.**

1. What goes in our time capsule is very important.

2. Whoever adds items chooses them for a reason.

3. Why my sister wants to include her phone is unknown to me.

4. That I will include sheet music for my flute will be no surprise to anyone.

5. Where we bury the capsule is the tricky part.

6. That my parents want it buried in the backyard is one idea.

7. That my dog can dig up the capsule needs to be considered.

8. Whether in the backyard or the front yard is what we must decide.

9. When we plan to reopen the time capsule is an exciting thought.

10. How long we wait may require much patience on my part.

APPLY IT NOW

Write sentences using each of the following clauses as the subject of a sentence:

why we want to make a time capsule

what I would like to put into my time capsule

whoever works with me

where we will put the time capsule

8.7 Noun Clauses as Subject Complements

Benjamin Franklin

Like nouns, noun clauses can be used as subject complements.

> **The problem was** *the choice of a subject for my report*.
>
> **The problem was** *that I couldn't decide on a subject for my report*.

In the first sentence, the subject is *problem*. The verb *was* links the subject to the subject complement, the noun *choice*. In the second sentence, *problem* is again the subject. The linking verb *was* joins the subject to the subject complement, the noun clause *that I couldn't decide on a subject for my report*.

What are the subject complements in the following sentences? Which one is a noun clause?

> **My goal is to find an interesting topic.**
>
> **My goal is that I will find an interesting topic.**

Both sentences contain subject complements. In the first sentence, the subject complement is the infinitive phrase *to find an interesting topic*. In the second sentence, it is the noun clause *that I will find an interesting topic*.

EXERCISE 1 **Identify the noun clause used as a subject complement in each sentence. Name the subject that the noun clause describes.**

1. One description of Benjamin Franklin is that he was "a jack of all trades and a master of many."

2. Proof of his importance as a statesman is when he signed both the Declaration of Independence and the U.S. Constitution.

3. Franklin became what few men ever think of becoming—a leader in many fields.

4. A favorite choice from his collection of published sayings is that "a penny saved is a penny earned."

5. His philosophy was that hard work and thrift were important qualities.

6. The result of one of his public-spirited campaigns was that the first public hospital in Philadelphia was built.

EXERCISE 2 Identify the noun clauses used as subject complements in these sentences. Not every sentence has such a clause.

1. Benjamin Franklin's vision for America was that it would be a free and independent democracy.
2. His interest in electricity was that of an amateur.
3. His curiosity about lightning is what many people remember.
4. Franklin's suspicion was whether or not lightning conducts electricity.
5. To test his theory, he used a toy that belonged to his son.
6. Franklin felt that lightning is powerful and dangerous.
7. He invented the lightning rod, which is still used.
8. The proof of the lightning rod's success appeared that it saved Franklin's own house during a lightning storm.
9. Another of his ideas was that two pairs of spectacles could be combined as one.
10. People still benefit from his invention of bifocals.

EXERCISE 3 Identify the noun clause in each sentence. Tell if the noun clause is used as a subject or a subject complement.

1. That fireplaces were dangerous was a commonplace concern of life.
2. Franklin's idea was that an enclosed fire would be much safer than an open fireplace.
3. That he then invented the iron stove became well known.
4. That he started the first fire insurance company seems less well known.
5. Franklin's greatest asset was how he never stopped being curious.
6. That Franklin was respected in many areas is quite an accomplishment.
7. That he founded the first library is well documented.
8. His hope was that Philadelphia would be made a better place.
9. Why his philosophies and inventions benefit us today is much celebrated.
10. Franklin's best lesson still remains how we should always strive to better things around us.

APPLY IT NOW

Write five sentences with subject complements. Here are some ideas for subjects:

the most important requirement
my philosophy
my best piece of advice
my safety suggestion
the chief difficulty
my chief concern

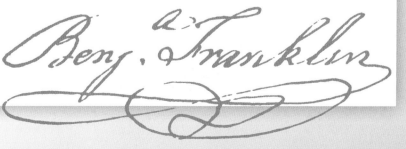

8.8 Noun Clauses as Appositives

Noun clauses can be used as appositives. An appositive follows a noun and renames it or gives more information about it.

Dr. King and his wife, Coretta, lead a civil rights march in Alabama in 1965.

> **In the 1960s many people's goal was** *that all Americans have equal rights.* (subject complement)
>
> **In the 1960s the goal** *that all Americans have equal rights* **became an important one to work for.** (appositive)

In the first sentence, the noun clause in red is a subject complement. It describes the subject *goal* and follows the linking verb *was.* In the second sentence, the noun clause in red is an appositive. It explains the noun that precedes it, *goal.*

Can you identify the noun clause used as an appositive in the sentence below and what it explains?

> **Many people's concern whether discrimination could be ended led them to take political action.**

You are correct if you said the noun clause is *whether discrimination could be ended* and that it follows and renames the noun *concern.*

Adjective clauses can be confused with noun clauses used as appositives. A noun clause used as an appositive renames the noun or pronoun it follows. An adjective clause describes a noun or pronoun.

> **The report** *that I wrote* **summarized the work of Martin Luther King Jr.** (adjective clause)
>
> **The report** *that King was assassinated* **shocked the world.** (noun clause)

In the first sentence, *that* acts as a relative pronoun. Its antecedent is *report,* and it is the direct object of the verb *wrote* in the adjective clause. In the second sentence, *that* introduces the noun clause but has no other function in the clause.

EXERCISE 1 Identify the noun clauses used as appositives in these sentences. Not all sentences have noun clauses.

1. Many leaders throughout history have held the belief that people can improve society.

2. Dr. Martin Luther King Jr. expressed the hope that both black and white children would one day judge each other according to character, not race.

3. The desire that we achieve this goal is expressed in his "I Have a Dream" speech.

4. African Americans were seeking the same rights that other Americans possessed.

5. President John F. Kennedy expressed the hope that more people dedicate themselves to public service.

6. The belief that we owed our talents to our country is stated in his inaugural address.

7. The fact that our country allows us to develop our talents gives us an obligation to do something in return.

8. It was King's and Kennedy's hope that their words would change people—and society.

9. It is a fact that we still remember their words today.

10. Theirs are speeches that we study in school.

EXERCISE 2 Complete each of the following with a noun clause used as an appositive.

1. My belief _____ is strong.

2. The theory _____ interests me.

3. The fact _____ is surprising.

4. Did you hear the news _____?

5. The report _____ was broadcast at noon.

6. The possibility _____ is exciting to me.

EXERCISE 3 Identify the noun clauses used as appositives in these sentences. Name the subject that each appositive renames.

1. The fact that the 1960s brought about social and scientific advances is well known.

2. Our nation's hope that we could send a man into space was realized in July 1969.

3. NASA's goal that they land a spaceship on the moon was achieved in an eight-day mission.

4. The crew of *Apollo 11* held the hope that they would be the first humans to walk on the surface of the moon.

5. The famous motto that it is one small step for man; one giant step for mankind will forever be remembered.

6. The fact that NASA ran a successful mission to the moon has never been forgotten.

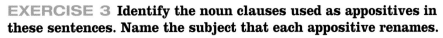

7. The question whether man can safely travel to the moon had been answered.

APPLY IT NOW

Write five sentences with noun clauses used as appositives. Use some of the following words as the nouns to which the appositives refer: *belief, fact, theory, hope, desire, dream,* and *goal.*

8.9 Noun Clauses as Direct Objects

Noun clauses can act as direct objects.

We often don't realize *what life was like before certain inventions.*
Imagine *what travel was like before the airplane.*

The introductory word *that* is often dropped from a noun clause used as a direct object.

I think *the Internet is the most important invention ever.*

When verbs such as *feel, learn, say, see,* and *think* are followed by noun clauses, omitting *that* may change the meaning of the sentence.

I can see *that you conduct experiments.*
I can see *you conduct experiments.*

Which sentence contains a noun clause used as a direct object?

Each student will research whatever interests him or her.
Each student will research an invention that interests him or her.

You are correct if you said the first sentence. The action of the verb *research* is received by the noun clause *whatever interests him or her.* In the second sentence, the noun *invention* is the direct object and is followed by the adjective clause *that interests him or her.*

The correct form of a pronoun is determined by its function within the noun clause.

We saw *who* **benefited most from the invention.**
We saw *whom* **the invention benefited most.**

In the first sentence, *who* is the subject of the noun clause *who benefited most from the invention.* In the second sentence, *whom* is the direct object in the clause *whom the invention benefited most.*

A laboratory petri dish for scientific experiments

EXERCISE 1 Identify the noun clause used as a direct object in each sentence.

1. I never really asked myself why things are invented.

2. A book I read explained how many things got started.

3. Did you know that many inventions resulted from chance?

4. Most people know that Alexander Fleming discovered penicillin after the chance formation of a mold on his experimental cultures.

5. I learned that the youngest person to get a patent on an invention—a toy truck—was only five years old.

EXERCISE 2 **Identify the direct object in each sentence. Tell whether the direct object is a noun or a noun clause.**

1. Do you know who invented the microwave oven?

2. In 1946 Dr. Percy Spencer was testing a vacuum tube.

3. Later he discovered that the candy bar in his pocket had melted.

4. The melted candy gave Dr. Spencer an idea.

5. He wondered what else the tube might affect.

6. He put some popcorn kernels near the tube, and they immediately popped.

7. Spencer thought that any food near the tube might cook.

8. He and a colleague placed an egg near the tube.

9. They wondered what would happen next.

10. It exploded and spattered hot yolk all over his colleague's face.

11. Dr. Spencer had invented a product that would revolutionize cooking.

12. At first, skeptics thought that microwave ovens would give people radiation poisoning.

13. By the 1970s, however, most people had discovered the benefits of this new kind of cooking.

14. Soon they decided that the microwave was a necessity.

15. Will you remember who invented this indispensable appliance?

EXERCISE 3 **Complete each of the following with a noun clause used as a direct object.**

1. Do you see _____?

2. Young adults feel _____.

3. Louis Braille invented _____.

4. He was 15 years old when he learned _____.

5. Most inventors think _____.

6. People don't realize _____.

7. Millions of people who were blind discovered _____.

APPLY IT NOW

Write a short letter to a friend, telling about a new or an unusual invention. Use noun clauses as direct objects in your writing by incorporating verbs such as *reported, said, explained, decided, think, know,* and *believe.*

Tech Tip With an adult, send your letter as an e-mail.

8.10 Noun Clauses as Objects of Prepositions

Noun clauses can function as objects of prepositions. In this sentence the noun clause serves as the object of *about*.

> **My father taught me about** *what I should do to ride my bicycle safely*.

What is the noun clause in this sentence? How is it used?

> **I was interested in what I learned about safe biking.**

The noun clause is *what I learned about safe biking*. The entire noun clause is the object of the preposition *in*.

Adjective clauses should not be confused with noun clauses used as objects of prepositions. An adjective clause describes a noun or pronoun in the independent clause, and the introductory word of the adjective clause has an antecedent in the independent clause.

> **The famous race** *in which cyclists travel through France* **is the Tour de France.** (adjective clause)
> **We talked about** *which cyclists might win the Tour de France*. (noun clause)

In the first sentence, *which* is a relative pronoun. Its antecedent is *race*, and it acts as the object of the preposition *in* in the adjective clause. In the second sentence, *which* introduces the noun clause but has no antecedent in the independent clause.

What is the correct choice of pronoun for this sentence?

> **The race is won by** (whoever whomever) **has the shortest total time.**

The clause *whoever has the shortest total time* is a noun clause. The word *whoever* is the subject of the verb *has*. The form of the pronoun is determined by its role in the subordinate clause. In sentences like these, don't be confused by the preposition.

EXERCISE 1 Identify each noun clause used as an object of a preposition. Not all sentences have noun clauses used in this way.

1. I was surprised by what I saw in the store window.
2. The sign announced what could be called a guessing contest.
3. Each entrant had to make a guess about how many jelly beans a certain container held.

4. A prize of a bicycle would go to whoever made the closest guess.

5. Since my current passion was for a fast bike, I wanted to enter the contest.

6. The problem of how I would make my guess came up.

7. I asked for ideas from whoever would listen.

8. I talked about why I wanted to win.

9. Finally, I got a jar of similar size and shape, filled it with jelly beans, counted them, and made an educated guess.

10. The total was near a number that was important to me.

11. The number 1243, my house number, was what I submitted as an answer to the contest.

12. Soon I was delighted with my prize bike and by what it could do.

EXERCISE 2 In each sentence, identify the noun clause. Tell whether it is the subject, the direct object, or the object of a preposition.

1. That the Tour de France is a grueling bicycle race is a fact.

2. I am impressed by how much determination the cyclists show.

3. Their success on the steep mountain legs of the race depends on what their training consisted of.

4. Whoever has the fastest time on each of the 20 race days receives a yellow jersey to wear the next day.

5. Did you know that the last leg of the race is along the Champs Elysées in Paris?

6. I hadn't realized that two Americans—Greg LeMond and Lance Armstrong—had each won the race several times.

7. I am amazed by how many miles they have to race.

8. That the bikers have to ride over 2,000 miles is unimaginable.

9. Do you realize that over 15 million people watch the race?

10. Whoever can ride that many miles through steep hills deserves much recognition and respect.

11. Spectators are astounded by how easy the riders make it look.

12. That these riders celebrate one another's victories is a bonus.

APPLY IT NOW

Find five sentences with noun clauses in a magazine, newspaper, or book. Copy these sentences and tell how each noun clause is used. Be sure to include the name of your source.

8.11 Simple, Compound, and Complex Sentences

Sentences can be classified according to their form, or structure. In the following examples, subjects are in red and verbs are underlined.

A **simple sentence** is an independent clause that stands alone. It has a subject and predicate, either or both of which can be compound.

> *Kathleen Mary Kenyon* <u>became</u> a famous archaeologist.
> *Kenyon* and *Mortimer Wheeler* <u>developed</u> a new excavation method.
> *They* <u>dug</u> down and <u>built</u> trenches.

A **compound sentence** contains two or more independent clauses.

> *Kenyon* <u>excavated</u> in England, but *she* also <u>worked</u> in the Middle East.
> *Kenyon* <u>worked</u> painstakingly; consequently, her *work* <u>was respected</u>.

The independent clauses in compound sentences are commonly connected in one of three ways: (1) by a comma and one of the coordinating conjunctions *and, or, but, nor,* or *yet*; (2) by a semicolon; or (3) by a semicolon followed by an adverb such as *therefore, however,* or *nevertheless*.

A **complex sentence** has one independent clause and at least one dependent clause, which may function as an adjective, an adverb, or a noun. In these sentences, subjects of clauses are in red and verbs are underlined.

> **Although many** *archaeologists* <u>excavated</u> **entire structures,** *Kenyon* and *Wheeler* <u>dug</u> **sites in vertical layers.** (adverb clause— *Although many archaeologists excavated entire structures*)
> **Their** *method, which* <u>showed</u> **changes over time,** <u>helped</u> **trace a site through its entire history.** (adjective clause beginning with the relative pronoun *which—which showed changes over time*)
> **Don't** *you* <u>think</u> **that** *archaeology* <u>is</u> **the most fascinating field of study?** (noun clause—*that archaeology is the most fascinating field of study*)

EXERCISE 1 **Tell whether each sentence is simple, compound, or complex.**

1. Kathleen Mary Kenyon, who was born in England in 1906, became interested in archaeology early on.

2. She attended Oxford University and became the first female president of its archaeological society.

3. She learned the method of excavating during her work in England.

King Tut's gold coffinette

4. In the 1950s and 1960s, Kenyon and her team worked in Palestine, and they uncovered areas in the town of Jericho.

5. Jericho, which is north of Jerusalem, is one of the world's most ancient cities.

6. When the city started, people were first learning about farming.

7. Kenyon's work traced the 4,000-year history of the city, and it resulted in much new scientific information.

8. She found dwellings that were constructed 10,000 years ago.

9. She learned about the city's inhabitants from ancient skulls.

10. Kenyon published reports of her excavations before she died.

EXERCISE 2 Complete each item by following the directions in parentheses. Then tell whether you wrote a simple, compound, or complex sentence.

1. I enjoy reading, _____. (independent clause with a coordinating conjunction)

2. Although I like archaeology, _____. (independent clause)

3. I enjoyed the book _____. (dependent clause)

4. I read a book _____. (dependent clause)

5. _____. (independent clause)

EXERCISE 3 Combine each of the following pairs of simple sentences into a compound or complex sentence. Tell whether you created a compound or complex sentence.

1. Howard Carter conducted digs in the Valley of Kings. He uncovered King Tut's tomb in 1922.

2. Carter worked in Egypt for over 30 years. He discovered the tomb after digging in the Valley of Kings for five years.

3. King Tut's tomb was one of the last ones found in the Valley of Kings. The tomb hadn't been touched in nearly 3,000 years.

4. It is believed that he became king when he was nine years old. King Tut is referred to as the Boy King.

5. Not much is known about his rule in ancient Egypt. Today he is the most widely known of ancient Egyptian kings.

APPLY IT NOW

Using this past weekend as your topic, write one simple sentence, one compound sentence, and one complex sentence. Identify each sentence type, circle the subjects, and underline the predicates.

Grammar in Action

Is the first sentence in the excerpt on p. 415 a simple, compound, or complex sentence?

Sentences • 161

Sentence Review

8.1 Add the correct end punctuation to each sentence. Identify it as declarative, interrogative, imperative, or exclamatory. Then name the complete subject and the complete predicate.

1. Vanilla ice cream is made primarily with vanilla beans, sugar, and cream

2. Do you know that there is also some salt in ice cream

3. This ice cream tastes delicious

4. Give me a double scoop of chocolate ice cream, please

8.2 Identify the adjective phrase or adverb phrase in each sentence. Tell whether each is a prepositional, a participial, or an infinitive phrase.

5. Helping build a fence, Celine learned about construction.

6. She and her father started in the morning.

7. Celine struggled to use the power drill.

8. Her father set the posts in concrete.

8.3 Identify the adjective clause in each sentence. Name the noun or pronoun that the adjective clause describes.

9. My friend, who is usually late, arrived on time.

10. The library is the place where we met.

11. Tanya located *Gentle Ben*, which is her favorite book.

12. She actually enjoys any story that involves animals.

8.4 Identify the adjective clause in each sentence and decide whether it is restrictive or nonrestrictive. Add commas to nonrestrictive clauses where necessary.

13. The view which showed the ocean was spectacular.

14. The Cliffs of Moher are crags that drop 700 feet to the sea.

15. The person who helped me find the area known as The Burren was named Maggie.

16. The Burren landscape is one of flat limestone which has been deeply eroded.

8.5 Identify the adverb clause in each sentence. Name the subordinate conjunction.

17. As soon as my family finished dinner, I cleared the table.

18. After Colin washed a plate, mom dried it.

19. Maggie doesn't wash dishes because she often breaks them.

20. Unless Maggie helps out, we won't do our part.

8.6 Identify the noun clause used as the subject in each sentence.

21. Whether there would be enough volunteers was our main worry.

22. How people help with the food drive depends on the amount of time each person has.

23. Whoever volunteers to help will be rewarded.

24. That they were able to feed some 100 families was amazing.

8.7 Identify the noun clause used as a subject complement in each sentence. Name the subject the noun clause describes.

25. A question that resulted in my research was why people admired John F. Kennedy.

26. A well-known quotation of Kennedy's was that you should "ask not what your country can do for you, but what you can do for your country."

27. His viewpoint was that young people should volunteer.

28. The idea of the Peace Corps is how young people can make a difference in people's lives.

8.8 Identify the noun clauses used as appositives.

29. The news that snow was on the way came from the report.

30. The announcement that school was canceled made us happy.

31. The question whether it would be dangerous to drive in the snowstorm occurred to us.

32. Mom's message that we might like to shovel the driveway was met with groans.

8.9 Identify the direct object in each sentence. Tell whether the direct object is a noun or a noun clause.

33. Ricardo studied only the chapters that the teacher had highlighted.

34. He decided that he would answer the short essays first.

35. Ricardo thought that he would remember enough information.

36. His teacher knew that Ricardo had not reviewed the notes.

8.10 Identify the noun clause used as the object of a preposition in each sentence.

37. The class is interested in whatever is known about earthquakes.

38. We read about how an earthquake occurs.

39. A video explained about why shifting tectonic plates cause seismic activity.

40. There are several warnings through which scientists can predict an earthquake.

41. The scientists reported on whether the likelihood of an earthquake in California was imminent.

8.11 Identify whether each sentence is simple, compound, or complex.

42. Guacamole, a popular dish from Mexico, consists of mashed and seasoned avocado.

43. Avocados, which grow on trees, are a tropical fruit.

44. Haas avocados, which are buttery and rich, make excellent guacamole.

45. Europeans discovered avocados in the 16th century, but Native Americans had eaten avocados for centuries.

 Tech Tip Go to www.voyagesinenglish.com for more activities.

Sentence Challenge

Read the selection and answer the questions.

1. Jason's ship, which was called the *Argo,* passed through the narrow channel. 2. He and his crew of 50 were now in the enemy's waters. 3. Every hand was prepared for a dangerous mission. 4. Were these veteran sailors hesitant in the face of danger? 5. No, their sworn oath was that they would capture the Golden Fleece. 6. What dangers awaited them! 7. First, they had to slip through the Cyanean rocks, two immense boulders that crushed everything between them. 8. This was accomplished through trickery, and then Jason and the Argonauts arrived in the land of the Golden Fleece. 9. There they subdued a race of skeleton warriors and gave a magic potion to the fire-breathing dragon that never slept. 10. Seeing the sought-after treasure, Jason and his crew executed their plan. 11. They seized the Golden Fleece, they concealed it aboard the *Argo,* and they headed for home. 12. As they sailed, Jason dreamed of when he would rule his homeland.

1. Which is the dependent clause in sentence 1? Is it an adjective or an adverb clause? If it is an adjective clause, is it restrictive or nonrestrictive?

2. Find an adjective phrase and an adverb phrase in sentence 2. What does each describe?

3. Identify the noun clause in sentence 5. How is it used in the sentence?

4. What is the dependent clause in sentence 7? Is it an adjective clause or an adverb clause?

5. Is sentence 8 simple, compound, or complex?

6. Is sentence 9 simple, compound, or complex?

7. Name the phrase in sentence 10. What kind of phrase is it?

8. Is sentence 11 simple, compound, or complex?

9. A dependent clause begins sentence 12. What is the clause? Is it an adjective clause or an adverb clause?

10. What is the noun clause in sentence 12? How is it used?

11. Find examples of these three kinds of sentences in the selection: exclamatory, interrogative, and declarative.

Conjunctions and Interjections

9.1 Coordinating Conjunctions

A **conjunction** is a word used to connect words or groups of words. The four types of connectors are coordinating conjunctions, correlative conjunctions, conjunctive adverbs, and subordinate conjunctions.

A **coordinating conjunction** joins words or groups of words that are similar. The coordinating conjunctions are *and, but, nor, or, so,* and *yet.*

Coordinating conjunctions connect words and phrases.

> **The North** *and* **the South fought in the Civil War.** (words)
> **They fought** **on land** *and* **on the sea.** (prepositional phrases)
> **The North fought** **to save the Union** *and* **to settle the question of slavery.** (infinitive phrases)

Coordinating conjunctions connect independent clauses to form compound sentences.

> **More than two million soldiers fought in the Civil War**, *and* **some 600,000 of them died.**
> **The South had few factories**, *but* **it hoped to get help from Europe.**
> **The North had to act to preserve the Union**, *or* **it could have let the South secede.**

Can you identify what is connected in these examples?

> **Robert E. Lee fought for the South,** *and* **Ulysses S. Grant fought for the North.**
> **Union** *and* **Confederate soldiers admired their leadership.**

The coordinating conjunction connects clauses in the first example and words in the second example.

EXERCISE 1 **Complete each sentence with a coordinating conjunction and an appropriate word, phrase, or clause as indicated.**

1. We will plant zucchini, tomatoes, _____. (word)
2. Tim read the directions carefully, _____. (clause)
3. Is this yours _____? (word)
4. The lights went out, _____. (clause)
5. Will you spend the summer in the city _____? (phrase)

EXERCISE 2 **Choose the correct coordinating conjunction to complete each sentence.**

1. We have had many great presidents in American history, (yet nor) one of the most famous is Abraham Lincoln.

2. Lincoln was president during the Civil War (and or) helped emancipate slaves.

3. Commemorated on May 30, 1922, the Lincoln Memorial is a well-known landmark in Washington, D.C., (nor but) it also serves to remind us of the great things this man did.

4. One of Lincoln's most famous speeches is the Gettysburg Address, (and or) it is often quoted in speeches today.

5. Lincoln was born in a backwoods cabin (and nor) he received little formal education, (but or) he went on to accomplish many things, such as becoming a lawyer and a lobbyist for the Illinois Central Railroad.

EXERCISE 3 **Find the coordinating conjunctions in these sentences and tell whether each joins words, phrases, or clauses.**

1. On the Boston Common is a sculpture of a soldier on a horse and of infantry troops around him.

2. The impressive statue, by Augustus Saint-Gaudens, shows Robert Gould Shaw and the 54th Regiment.

3. The 54th Regiment was the first company that included former slaves in the Civil War, so its formation was somewhat controversial.

4. The Civil War was fought in part to end slavery, yet prejudice existed even in the Union Army.

5. Shaw was asked to raise a regiment including former slaves and to command it.

6. Once the company was formed, the loyalty of the troop or its leader was never in question.

7. During the battle, Sergeant W. H. Carney impulsively but bravely ran through a hail of bullets to raise the flag.

8. Carney was the first African American to receive the Congressional Medal of Honor, but it was not awarded until 1900.

9. After a fearsome assault, Shaw and 270 of his men were dead.

APPLY IT NOW

Think back about a project you worked on at school or at home. Write three or four sentences describing the project. Use coordinating conjunctions as you explain everyone's role and actions. Identify each conjunction.

Grammar in Action
In the p. 453 excerpt, find the first coordinating conjunction. What is it connecting?

9.2 Correlative Conjunctions

Correlative conjunctions are conjunctions that are used in pairs to connect words or groups of words that have equal importance in a sentence. The words or phrases should have parallel structure. Correlative conjunctions emphasize the relationship between the words or groups of words that are connected.

> A goldfish *or* a gerbil is a good pet for most children.
>
> *Either* a goldfish *or* a gerbil is a good pet for most children.

In the first sentence, the coordinating conjunction *or* joins the two nouns, *goldfish* and *gerbil*. In the second sentence, the pair of conjunctions, *either* and *or*, also connects *goldfish* and *gerbil* but gives greater emphasis to the relationship.

The following are the most commonly used correlative conjunctions:

both . . . and	**not only . . . but also**
either . . . or	**whether . . . or**
neither . . . nor	

Each correlative conjunction appears immediately in front of one of the words or phrases that are connected. In sentences with *neither . . . nor* connecting the subjects, the verb agrees with the noun closer to it.

> *Neither* the lizard *nor* those gerbils require a lot of care.
>
> I can't decide *whether* a snake *or* a lizard is my favorite pet.
>
> *Not only* does my friend have a dog, *but* he *also* has a rab bit.

EXERCISE 1 Identify the correlative conjunctions in each sentence.

1. I can't decide whether a dog or a cat is the better pet for me.
2. Both dogs and cats are appealing.
3. Cats are both cute and cuddly.
4. Not only can dogs be friendly, but they can also be helpful.
5. Neither our dogs nor our cat is difficult to care for.
6. Dogs require both walking and grooming.
7. Cats need neither haircuts nor baths.
8. Either a dog or a cat is actually a good choice for a pet.

EXERCISE 2 Identify the correlative conjunctions in these sentences and tell the words they connect. Not all sentences have correlative conjunctions.

1. Either a Labrador retriever or a Chesapeake Bay retriever can be a good companion.

2. These two breeds of dogs are both sweet-tempered creatures and strong swimmers.

3. Webs between their toes help make both Labradors and Chesapeakes excellent swimmers.

4. Neither the Labrador nor the Chesapeake is a small dog; as an adult each weighs between 50 and 75 pounds.

5. Their thick, oily coats protect them against either cold weather or icy waters.

6. Labradors' coats are yellow, brown, or black and smooth; Chesapeakes' are dark brown and curly.

7. Tales of saving people at sea are told not only of the Labrador but also of the Chesapeake.

8. A Labrador can be used as a guide dog for people who are visually impaired.

EXERCISE 3 Complete the sentences with either coordinating or correlative conjunctions.

1. Cats make nice pets, _____ for people on farms, dogs are even better.

2. Cats and dogs may live _____ in the house or in the barns.

3. Some dogs herd _____ sheep and cows.

4. Dogs may guard both house _____ yard.

5. Indoors _____ outdoors, dogs are good pets, _____ some people find them helpful too.

6. _____ are cats good pets, _____ they have a presence in stories and nursery rhymes, such as *Puss in Boots* and *The Cat and the Fiddle*.

7. Cats have _____ a keen sense of smell _____ a curious nature.

APPLY IT NOW

Write four sentences about animals that interest you as pets. Use both coordinating and correlative conjunctions.

Tech Tip With an adult, research other types of pets online.

169

9.3 Conjunctive Adverbs

Conjunctive adverbs connect independent clauses. A semicolon is used before a conjunctive adverb and a comma is used after it.

> **Many Amish live in Pennsylvania;** *nevertheless*, **they have communities in other parts of the United States.**
>
> **Pennsylvania still has many Amish communities;** *moreover*, **Ohio and Indiana also have Amish communities.**

Common conjunctive adverbs include the following:

also	hence	likewise	otherwise
besides	however	meanwhile	subsequently
consequently	indeed	moreover	still
finally	instead	nevertheless	therefore
furthermore	later	nonetheless	thus

Parenthetical expressions, also called explanatory expressions, are used in the same way as conjunctive adverbs. Among these are *for example, namely, on the contrary, in fact, that is,* and *on the other hand.* When such an expression joins independent clauses, it must be preceded by a semicolon and followed by a comma.

> **Luis is a very good diver;** *in fact*, **he ranks first in the state.**

EXERCISE 1 Identify the conjunctive adverb in each sentence.

1. The Amish were persecuted in Europe for years; finally, in the 1700s they began to move to America.

2. Pennsylvania was noted as a place of religious tolerance; therefore, many Amish moved there at first.

3. The Amish are committed to a simple lifestyle; hence, many of them are farmers or craftworkers.

4. The Amish live by a set of rules called *Ordnung*; however, these rules vary from community to community.

5. Many Amish communities reject electricity; thus, they live in houses without electric lights.

6. The Amish dress in a simple style; consequently, they wear plain fabrics and dark colors.

EXERCISE 2 **Rewrite the following sentences, choosing the correct conjunctive adverb. Add semicolons and commas where needed.**

1. Many Amish communities reject the use of motorized vehicles (nevertheless thus) many Amish drive horse-drawn buggies.

2. Many Amish communities do not have telephones (still moreover) there may be one central phone for the entire community.

3. Some Amish communities accept electricity (furthermore still) some even have modern farming equipment.

4. The Amish set up their own schools (indeed also) formal education is provided through the eighth grade.

5. The basics of writing, reading, and math are stressed in school (likewise therefore) farming and homemaking are also emphasized.

6. Typically, German is spoken in Amish homes (thus nevertheless) English is taught in school.

7. Simplicity and lack of ego mark the Amish way of life (moreover however) this emphasis on simplicity carries over into their arts.

8. Furniture making is one common craft (also furthermore) quilt making is quite important.

9. Visitors make special trips to buy Amish craftwork (therefore still) a bit of Amish culture is introduced into the world outside their communities.

10. Over time the patterns for Amish quilts have changed somewhat (besides however) the quilts remain works of art.

11. Quilts may have elaborate geometric patterns with some pieces in bright colors (consequently finally) some quilts seem almost three-dimensional rather than flat.

12. Amish quilts are known for durability (nonetheless therefore) many people display the quilts for their beauty.

13. The Amish quilting bee is a way for women and girls to relax and socialize (moreover therefore) it reflects the Amish belief in community and cooperation.

14. Barn raising is another community event where all the men gather to build a barn (therefore likewise) all the women gather to feed the men.

APPLY IT NOW

Choose five conjunctive adverbs from the list on page 170 and look up their meanings in a dictionary. Then use each in a sentence.

With an adult, use an online dictionary.

9.4 Subordinate Conjunctions

A **subordinate conjunction** is used to join an independent clause and a dependent clause. Subordinate conjunctions typically introduce adverb clauses, which tell *how, why, to what extent,* and *under what condition.* The subordinate conjunctions *where* and *when* may introduce adjective clauses. Noun clauses may be introduced by subordinate conjunctions such as *how, when,* and *whether.* The only function of a subordinate conjunction is to connect a dependent clause and an independent clause while indicating their proper relationship.

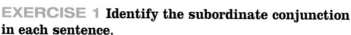

When we studied ancient Greece, we learned about the Acropolis.
I wonder about the time <u>when</u> this great fortress was created.

In the first sentence, the subordinate conjunction *when* introduces the dependent clause *When we studied ancient Greece.* The dependent clause is an adverb clause, and it modifies *learned* in the independent clause. In the second sentence, *when* introduces an adjective clause that modifies *time* in the independent clause.

Common subordinate conjunctions include the following:

after	even though	though
although	if	unless
as, as if	in order that	until
as long as	since	when, whenever
because	so that	where, wherever
before	than	while

EXERCISE 1 Identify the subordinate conjunction in each sentence.

1. When we look at the sculpture of ancient Greece, we see beautiful white marble.

2. We see the greenish gold of metal if the sculpture is bronze.

3. While this is true today, the appearance of the works was different for the ancient Greeks.

4. Although many statues were made of marble, they were often painted in bright colors.

5. Scholars know this because traces of paint remain on some pieces.

6. Even though our image of the Parthenon in Athens is of a white monument, it was originally richly colored.

Illustration of a statue of Athena in the Parthenon

EXERCISE 2 **Identify the subordinate conjunction(s) in each sentence. Then identify the dependent clause(s) in each.**

1. The magnificence of some ancient Greek artworks would probably overwhelm us if we could see them in their original form.
2. Phidias's statue of Zeus, for example, was 42 feet high so that it would dominate the temple of Olympia.
3. Although the body of the god was gold, the flesh was ivory.
4. The statue of Athena in the Parthenon in Athens was of the same rich materials even though it was somewhat shorter.
5. On some marble statues, the facial features were colored with paint, while in others they were of different-colored metals.
6. As the centuries passed, the colors faded or were damaged.
7. If you visit certain museums, you can see reproductions of the statues or temples as they looked originally.
8. After you see these reproductions, you will have a better idea of the nature of Greek art.

EXERCISE 3 **Complete each sentence with an appropriate dependent clause beginning with a subordinate conjunction.**

1. Everyone gazed wide-eyed _____.
2. The afternoon passed quickly _____.
3. It was very late _____.
4. _____, I have become very interested in the topic.
5. I worked on my report _____.

EXERCISE 4 **Rewrite the following sentences, using an appropriate subordinate conjunction to join the clauses.**

1. Music was important to the people of ancient Greece. We do not know what it sounded like.
2. Historians have said that many people in ancient Greece were taught to sing and play music. Little music of this time period still exists for us to hear today.
3. The ancient Greeks were the first to perform dramas. Many later civilizations developed a culture of drama.
4. Life in ancient Greece ended centuries ago. Artifacts in museums give us a sense of what life was like.

APPLY IT NOW

Write four sentences about one or more pieces of art that impressed you. Describe the artwork and why it had an effect on you. Use subordinate conjunctions in your writing.

9.5 Troublesome Conjunctions

Some conjunctions are frequently misused or confused.

Without and *Unless*

The word *without* is a preposition and introduces a prepositional phrase. In this sentence *without* introduces the prepositional phrase *without my parents' permission*.

>**I cannot go on the trip *without* my parents' permission.**

The word *unless* is a subordinate conjunction, and it introduces a clause. In this sentence *unless* introduces a dependent adverb clause.

>**I cannot go *unless* my parents give their permission.**

Which word correctly completes the following?

>**Don't go** (without unless) **I accompany you.**

The correct answer is the subordinate conjunction *unless*, used to introduce a clause.

Like, As if, and *As*

The word *like* is a preposition, and it introduces a prepositional phrase.

>**Jake prefers a game *like* football.**

As if is a subordinate conjunction, and it introduces a clause. It is often easy to confuse *like* and *as if*. When in doubt, substitute *similar to* in the sentence. If the sentence makes sense, *like* is the correct choice.

>**Jake looks *as if* he is very tired.**

As can be a conjunction or a preposition, depending upon its use.

>**I stayed with my brother *as* my parents asked.** (conjunction)
>**My brother visited New York *as* a member of the school band.** (preposition)

EXERCISE 1 Choose the correct item to complete each sentence.

1. Many argue that a person hasn't lived (unless without) he or she has seen New York City.

2. I felt (as if like) my dreams had come true when my parents announced that we would go there on vacation.

3. My older brother acted (as if like) it was no big deal; after all, he had been there once before.

4. I must admit that some sights, (as if like) Radio City Music Hall, were even better than I expected.

5. The Chrysler Building rose into the air (as if like) the spire of a cathedral.

6. Even the street performers in the city seemed (like as if) they were professionals.

7. My trip wouldn't have been complete (without unless) I had a chance to visit Central Park.

8. Don't visit Manhattan (without unless) attending a Broadway show.

9. The beautiful interior of St. Patrick's Cathedral made us feel (as if like) we had entered a new and different world.

10. (As Like) my dad said, you really must see this greatest of American cities.

EXERCISE 2 Rewrite the following sentences to correct the use of conjunctions and prepositions. Not all the sentences have errors.

1. Unless you are terribly frightened of heights, you should see the view from the top of the Empire State Building.

2. The cars below look like they are tiny dots.

3. You can even see the distant Statue of Liberty from the Empire State's observation deck, like my friend told me.

4. People in the city streets looked like they were rushing.

5. The lights on top of the Empire State Building twinkle as stars in the night sky.

6. Unless you studied architecture, you might not know that the Empire State Building reflects the architecture style called art deco.

7. I would visit there again without any hesitation.

EXERCISE 3 Use an appropriate conjunction to complete each sentence.

1. Many people say that a trip to New York City isn't complete _____ buying food from a vendor.

2. My sister went to New York City and ate at the Rainbow Room restaurant _____ my grandparents suggested.

3. Don't go to New York City _____ you're willing to try new and exciting foods.

4. To celebrate their anniversary, my parents ate dinner at Tavern on the Green, a famous restaurant in Central Park, _____ my sister and me.

APPLY IT NOW

Complete these sentences to show you can use the troublesome conjunctions correctly.

She won't go unless _____.

He looks like _____.

The dog won't go without

_____.

She looks as if _____.

9.6 Interjections

An **interjection** is a word or phrase that expresses a strong or sudden emotion. Interjections can be used to convey happiness, delight, anger, disgust, surprise (of a good or an unpleasant sort), impatience, pain, wonder, and so on. They can also be used to get or hold attention.

> *Hey!* **Don't cross the street without checking the traffic.**

What do you think is expressed by the above interjection? It might be used to get attention or perhaps to express annoyance.

Interjections may be set off from the rest of a sentence by an exclamation point. They may also be part of an exclamatory sentence. If the sentence is exclamatory, the interjection is followed by a comma, and the exclamation point is put at the end of the sentence.

> *Oh!* **The wind just blew off my hat.**
> *Ouch!* **The sand is too hot to walk barefoot.**
> *Ah*, **how nice and cool the water is***!*

These are some common interjections:

Ah!	Great!	Oh!	Ugh!
Beware!	Ha!	No!	Well!
Bravo!	Hello!	Oh dear!	What!
Cool!	Hey!	Oh, no!	Whew!
Enough!	Hooray!	Oops!	Wow!
Good grief!	Hush!	Ouch!	Yes!
Goodness!	Indeed!	Rats!	Yikes!
Gosh!	My!	Sh!	Yum!

EXERCISE 1 **Identify the interjection in each of the following sentences.**

1. Hooray! We arrive at the train station in five minutes.
2. Wow! Look at the long line of people waiting.
3. Goodness! I hope we are able to get a taxi.
4. Great! Let's go to the top of the John Hancock Center first.
5. Yes! I get to take a really long elevator trip up.
6. Ah, look at this magnificent view of the city and lake!
7. No! I forgot my camera.
8. Oh, the weather surely changes quickly here!
9. Cool! We can take a ride on the subway.

10. Yum! Let's go for deep-dish pizza for lunch.

11. Oops! I got some tomato sauce on my new T-shirt.

12. Bravo! The Lincoln Park Zoo is next.

13. Sh! I want to hear the guide tell us about the gorillas.

14. Hey, there's a heron! Can you see it?

15. Enough! It's already time to go back to the hotel.

EXERCISE 2 Write an interjection to go with each sentence. Use an exclamation point at the end of each interjection.

1. _____ We're going to the visit the natural history museum.

2. _____ That dinosaur skeleton is huge.

3. _____ I'd never seen a *Tyrannosaurus rex* before.

4. _____ The planetarium is our next stop.

5. _____ There's a film about the planets.

6. _____ I think I lost my ticket.

7. _____ I just found it.

8. _____ I can't hear the sound.

9. _____ I left my sweater in the auditorium.

10. _____ We should go to the aquarium next.

EXERCISE 3 Write a sentence for each interjection below. Indicate the emotion expressed by each interjection.

1. Oh, no!
2. Cool!
3. Gosh!
4. Yum!
5. Enough!
6. Yes!
7. Hooray!
8. Wow!
9. Ha!
10. Beware!

APPLY IT NOW

Write sentences using interjections to show these emotions:

pain
fear
excitement
caution
disappointment
contentment

Grammar in Action. Identify the emotion conveyed in the p. 457 excerpt. What interjection could be used there?

Conjunction and Interjection Review

9.1 Identify the coordinating conjunctions in these sentences and tell whether each joins words, phrases, or clauses.

1. The east and west windows were open during the rain.
2. Water collected on the floor and on the dresser.
3. The framed pictures on the dresser got wet, but Elliott was able to dry them off with a large towel.
4. The rainwater also soaked some papers and books sitting on the dresser.
5. The rain splashed on the sill, but it didn't ruin its finish.
6. Elliott tried several remedies, but he finally decided to call a professional.
7. Now Elliot always closes the windows when it rains, so he's sure it won't happen again.

9.2 Identify the correlative conjunction in each sentence.

8. Either breakfast or lunch is included with the tour.
9. Neither the oatmeal nor the eggs looked appetizing.
10. Erin can't decide whether blueberry muffins or croissants taste better.
11. Simon ate not only a waffle but also French toast.
12. Both Kyle and Chris ordered orange juice.
13. Neither Jack nor Louise ate breakfast because they were not hungry.

9.3 Revise the following sentences, choosing the correct conjunctive adverb. Add the correct punctuation.

14. Humans use trees for lumber (later consequently) many forests have been destroyed.
15. Forests are razed (thus besides) the habitats of many animals have become smaller.
16. Some animal populations have dwindled (however furthermore) conservationists continue to try to save them.
17. Many people today are environmentally aware (finally therefore) they use renewable resources.
18. Bamboo is hard like wood (however thus) it is a renewable grass.
19. The U.S. Green Building Council promotes environmentally friendly building practices (therefore, moreover) the organization promotes architecture that incorporates sustainability in houses and offices.
20. Some builders recycle wood from older buildings (indeed moreover) some builders try to protect natural resources.
21. Many builders try to use biodegradable or recycled materials; (hence, unless) these practices will have less of an impact on the environment.

9.4 **Identify the subordinate conjunction and dependent clause in each sentence.**

22. Before Margaret goes outdoors, she puts on a large-brimmed hat.

23. As long as she applies sunscreen, Margaret can play outside.

24. Though she applied sunscreen in the morning, she reapplied the lotion after swimming.

25. The suns rays are the most intense when the sun is directly overhead.

26. She puts on mosquito repellent after the sun goes down.

27. So that mosquitoes don't bite her legs, Margaret wears long pants.

28. If mosquitoes begin to bite, she goes inside the house.

29. Margaret and her family will eat dinner on the patio as long as the citronella candles are lit.

30. Since citronella candles keep mosquitoes away, the family can enjoy the sunset and a delicious meal.

9.5 **Choose the correct item to complete each sentence.**

31. It looks (as if like) I won't finish the book tonight.

32. I won't know the ending (unless without) I stay up well past my bedtime.

33. I turned off the light (as if as) my mother asked.

34. It will be hard to sleep (unless without) knowing the ending.

35. Some stories, (as like) this one, have unexpected endings.

36. I chose the book (as like) part of the library's summer reading program.

37. If the library didn't offer a summer reading program (like as if) this one, I wouldn't discover wonderful books to read.

38. I cannot go to the library (without unless) my brother James because he loves to read books too.

9.6 **Rewrite each sentence twice, showing two ways to punctuate it correctly.**

39. Hooray we're going to the zoo

40. Wow look at the size of that elephant

41. Cool the caretaker is feeding the tigers

42. Sh don't disturb the animals

43. Goodness look at how much food the rhinoceros eats

44. Hey let's see the penguins swim in the water

Tech Tip   Go to www.voyagesinenglish.com for more activities.

Conjunction and Interjection Challenge

EXERCISE 1 Read the selection and answer the questions.

1. Today long-distance trucking on interstate highways, shipping on the St. Lawrence Seaway, and air travel and air freight are the established means of transportation in this country. 2. Previously, the railroads were our busiest and best form of travel and shipping. 3. Before Amtrak consolidated U.S. railroads under one management, this country had a long-standing love for both trains and train travel. 4. Trains offered romance and adventure; moreover, they were a relatively fast way to get around.

5. Various train companies created their own identities; consequently, boxcars were usually painted with the special logos of the railroads. 6. Seaboard Airline Railroad, which served the East Coast, had "Through the Heart of Dixie" on its cars. 7. They added an orange-red heart so that there could be no mistake about its identity. 8. The Chesapeake & Ohio adopted the image of a sleeping kitten because it suggested both the comfort and the safety of that line. 9. Oh, what a fascinating part of our history!

1. What are the two coordinating conjunctions in sentence 2? They each join words. Tell what part of speech each set of words is.

2. Identify the correlative conjunction in the first paragraph. What words does it join?

3. Identify the conjunctive adverb in the first paragraph.

4. Identify the subordinate conjunction in the first paragraph. Identify the dependent clause that it introduces.

5. Identify the conjunctive adverb in the second paragraph.

6. Is the conjunction in sentence 7 a coordinating conjunction, a correlative conjunction, or a subordinate conjunction?

7. Name the correlative conjunction in the second paragraph.

8. What kind of conjunction is *because* in sentence 8?

9. Identify an interjection in the selection.

EXERCISE 2 Think of a place you'd like to visit or have visited. Write your own four- or five-sentence paragraph describing it. Include and identify the following:

1. a coordinating conjunction, a correlative conjunction, and a subordinate conjunction

2. a conjunctive adverb

3. two troublesome conjunctions

4. an interjection

Punctuation and Capitalization

10.1 Periods and Commas

A **period** is used at the end of a declarative or an imperative sentence, after an abbreviation, and after the initials in a name.

> I went to New York by train. Tell me about the trip.
> Mrs. Eleanor Roosevelt   Dr. Watson   John F. Kennedy

Commas are used for the following:

- to separate words in a series of three or more and to separate adjectives of equal importance in front of a noun

> We need water, snacks, and magazines for the trip.
> The tall, dignified, gray-haired speaker rose.

- to set off the parts of addresses, place names, and dates

> We started our trip on May 30, 2009, in Akron, Ohio.

- to set off words of direct address and parenthetical expressions. A noun in direct address is the name of the person being spoken to. A parenthetical expression is a word or a group of words inserted as a comment not necessary to the sentence.

> Letty, it is time to get on the train. Yes, I know.

- to set off nonrestrictive phrases and clauses

> Amtrak, the National Railroad Passenger Corporation, began service on May 1, 1971. (nonrestrictive appositive)
> My mom, who has never taken a long train ride, is as excited as we are about the trip. (nonrestrictive clause)

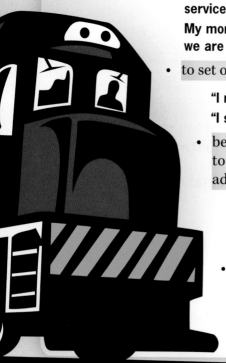

- to set off a direct quotation or parts of a divided quotation

> "I remember my first train trip," my grandfather said.
> "I slept," he continued, "on an upper bunk in a sleeping car."

- before coordinating conjunctions when they are used to connect clauses in a sentence and after conjunctive adverbs in compound sentences

> Passenger trains may have lost riders, yet the amount of freight carried by train is at its highest level ever.
> We waited for hours; however, we finally had to leave.

- after the salutation in a friendly letter and after the complimentary closing in all letters

> Dear Jessica,   Very truly yours,
> Sincerely,   Cordially,

EXERCISE 1 **Rewrite the following sentences. Add periods and commas where needed.**

1. "The romance of the railroads" Mr Cusick our history teacher said "lies to a great extent in their names"

2. "Class the railroads' very names" he said "evoke this vast country"

3. Find the names of some of the railroads and trains

4. Some passenger trains have special names such as the Broadway Limited the Crescent or the Denver Zephyr

5. The California Zephyr which travels between Chicago and San Francisco climbs the Rockies and it might offer the most spectacular train ride in the country

6. A popular song about the City of New Orleans a train between New Orleans Louisiana and Chicago Illinois was written by Steve Goodman.

7. The Twentieth Century Limited one of the most luxurious trains ran between New York City and Chicago

8. It had sleeping cars a dining car and even a library

9. George M Pullman invented the modern sleeping car in the 1850s

EXERCISE 2 **Rewrite the following sentences to correct any errors in punctuation.**

1. Find recordings of "The Wreck of the Old '97" and "John Henry"

2. The Library of Congress which is in Washington D.C. offers recordings of many traditional songs

3. A review of Leonard E Fisher's *Tracks Across America*, states "The author clearly shows how and why railroads came to be pivotal in our history and society"

Brownie McGhee (left)

4. There have been many other famous songs that explore the lure of trains such as "Lonesome Train" by Woodie Guthrie "Freight Train" by Elizabeth Cotton and "Freight Train Blues" by Brownie McGhee.

5. "A famous train called the John Bull is on display at the Smithsonian in Washington, D.C." said our teacher "We will be sure to see it on our field trip to this incredible museum."

6. Train travel may not compare to a trip on an airplane to some people but other people enjoy the thrill of simply being on a train.

APPLY IT NOW

Write a short letter to a friend, describing a place your family went on vacation or where you would like to go on vacation. Check your usage of periods and commas.

Tech Tip Send your letter as an e-mail.

10.2 Exclamation Points, Question Marks, Semicolons, and Colons

An **exclamation point** is used after some interjections and at the end of exclamatory sentences.

> Hooray! I know the answer.
> No, I can't find my notebook!

Question marks are used at the end of interrogative sentences.

> Who will be first to find the answer?

A **semicolon** is used for the following:

- to separate clauses in a compound sentence when they are not joined by a conjunction

> We called early this morning; nobody was at home.

- to separate clauses in a compound sentence that are connected by conjunctive adverbs

> Leo was here early; consequently, we started right away.

- to separate phrases or clauses of the same type that contain internal punctuation

> The train stopped at Boston, Massachusetts; Providence, Rhode Island; Fairfield, Connecticut; and Trenton, New Jersey.

- before expressions such as *for example* and *namely* when they are used to introduce examples

> Several students earned the highest honors; namely, Ricardo, Jenna, Sheila, Kristen, and Paul.

A **colon** is used for the following:

- before a list when terms such as *the following* or *as follows* are used

> The following students are in our study group: Leo, Alicia, Julio, Paige, Emily, Jason, and Louis.

- after the salutation of a business letter

> Dear Professor Rosenfeld:

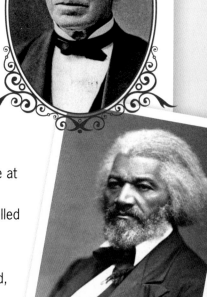

EXERCISE 1 Rewrite the following sentences. Add punctuation where needed.

1. Are all of you studying for exams

2. Step over those piles of books. Look out

3. We need to have the following our textbooks, our notes, paper, and pencils

4. Which group is reviewing history

5. According to my notes, we should study the following topics the abolitionists, industrialization, the West, and the Civil War

6. The textbook has good review questions the questions are at the end of each chapter

7. William Lloyd Garrison was an abolitionist moreover, he called for immediate freedom for all slaves

8. Who were some prominent abolitionists

9. They included the following Sojourner Truth Theodore Weld, Frederick Douglass and William Lloyd Garrison

10. Frederick Douglass had been a slave however he escaped to the North

11. Sojourner Truth spoke out for the freedom of slaves furthermore she spoke out for women's rights

12. What amazing people they were

EXERCISE 2 Rewrite the following sentences, using correct punctuation.

1. "Wow. The Underground Railroad is fascinating" said my classmate Nora.

2. The Underground Railroad was neither underground nor a train line, it was a system meant to sneak slaves safely to the North or to Canada.

3. Did you know Harriet Tubman and Thomas Garrett were involved with the Underground Railroad.

4. The Underground Railroad used railway terms to reference this system for example travel routes were called lines stopping places were called stations and helpers were called conductors.

APPLY IT NOW

Think of a current event that interests you. Write four sentences about the event, using an exclamation point, a question mark, a semicolon, and a colon. Circle each punctuation mark.

With an adult, research your event online.

185

10.3 Quotation Marks and Italics

Quotation marks are used for the following:

- before and after direct quotations and around the parts of divided quotations

> "Everybody is welcome!" Peter exclaimed.
> "Here," Greta called, "is a good spot for a picnic."

Sometimes a quotation includes another quotation. The included quotation is marked with single quotation marks.

> Marisela asked, "Was it Lincoln who said, 'With malice toward none; with charity for all'?"

Indirect quotations do not use quotation marks.

> He said that we should visit Lincoln's birthplace.

- to set off the titles of stories, poems, songs, magazine and newspaper articles, individual episodes of TV series, and radio programs

> She suggested we learn all the verses to "America the Beautiful."
> "Stopping by Woods on a Snowy Evening" is my favorite poem.

Italics are used for the titles of books, magazines, newspapers, movies, TV series, works of art, and for the names of ships and aircraft. If you are handwriting, use underlining to indicate italics.

> Have you read *Across Five Aprils*?
> The inauguration of *Queen Mary 2* took place in 2004.

EXERCISE 1 Rewrite each sentence, using quotation marks.

1. Thomas Jefferson said, All men are created equal.
2. I regret, declared Nathan Hale, that I have but one life to give for my country.
3. Lafayette, we are here, stated General Pershing.
4. Give me liberty or give me death! shouted Patrick Henry.
5. All we have to fear, said Franklin Roosevelt, is fear itself.

Patrick Henry

Paul Revere

EXERCISE 2 Rewrite each sentence, using quotation marks and italics as needed. Remember that you can use underlining to show italics.

1. Last Sunday the Los Angeles Times ran a feature on summer entertainment.
2. Called The Best of Summer, it reviewed books and movies.
3. The writer said that The Adventures of Tom Sawyer is a great read.
4. The movie Teen Alien should be this summer's big hit.
5. The writer recommended that babysitters read children nursery rhymes such as Humpty Dumpty and Little Boy Blue from The True Book of Mother Goose.
6. This summer our class will travel to London, England, on the Queen Elizabeth 2.
7. I plan to read the novel Another Spring on the trip.
8. The ship gets satellite TV, so I'll watch reruns of I Love Lucy.
9. Are America and God Save the Queen sung to the same tune?
10. We can see van Gogh's painting Sunflowers at the National Gallery.

EXERCISE 3 Rewrite each sentence, using correct punctuation and italics.

1. A summer without books Mom says is like a day without light
2. My dad stated that a Chicago Tribune reviewer said that The Fall of Rome is a great book
3. I'm going to the movies my brother declared to see Troy
4. Let's watch the rerun of the Molly and Me episode on the Guess Who's Here TV show suggested my aunt
5. My favorite movies are Sleeping Beauty and Batman said my brother
6. Anna's teacher recommended that she read Little Women by Louisa May Alcott and the poem Paul Revere's Ride by Henry Wadsworth Longfellow

APPLY IT NOW

What is your favorite book, magazine, and movie? Write a sentence about each, stating the names. Then write a sentence using a quotation that appeared in either your favorite book, magazine, or movie.

Grammar in Action. How would you punctuate the titles of Gauguin's paintings described on p. 450?

10.4 Apostrophes, Hyphens, and Dashes

An **apostrophe** is used for the following:

- to show possession

   Rebecca's shoes
   My brothers' plan

- to show the omission of letters as used in contractions or numbers

   wouldn't   we'll   spirit of '76

- to show the plurals of lowercase letters (but not of capital letters unless the plural could be mistaken for a word)

   i's   a's   Rs   Ms   (but **U**'s and **I**'s)

A **hyphen** is used for the following:

- to divide a word between syllables at the end of a line

   Many locomotives run on power supplied by elec-tricity from overhead cables.

- in compound numbers from twenty-one to ninety-nine

   fifty-eight   eighty-four

- to separate parts of some compound words

   sister-in-law   drive-in

- to form some temporary adjectives

   This stove uses *natural gas*. (noun)
   The *natural-gas* **pipeline is being laid this week.**
   (adjective before a noun)

A **dash** is used for the following:

- to set off words that indicate a change in thought

   Mr. Blair—I believe he drives an SUV—teaches math.

- to set off an appositive that contains commas

   His wife studies languages—Danish, Norwegian, and Swedish.

EXERCISE 1 Find each of these words in a dictionary. Use hyphens to show where the words could be divided if necessary at the end of a line.

1. accommodate
2. musician
3. improvement
4. persuasion
5. locomotive
6. punctuation
7. possession
8. illustration
9. instruments

EXERCISE 2 Rewrite each sentence, using apostrophes, hyphens, and dashes where needed.

1. My aunts twenty fifth birthday is coming soon.
2. Her mother in law is planning a big celebration.
3. She bought twenty five different colored balloons.
4. Shell hang the balloons in the backyard.
5. We hope her sisters in law wont ruin the surprise.
6. My brother offered to help an unusual thing for him.
7. He and my great grandmother will bake a chocolate cake.
8. Our neighbors Emma, Rose, and Jessie cannot come to the party.
9. My aunts husband invited fifty five people to the party; wouldnt it be great if they all showed up?
10. He also plans to buy her flowers roses, lilies, and pansies.

EXERCISE 3 Rewrite each sentence, adding the correct punctuation and italicizing as appropriate.

1. The Daily Herald had an article about its readers favorites
2. One person nominated Shirley Jacksons short story The Lottery
3. One reader wrote I was deeply moved when Martin Luther King Jr declared I have a dream
4. That seventy two people mentioned Beethovens Ninth Symphony was a big surprise to the editor
5. The editor exclaimed I am surprised that no one mentioned the song Chicago or the book The Adventures of Tom Sawyer.
6. The newspaper received seventy eight letters and over ninety nine calls for nominations.

APPLY IT NOW

Using your family as the subject matter, write three sentences describing them. Use an apostrophe, a hyphen, and a dash in separate sentences.

Grammar in Action

Why is the first apostrophe used in the excerpt on p. 450?

10.5 Capitalization

Use **capital letters** for the following:

- usually the first word of lines of poetry and songs, the first word in a sentence, and the first word in a direct quotation

  > Life has loveliness to sell,
  > All beautiful and splendid things,
  > Blue waves whitened on a cliff . . . —Sara Teasdale

  > He shouted, "Run for cover!"

- proper nouns and proper adjectives—names of people, groups of people, buildings, particular places, months, and holidays

Georgetown University	Thai food
the Museum of Natural History	American universities

- a title when it precedes a person's name

  Senator Vlasic (*but* The senator said . . .)

- the directions North, South, East, and West, when they refer to sections of the country

  My brother went to college in the West. (*but* Go east on Elm Drive.)

- the names of deities and sacred books

  Holy Spirit   Bible   Koran   Old Testament

- the principal words in titles of works (but not the articles *a, an,* and *the,* coordinating conjunctions, or prepositions unless they are the first or last words)

A Tale of Two Cities	*The Call of the Wild*
"The Raven"	"Macavity: the Mystery Cat"

- abbreviations of words that are capitalized

  U.S.A.   Dr.   Ave.   Jan.

Do not capitalize the names of subjects unless they come from proper names.

science   math   Spanish

EXERCISE 1 Rewrite these items, using correct capitalization.

1. general john j. pershing

2. museum of contemporary art in los angeles, california

3. the short story "all summer in a day" by ray bradbury

4. the novel *harry potter and the goblet of fire* by j. k. rowling

5. jack and jill went up the hill to fetch a pail of water.

6. the united nations in new york city

7. crossing the rocky mountains

8. eating in a mexican restaurant and ordering in spanish

9. the field museum of natural history in chicago, illinois

10. the CDs *yellow submarine* and *abbey road* by the beatles

EXERCISE 2 Rewrite these sentences, using capital letters where needed.

1. mr. allen, our social studies teacher, has won an award.

2. he is one of only 20 teachers in all the united states to be chosen.

3. They will meet at a university in the east for several weeks in june.

4. they will stay in washington, d.c., and visit baltimore, maryland, and williamsburg, virginia.

5. they will meet with professors from such schools as harvard university and columbia university.

6. the group will meet congresswoman smythe and senator merton, who sponsored this program.

7. our class gave mr. allen several gifts, including early editions of c. s. lewis's *the lion, the witch and the wardrobe* and walt whitman's *leaves of grass.*

8. Our class received a postcard from mr. allen, and it said, "washington, d.c., is great! what a historic town!"

APPLY IT NOW

Write your own examples that include using capital letters for a proper noun, a proper adjective, the name of a deity or sacred book, a title of a work, and an abbreviation of a word that is capitalized. Then write a sentence using a direction that should begin with a capital letter and one that should not.

Punctuation and Capitalization Review

10.1 **Rewrite these sentences, adding periods and commas where needed.**

1. The homeowners hired R R Smith Landscaping for the yard work

2. The landscapers have offices at 311 N Primrose Avenue and 15 E Elm Street

3. The landscapers mowed fertilized and watered the lawn

4. They planted evergreen trees rosebushes and flats of pansies

5. Gerald didn't the landscapers do a good job?

6. Yes I am impressed

7. The landscape architect who studied for many years designed the award-winning plan

8. "I'm happy to accept this award" she said

9. There were only a few minutes yet she had many people to thank

10.2 **Rewrite these sentences, adding exclamation points, question marks, semicolons, and colons as needed.**

10. What do we need at the grocery store

11. The following are the items on my grocery list milk, bread wheat bread and eggs.

12. Oh no I forgot the list

13. The list was in my pocket it must have fallen out.

14. Please find a few things in the dairy aisle namely sour cream, butter, and cheese.

15. I did not have the list therefore I forgot a few things at the store.

16. Do you need help unloading the groceries

17. Wow you certainly bought a lot of food

18. We were at the grocery store for two hours consequently we did not finish our other errands.

19. I rushed to get to the bank it closed at noon.

10.3 **Rewrite these sentences, using quotation marks and italics as needed.**

20. What are you reading? asked Rodrigo.

21. Sheila reads the Daily News every morning before school.

22. We listened to This American Life on the radio.

23. I plan to read the novel Animal Farm this summer.

24. That, said Tommy, is my favorite painting.

25. I went to the library and checked out War and Peace, Pride and Prejudice, and Frankenstein for my Aunt Lily said John.

26. Rebecca plans to sing Danny Boy and read a passage from The Raven by Edgar Allen Poe for the school talent show next month.

27. Jenny plans to see Edward Hopper's painting Nighthawks and Pierre August Renoir's The Rower's Lunch.

10.4 Rewrite these sentences, using apostrophes, hyphens, and dashes where needed.

28. This is the only drive in movie theater left in the state.

29. The theater celebrated its forty fourth anniversary this year.

30. The theater is so old that the is on the sign are no longer dotted.

31. The theater I think it's a historic place has a lot of charm.

32. My dad said old time movies were shown there.

33. My mom said that she celebrated her twenty first birthday at this drive in with her friends.

34. She saw many movies here romantic films, comedies, and mysteries.

35. My dad said that his mother in law has never been to this theater before.

10.5 Rewrite these sentences, using capital letters where needed.

36. there are thunderclouds gathering over the great plains.

37. juan studied meteorology, the science of weather, at florida state university.

38. the risk of tornadoes increases after april 1.

39. monica shouted, "head for the basement!"

40. the residents received help from the red cross and other organizations.

41. l. frank baum's book *the wizard of oz* mentions a tornado.

42. The federal emergency management agency helps people who have been in disasters.

43. My sister wants to work for the national oceanic and atmospheric administration when she graduates in june.

Tech Tip Go to www.voyagesinenglish.com for more activities.

Punctuation and Capitalization Challenge

EXERCISE 1 **All the punctuation marks and capital letters are missing from the selection below. Copy the paragraph and insert the proper punctuation and capitalization.**

a fox once saw a crow fly off with a piece of cheese and settle on a branch in a tree that's for me said master reynard and he walked up to the foot of the tree

good day mistress crow he cried how well you are looking today how glossy your feathers how bright your eyes I feel sure that your voice must surpass that of the other birds just as your figure does let me hear but one song from you

the crow lifted her head and began to caw her best but the moment she opened her mouth the piece of cheese fell to the ground only to be snapped up by master reynard

that will do he said that was all i wanted in exchange for your cheese i will give you a piece of advice for the future do not trust flatterers

—*the fables of aesop* by joseph jacobs

EXERCISE 2 **Write a sentence illustrating each rule below.**

Use a comma in each of the following ways:

1. to separate words in a series
2. to separate adjectives of equal importance in front of a noun
3. to set off the parts of addresses, place names, and dates
4. to set off words of direct address and parenthetical expressions
5. to set off a nonrestrictive phrase or clause
6. to set off the parts of a divided quotation
7. before a coordinating conjunction when it is used to connect clauses in a sentence
8. after a conjunctive adverb in a compound sentence

Diagramming

11.1 Simple Sentences

A **diagram** is a visual outline of a sentence. It shows in a graphic manner the relationships among words in a sentence. Diagramming serves two purposes. First, it helps a person understand how a sentence is put together. Second, it identifies errors in a sentence and makes clear why they are errors.

In a diagram the subject, the verb, the direct object, and the subject or object complement go on the main horizontal line. The subject is separated from the verb by a vertical line that cuts through the horizontal line. The line to separate a direct object from the verb is also vertical but does not cut through the line; the line to separate a subject complement from the verb slants left.

SENTENCE **Elephants eat plants.**

| Elephants | eat | plants |

SENTENCE **Lemurs are mammals.**

| Lemurs | are \ mammals |

An object complement is placed on the horizontal line after a line that slants right.

SENTENCE **The mayor appointed Mr. Edmonds zookeeper.**

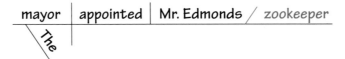

An indirect object is placed under the verb on a horizontal line.

SENTENCE **The children are giving the monkeys peanuts.**

Lemur

Adjectives and adverbs are placed under the words that they describe. Prepositional phrases can act as adjectives or as adverbs. They also are positioned under the words they describe.

SENTENCE **The big, glossy raven cawed very loudly.**

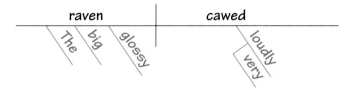

SENTENCE **A plant with pink flowers hung in the window.**

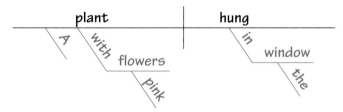

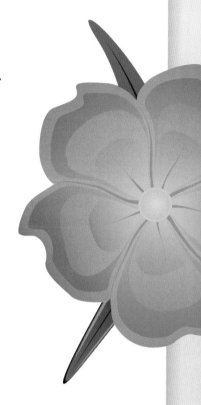

EXERCISE 1 Diagram the sentences.

1. Jupiter was the principal god in Roman mythology.
2. Peggy celebrated her thirteenth birthday.
3. The set of dusty books tumbled from the bookcase.
4. We quickly decorated our house with blue lights.
5. Our group appointed Chang spokesperson.
6. Cliff washed the dirty car thoroughly.
7. Ogden Nash was a writer of humorous verse.
8. A large brass band entertained the crowd at halftime.
9. The guide gave the guests a tour of the crayon factory.
10. The critic called the film the best comedy of the year.
11. Pablo painted Sarah pictures in art class.
12. The librarian read storybooks to the children.
13. I baked blueberry pie for the fund-raiser.
14. LaToya purchased new markers for her brother.
15. Dad gave me a new bicycle with a brown wicker basket.
16. Juan washed the dirty dishes in the kitchen sink.
17. Nora put money on the coffee table.
18. The happy coach gave the soccer team trophies.

APPLY IT NOW

Write and diagram five simple sentences, using your home as the topic. Be sure to include at least one object complement, one prepositional phrase used as an adjective, and one prepositional phrase used as an adverb.

11.2 Appositives

An **appositive** is a word or a group of words that follows a noun or a pronoun and further identifies it or adds information. An appositive names the same person, place, thing, or idea as the word it explains.

In a diagram an appositive is placed in parentheses to the right of the word it identifies. Words that describe the appositive go under it. In this sentence the appositive renames and describes the proper noun *Milky Way*, which is the subject.

SENTENCE **The Milky Way, our galaxy, has billions of stars.**

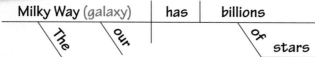

Milky Way (galaxy) | has | billions
The | our | of stars

Appositives can appear in any place where nouns occur. In this sentence, the appositive explains the word *nickname*, the direct object.

SENTENCE **People from Indiana have the nickname Hoosiers.**

People | have | nickname (Hoosiers)
from Indiana | | the

This sentence contains an **intensive pronoun.** What word is it emphasizing? What word does the appositive in this sentence rename? How does that word function?

SENTENCE **We ourselves read stories by Joseph Bruchac, a Native American writer.**

We (ourselves) | read | stories
by Joseph Bruchac (writer)
a Native American

The appositive, *writer*, explains the proper noun, *Joseph Bruchac*, which is the object of a preposition. The intensive pronoun, *ourselves*, emphasizing *we*, is placed in parentheses to the right of the word it emphasizes.

EXERCISE 1 Diagram the sentences.

1. Charlie Chaplin, a famous comedian, was the star of many silent movies.
2. In the Revolutionary War, the colonists were aided by a Polish patriot, Casimir Pulaski.
3. Margaret reviewed J. R. R. Tolkien's novel *The Hobbit*.
4. My brother's backpack is in the shape of Kermit, the famous frog.
5. For my science project, I drew a picture of a mite, a spiderlike insect.
6. Events in the novel *Johnny Tremain* occur during the American Revolution.
7. The kiwi, a flightless bird, is native to New Zealand.
8. My cousin Anna is a philatelist, a collector of stamps.
9. The story "The Most Dangerous Game" is suspenseful.
10. A popular resort in the summer is Nantucket, an island off Massachusetts.
11. Jim's birthday present, a new bike, is hidden in the garage.
12. Coral's latest recipe, a persimmon cake, was a disaster.
13. The twins enjoyed their new DVD, *The Princess Diaries*.
14. Hal's new car, a red convertible, is certainly eye-catching.
15. Mr. Tomasek, our math teacher, announced a new competition.
16. My favorite room, the computer lab, was closed for the afternoon.
17. Scrabble, a word game, is on sale at the Game Corner.
18. The vintage movie *Citizen Kane* is playing at the Palace Theater.
19. Valentine's Day, February 14, is Mark's birthday.
20. It is time for our yearly vacation, a trip to a beach resort.

Charlie Chaplin

Charlie Chaplin and Paulette Goddard in *Modern Times*, 1936

APPLY IT NOW

Using your friends as the topic, write and diagram four sentences with appositives: one describing a subject, one describing a direct object, one describing a subject complement, and one describing an object of a preposition.

11.3 Compound Sentences

A **compound sentence** contains two or more independent clauses. An independent clause has a subject and a predicate and can stand on its own as a sentence. Clauses in a compound sentence are usually connected by a coordinating conjunction.

In a diagram each independent clause has its own horizontal line with its subject and verb as well as any complements and objects.

- The coordinating conjunction is placed on a dashed line at the left edge of the diagram.
- The line connects the main horizontal lines of the two clauses.

In the first clause of this sentence, *camel* is the subject, *is* is the verb, and *ship* is the subject complement. In the second clause, *reindeer* is the subject, *is* is the verb, and *camel* is the subject complement.

SENTENCE **The camel is the ship of the desert, and the reindeer is the camel of the snow land.**

Independent clauses connected by a conjunctive adverb and a semicolon are also compound sentences. A conjunctive adverb is diagrammed in the same way as a coordinating conjunction.

SENTENCE **Gorillas may look frightening; however, they are quite timid.**

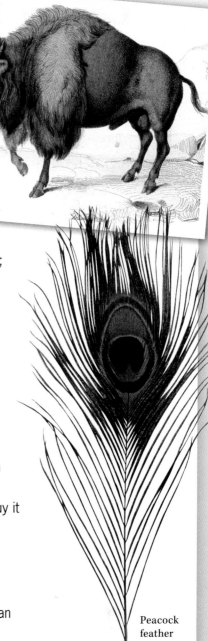

Bison

EXERCISE 1 Diagram the sentences.

1. Participants in rodeos rope calves, and they ride wild horses.

2. The students were waiting, but the bus had not arrived.

3. Many animals cannot survive cold weather; therefore, they move south during the winter.

4. Zoology is the study of animals, and botany is the study of plants.

5. Many American places are named for cities in Europe; furthermore, many have Native American names.

6. Kindergarten originated in Germany in the 19th century, and the word means "a garden for children."

7. Bison were once almost extinct, but now they are thriving in places on the Great Plains.

8. Melissa saw the movie *The Black Stallion*; moreover, she had read the book.

9. The mansion is beautifully furnished, but the gardens are more remarkable.

10. Coach Lane's birthday is on Friday, and we will have a surprise party for him.

11. I'll go to the convenience store for milk, or you can buy it at the supermarket.

12. Miguel likes video games, but Kayla prefers movies.

13. Peacocks are elegant birds; however, they have an aggressive nature.

14. Mason will paint scenery for the play, and Katherine can sew the costumes.

15. Justine ordered spinach lasagna, but she wanted cheese pizza.

Peacock feather

APPLY IT NOW

Write and diagram six compound sentences about this past weekend. Use coordinating conjunctions in three sentences and conjunctive adverbs in the other three.

Grammar in Action.

What is the first compound sentence in the student report on p. 489?

11.4 Compound Sentence Elements

The subject and the predicate in a sentence may be compound. They may consist of two or more words connected by a coordinating conjunction. Remember that a sentence with a compound subject or a compound predicate is still a simple sentence.

In a diagram the compound parts appear on two separate lines with the conjunction on a vertical dashed line between them. In the first sentence, the subject is compound. In the second sentence, the verb is compound.

SENTENCE **Bridget and Helen competed in the sprint race.**

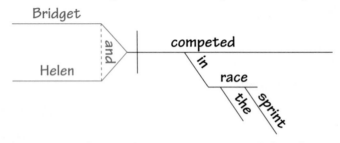

SENTENCE **The performer composes and sings her own songs.**

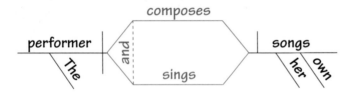

Both the subject and the verb may be compound, and each verb may have its own object.

SENTENCE **My sister and I visited the hospital and brought colorful balloons for the children.**

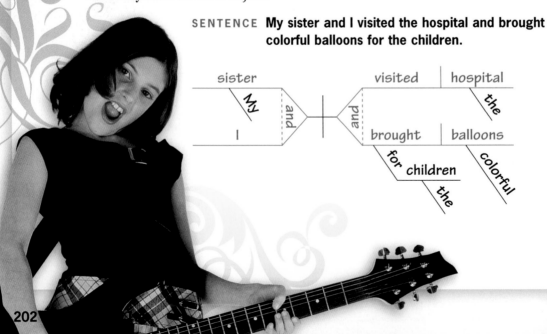

Words other than subjects and predicates may also be compound, and they are diagrammed in a similar way. In this sentence compound adjectives function as subject complements.

SENTENCE **The day was cool and rainy.**

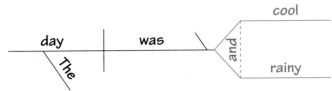

EXERCISE 1 Diagram the sentences.

1. Mom and I made the meal.

2. I peeled and cut a bag of potatoes.

3. The wild horses and the buffalo roamed the Western plains and grazed on them.

4. Spiders spin webs and weave cocoons.

5. I wrote and typed my report on the computer.

6. The fans and the players on the bench stood and applauded.

7. The Navajo artist cut the turquoise stone and set it into the silver bracelet.

8. Sara and I folded the tent and put it into the van.

9. Tanya stopped playing and went to the mall.

10. Those books and videos are overdue.

11. Kelly and I will wash the car and the van.

12. Jerry and the boys want hamburgers and potato salad.

13. Leo and Jill enjoyed the carnival and bought lemonade for their friends.

14. I ate vegetable tacos and Spanish rice.

15. Aimee washed and dried the dinner dishes.

16. Arletrice won the geography bee and received a blue ribbon.

17. Chan and Erin are talented singers and creative dancers.

APPLY IT NOW

Using your school as the topic, write and diagram four sentences: two with compound subjects and two with compound predicates.

11.5 Participles

A **participle** is a verb form that is used as an adjective. A participial phrase is made up of the participle, its objects or complements, and any modifiers. The entire phrase acts as an adjective.

In a diagram a participial phrase goes under the noun or the pronoun that it describes. It is placed on a slanted line connecting to a horizontal line.

- The participle starts on the slanted line and extends onto the horizontal line.
- A direct object or a complement is placed after the participle.
- Any word that describes the participle or its object or complement goes on a slanted line under the correct word.

In the following sentences the participial phrases describe the pronoun *I*, the noun *cards*, and the noun *Leon*.

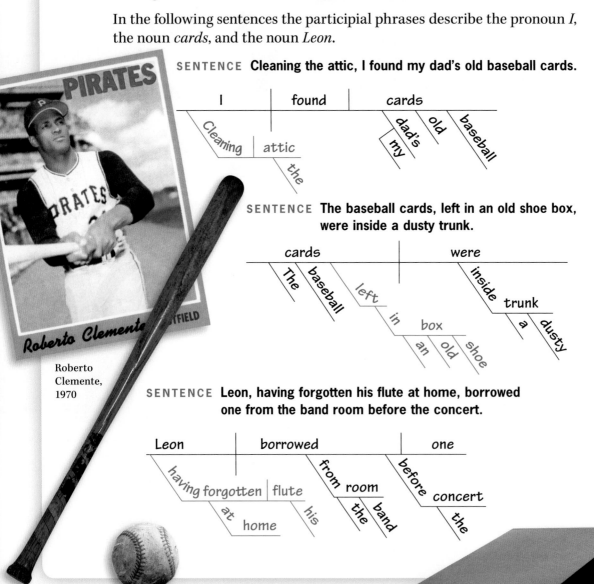

SENTENCE **Cleaning the attic, I found my dad's old baseball cards.**

SENTENCE **The baseball cards, left in an old shoe box, were inside a dusty trunk.**

SENTENCE **Leon, having forgotten his flute at home, borrowed one from the band room before the concert.**

Roberto Clemente, 1970

Participial adjectives, which often precede the nouns they describe, are placed just as other adjectives are.

SENTENCE **The running water wore away the stone.**

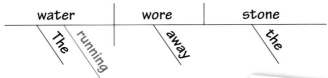

EXERCISE 1 **Diagram the sentences.**

1. Having studied thoroughly for the test, Michael got a good grade.

2. The boy, whistling softly, walked down the dark street.

3. The broken vase was fixed with glue.

4. Spread by rodents, the Black Death killed many people in Europe in the 1300s.

5. "The Lottery," written by Shirley Jackson, is a chilling short story.

6. The missing stamp is a rare one.

7. Searching the Internet, I found information on terrariums.

8. The cat sleeping in the sun belongs to my sister.

9. Walking through the rain forest, the tourists saw parrots.

10. Held at four-year intervals, presidential elections are important in our democratic process.

11. Running for the bus, I tripped on my untied shoelace.

12. The lioness, purring contentedly, resembled a big kitten.

13. The leaking water jug was soon empty.

14. Painting the scenery, I forgot the time.

15. Covered with mud, Josh slowly limped to the school bus.

16. Hung on the line, the colorful swimsuits caught my eye.

17. Having run the race, Hosea was tired.

18. Joe cut his finger chopping onions.

19. Using library books, Alonzo wanted information on fossils.

20. The yapping puppy woke the napping toddler.

APPLY IT NOW

Using a family vacation or an outing with friends as the topic, write and diagram four sentences with participial phrases.

11.6 Gerunds

A **gerund** is a verb form ending in *ing* that is used as a noun. A gerund can be used in a sentence as a subject, a subject complement, an object of a verb, an object of a preposition, or an appositive.

In a diagram a gerund is placed according to its function.

- The gerund is placed on a stepped line that extends onto a horizontal line.
- A direct object or a complement is placed after the gerund.
- Words that describe the gerund or its object or complement go on slanted lines.

A gerund that acts as a subject, a direct object, or a subject complement is placed on a stepped line above the main horizontal line. The gerund in this sentence is used as the subject.

SENTENCE **Painting pictures is my favorite hobby.**

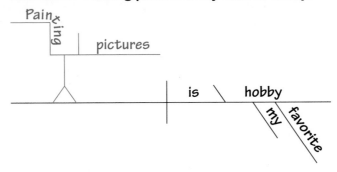

The gerund in this sentence is used as the direct object. A gerund used as a subject complement would go in a similar position, but the line before it would be slanted left. A gerund used as an appositive goes next to the word it describes in parentheses, as other appositives do.

SENTENCE **We enjoyed visiting the science museum.**

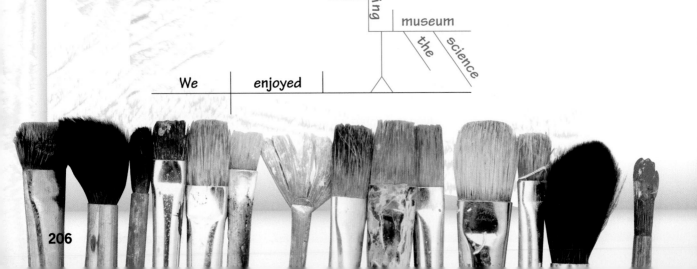

A gerund used as the object of a preposition is part of the prepositional phrase, which goes under the word it describes. A stepped line is still used, but it is not raised.

SENTENCE **A telescope is an instrument for viewing distant objects.**

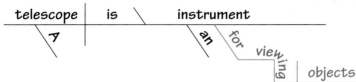

EXERCISE 1 **Diagram the sentences.**

1. My favorite hobby is playing computer games.
2. Our art assignment, making a collage, was fun.
3. We were worried about arriving late.
4. Having brilliant colors protects some animals.
5. We considered organizing a class picnic.
6. I learned some words in Spanish by listening to a CD.
7. Jenna has a big goal, starting a babysitting service.
8. Making colorful blankets is a craft of the Navajo.
9. The Greeks won the Trojan War by constructing a large wooden horse.
10. Skating and jogging are good forms of exercise.
11. Working hard in school can be rewarding.
12. Chloe dislikes peeling potatoes for dinner.
13. Aaliyah wrote an article about running marathons for the school paper.
14. Drinking orange juice is good for you.
15. Our science experiment, studying photosynthesis, was incredible.

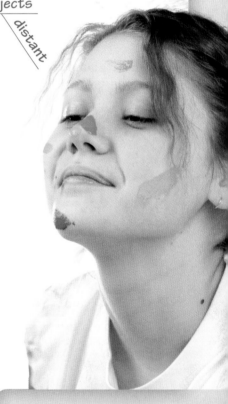

APPLY IT NOW

Using someone you admire and respect as the topic, write and diagram four sentences with gerunds. Use one gerund for each of these functions: subject, direct object, object of a preposition, and appositive.

11.7 Infinitives

An **infinitive** is a verb form, usually preceded by *to*, that is used as a noun, an adjective, or an adverb.

In a diagram an infinitive phrase is placed according to its function in the sentence.

- An infinitive is diagrammed like a prepositional phrase. The *to* goes on a slanted line, and the verb goes on a horizontal line.
- A direct object or a complement is placed after the verb on the horizontal line.
- A word that describes the infinitive, such as an adverb, goes under the horizontal line.

An infinitive used as a subject, an object, a subject complement, or an appositive is placed on a set of lines above the main horizontal line. In the first sentence, the infinitive is a direct object, and in the second sentence, the infinitive is an appositive.

SENTENCE **We decided to go to the zoo.**

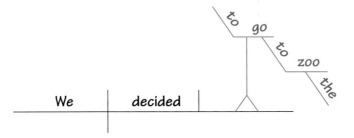

SENTENCE **My goal, to speak Spanish, requires hard work.**

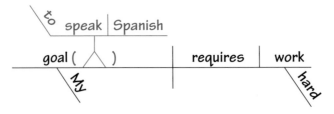

Infinitives used as adjectives or adverbs are placed under the words they describe. This is shown in the example on the next page.

SENTENCE **We had an opportunity to visit a film studio.**

We | had | opportunity
        an   to visit | studio
                            a film

EXERCISE 1 Diagram the sentences.

1. To litter is a minor crime.
2. We were anxious to leave.
3. The smoke alarm began to shriek.
4. Radar is used to track storms.
5. The purpose of the trip was to see my grandparents.
6. We need a way to raise money for new computers.
7. My suggestion, to start a French club, is being discussed.
8. *A Wrinkle in Time* is a great book to read.
9. The gardener used a saw to remove the dead branches.
10. My goal, to play the trumpet, requires good lungs.
11. To be, or not to be: that is the question.
12. I wanted to memorize my lines and to press my costume.
13. The hot, savory casserole is ready to be put on the table.
14. Your article should describe two ways to create a safety poster.
15. His lifelong dream, to play at Carnegie Hall, will certainly happen.
16. My first priority is to care for the baby.
17. To make toffee will require buying more sugar.
18. Jaden's goal, to learn Latin, requires discipline.
19. The sweet, moist chocolate cake is ready to be frosted.

APPLY IT NOW

Using yourself as the topic, write and diagram six sentences with infinitives. Use one infinitive for each of these noun functions: subject, direct object, object of a preposition, and appositive. Also include one infinitive used as an adjective and one as an adverb.

11.8 Adjective Clauses

An **adjective clause** is a dependent clause that describes a noun or a pronoun. An adjective clause begins with a relative pronoun *(who, whom, whose, which,* or *that)* or with a subordinate conjunction *(when, where,* or *why).*

In a diagram the adjective clause and the independent clause go on separate lines, with the dependent clause beneath the independent clause.

- A dashed line connects the relative pronoun or subordinate conjunction in the dependent clause to the word in the independent clause that is modified by the adjective clause.
- A relative pronoun is placed in the diagram according to its function in the adjective clause.

In the first sentence, *Pueblo* is the antecedent of *who,* which acts as the subject of the adjective clause. In the second sentence, *pie* is the antecedent of *that,* which acts as the direct object of the verb *made* in the adjective clause.

SENTENCE **The Pueblo, who live in the Southwest, have a very old culture.**

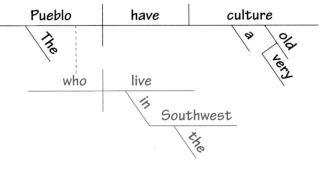

SENTENCE **I finished the pie that Carlotta made.**

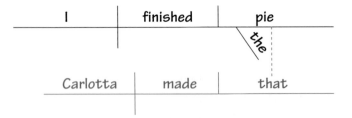

Ancient Pueblo village (below) and kachina doll (left)

The relative pronoun *whose*, like other possessives, goes under the noun it is associated with.

SENTENCE **Odysseus, whose adventures are told in an epic poem, was a legendary hero of the ancient Greeks.**

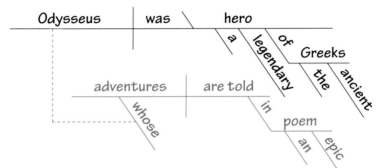

EXERCISE 1 Diagram the sentences.

1. Any student who participated in the bike-a-thon received a special certificate.
2. The poster that I bought shows Mount Fuji.
3. That is the jockey whose horse won the race.
4. Mary Shelley, whose works include *Frankenstein*, was born in 1797.
5. A shot that shows a person's face is called a close-up.
6. Iris, which refers to the colored part of the eye, comes from the Greek word for rainbow.
7. The movie that we saw had a very sad ending.
8. A figure that has five sides is a pentagon.
9. Polaris, which people also call the North Star, is always to the north.
10. A special award was given to the student whose project won the science fair.
11. Rio de Janeiro, which hosts Carnival, is a large city in Brazil.
12. Carver is returning the reference book that he borrowed from the teacher.
13. Louis Armstrong, who was famous for playing the trumpet, sang in the movie *Hello Dolly*.
14. The muffins that Kyle brought to the bake sale were delicious.

APPLY IT NOW

Using a school vacation such as summer or spring break as the topic, write and diagram five sentences with adjective clauses. Use *whose* in at least one sentence.

11.9 Adverb Clauses

An **adverb clause** is a dependent clause that acts as an adverb; it describes a verb, an adjective, or another adverb. Adverb clauses begin with subordinate conjunctions, such as *after, although, as, because, before, if, since, so that, unless, until, when, whenever, wherever,* and *while.*

In a diagram an adverb clause goes on its own horizontal line under the independent clause.

- The subordinate conjunction is placed on a slanted dashed line that connects the two clauses.
  - The line goes from the verb in the adverb clause to the word in the independent clause that the adverb clause describes, which is usually the verb.

In the first sentence, the subordinate conjunction is *Because.* The dependent clause modifies *postponed.* In the second sentence, the subordinate conjunction is *after.* The dependent clause modifies *bought.*

SENTENCE **Because the weather was stormy, the campers postponed the hike.**

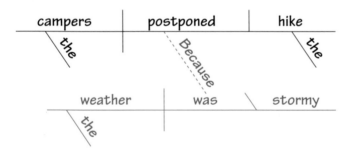

SENTENCE **Our coach bought us pizza after we won the basketball tournament.**

EXERCISE 1 Diagram the sentences.

1. Buttery popcorn scattered everywhere after I tripped in the dark theater.

2. When it was first rung, the Liberty Bell cracked.

3. Because Angie loved basketball, she practiced frequently with her older brother.

4. Wherever Johnny Appleseed went, he planted apple trees.

5. You should stir the custard mixture constantly until it thickens.

6. If you want to see the secret message, you should put the paper under a red light.

7. Eric probably wrapped this package since he can never tie a good bow.

8. A national park was established in California so that the giant redwood trees would be preserved.

9. Although the brownies were burned on the bottom, the boys and the girls ate them hungrily.

10. I can't finish these costumes until I get more gold braid and scarlet ribbon.

11. If we can finish this project quickly, we'll be able to play ball while it is still daylight.

12. Because the movie was sad, the audience cried.

13. Water spilled on the floor when the vase broke.

14. As Marta entered the room, the dog barked.

APPLY IT NOW

Describing a book you have recently read or a movie you have recently seen, write five sentences with adverb clauses. Diagram the sentences. Use a different subordinate conjunction in each sentence.

Grammar in Action. What is the first adverb clause used in the p. 488 excerpt?

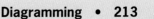

11.10 Noun Clauses

Dependent clauses can be used as nouns. **Noun clauses work in sentences in the same way that nouns do.** Among the words that commonly introduce noun clauses are *that, who, whom, whose, whoever, whomever, how, whether, what, whatever, when, where, which,* and *why.*

In a diagram the noun clause is placed according to its function in the sentence.

- The clause has a horizontal line for its subject and verb and for any direct objects or complements.
- Words or phrases that describe the subject and verb are diagrammed as in a simple sentence.
- If the word that introduces a noun clause has no function in the clause, it is placed on the vertical line connecting the noun clause to the main horizontal line of the independent clause. If the word that introduces the noun clause has a specific function in the noun clause, it is placed in the diagram according to that function.

In this sentence the noun clause is the subject. Noun clauses used as complements or direct objects are diagrammed in a similar way but in their appropriate place on the main horizontal line. A noun clause used as an appositive goes in parentheses next to the noun it describes.

SENTENCE **That we need new uniforms is obvious.**

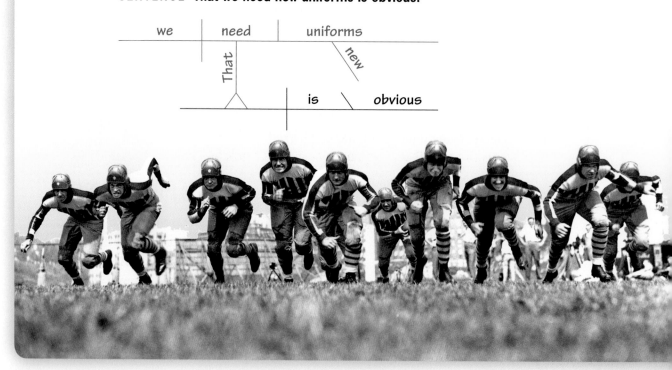

In this sentence the noun clause is the object of the preposition *to*. The word *whoever*, which introduces the noun clause, acts as its subject.

SENTENCE **We should give the extra T-shirt to whoever likes the band.**

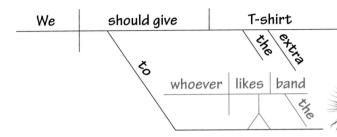

EXERCISE 1 **Diagram the sentences.**

1. I learned that the tickets to the game are free.
2. That Tallahassee is the capital of Florida is a good trivia question.
3. Mason told me about what he saw at the museum.
4. The suggestion that everyone should read the classics seems a good one.
5. I think that we should start our project soon.
6. What you suggest makes good sense.
7. I can't remember where I put my skates.
8. The idea that everyone is equal is stated in the Declaration of Independence.
9. The photographer took pictures of whatever captured her interest.
10. The store offered a discount to whoever had a coupon.
11. Thom told me that he needs help with all the books and magazines.
12. In the summer I certainly wish that we had a power mower.
13. Alexandra hopes that the school play will be popular.
14. That we won the contest was a surprise.
15. Jonathon hopes that he can be the class treasurer.
16. Does Lauren know who will be in the school play?

APPLY IT NOW

Using a current event as the topic, write and diagram six sentences with noun clauses. Use at least three different words to introduce the clauses.

11.11 Diagramming Practice

Let's review some of the basics of diagramming. Subjects, verbs, direct objects, subject complements, and object complements go on the main horizontal line. Adjectives, adverbs, prepositional phrases, participles, and some infinitives go under the main horizontal line.

Gerunds and infinitives used as subjects, objects, or complements go on the main horizontal line of a diagram, on lines rising above it. Gerunds used as objects of prepositions and infinitives used as adverbs and adjectives go on lines below the main horizontal line.

SENTENCE **To buy a new pet was our intention in going to the store.**

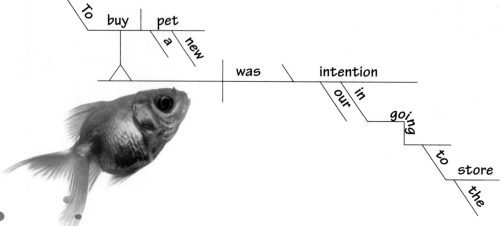

Diagrams of compound sentences and of sentences with adjective clauses, adverb clauses, and noun clauses have two horizontal lines.

SENTENCE **Whenever I am really hungry, I eat a submarine sandwich.**

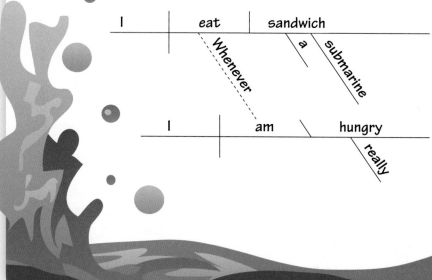

Write out the sentences.

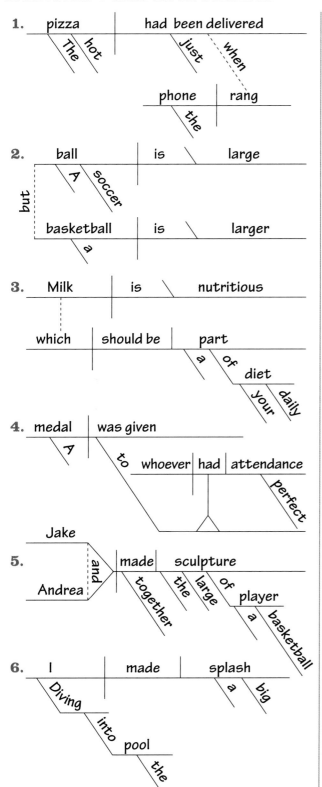

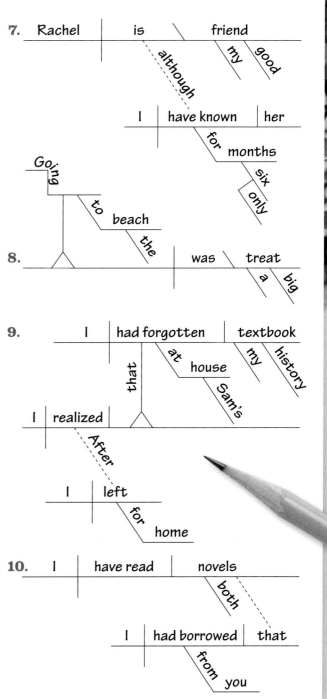

APPLY IT NOW

Choose 10 sentences from this book or another textbook and diagram them.

Diagramming Review

Diagram the sentences.

11.1

1. The brave beekeeper is collecting the honey.

11.2

2. The sun, a star, burns brightly.
3. We traveled to Tallahassee, the capital of Florida.

11.3

4. The Irish wolfhound is the tallest breed, and the Chihuahua is the shortest.

11.4

5. My friend and I volunteered at the animal shelter and walked dogs.

11.5

6. Walking to the store, I saw my neighbors in their new car.
7. The hybrid, purchased by Mr. Juarez, was shiny and spotless.

11.6

8. My hobby, knitting scarves, is difficult for some people.

11.7

9. We tried to get into the movie.
10. Henry's ambition, to make movies, requires dedication.

11.8

11. The musician, who wrote many popular songs, lives in Mexico.
12. I wanted the last CD that the band released.

13. Because Emma was hungry, she wanted a snack.

14. Emma's mom fixed a quick bite before they ate dinner.

11.10

15. The mayor will give certificates to whoever performed a heroic act.

16. That the firefighters are brave is obvious.

11.11 **Write out the sentences.**

17.

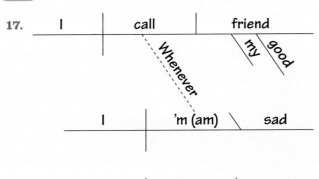

18.

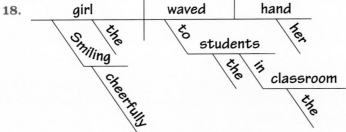

Diagramming Challenge

Study the diagram and answer the questions.

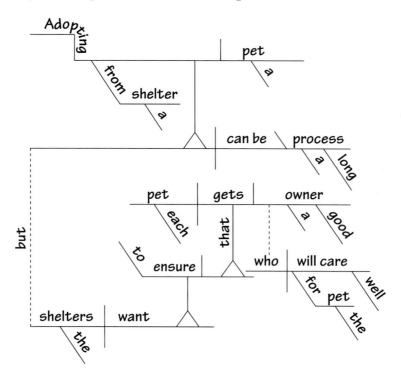

1. What is compound in the sentence?
2. How is the word *adopting* used?
3. How is the word *process* used?
4. What is the noun clause in the sentence?
5. What is the adjective clause in the sentence?
6. What are the prepositional phrases in the sentence? What kind is each—an adjective phrase or an adverb phrase?
7. Identify all the adjectives used in the sentence.
8. Name the conjunction used in the sentence.
9. What is the infinitive used in the sentence?
10. Write out the sentence.

WRITTEN AND ORAL COMMUNICATION

Chapters

Personal Narratives

LiNK

The Land I Lost

by Huynh Quang Nhuong

One day when I was in the field with the herd, fierce fighting between the French forces and the Resistance led by Ho Chi Minh erupted in our hamlet. The battle was so close that I tried to run away and find shelter in the river.

I led Tank and the rest of the herd toward the river, but suddenly I noticed that Tank was lagging behind and limping. He had been hit by a stray bullet which had passed through his chest. With my urging, Tank made it to the river, but he looked very weak when he lay down. I tapped Tank's neck slightly to let him know I was still with him, and I also tried to tell him that he would be okay. . . . When the battle was over, Tank could not get up. He died about an hour later.

We buried Tank in the graveyard where we buried all the dead in our family, and every Luna New Year my father burned incense in front of all those tombs, including Tank's.

> Published in 1982, *The Land I Lost* tells of the splendor, heartache, and danger in Huynh Quang Nhuong's youth, growing up in the highlands of Vietnam.

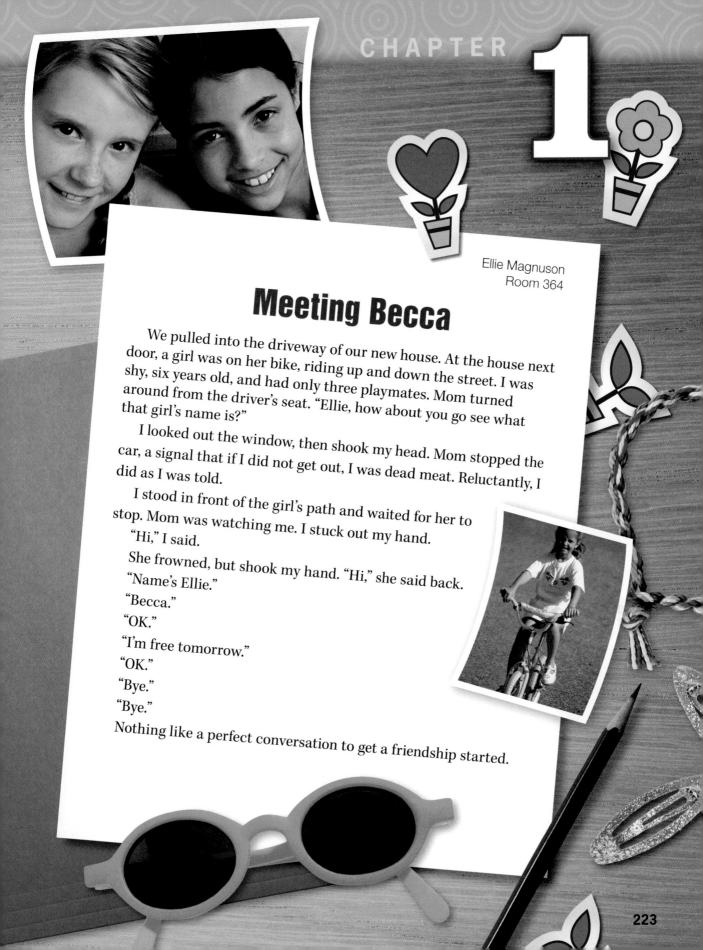

CHAPTER 1

Ellie Magnuson
Room 364

Meeting Becca

We pulled into the driveway of our new house. At the house next door, a girl was on her bike, riding up and down the street. I was shy, six years old, and had only three playmates. Mom turned around from the driver's seat. "Ellie, how about you go see what that girl's name is?"

I looked out the window, then shook my head. Mom stopped the car, a signal that if I did not get out, I was dead meat. Reluctantly, I did as I was told.

I stood in front of the girl's path and waited for her to stop. Mom was watching me. I stuck out my hand.

"Hi," I said.

She frowned, but shook my hand. "Hi," she said back.

"Name's Ellie."

"Becca."

"OK."

"I'm free tomorrow."

"OK."

"Bye."

"Bye."

Nothing like a perfect conversation to get a friendship started.

What Makes a Good Personal Narrative?

The excerpt from *The Land I Lost* on page 222 shares a tense and emotional time in Huynh's childhood. The personal narrative on page 223 was written to share the story of how Ellie, the author, had a funny experience when she moved to a new neighborhood years ago. These stories are written from the authors' point of view, which makes them personal narratives. Another type is an informal business report, such as when you share a "story" of what happened when you met with the school green committee about starting a special recycling project.

A personal narrative is a true story written about a particular event by the person who experienced it. Personal narratives are written in the first person, using the personal pronouns *I* and *me*. Here are some things to keep in mind when writing a personal narrative.

Audience

Ask yourself, *Who is my audience?* and *What will my readers want to know or understand about this?* Think of your audience and these questions as you write.

Structure

Attract your audience's attention with an opening sentence that gives the reader an idea of the topic of your narrative. Then relate the events of your experience in chronological order. Maintain your audience's attention by staying focused on your topic and not giving any irrelevant information. Conclude with a sentence that completes, sums up, or expands on the narrative.

Flow

Focus on the fluidity of your sentences and thoughts. Does your narrative move smoothly from one fact to the next? Does it flow from the beginning to the middle to the end?

ACTIVITY A Below are sentences taken from an e-mail about a meeting. They are listed out of order. Rewrite the personal narrative by listing the sentences in chronological order and then writing them in paragraph form.

1. First, I presented my idea on making a section of the school grounds a native flower preserve.

2. I met with the head of the committee, Ms. Borowski.

3. I ended the meeting by saying I would be happy to outline our meeting for her so that she can present the ideas to the rest of the committee to be discussed at their next meeting. She was thrilled.

4. She was particularly interested in recycling used cell phones, batteries, and printer cartridges.

5. Mom, before you come home from work, I wanted to let you know about the exciting meeting I had with the school green committee today after classes.

6. Before I prepare the outline, I will send her a quick e-mail thanking her for her time and for considering my ideas. Thanks, Mom, for helping me practice this meeting with you.

7. I then presented to her three additional ideas on how to help our school be more energy efficient and environmentally friendly.

ACTIVITY B Reread the organized e-mail from Activity A. Imagine that you are the head of the school green committee, Ms. Borowski. Write a note to the principal, explaining what was discussed at the meeting with the student. Be sure to tell whether or not you will be using these suggestions.

WRITER'S CORNER

Reread the excerpts on pages 222 and 223. Choose a topic below or think of something you experienced that would make an interesting personal narrative. Write who the audience would be and then list the events in chronological order.

A. a severe storm in your neighborhood

B. volunteering at an event

C. a family road trip

D. a day at an amusement park or water park

E. a sporting event

Choosing Your Topic

Before you can write a personal narrative, you need to decide which life experience you want to write about. Think about experiences that have caused you to feel a strong emotion. Some of your memorable experiences might make you laugh or smile, while others might make you feel sad or angry.

One way to choose a topic for your personal narrative is to brainstorm a list of memorable experiences. Then narrow down the list by choosing the ones you like the best. Here are a few questions to ask yourself when choosing an experience to write about.

- Do I have enough to write about this experience in the form of a personal narrative?
- Do I have strong feelings about this particular experience?
- Who is my audience? Will the topic be interesting to my audience?

Tone

When selecting an idea to write about, think about your tone, how you as the writer feel about your subject. You will convey that tone to your audience through your language. For example, look at the line on page 223 that says "dead meat." How does this exaggeration connect the writer to her audience? Can you find another line where the writer's exaggeration clearly reveals her tone?

LiNK

The Land I Lost

It took me a long time to get used to the reality that my grandmother had passed away. Wherever I was, in the house, in the garden, out on the fields, her face always appeared so clearly to me.

Huynh Quang Nhuong

ACTIVITY C Read the following lines from a variety of narratives and decide what tone is being conveyed.

1. She thought the bell would never ring.
2. As the sun set, John wondered if he'd ever see Lucky again.
3. Nicole walked by the old house, and something caught her eye in the window.
4. Again my parents thought that I had made the mess.

ACTIVITY D Using what you have learned about choosing a topic, decide whether the following ideas would be appropriate topics for a personal narrative.

1. my sister's bike trip
2. losing and then finding my new puppy
3. making friends with a new neighbor
4. babysitting for the first time
5. how our neighbor's house was built
6. my frustrating math problem
7. a friend's family history
8. great places to ski
9. techniques for playing the violin
10. finding a mysterious backpack

ACTIVITY E This writer ran into trouble while she was writing e-mails to her art teacher and her friend. Her sentences got mixed into one e-mail. Read her e-mail and decide which sentences were meant for her teacher and which sentences were meant for her friend. Rewrite the e-mail below to make two separate e-mails—one for the art teacher and one for the friend.

You always encouraged me to be as creative as I could with my art, so I wanted to share my good news with you. You won't believe what happened! Remember that crazy painting I did with those funky colors? Thanks to your inspiration, I entered my *Joy* painting in the art contest at the library and won a first-place ribbon for my age group. Well, the judges at the library must think those colors are cool because I got first prize—a blue ribbon and 25 bucks!

Thanks again for teaching me how to paint and having confidence in my abilities. I can't wait to use my prize money to treat us to a movie and some ice cream.

WRITER'S CORNER

Look at the story on page 223. How might the language be different between two seventh graders meeting for the first time? Rewrite a few of the sentences to show the difference in tone for your new audience.

Tech Tip How can you express tone in an e-mail?

Introduction, Body, and Conclusion

A good personal narrative has an introduction, a body, and a conclusion. While they may be identified as distinct parts of the story, they should flow into one another seamlessly.

Introduction

The introduction sets the scene for the narrative. It can be as short as one sentence or as long as a paragraph. The introduction should be engaging and lead the reader into the body of the narrative. Read a chapter's introduction sentence from *The Land I Lost* on your left. How does that catch your attention and make you wonder where this story is going?

Body

The body is the main part of the narrative. It tells the story of what happened during the experience. The body should tell the facts one by one, in chronological order. It should include only the thoughts and details that relate to the topic of the narrative.

Conclusion

The conclusion is the end of the writer's story. The conclusion should do one of the following:

- emphasize one last fact or detail to leave a lasting impression on the reader
- summarize or make a statement that draws together the information from the body
- make a personal comment or a reflection that imparts the writer's reactions or feelings toward the narrative's topic

A good conclusion leaves the reader with a feeling of satisfaction and sometimes prompts him or her to think about what the writer has written.

ACTIVITY A **Identify the introduction and conclusion in this narrative. Discuss whether or not they are effective. Then find one detail that is not necessary to the story.**

Have you ever had an ordinary day turn out to be quite memorable? That's what happened to me one summer day, when several of my friends decided to go swimming in the river. I went along to watch because I cannot swim very well. As I sat on the bank, I dangled my feet in the water and waved at my friends who were wading in it. Suddenly, I realized that my bracelet had slipped from my arm and fallen into the water. I bent over to grab it and immediately fell headfirst into the river. I panicked until my friend Susan pulled me to safety. She was wearing a crimson red swimsuit. That experience convinced me to start swimming lessons the next day.

ACTIVITY B **Read each pair of sentences. Which sentence makes a better introduction for a personal narrative?**

1. **a.** I grabbed my suitcase and I was ready to pack for the trip.
   b. I'll never forget my family road trip to the Florida Everglades.

2. **a.** I've been on long, hot parade routes before, but the Fourth of July parade topped them all.
   b. I marched with the band in the Fourth of July parade.

3. **a.** My cousin and I enjoy riding roller coasters.
   b. My cousin and I have never been on a roller coaster we didn't like.

4. **a.** Have you ever had a tomato juice shower?
   b. There was this one time when I had to take a tomato juice shower one night.

5. **a.** I enjoy riding bikes, but I don't like repairing them.
   b. If you ever need a bike mechanic, don't call me.

6. **a.** All week I heard that noise while trying to fall asleep.
   b. I grabbed my flashlight and decided that this was the night I would find out what was making that noise.

WRITER'S CORNER

Write a new introductory sentence and concluding sentence to the paragraph in Activity A. Did your new sentences improve on the original?

Tech Tip Post work on a classroom blog or wiki for peer review.

Personal Narratives • 229

ACTIVITY C Which sentence in each pair is a better conclusion for a personal narrative? Keep in mind the characteristics of a good conclusion.

1. a. Learning how to play the piano takes a great deal of practice.
   b. After a great deal of practice and determination, I had the satisfaction of finally knowing how to play the piano.

2. a. Once we tasted the yummy blackberry sundaes, we completely forgot about our scratches and itchy mosquito bites.
   b. Picking blackberries wasn't as much fun as we thought it would be.

3. a. I was totally exhausted after the whole cookie sale experience.
   b. After hearing that I had sold the most boxes of cookies in the group, I knew I had finally conquered my fear of selling.

ACTIVITY D Carefully read the following concluding sentences. Which kind of conclusion does each sentence represent: a last detail, a summary, or a personal comment?

1. This first acting experience made me determined to try again and to overcome stage fright.

2. Now that I know what to look for, I can check my houseplants for signs of these pests.

3. No doubt about it, this was the sport for me.

4. I finished the race in first place, surprising everyone who was there.

5. When I am as old as she is, I hope to be as full of joy.

6. It was the many late practices and self-discipline that enabled me to win the most coveted prize.

7. That was the funniest movie I had ever seen.

8. The words "consider all the avenues of life" were the last words he said to me as I left the room.

9. I had walked four adventure-filled miles in the pouring rain, ridden the train to the end of the line, and taken a crowded bus before reaching my final destination.

10. Finally, the customer agreed to buy the books from me after I promised a 40 percent discount on all of them.

11. After all the training, the marathon was canceled due to the severe heat.

ACTIVITY E **Read the personal narratives and then write a concluding sentence for each one.**

1. A Green Centerpiece

Rush hour is a dangerous time for carrying something as delicate as a bouquet of flowers on the subway. I learned this lesson the painful way the evening I brought home a centerpiece for my mother's book club. By the time I finally made it onto a crowded train, my huge bouquet had shed its wrappings. As people squeezed by me getting on and off the train, my colorful bundle gradually lost its brightness. Flowers took root in umbrella spokes, shopping bags were transformed into floral baskets, and suited executives acquired decorations in their lapels. When the train finally reached my stop and I emerged into the open spaces, my hands clutched a bunch of blossomless stems.

2. What a Ride!

Fear and excitement clashed in my stomach when I stepped into the roller coaster. As the little car chugged confidently up the first steep incline, my timidity increased. I peeped over the edge of the miniature train to look down on the park, and I realized that we had reached the top. With mounting terror, I prepared to fly into space. Down rushed the car to the accompaniment of my frantic screams. Hardly had I regained my breath when the chariot again ascended, intent on dropping me once more into the yawning abyss. Whoosh! Abruptly the ride ended.

3. Cooling Off at the River

On one particularly hot day, Jake and I went to the river to swim. On the way, we passed Max and asked him to join us. He went along to watch because he couldn't swim very well. When we got there, Jake and I ran into the water and yelled in shock at the cold temperature. But soon enough we adjusted to the cold and had a great time. Max was throwing rocks in the shallow end, but suddenly he walked into an area with a deep drop-off. He became panicky and started bobbing up and down. Jake quickly swam toward Max and pulled him to safety.

Revising Sentences

Rambling Sentences

Sometimes sentences ramble and lose their focus. This can happen when a number of short sentences are strung together with conjunctions such as *and* and *but.* Here is an example of a rambling sentence.

> **A group of beautiful spruce trees adorns the lawn outside our home, and last Tuesday a swarm of bees selected one of these trees and built a hive in it, but my mom had to have the troublemakers removed.**

To avoid rambling sentences, create shorter sentences and combine ideas where possible.

> **A group of beautiful spruce trees adorns the lawn outside our house. Last Tuesday a swarm of bees selected one of these trees for a new hive, but my mom had to have the troublemakers removed.**

LiNK
The Land I Lost

So the people of our hamlet built a little altar on the side of the road leading to the graves of the son and mother and father, and during the holidays someone always burned incense at their altar, and from time to time travelers stopped by and prayed at the roadside altar, hoping their prayer would make their long journey less hazardous.

Huynh Quang Nhuong

Run-on Sentences

Sometimes sentences are too long because two or more sentences run together without the proper punctuation or with no punctuation between them. They should actually be two or three separate sentences. Here is an example of a run-on sentence.

> **Tigers inhabit the forests of Asia, some kinds of tigers are actually larger than their cousins, the lions.**

To avoid run-on sentences, decide where each complete thought should stop. Put a period at the end and begin the next word with a capital letter.

> **Tigers inhabit the forests of Asia. Some kinds of tigers are actually larger than their cousins, the lions.**

ACTIVITY A **Revise these rambling sentences.**

1. After we went through the park, we went across Pleasant Street, and then we walked for five blocks to where the Ketters live.

2. I had a large part in the school play last year, and this year I will have only a minor part, but next year I hope to be the lead singer in a musical.

3. Last night as we were having dinner we heard fire engines, and we ran to the window and saw the house across the street on fire.

4. The bus I was on was going too fast, and it was packed to capacity, and when it reached a traffic light, it stopped so suddenly that people lurched forward.

5. The music teacher told us to stand up straight and breathe deeply, and she wanted us to look forward, not downward, when we sang.

6. We were excited to take the ferry across the lake to the island but as we neared the port we couldn't find the ferry crossing signs and we were afraid we missed the last ferry for the day.

ACTIVITY B **Correct the following run-on sentences by breaking them into separate sentences.**

1. I shelve books at the library every Tuesday after school then I babysit a two-year-old boy.

2. We organized a club and called it Northeastern Athletic Society its purposes are to uphold the ideals of honorable sports conduct and to arrange games between schools.

3. Yolanda and I practiced our violin duet every day after school for a whole semester, her suggestions helped me improve.

4. My mother does volunteer work on Wednesdays she works at a food pantry in the morning and tutors students in the evening.

5. Ice-skating is no longer a sport limited to colder climates, now I can go to an indoor rink with artificial ice here in Florida.

WRITER'S CORNER

Using the topic chosen for the Writer's Corner on page 225, write a short body paragraph about it. Use conjunctions to connect sentences. Then find a partner and take turns reading each other's paragraphs aloud. Listen for rambling or run-on sentences. Make changes to your sentences and then read them aloud again.

Grammar in Action. Find the fourth noun used in the p. 232 excerpt.

Redundant Words

Another way to trim a sentence is to remove words that repeat ideas already stated. Redundant words lengthen a sentence and do not add to its meaning. Which word is redundant in the following sentence?

> **When we looked out at the Caribbean Sea, we were impressed with the blue, azure water.**

The words *blue* and *azure* have similar meanings. In revising the sentence, you might substitute a word that describes another quality of the water, such as *sparkling*.

> **When we looked out at the Caribbean Sea, we were impressed with the sparkling, azure water.**

Some sentences have a redundant clause that is near a word with the same meaning. What clause is redundant in the following sentence?

> **The book's unique plot, which was unlike any other I had ever read, made me want to keep reading the book without stopping.**

You are correct if you said *unlike any other I had ever read.* The clause is redundant because it restates the meaning of the adjective *unique*.

ACTIVITY C Remove the redundant words from the following sentences.

1. The two of us shared the huge, enormous submarine sandwich.
2. That was the most boring and dull program I've seen all year.
3. I'm writing a short one-page biography about the life of the baseball player Roberto Clemente.

Roberto Clemente

4. After reading the chapter for history class once, I reread it again.
5. The cheerful, upbeat music made me want to dance.
6. My friend Jenna lay and reclined on the sandy beach, watching her brothers build sandcastles.
7. A drowsy Christopher, who was quite sleepy, had to pull the car over and ask my dad to drive.
8. Our chess team has won 10 consecutive tournaments in a row.
9. Alex's victory in the essay contest was astonishing news that surprised everyone.
10. The wet weather, which was very rainy, kept us from going outside to play soccer.

ACTIVITY D Identify the error or errors in each sentence. Is it a rambling sentence, a run-on sentence, or a sentence with redundant words? Rewrite each sentence so it is clear and focused.

1. I went snow skiing down a hill, and two other kids were there, and they were skiing fast.
2. We thought the football game would never end the other team's score kept increasing while our team's score never changed.
3. As our plane ascended upward, I began to feel sad about leaving my grandparents' house.
4. Isabelle and I tiptoed down the hall and picked up the cake and then tiptoed to Mom's room and said, "Surprise!"
5. The movie actors kept my attention all the time throughout the whole movie.
6. I was approached by an aggressive salesperson who was very pushy trying to sell me a new MP3 player.
7. After Mason came home from school, he took his dog for a walk and threw the ball to it in the backyard and then filled its bowls with dog food and fresh water.
8. To study for her Spanish class, Krista reread her vocabulary list again.
9. Daniella wore her favorite T-shirt three consecutive days in a row.
10. The East Indies lie between southern Asia and Australia this chain of beautiful green islands is rich in natural resources.

ACTIVITY E The following paragraph contains redundant words and rambling sentences. Rewrite the paragraph by dividing and revising sentences as necessary.

With the first spring thunderstorm of rain, the water made the grass begin to spring up from under the ground. The earth felt soft, mushy, and wet underfoot as we walked across the swampy baseball diamond. Before too long the glaring light of the sun would be beating down on the dry and dusty earth, and we would hear the sound of bats and balls and tramping feet on solid, hard, dry, dusty ground, but for a while, a few months anyway, we and the birds and mosquitoes would have this lagoon all to ourselves alone.

WRITER'S CORNER

Look back at the sentences you revised in the Writer's Corner on page 233. Work with a partner to find a new way to revise the sentences, such as combining short, choppy sentences or eliminating any redundant words.

Exact Words

LiNK

The Land I Lost

My good friend, you should not only chain your monkey to a tree but also inspect the chain every day. You came to live in our hamlet only a short while ago and you may not know how mischievous, malicious, and unpredictable these monkeys can be.

Huynh Quang Nhuong

Good writers know the importance of word choice when trying to convey a specific, intended meaning to their readers. Exact words also help create visual images for the reader.

Nouns

General nouns, such as *fruit* and *clothes,* often produce an incomplete picture for the reader. More specific nouns, such as *blueberries* and *raincoat,* create a detailed picture. Compare the nouns in the following sentences:

> **We ate *vegetables* for a snack.**
> **We ate *carrot sticks* and *green pepper strips* for a snack.**

Verbs

Choosing an exact verb can intensify an action and make your sentences come alive. Instead of using a common verb, such as *run,* consider using more specific verbs, such as *sprinted, raced,* and *jogged.* Which sentence creates the more vivid picture?

> **Henry *walked* slowly across the gym.**
> **Henry *lumbered* across the gym.**

Adjectives

Adjectives are modifiers that can make the nouns they accompany clearer. However, some adjectives are so common that they add little meaning to a sentence, for example, *big, small,* and *good.* Examples of colorful adjectives include *gigantic, miniscule,* and *breathtaking.* Read the following example sentences:

> **We entered the attic, hoping to find Grandma's lamp.**
> **We entered the *musty* attic, hoping to find Grandma's *antique* lamp.**

Adverbs

Adverbs give more specific meaning to the verbs they modify. Use adverbs when you think they can add detail or color to the action.

> **Mia placed the figurines on the shelf.**
> **Mia** *delicately* **placed the figurines on the shelf.**

ACTIVITY A Complete the following exercises to practice choosing more effective and specific words.

1. Think of one vivid verb that could replace *walk*. Use this verb in a sentence.

2. Write a sentence to describe a mountain or a park you have seen. Use adjectives that paint a picture.

3. Use an adverb to describe an activity that you do, such as playing soccer or painting a picture.

4. Think of a specific noun that could replace *toy*. Use this noun in a sentence.

5. Write a sentence using the sound a machine makes as a verb.

6. Rewrite the sentence in number 5 by adding an adverb to describe the sound.

7. Use an adjective in a sentence to describe your favorite animal.

8. What adjectives would you use to describe your family?

ACTIVITY B Rewrite the personal narrative *Taking Off* using exact words to make the images more vivid.

Taking Off

My first plane trip was very fun. The engines made a lot of noise, and the plane shook as it prepared for takeoff. The ground went by quickly as the plane went down the runway. It was a nice moment when the plane rose from the ground.

WRITER'S CORNER

Think of a funny or scary experience and write five sentences about it. Practice using exact words in your description of the experience.

Grammar in Action, What adjectives describe monkeys on p. 236?

Homophones

Sometimes writers confuse words that sound alike but have different meanings. These words are called *homophones*. Notice the difference in meaning and spelling in the following examples of homophones:

> Did you *hear* a strange noise?
> I saw a raccoon *here* yesterday.

> Do you *know* the man wearing the black shirt?
> *No*, I don't *know* him, and he has *no* nametag.

Sometimes contractions that are homophones cause difficulty in writing too. The following examples can be particularly tricky:

it's–its	they're–there–their
you're–your	who's–whose

ACTIVITY C **Select the homophone that correctly completes each sentence.**

1. (Who's Whose) responsible for knocking over the dog's water bowl?
2. (Who's Whose) skateboard is by that tree?
3. (It's Its) important for you to proofread your writing.
4. Could I please borrow (you're your) dictionary?
5. The dog was running in circles, trying to catch (it's its) tail.
6. (They're There Their) is a fancy restaurant on the corner of Oakley and Waveland streets.
7. (You're Your) going to sing a song, aren't you?
8. The Martins are trying to sell (they're their there) house to the highest bidder.
9. (They're Their, There) waiting patiently for the hamburgers to be ready.
10. Denzig, (who's whose) father is a teacher, has decided that he would like to be a teacher someday too.
11. Are you going to (there their) house after school today?
12. I see that you remembered to bring (you're your) book to the book club.
13. Jake kicked the soccer ball over (their there).
14. Sophia can't remember (who's whose) coming to her birthday party.
15. Do you think the orphaned rabbit will eat (its it's) food?

ACTIVITY D Use the following list of homophones to name what each numbered statement is describing. Use your dictionary if necessary. Define the remaining homophones.

slay–sleigh   maize–maze

cash–cache   core–corps

taught–taut   principal–principle

cue–queue   current–currant

1. I am a basic rule or truth.
2. I am a way to get around in the snow.
3. I am a line of people.
4. I am a sour berry that grows on a bush.
5. I am another name for corn.
6. I am money in your pocket.
7. I am a confusing path.
8. I am recent.

ACTIVITY E Complete each sentence with the correct homophone from the list in Activity D.

1. The knight grabbed his sword to _____ the dragon.
2. Algernon, the mouse, had to find his way through a _____ to be rewarded.
3. The canoe was carried along by a swift-moving _____.
4. Our neighbor _____ us karate.
5. The hospital is staffed by a _____ of doctors and nurses.
6. The mountain climber tugged on the rope so that it was _____.
7. The explorer prepared a _____ of food to use when he returned from his journey.
8. His _____ temperature was low.

WRITER'S CORNER

Choose four pairs of words below and write a sentence using each word, or use the pair in one sentence, such as *I did* not *tie the* knot.

bough–bow

coarse–course

knot–not

patience–patients

piece–peace

stationery–stationary

sum–some

through–threw

With an adult, look up a word, using an online dictionary.

Tech Tip

Graphic Organizers

Time Lines

A time line is a graphic organizer that writers use to arrange the events of a story or an experience. Time lines are constructed by listing events in chronological order on a vertical, horizontal, or diagonal line.

Suppose the writer chose "my first hiking experience" as the topic for a personal narrative. Here's an example of the writer's time line.

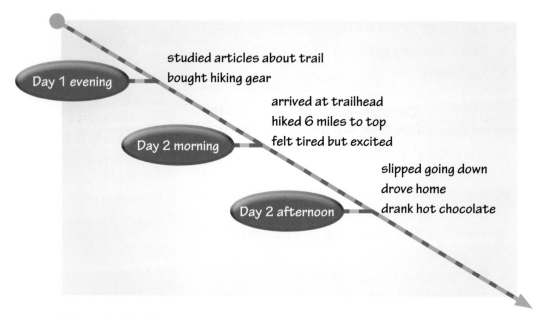

Day 1 evening
studied articles about trail
bought hiking gear

Day 2 morning
arrived at trailhead
hiked 6 miles to top
felt tired but excited

Day 2 afternoon
slipped going down
drove home
drank hot chocolate

Word Webs

A word web is a type of graphic organizer that helps writers map out the subtopics and details related to their chosen topics. It also keeps writers from introducing unnecessary details.

The following three steps are examples of how a writer might construct a word web to organize the topic "my first hiking experience":

1. Write your topic idea and draw a box around it.
2. Around the box, name things that are related to the topic "my first hiking experience." These ideas are called subtopics. Draw lines connecting each subtopic to the topic in the center.
3. Around each subtopic, write any details relating to that subtopic.

ACTIVITY A **Refer to the graphic organizers to write one or two sentences for each of the subtopics below. Include the details connected to the subtopics in the word web. Feel free to add your own details for creativity. The first one has been done as an example.**

1. Preparation—A day before the hike we read an article about the trail and then bought backpacks, hiking boots, and trail mix.

2. Hiking to Eagle Ridge—

3. Hiking back—

WRITER'S CORNER

Create a time line for the topic "my last day of summer vacation" or choose a topic of your own.

Tech Tip Use a computer tool to help you create your time line.

Using Your Graphic Organizer

Now that the subtopics and details of the experience have been organized, here's an example of how one writer chose to write a draft of the body of a personal narrative based on a graphic organizer.

The day before the hike my brother and I read an intriguing article about Eagle Ridge. Then we eagerly shopped for backpacks, hiking shoes, and trail mix. We could hardly wait until our hike would begin. The next morning when the alarm clock went off, I excitedly jumped out of bed and woke up my brother. We were at the trail to begin our hiking adventure by 8:00 a.m. on a cool, sunny day.

The sign at the beginning of the trail said Eagle Ridge was six miles to the west. We had read that this trail was one of the easiest trails to hike in the area. However, we found the slippery rocks and steep climbs to be difficult. When we finally climbed to the top of Eagle Ridge, we felt fatigued but also satisfied about reaching our goal.

Coming down Eagle Ridge was no easier than ascending it. On the steepest part of the trail, I took a wrong step and fell to my knees. I don't have to tell you how thrilled we were to see our car and later sip hot chocolate while we rested our sore muscles.

ACTIVITY B **Choose three or four points from the time line you made in the Writer's Corner on page 241. Use the information to write a body paragraph for a personal narrative.**

ACTIVITY C Below is a word web that's in need of subtopics and details relating to the topic "a day at the beach." Use what's already been written to help you extend and develop the partial word web.

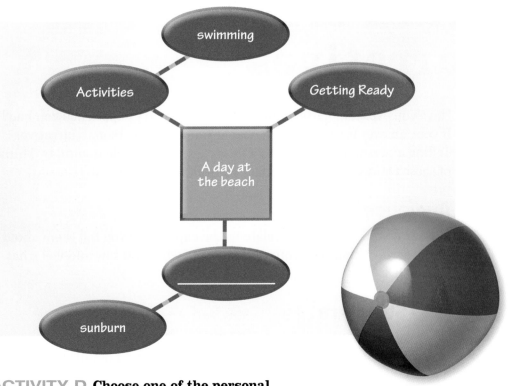

ACTIVITY D Choose one of the personal narrative topics below or choose a topic of your own. Use either a time line or a word web to help you organize the events.

1. a holiday
2. game day
3. my birthday
4. Saturday morning
5. a busy afternoon after school

WRITER'S CORNER

Use the graphic organizer you created in Activity D to write a short body paragraph of a personal narrative. Ask yourself the following questions: Do all the subtopics relate to the topic? Are any of the details irrelevant to the topic? Does the writing flow in chronological order?

Oral Personal Narratives

Have you ever told a friend about a funny or scary experience you had? If your answer is yes, then you have given an oral personal narrative. Telling a personal narrative to a larger group of people is similar. Think of these things when you prepare an oral personal narrative.

Audience

You want your audience to relate to the experience you tell them about. Choose words that help your audience see what you saw and feel what you felt.

Structure

Capture your audience's attention with an intriguing introductory sentence. Then give interesting details that tell what happened in chronological order. Be sure that all the details relate to the topic of the narrative. Conclude your narrative by giving one last detail, summarizing the narrative, or stating your own reaction to the experience described.

Expression

When you speak, it is important to engage the audience by changing the expression in your voice to convey the appropriate emotions. It also helps to use gestures that correspond to what you are saying. Always make eye contact with your audience.

Visual Aid

Whenever possible, present a visual aid related to the topic of your personal narrative. A visual aid could be a photograph, an illustration, a map, charts, graphs, or an object. Before you give your oral personal narrative, decide when you want to show the visual aid.

Preparing an Oral Personal Narrative

Writing your notes on note cards will help you organize the important details you wish to speak about. You should not read your notes word for word. Instead, write keywords or phrases that will help you remember your main points. Below are ways to prepare your oral personal narrative.

1. Write the introductory sentence on the first card.
2. Write each event or subtopic on a separate card along with keywords that will help you remember details.
3. Write your concluding sentence on the last card.
4. Plan when you will show your visual aids.

ACTIVITY A These are note cards for an oral presentation on the personal narrative from page 242. Complete the note cards by adding more details and subtopics to each one. Write a colorful introduction and conclusion on separate cards.

2. Preparations
-
- backpacks
-

3.
- start time 8:00 a.m.
- cool, sunny
-
-

4.
-
- thrilled to see car
-
- sore muscles
-

SPEAKER'S CORNER

Use the graphic organizer you made for one of the topics in Activity D on page 243. Write note cards for an oral personal narrative on the topic. Brainstorm possible visual aids that you'd like to use for your presentation.

Practice

You'll feel confident when giving an oral personal narrative if you practice with your notes and visual aids ahead of time.

Try practicing your presentation in front of a family member, a friend, or even a mirror. Here are some questions that you and those watching you should consider as you practice:

- Does my introduction get the audience's attention?
- Do I present the events of my narrative in the order in which they happened?
- Do I speak clearly?
- Do I speak with feeling?
- Do I use exact words?
- Is my visual aid appropriate? Do I share it at the correct time?
- Does my conclusion provide an ending that ties the rest of the narrative together?

Listening Tips

When someone else is giving an oral personal narrative, it is important to be a good listener. Here are some tips to follow:

- Be respectful of the speaker and show that you are listening by looking at him or her.
- Do not interrupt the speaker.
- Write down any questions you may want to ask at the end of the speech.
- Listen for the speaker's subtopics and details.
- If a visual aid is displayed, think of how it connects to what the speaker is talking about.
- When the speaker has finished speaking, provide feedback on the content of the narrative. Say things such as, "I've never been on a hike, but now you've given me an idea of what to expect."

ACTIVITY B Follow the tips in this lesson to prepare note cards for your own oral personal narrative. You may choose a topic of your own or refer back to the note cards you started writing in the Speaker's Corner on page 245. Whether you're building on your notes from the Speaker's Corner or beginning something new, keep in mind that your classmates will be your audience.

ACTIVITY C Look over your completed note cards from Activity B as well as the visual aid suggestions given below. Which visual aid or aids do you think would make your oral personal narrative more interesting? When would be the appropriate time to show the visual aids during your presentation?

1. photographs
2. illustrations
3. maps
4. charts or graphs
5. a few objects
6. newspapers or magazines

ACTIVITY D Practice using the note cards you prepared for Activity A on page 245. With a partner, take turns giving the oral presentation as well as listening to it. When you are the listener, follow the Listening Tips on page 246, including follow-up questions or comments.

SPEAKER'S CORNER

Use the note cards that you made in Activity B and the visual aids that you selected in Activity C to continue preparing for your own oral personal narrative. Practice your presentation with a friend or a family member. Then present the oral personal narrative to your classmates. Remember to follow the Listening Tips when it is your turn to listen to another classmate's oral personal narrative.

Tech Tip Record a podcast of yourself and critique it.

Writer's Workshop

Prewriting and Drafting

Have you ever had an experience that was so funny or unusual that you couldn't wait to tell your friends or family about it? Has anyone ever asked you to tell the story of an experience you have had? Experiences such as these are great topics for personal narratives.

Prewriting

 Ideas To begin the writing process, writers will use prewriting techniques to brainstorm topics, to freewrite ideas, and to organize and structure their writing.

Brainstorming

For a personal narrative, brainstorming helps the writer remember and list personal experiences he or she has had. After brainstorming, the writer looks over the list and chooses the topic that will probably be most appealing to your audience.

Writer's Tip Brainstorming means listing all the ideas that come to mind. Freewriting means exploring and expanding on your selected topic.

Freewriting

After choosing a topic, begin freewriting. When freewriting for a personal narrative, record everything that you can remember about an event, including how you felt. The more ideas you have, the more you have to choose from when writing your first draft.

Here's an example of freewriting notes written by Jason, a seventh grader. He writes about a frustrating day.

Notice that Jason wrote in phrases to quickly capture his ideas. Jason knew that he could organize his thoughts later in the writing process.

I felt frustrated at neighborhood fair popcorn stand.
Dog knocked over bags—big mess.
Popcorn burned when I answered the phone.
Smelled bad.
Made more popcorn. Friend poured too much salt.
We made pink lemonade.
When life gives you lemons, make lemonade.
Made $86.00 for family with kid in hospital.

Your Turn

Today you will begin to write a personal narrative, and your classmates will be your audience. To select a topic for your personal narrative, practice brainstorming by completing one or two of the following sentences:

I was quite surprised/scared when . . .
I felt proud/brave/frustrated when . . .
The best/worst day of my life was . . .
My most embarrassing moment was . . .

Select a topic that will appeal to both you and your audience. Next, use freewriting to help you recall details about your topic. Write as much as you can in five minutes.

Organizing Your Ideas

Once a writer has chosen a topic and has recalled several details about the topic, he or she can

Organization use a graphic organizer to organize thoughts and possibly add more details. Earlier in this chapter, you learned to organize events by using word webs and time lines.

Because the events of a narrative often appear in chronological order, creating a time line is a great way to organize details. Look at Jason's time line. Notice that he expanded on his ideas more here than in the freewriting exercises.

Your Turn

Look at your freewriting notes. Make a time line to show what happened in chronological order.

Prewriting
Drafting
Content Editing
Revising
Copyediting
Proofreading
Publishing

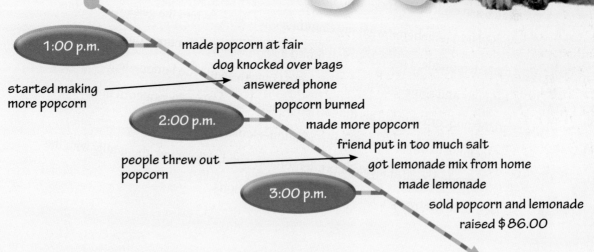

1:00 p.m.
made popcorn at fair
dog knocked over bags
started making more popcorn → answered phone
popcorn burned
2:00 p.m.
made more popcorn
friend put in too much salt
people threw out popcorn → got lemonade mix from home
made lemonade
3:00 p.m.
sold popcorn and lemonade
raised $86.00

Drafting

A draft is a writer's first chance to develop and organize his or her prewriting notes into a coherent narrative. After Jason reviewed his time line, he wrote his first draft. In addition to putting his thoughts into paragraph form, Jason added an introduction and a conclusion.

Writer's Tip As he wrote, Jason kept in mind that he wanted his narrative to appeal to his peers, so he wrote using an informal tone.

A Frustrating and Rewarding Day

It was a hot day in July when our neighborhood held a fare to raise money for medical treatments for a child who was sick in the hospital. We were surprised at the big number of people who came to eat food and play games like water balloon toss. Even my cousins from across town came.

My job was to make popcorn in a popcorn popper and to sell a lot of it, however, I had a lot of bad luck. First, my dog, Bailey, who is a golden retriever, got so interested in the bags of popcorn that he knocked them onto the ground so he could sniff them. Then the phone rang. It was Ricardo, he made me burn the popcorn. It smelled so bad that I threw it out and made more popcorn.

I asked my friend Greta to put salt on the new batch of popcorn but she put too much salt on it and people who bought it ate just one bite and threw it away. Suddenly, I remebered what my Grandma often says: "When life gives you lemons, make lemonade. I ran home and found a lot of pink paper cups from my little sister's birthday and some pink lemonade mix. I quickly made the lemonade and took it to the popcorn stand. This time when people tasted the salty popcorn and needed something to drink, I had just the solution—lemonade.

I made $86.00 at my popcorn/lemonade stand. Altogether, the family with the sick child got over $4,000.00 in sales and donations.

Your Turn

Jason's draft pulls together the ideas he wrote during his prewriting exercises. He also added a few other details and an introduction and a conclusion.

Now it's your turn to look at your prewriting exercises and write your first draft. Make sure that you have included all the relevant details about your chosen experience as well as any new details that come to mind before you begin writing.

When you add an introduction and a conclusion, remember what you have learned about the purpose of each in a personal narrative.

Writer's Tip When you write, double-space between lines so that you have room to add revisions.

Writing with a "Voice"

How does a writer use expression? In writing, voice is heard through your choice of words and in the way you compose your sentences.

Writers who write with a strong voice use specific words to express their thoughts. Their paragraphs are not lists of sentences. Instead, their paragraphs engage the reader with clear sentences of varying lengths and types.

How strong is the voice in your writing? It takes effort on your part to produce a strong, effective voice. As you keep writing, your voice will become stronger.

Voice

Prewriting

Drafting

Content Editing

Revising

Copyediting

Proofreading

Publishing

Content Editing

Good writers know that their first drafts are not perfect. Drafts need to be edited for content and revised to make them better. A content editor notices how well the ideas of a piece are expressed. Is all the necessary information included? Do the ideas flow clearly and logically?

Jason tried to edit his own writing with the help of the Content Editor's Checklist. However, he knew that some things in the story that appeared clear to him might not be as clear to the reader.

Jason decided to find a fresh pair of eyes to read his draft. His classmate Olivia agreed to have a peer conference with him. She would give him feedback on the content of his draft in a kind and respectful way. Jason said he would do the same for Olivia's personal narrative. First, Olivia carefully read Jason's narrative. Then she checked it against the Content Editor's Checklist and read it a second time.

Writer's Tip As content editors find things they can improve, they carefully mark them on the draft, as near as possible to the location of the error. Editing with a colored pencil will help the writer note the needed revisions.

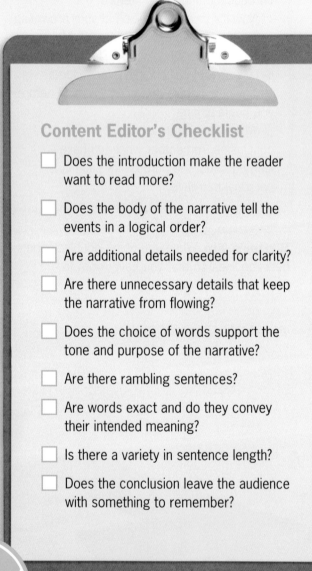

Content Editor's Checklist

- [ ] Does the introduction make the reader want to read more?
- [ ] Does the body of the narrative tell the events in a logical order?
- [ ] Are additional details needed for clarity?
- [ ] Are there unnecessary details that keep the narrative from flowing?
- [ ] Does the choice of words support the tone and purpose of the narrative?
- [ ] Are there rambling sentences?
- [ ] Are words exact and do they convey their intended meaning?
- [ ] Is there a variety in sentence length?
- [ ] Does the conclusion leave the audience with something to remember?

Olivia then shared with Jason the things in the narrative she thought could be improved. Here are her comments.

- I like the expression you wrote in the body of the narrative: "If life gives you lemons, make lemonade." I wonder if that could become the conclusion. If not, you need a more memorable conclusion because the one you wrote seems a little dull.

- The same is true of the introduction. Your first sentence sets the scene, but it also needs to make me want to read more. Perhaps you could add a catchy introductory sentence.

- There are a few missing details that I'd like to know. What was the child's illness? How did Ricardo cause you to burn the popcorn?

- You might want to replace words like *food*, *threw away*, *ran*, and *took* with more precise words that interest your audience.

Jason valued Olivia's feedback, so he decided to work on fixing the things she mentioned. He clarified the sentences about the phone call and the burnt popcorn. He also worked on improving the introduction and conclusion.

Your Turn

Look for ways to improve your first draft.

- Will your introduction make readers want to keep reading?
- Do you have enough details to make the story clear for all classmates reading the story?
- Are only the essential details in the body?
- Is your conclusion strong enough so that your readers will know it's the end of the narrative?

Trade personal narratives with a classmate. Read your classmate's narrative several times and go over the Content Editor's Checklist.

Writer's Tip After you finish reading your partner's first draft, first tell your partner the good things that you read. Then give your opinion of how you think the narrative could be improved. Your partner will do the same for you.

Prewriting

Drafting

Content Editing

Revising

Copyediting

Proofreading

Publishing

Writer's Workshop

Revising

Here are the revisions Jason made to his draft after he met about content editing with Olivia.

A Frustrating and Rewarding Day

Have you ever had a day that was really frustrating. I have, but fortunately everything turned out OK in the end.

It was a hot day in July when our neighborhood held a fare to raise money for ~~medical treatments for a child who was sick in the hospital.~~ for a girl who was ill with leukemia. We were surprised at the the concession stand to ~~big number~~ hundreds of people who came to eat food and play games like water balloon toss. ~~Even my cousins from across town came.~~

My job was to make popcorn in a popcorn popper and to sell ~~a lot of it~~ as much as I could, however, I had a lot of bad luck. First, my dog, Bailey, ~~who is a golden retriever,~~ got so interested in the bags of popcorn that he knocked them onto the ground so he could sniff them. ~~Then the phone rang. It was Ricardo, he made me burn the popcorn.~~ Then I got a call from Ricardo. While we were talking, the popcorn burned. It smelled so bad that I threw it out and made more popcorn.

I asked my friend Greta to put salt on the new batch of popcorn but she put too much salt on it and people who bought it ~~ate just one bite and threw it away.~~ tossed it in the garbage after eating just one bite.

Suddenly, I remebered what my Grandma often says: "When life gives you lemons, make lemonade. I ~~ran~~ dashed home and found a lot of pink paper cups from my little sister's birthday and some pink lemonade mix. I quickly made the lemonade and ~~took it~~ lugged it over to the popcorn stand. This time when people tasted the salty popcorn and needed something to drink, I had just the solution—lemonade.

I made $86.00 at my popcorn/lemonade stand. Altogether, the family with the sick child ~~got~~ received over $4,000.00 in sales and donations. In the end I could finally laugh at my frustrating popcorn episode and find joy in "making lemonade out of lemons."

Look at the revisions Jason made to his draft. He used some of Olivia's suggestions and found more ways to improve his narrative.

- Jason agreed with Olivia that he needed a conclusion that would pull together ideas from the body. He just had to think about it for a while. What could he focus on to help him come up with a new concluding sentence?

- What should he revise to better capture the attention of his readers?

- Olivia's comments helped Jason see that there were a few missing details in his narrative. What were the missing details and where should he place them in his story?

- Jason also noticed that he had used the phrase *a lot of* twice in consecutive sentences. Should he reword one of the sentences? Which one?

Then he realized that several common words could be replaced with more exact words, such as *hundreds* for *big number*, *tossed in the garbage* for *threw away*, and *dashed home* for *ran home*.

Word Choice

After Jason incorporated Olivia's suggestions, he read his revised draft again. He made additional changes when he noticed some details that did not support the purpose of the narrative. Were the references to his cousins and to the breed of his dog, Bailey, necessary to the story?

Grammar in Action

Identify the appositive in the second paragraph in Jason's draft on page 254. Is it restrictive or nonrestrictive? See Section 1.5.

Your Turn

Use your ideas about the content and the ideas you got from your classmate to revise your personal narrative.

Write your changes as neatly as you can next to the text you are changing. That will make it easier to read the edited parts when you rewrite your story.

When you have finished making revisions, use the Content Editor's Checklist again.

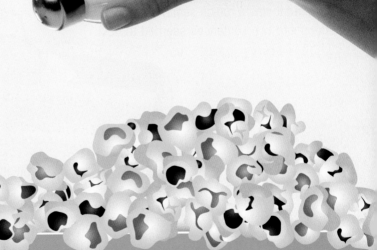

Prewriting

Drafting

Content Editing

Revising

Copyediting

Proofreading

Publishing

Copyediting and Proofreading

Copyediting

The day after Jason revised his draft for content, he read the revised draft again. He knew that the content was greatly improved, but he wanted to make the draft even better. He decided to copyedit his draft and pay closer attention to his choice of words and sentence structure.

When you copyedit, you look for accuracy in word meaning, word choice, sentence structure, and the overall logic of the piece. Check for any overused words that could be replaced with more precise words that better convey your intended meaning. Remembering the lesson on run-on and rambling sentences, Jason decided to see if his draft had any of those kinds of errors. Jason thought the sentence about the dog in the third paragraph was too long and awkward, so he changed it to read like this:

First, my dog, Bailey, became so interested in sniffing the bags of popcorn that he knocked them onto the ground.

Jason found another sentence that looked too long at the beginning of the second paragraph. He realized it was a run-on sentence. Separating the ideas into two sentences seemed to help.

My job was to make popcorn in a popcorn popper and to sell as much as I could. However, I had a lot of bad luck.

Jason used the checklist at the bottom of the page to copyedit his draft.

Your Turn

Look over your revised draft and use the Copyeditor's Checklist. A good way to catch sentence construction mistakes is to read the narrative aloud. You might ask someone else to read your draft aloud to let you know if any sentences sound awkward.

Proofreading

Before writing the final copy of a personal narrative, a good writer proofreads the draft for mistakes in spelling, capitalization, punctuation, and grammar. He or she also checks to make sure that no new errors have been introduced during the revising

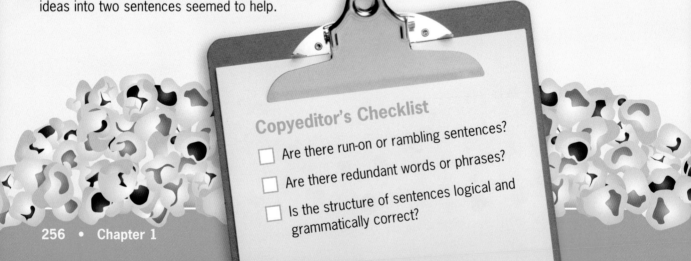

Copyeditor's Checklist

- ☐ Are there run-on or rambling sentences?
- ☐ Are there redundant words or phrases?
- ☐ Is the structure of sentences logical and grammatically correct?

steps. Good writers also ask someone else to

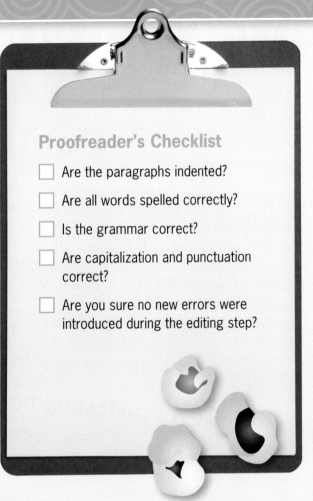

proofread their draft, because another proofreader may catch errors that the writer missed.

Jason asked another classmate, William, to read his personal narrative. William followed the Proofreader's Checklist and found a spelling error, one homophone error, one word that should be capitalized, a missing question mark, a missing quotation mark, and a paragraph that was not indented. He also found a redundant word, *finally*, just after the phrase *In the end*.

Your Turn

Read your revised draft carefully against the Proofreader's Checklist. When you have gone through the list, trade papers with a partner. Check your partner's paper in the same way. Be sure to use a dictionary if you are unsure of a word's definition or correct spelling.

Proofreader's Checklist

- [ ] Are the paragraphs indented?
- [ ] Are all words spelled correctly?
- [ ] Is the grammar correct?
- [ ] Are capitalization and punctuation correct?
- [ ] Are you sure no new errors were introduced during the editing step?

Common Proofreading Marks

Symbol	Meaning	Example
¶	begin new paragraph	over. Begin a new
◡	close up space	close u p space
∧	insert	students think *should*
℘	delete, omit	that the the book
/	make lowercase	Mathematics
∼	reverse letters	reversre letters
≡	capitalize	washington
∨ ∨	add quotation marks	I am, I said.
⊙	add period	Marta drank tea

Publishing

Publishing is the moment when you decide to share your finished work. You know it is your best work, and you are ready to share it with your audience. As Jason prepared to publish his narrative, he read his draft again to make sure he had written all the necessary revisions and corrections. Then he used a computer to type his finished piece. Since his narrative was to be published in the form of a booklet, Jason wanted to make it look as polished as he could. Jason used a large font to type the narrative's title at the top of the first page. Jason then created a booklet by placing his finished piece between a front and back cover and stapling the pages together along the left side.

A Frustrating but Rewarding Day

by Jason Brady

Have you ever had a day that was really frustrating? I have, but fortunately everything turned out OK in the end.

It was a hot day in July when our neighborhood held a fair to raise money for medical treatments for a girl who was ill with leukemia. We were surprised at the hundreds of people who came to eat concession stand food and play games like water balloon toss.

My job was to make popcorn in a popcorn popper and to sell as much as I could. However, I had a lot of bad luck. First, my dog, Bailey, became so interested in sniffing the bags of popcorn that he knocked them onto the ground. Then I got a call from Ricardo. While we were talking, the popcorn burned. It smelled so bad that I threw it out and made more popcorn.

I asked my friend Greta to put salt on the newest batch of popcorn, but she used too much salt. The people who bought the popcorn tossed their bags in the garbage after eating just one bite.

Suddenly, I remembered what my grandma often says: "When life gives you lemons, make lemonade." I dashed home and found a lot of pink paper cups from my little sister's birthday and some pink lemonade mix. I quickly made the lemonade and lugged it over to the popcorn stand. This time when people tasted the salty popcorn and needed something to drink, I had the perfect solution—lemonade. I made $86.00 at my popcorn/lemonade stand. Altogether, the family with the sick child received over $4,000.00 in sales and donations. In the end, I could laugh at my frustrating popcorn episode and find joy in "making lemonade out of lemons."

A publisher prints a written work and then sells or distributes it to the public. Completing the final version of something that will be published is a writer's last step in the writing process.

 Presentation

There are many ways you can publish your personal narrative.

 Create a class book or scrapbook. Put together all the personal narratives from your class. Use a digital camera to add photos. You might also include original illustrations or souvenirs.

 Film your personal narrative. Present it using a video of each student reading his or her narrative aloud and show it at Parents' Night to an even larger audience.

 Create a class newsletter. Use a digital camera or a scanner to add your photo to your piece.

 Post your personal narrative to a Web site that publishes student writing. Work with an adult to find an appropriate site.

 Make a pop-up book. Add illustrations by drawing them yourself or using a digital camera.

Your Turn

Choose one of the publishing options. Carefully type your narrative on a computer or write it using your neatest handwriting to make a final copy of your revised draft. Proofread your final copy one more time.

Writer's Tip Your computer's spell checker can help you find spelling errors, but remember that it won't find incorrect homophones.

A Frustrating but Rewarding Day

by Jason Brady

Prewriting

Drafting

Content Editing

Revising

Copyediting

Proofreading

Publishing

Business Letters

LiNK

Hugh Walsh
Allardyce Associates
2426 Lawrence Ave.
Chicago, IL 60618

August 29, 20–

Ferdinand Brostrom
Customer Service Manager
Brostrom Cable Company
4218 W. Keeler Ave.
Chicago, IL 60657

Dear Mr. Brostrom:

This letter is to notify you of the poor cable installation done on August 20. I gave the installer specific instructions myself of how I needed the work done, but instead there are cables suspended everywhere. I was told that it would take three weeks and cost $300 to come out again and make changes to the cables. I have enclosed photographs of the poor work.

I am requesting that you send an installer to correct the problems within two business days, make corrections at no charge, and refund the original installation fee.

Please contact me immediately at 312.555.1111. If you do not, I will file a complaint with the Better Business Bureau.

Sincerely,

Hugh Walsh

Hugh Walsh

> This letter of complaint has a clear purpose and employs a proper heading, salutation, and closing.

CHAPTER 2

Queen Victoria Middle School
123 Flower St.
Honolulu, Hawaii 96813

January 15, 20–

Ms. Laura Ramirez
Editor
NewLight Publishing
123 Avenue of the Americas
New York, NY 10010

Dear Ms. Ramirez:

My name is Kalani Ahana, a seventh grader from Hawaii, the 50th state of our country. I am writing to you in hopes that you will consider my story "Kimo and the Papaholua Sled" for publication in your student collection *Young Voices Across America*.

My story is about an ancient Hawaiian traditional sport we have here called lava sledding, or he'eholua. It is about a Hawaiian boy who proves his bravery by sledding down Kilauea, which is the earth's most active volcano, to save his little sister Leilani.

As a seventh grader at Queen Victoria Middle School, I have written several articles for our school newspaper and also won my school's creative writing contest for sixth graders last year. Furthermore, I take writing classes in an after-school program.

I have included a copy of my story with this letter. I would be happy to receive any criticism or advice about how to improve it for publication. It would be a great honor to be published in *Young Voices Across America*.

Sincerely,

Kalani Ahana

Kalani Ahana

Aloha from HAWAII

What Makes a Good Business Letter?

Hugh Walsh wrote a letter of complaint and Kalani Ahana wrote a letter of request, both of which are types of business letters. A business letter is a formal letter with a specific business-related purpose. Business letters also can include letters of application and gratitude. In the case of a letter of request, the purpose is to ask for information or action about a product or an event. Look at Kalani's letter, shown below, to see where the parts of a business letter are placed.

Heading
The writer's return address is in the top left-hand corner of the paper. The date should be placed two lines below the return address.

Salutation
The salutation is a greeting. It should read "Dear" (followed by the name of the receiver) or "To whom it may concern" and be followed by a colon.

Body
The body is the main part of a letter. The body is single-spaced, with a line between paragraphs and an extra line after the last paragraph. The paragraphs are not indented.

Closing
Use a complimentary closing such as "Sincerely" or "Sincerely yours," followed by a comma. Type your name four lines below the closing. Write your signature directly above your name.

Inside Address
The inside address includes the receiver's name and job title, as well as the company's name and address.

Queen Victoria Middle School
123 Flower St.
Honolulu, Hawaii 96813

January 15, 20–

Ms. Laura Ramirez
Editor
NewLight Publishing
123 Avenue of the Americas
New York, NY 10010

Dear Ms. Ramirez:

My name is Kalani Ahana, a seventh grader from Hawaii, the 50th state of our country. I am writing to you in hopes that you will consider my story "Kimo and the Papaholua Sled" for publication in your student collection *Young Voices Across America*.

My story is about an ancient Hawaiian traditional sport we have here called lava sledding, or he'eholua. It is about a Hawaiian boy who proves his bravery by sledding down Kilauea, which is the earth's most active volcano, to save his little sister Leilani.

As a seventh grader at Queen Victoria Middle School, I have written several articles for our school newspaper and also won my school's creative writing contest for sixth graders last year. Furthermore, I take writing classes in an after-school program.

I have included a copy of my story with this letter. I would be happy to receive any criticism or advice about how to improve it for publication. It would be a great honor to be published in *Young Voices Across America*.

Sincerely,

Kalani Ahana

Kalani Ahana

Structure of a Business Letter

The best business letters are confident, polite, and concise. A good business letter can be easy to recognize, but challenging to write. Here are some guidelines for writing effective business letters.

- Begin the first paragraph with a professional and polite opening sentence that states the purpose of the letter. Get right to the point, leaving out any unnecessary details.
- In the next paragraph or paragraphs, offer persuasive reasoning, examples, or other information to support your main point.
- In the closing paragraph, restate the purpose of the letter and ask for action if appropriate. If you are making a request, thank the recipient in advance for his or her help.

ACTIVITY A **Read the following sentences from letters of application. Evaluate them using the guidelines above. Which openings do not use a professional and polite tone? Which openings include information unrelated to the purpose of the letter?**

1. Jessica Kim mentioned that your babysitter moved out of state and will no longer be able to babysit, and she suggested that I contact you.

2. I'm a big fan of your store. I must spend $100 there every month.

3. Recently, I was let go from my job. It wasn't that I did bad work or anything; in fact, I was a really good worker. But now I need to find a new job.

4. I understand that your company is in search of customer service representatives who are bilingual in Spanish and English. My résumé will show you that I am a highly qualified candidate.

5. When you're done reading this letter, you'd be crazy not to hire me.

6. I would like to join my friends on a camping trip, so I am trying to earn as much money as I can by dog walking. I'm great with dogs, so I'm trying to walk as many as I can after school.

WRITER'S CORNER

Imagine that you are writing a business letter. Use your school's address as the return address. For the inside address, use the address of the person to whom you are writing. Write the return address, date, inside address, and salutation in the proper business-letter format.

Grammar in Action. Check pronoun usage in your letters. See Section 3.

Stating the Facts

When writing a letter of application, it is important to describe your qualifications. Begin with a summary, or a brief statement, of your experience, skills, and abilities. Be sure to focus on the qualifications that are most relevant to the position you seek.

You may wish to provide a concrete example to highlight a specific ability. Don't simply note that you can handle multiple tasks at once, for example, but mention that when babysitting, you sometimes supervise two active children, feed a baby, and make snacks at the same time.

When stating your qualifications, keep in mind that the reader has limited time and many application letters to read. Keep the letter short, highlighting only the skills that relate to the job opening. You don't want to bore your reader with every aspect of your life!

ACTIVITY B **The paragraphs below and on page 265 were taken from letters three people wrote to apply for a job at Guitar Mania. In each, the writer tried to summarize his or her qualifications for the job. Read the summaries, then answer the questions that follow them on page 265.**

1

I was walking through the mall yesterday when I saw that you were hiring new employees at Guitar Mania. I've always had a great love of guitar music and it's always been my dream to work in a big guitar store with a selection as large as yours. I think that guitars are one of the greatest creations. Aside from the fact that I've studied music (playing both guitar and drums), I have a really mixed taste—from rock to classical, country to rap, and R & B to metal. I love all types of music. When I was a kid, my parents always had the radio going. I was listening to the Ocean Dreams when I was five!

Additionally, I have always been a good salesman. Last year I sold the most raffle tickets for the homecoming festivities at our school, and I have helped out in numerous events where I've had to deal with lots of people. I volunteer at the school radio station on the weekends and have been able to spin in the DJ booth on several occasions. I'm sure that I'd be great working for you.

2

I have a strong background in music. I am an avid CD collector with more than 200 CDs, ranging from jazz to heavy metal. I listen to my MP3 player constantly and read music industry magazines, so I would be able to answer most of your customers' questions.

I also have experience as a receptionist and in customer service. Last year I helped out at my father's real estate office, greeting clients and providing them information as they waited to be helped. I also spent time putting his client lists in alphabetical order, a skill that would help me keep track of guitar inventory.

3

One reason I might be good for this position is that I love music. I have been playing the violin since I was four and am now in the school symphony. Brahms and Mahler are my favorite composers. I am working on a Brahms piece right now with my teacher. I will play it in a recital this spring. It is a difficult piece, but I like the challenge.

Another challenge that I enjoy is playing chess. I am a great chess player—able to concentrate for long periods of time and to think strategically. I also have lots of other great qualities, but I won't bore you with a list. I have all the qualities that a good employee should have.

1. Which summaries are not clear and concise?
2. What unrelated or unnecessary details are included in the summaries?
3. Which summaries include concrete examples of the person's qualifications? In what places could more concrete examples be included?
4. If you were the manager of Guitar Mania, which applicant would you be most likely to hire for the position? Why?

ACTIVITY C **Choose one of the summaries from Activity B that you think needs improvement. Rewrite the summary, making it clear and concise, removing unnecessary details, and adding concrete examples to improve it.**

WRITER'S CORNER

Imagine that you are competing for an interesting position you might want. In three or four sentences, summarize your qualifications for the job, using concise language and concrete examples.

Purpose, Audience, and Tone

Purpose

The first step in writing a good business letter is having a clear purpose and communicating it to your audience. Business letters can be written with many different purposes in mind. Here are a few common types of letters with a specific purpose.

- A letter of application is written to ask an employer to consider the sender for a job opening.
- A letter of request is written to ask for information about a product, an event, or a particular place.
- A letter of gratitude, such as the example on the right, is written to thank a person or company for a gift or service.
- A letter of complaint is written to complain about a faulty product, poor service, or misinformation.

LiNK

Dear Ms. Darnell:

Thank you for your confidence in Concord Advertising to promote your new business venture. We welcome the opportunity to assist you by providing top-quality marketing and advertising services. Our staff is available to you. I look forward to our meeting on Thursday to discuss details.

Sincerely,

Claire Johansson

Claire Johansson
President
Concord Advertising

Once you know what type of letter is called for, you can clarify the purpose by writing a purpose statement. You might not include this statement in the letter, but keep it in mind when writing the letter. In particular, remember the purpose statement when you write the opening and closing paragraphs of the letter, which state the purpose and sum it up.

Read the following purpose statement for someone writing a letter of complaint:

Watch the Time should know that the watch I purchased from them has stopped three times since I bought it two months ago, and I want them to replace it.

If you write a clear purpose statement before you begin the body of your letter, you will find it easier to organize and write your letter. When you finish writing your letter, look back at your purpose statement to make sure every sentence of your letter supports its purpose.

At the right is the body portion of one student's letter of request.

> Our class of 25 students would like to visit the police station. We have been studying people who work in the service professions, and we want to get a better idea of how the police department actually works. Our teacher has told us that you regularly give tours on Wednesday afternoons, and that is a good time for us. Please let us know what specific date would be best for us to come.

ACTIVITY A **Decide whether each sentence belongs in a letter of application, request, gratitude, or complaint.**

1. Everyone was thrilled with the picture you sent.

2. I know I would be the perfect candidate for this position.

3. Not only was the cover misleading, but the story was also poorly written.

4. I would be grateful if you could send me this hard-to-find CD.

5. The speech you gave left us at the edge of our seats.

6. I will call you later this week to set up an interview.

ACTIVITY B **Read the purpose statements below and use them to write an opening sentence for a business letter.**

1. I want to invite the author Lisa Lopez to visit our school.

2. The computer game I bought is missing the disk, and I need the manufacturer to send me a new one.

3. I had a great time at my birthday party at your restaurant last week, and I want to thank the restaurant's owner for the great service.

4. I want to complain about the rude service that I experienced recently at the Crafts 'n' More arts and crafts store.

5. I want to apply for a job as a cashier at the Food Town supermarket on Cedar Street.

WRITER'S CORNER

Think of a company to which you could write a business letter. Write a purpose statement describing why you would write the letter. What type of letter would it be?

Dear Representative Doakes:

My class is studying the rules on voting used by Congress. We are puzzled by the way Congress allowed itself to be given a raise in salary without voting for it...

With respect, Sir, we do not understand how you could accept a raise in salary and vote against school lunches...

If you have an explanation, my class and I would like to hear it.

Respectfully,

Daniel Shaftell

Daniel Shaftell

Audience

When writing a business letter, keep in mind that your audience is usually one person or at most very few people. Remember that your reader is likely to be busy, so be sure to get to the point quickly. If you are writing about a product or a job opportunity, your reader will probably be familiar with the subject of your letter.

Tone

The tone of a business letter should be polite and formal. If the purpose of the letter is to make a complaint, such as the example above, be careful not to be insulting or threatening. If the purpose of your letter is to apply for a job, be direct and confident as you explain why you are the right person for the job. Once you have written your letter, reread it with both its tone and your audience in mind. For a letter of application, ask yourself these questions.

- What might the reader think or feel about what I write?
- Will the reader think that my word choice is appropriate?
- Am I stating my qualifications in a way that is believable, or does it sound as though I am exaggerating?
- Is my tone confident and direct without sounding pushy?

When setting your tone, word choice is one of the most important things to consider. Though your tone should be formal, always choose the words that make your point most simply and clearly. If you are unsure if your words have the exact meaning that you intend, consult a dictionary.

ACTIVITY C **Under each business below are sentences from letters students sent to apply for jobs. Determine whether each set of sentences is appropriate for its audience. If not, suggest a way to improve it.**

1. Liberty Public Library

   I have almost two years of experience working in a stockroom of a sporting goods store. In my free time, I ride my bike and play games on a computer.

2. Daily Food Service

I'm familiar with the food industry because last year I worked part-time in a school cafeteria. My duties there included checking tickets and cleaning off tables.

3. Newton Ice-Skating Rink

I stocked shelves at a grocery store for two months. I think passing out skates at your rink will be more fun because I'll get to meet a lot of new people. I am definitely a person who does not care for boring jobs.

4. Maple Park Animal Shelter

My mother is a veterinarian, so most of my life has been spent around animals. I spent three months working at a music store last summer, where I learned how to help customers find what they were looking for.

5. Freezone Bike Shop

There is nothing more fun than riding a bike. I've been riding one since I was seven, and my older brother has taught me some great tricks. I could teach your customers new tricks too.

ACTIVITY D **Revise the sets of paragraphs below that are taken from business letters. Use a more appropriate tone.**

1. I'm so excited to hear from my friend Connor that I might have a chance to get a job at your store. I shop there all the time because you guys have the coolest clothes.

Just give me a call whenever you're free. I'll be totally thrilled if you hire me.

2. When I opened my spy kit that I bought last Wednesday, I was appalled. Even though the box said there would be a secret decoder inside, there was not. How am I supposed to decode secret messages without a decoder?

I'll be very angry if you don't send me a replacement right away. I'll have to tell my friends never to buy your products again.

WRITER'S CORNER

Imagine that you are writing two letters: a letter to a bike repair shop to explain your disappointment about the poor quality of the bike tune-up you received and a letter of application for a junior camp counselor position. Using examples, write two to three sentences to explain how your tone would differ for each audience.

Grammar in Action, Find the third personal pronoun in p. 268 excerpt.

Adjective Clauses

Mary McLeod Bethune

Like a cook with a rack of spices at hand, writers can choose from many options to spice up their sentences. A clause such as an adjective clause is one ingredient that can make your writing livelier.

A clause is a group of words containing a subject and a predicate. There are two main types of clauses: independent clauses and dependent clauses. An independent clause expresses a complete thought, and it can stand alone. A dependent clause, which does not express a complete thought, cannot stand alone.

Mary McLeod Bethune opened a school for girls in 1904, and she worked all her life to provide African Americans with an education.

Mary McLeod Bethune, who opened a school for girls in 1904, worked all her life to provide African Americans with an education.

Both sentences provide the same information, but their structure is different. The first sentence includes two independent clauses separated by a conjunction. In the second sentence, one independent clause becomes the dependent clause *who opened a school for girls in 1904.* Because the clause modifies the noun *Mary McLeod Bethune,* we call it an adjective clause.

Like adjectives, adjective clauses can modify a noun or a pronoun. They usually begin with relative pronouns such as *who, whom, which,* or *that.*

When to Use Adjective Clauses

Adjective clauses can improve your writing by shifting the emphasis, deepening the meaning, or increasing the variety of your sentences.

Shifting the emphasis: In the examples above, the use of an adjective clause shifts the emphasis of the sentence. In the first sentence, both facts about Mary McLeod Bethune are equally important. In the second sentence, the emphasis is shifted to the independent clause, which focuses on her life's work. The adjective clause *who opened a school for girls in 1904* becomes less important. Since it now merely gives extra information, it is set off by commas.

Deepening the meaning: Adjective clauses can also deepen the meaning of a sentence by giving more information.

> Bethune allowed parents who could not afford her school's tuition to send their children to her school for free.
>
> Bethune allowed parents who could not afford her school's tuition, which was 50 cents a week, to send their children to her school for free.

In the first sentence above, the writer included the essential information, but she wanted to tell more about the school's tuition. She included the information in an adjective clause. Since the new information was not essential to the sentence, she set it off by commas.

Adding variety: Finally, an adjective clause can be used to add variety to your sentences. In the examples below, three simple sentences are varied by making one of them an adjective clause.

> Bethune was born to former slaves. She rose to the highest positions in society. She worked for Presidents Calvin Coolidge, Herbert Hoover, and Theodore Roosevelt.
>
> Bethune, who was born to former slaves, rose to the highest positions in society. She worked for Presidents Calvin Coolidge, Herbert Hoover, and Theodore Roosevelt.

ACTIVITY A **Look back at the student letter of request on page 261. Find two adjective clauses. Why do you think each adjective clause was used instead of a separate sentence?**

Mary McLeod Bethune with her students, circa 1905

WRITER'S CORNER

Skim through a nonfiction selection, such as a book or a newspaper article, for examples of adjective clauses beginning with the relative pronouns *who, whom, which,* and *that.* Write down the examples you find.

Self-portrait of
Vincent van Gogh

ACTIVITY B **Name the independent clause in each of the following sentences with adjective clauses.**

1. My résumé, which is attached, includes some details about my work experience.
2. Kelly Taylor, who recommended I get in touch with you, believes I have the necessary skills for the job.
3. Brandon Paul, who works in the accounting office, spoke with me yesterday.
4. The job ad that I read on the Internet calls for someone with computer skills.
5. The person who informed me of the job is a former employee of yours.
6. My favorite instrument is a French horn, which is made of brass.
7. The painting that the student is copying was painted by van Gogh.
8. The woman who is waving at everyone from a car is the governor.
9. Greenland, which is on the Arctic Circle, is not green but mostly white with ice.
10. The horse that is whinnying is an Appaloosa.

ACTIVITY C **Revise the following sentences to change the emphasis.**

Bedroom in Arles, Vincent van Gogh, 1888

1. The cardboard box, which is clearly labeled, contains bandages and iodine.
2. Anna Spokane, who drives the ice-cream truck, lives in my neighborhood.
3. My father's watch, which is a family heirloom, hasn't run for 20 years.
4. Our vacation, which was the best vacation ever, took place on the coast of California.
5. The rabbit, which was my brother's pet, escaped yesterday.
6. Polaris, which is often called the North Star, is always due north.
7. Li, who is 12, has a paper route.
8. Orangutans, which are a kind of ape, walk along tree branches.
9. *The Nutcracker,* which is a famous ballet, is often performed during the holiday season.
10. Vatican City, which is in Rome, is the smallest independent state in the world.

ACTIVITY D Combine each pair of sentences to form a longer sentence with an adjective clause. Let the first sentence of the pair be the main idea of the new sentence.

1. Nadia dreams of participating in the Olympics. Nadia has won two first-place awards in gymnastics.

2. Playing tennis is Sam's favorite activity. Playing tennis requires great concentration.

3. The llama does not have a hump. The llama is in the camel family.

4. Meerkats inhabit the Kalahari Desert in southern Africa. Meerkats are relatives of the mongoose.

5. That computer is on sale this week. Jack likes that computer best.

6. In winter some mammals go into a deep sleep. This sleep is called hibernation.

7. Grammar is taught in schools throughout the world. It is the study of the structure of a language.

8. The first working submarine was built in 1620. It was a wooden frame covered with greased leather.

9. Graffiti refers to writing on walls. It comes from the Italian word for "scratchings."

10. The labradoodle is a new breed of dog. It is a combination of a Labrador retriever and a poodle.

ACTIVITY E Rewrite the following paragraph by combining some of the sentences with adjective clauses.

Some products may no longer be readily available. These products were once easy to buy. For example, when Mom was little, she ate a product called a push-up. This wasn't ice cream. It was orange sherbet in a striped tube. At the bottom of the tube was a stick. You pushed the stick to raise the sherbet. There is another product that can no longer be bought in most places. The candy consisted of small, multicolored gobs of sugar. The gobs were hard and sweet. The gobs were attached to a narrow sheet of white paper. The paper was a little like the tape from a cash register. Can you buy these products where you live?

WRITER'S CORNER

Write a five-sentence paragraph that describes yourself or a friend. Then expand it, adding an adjective clause to each sentence.

Roots

A root is the base from which a word is built. Finding a root inside a word can help you understand its meaning. For example, suppose you read the word *various* in a book. You realize that the root *vari* looks similar to the word *vary*. *Vary* means "to change" or "to make different," and *various* means "differing from one another." When you see or hear words with the same root, such as *variable* and *variety,* you'll have a better idea of what the words mean.

Many roots come from the Latin and Greek languages. Some roots, such as *photo,* can stand alone as a word. Other roots are used only with other word parts, such as prefixes and suffixes, added to them. Below are some common roots and their meanings. Which of them can stand alone as a word?

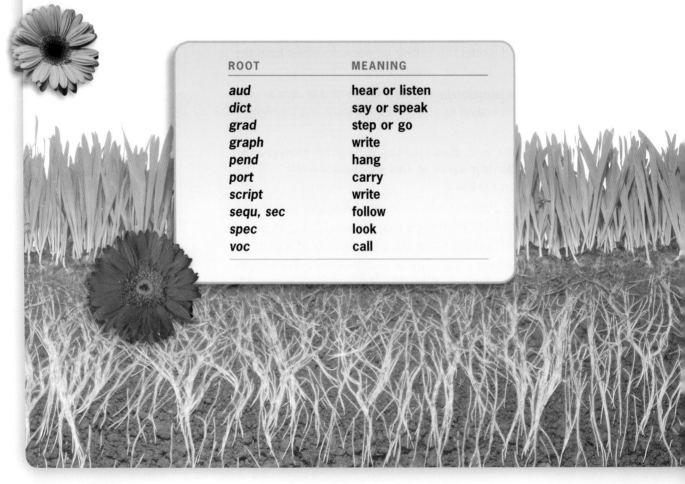

ROOT	MEANING
aud	hear or listen
dict	say or speak
grad	step or go
graph	write
pend	hang
port	carry
script	write
sequ, sec	follow
spec	look
voc	call

ACTIVITY A **Complete each of the following sentences, using a word with the root shown in parentheses.**

1. When you get the job, you will (*port*) to a supervisor.
2. When writing a business letter, it is important to consider your (*aud*).
3. Be sure to state your purpose in the opening (*graph*).
4. When you finish your letter, be sure to (*spec*) it for any misspellings or other errors.
5. It helps to take an internship to see if a particular job might become your (*voc*).
6. After purchasing special pens, Isabel created her own summer job by doing (*graph*) for formal invitations.
7. Be careful filling out a form, such as dates, so that your answers do not (*dict*) themselves.

ACTIVITY B **The following words use roots from the chart on page 274. Using the chart, write down what you think each word might mean. Then use a dictionary to check each definition.**

1. audiophile
2. speculation
3. gradual
4. impending
5. dictatorial
6. invocation
7. telegraph
8. prescription
9. sequential
10. portage
11. pendulum
12. suspend

WRITER'S CORNER

Reread the letter on page 260 and identify words that contain roots from the chart on page 274. Write down the words, then write a sentence using each word.

More Common Roots

Here are several more commonly used roots.

ROOT	MEANING	EXAMPLE
aqu	water	aqueduct
bio	life	biography
cise	cut	incision
dem	people	demographic
fin	end	finite
man	hand	manual
scope	see or watch	periscope

ACTIVITY C **Use a dictionary to find the definition for each example word above. Then find another word that contains each root.**

ACTIVITY D **Identify the words in the following paragraph that contain the roots you have studied throughout this lesson. Then write a definition for each word.**

After I graduate from college, I think my vocation will be in the field of biology. As a biologist, I can use a microscope to inspect the characteristics of aquatic microorganisms. Or I can study the germs that could cause an epidemic. After I am famous, I can write my autobiography and have it exported to other parts of the world.

ACTIVITY E **Use the root to help you find the appropriate word to complete each sentence.**

1. *port*

   a. One basic _____ of the United States to other countries is technology.

   b. Nikki has a _____ TV, which goes with her everywhere.

   c. The island of Hawaii _____ many items from the mainland.

2. *graph*
   a. Marcos draws pictures on his computer, which are called computer _____.
   b. That famous movie star, who likes to keep her privacy, seldom signs _____ for fans.
   c. She addressed the wedding invitations in _____.

3. *pend*
   a. The clouds quickly darkened, and we sensed the _____ storm.
   b. The swinging _____ on the grandfather clock is hypnotic.
   c. Malia wore her grandmother's _____ on her anniversary.

4. *dict*
   a. Look up words you don't know in a _____.
   b. Speak clearly and use good _____ when giving a speech.
   c. The _____ spoke with force to the crowd.

5. *grad*
   a. Will you be 17 or 18 when you _____ from high school?
   b. French was difficult to learn, but _____ I was able to say more and more words.
   c. Do you have your cap and gown for your _____ ceremony?

6. *aud*
   a. The _____ clapped loudly after the play.
   b. You must speak in an _____ voice when giving a speech.
   c. We put on headphones to participate in the _____ part of the tour.

7. *script*
   a. My aunt added a _____ about my cousin to the end of her letter.
   b. Tom just finished writing a 200-page _____ for a book on crime.
   c. My father renewed his _____ to the newspaper.

WRITER'S CORNER

capture • captivate • capacity

What is the root that these words have in common? What do you think the root means? What makes you think so? Look up the words in a dictionary to check if you are right.

Tech Tip With an adult, use an online dictionary.

Writing Tools

Summary

A **summary** is a condensed version of a text or other source, written in your own words. When you summarize an informational text, you restate only the main points.

To summarize a story, you restate only important elements such as the main characters, the main events, the plot, and the theme. In a business letter, you may want to summarize only the main points. In the student's letter presented at the beginning of this chapter, the student summarizes the story she wrote for submission to the publisher, as well as her experience as a writer.

A summary can be as long as one-third the length of the original or as short as one sentence.

> **Over the past two years, I have had several jobs that I believe have given me the experience to take on the position of beach attendant for your country club.**

Paraphrasing

Paraphrasing is restating individual passages of a work in your own words. It is more detailed than a summary. Researchers, book reviewers, and other writers generally paraphrase the supporting details of a work's main ideas. It also helps writers avoid using too many direct quotations.

Direct Quotation

A **direct quotation** contains words that are identical to the original text. It must match the original text word for word. A quotation should be enclosed in quotation marks.

Whether you summarize, paraphrase, or quote, you must attribute your information to its original source. Taking someone else's research, words, or ideas and presenting them as your own is plagiarism. It is considered stealing. Be sure to cite others' work no matter what type of medium it comes from, including Web sites, blogs, or films.

Below is a brief summary of a novella called *The Old Man and the Sea* by Ernest Hemingway.

> **The Old Man and the Sea takes place in Cuba. It is a story about a poor, old fisherman named Santiago and his epic struggle with a giant marlin. Santiago is considered an unlucky fisherman by others in his village because he has gone many days without being able to catch a fish. Finally, one day he hooks a giant marlin, but it is so large that it drags him out to sea. Santiago and the fish fight for many days, and Santiago gains a feeling of love and respect for the fish.**

Reread the personal narrative "Meeting Becca" in Chapter 1 on page 223. How would you summarize it? Here is a summary of "Meeting Becca."

> **"Meeting Becca" is about a six-year-old girl, Ellie, who has moved to a new house and meets a new friend named Becca.**

ACTIVITY A **In two or three sentences, summarize the following fable.**

The Raven and the Fox

Mr. Raven was perched upon a limb,
And Reynard the Fox looked up at him;
For the Raven held in his great big beak
A morsel the Fox would go far to seek.

Said the Fox, in admiring tones: "My word!
Sir Raven, you are a handsome bird.
Such feathers! If you would only sing,
The birds of these woods would call you King."

The Raven, who did not see the joke,
Forgot that his voice was just a croak.
He opened his beak, in his foolish pride—
And down fell the morsel the Fox had spied.

Ha-ha!" said the Fox. "And now you see
You should not listen to flattery.
Vanity, Sir is a horrid vice—
I'm sure the lesson is worth the price."

Tech Tip With an adult, find a book review online.

To paraphrase, read and then reread the original text until you are sure you understand it. Then explain what you have learned in your own words. Follow these tips:

- Highlight or flag important words, phrases, or sentences central to the meaning of the text.
- Do not change special terms or proper names.
- Do not "copy-and-paste" from online sources.
- Check your paraphrase against the original to make sure you did not miss any important information.
- Put quotation marks around any phrase you quoted directly from the original source.

Read the following original source and the paraphrase.

Original Source
Each year, more than 700,000 children ages 14 and under are treated in hospital emergency rooms for sports-related injuries. Most of the injuries are the result of falls, being struck by an object (like a bat or a ball), collisions with other participants, and overexertion during informal sports activities. If all children were trained to properly warm up before all such activities, and properly educated in the use of safety equipment, this number could be drastically reduced. ("Children's Injuries in Sports Focus Study Results," Dr. R.J. Banger)

Paraphrase
Many childhood injuries are due to participating in unsupervised sports activities. Doctors recommend that children be taught to stretch properly and to wear safety equipment to prevent injuries.

Good writers often combine summarizing, paraphrasing, and direct quotations. Read the following scientific summary that has a summary, a paraphrase, and a direct quotation.

According to researchers at the International Climate Institute, the last decade has been the warmest decade ever recorded and is causing massive changes to our planet. — **Summary**

Dr. Hans Stein uses examples such as the melting ice caps and the often fatal heat waves of Europe to support his assertion that this climate change has deadly consequences for the planet. — **Paraphrase**

"With the melting ice caps on many of the world's mountain peaks, people in some regions are already running out of fresh water," Stein states in his report. — **Direct Quotation**

280

Remember that if you use the original language—even in a paraphrase—it is still considered plagiarism unless you use quotation marks.

To avoid plagiarizing, follow these steps.

1. Use many different sources when conducting research on a topic. Different experts present similar information in different ways and in different words.
2. Set aside your research material.
3. Think critically about what you have read. How was the information from different sources similar? How was it different?
4. Draw your own conclusions and then start making notes. Find your own words to express your thoughts.
5. Go back to your sources to make sure you have not plagiarized anyone's words.

ACTIVITY B **In two or three sentences, paraphrase the following excerpt from Paul Lacroix's "Manners, Customs and Dress During the Middle Ages and During the Renaissance Period."**

Heads of families, on becoming attached to the soil, naturally had other wants and other customs than those which they had delighted in when they were only the chiefs of wandering adventurers. The strength of their followers was not now so important to them as the security of their castles. Fortresses took the place of armed bodies; and at this time, every one who wished to keep what he had, entrenched himself to the best of his ability at his own residence. The banks of rivers, elevated positions, and all inaccessible heights, were occupied by towers and castles, surrounded by ditches, which served as strongholds to the lords of the soil. These places of defence soon became points for attack. Out of danger at home, many of the nobles kept watch like birds of prey on the surrounding country, and were always ready to fall, not only upon their enemies, but also on their neighbours, in the hope either of robbing them when off their guard, or of obtaining a ransom for any unwary traveller who might fall into their hands. Everywhere society was in ambuscade, and waged civil war—individual against individual—without peace or mercy. Such was the reign of feudalism.

WRITER'S CORNER

Write a five-sentence review of your favorite book. Include a summary of the book and either a paraphrase or use one direct quotation.

Tech Tip Post your review on the class blog.

Job Interview

Have you ever interviewed another person? You may have interviewed a classmate or an adult for a school assignment. Has anyone ever interviewed you? An interview is an arranged meeting with one or more people for the purpose of asking questions to gain information. More specifically, the purpose of a job interview is to meet a job applicant and evaluate his or her qualifications for the job.

Making a positive first impression is important because the employer may have several other job candidates to interview besides you.

Tips for a Positive First Impression

- Be sure to arrive for the interview on time.
- Remember to smile and make eye contact with your interviewer.
- Introduce yourself and shake hands with the interviewer when you first meet.
- Shake hands with the interviewer at the end and thank him or her for meeting with you.
- Answer questions in complete sentences, giving examples of your accomplishments as they relate to the question.

Preparing for the Interview Questions

To prepare for an interview, it's always a good idea to practice how you will answer the interviewer's questions. As you practice, speak in a confident, businesslike tone and use examples to highlight your qualifications. Think about how you would answer these questions.

1. What can you tell me about yourself?
2. Why should we hire you?
3. What are your strengths and weaknesses?
4. What are your plans for the future?
5. What do you know about our organization?

ACTIVITY A Read each interview question and decide which of the two answers is better. Explain why.

1. Tell me about yourself.
   a. I was born in a small town. I have two sisters.
   b. I am a senior in high school. The subjects I excel in are math and Spanish.

2. What are your strengths?
   a. I'm hardworking. I like the satisfaction of doing something well.
   b. I'm not sure. I guess I'm good at skateboarding and soccer.

3. What are your plans for the future?
   a. I'll definitely be going to Notre Dame in the fall.
   b. I'd like to make lots of money so I can retire early.

4. What are your weaknesses?
   a. I don't think I have any weaknesses.
   b. I haven't always been very neat, but I'm getting better at keeping things tidy.

5. Why should we hire you?
   a. I have the kind of education and work experience you are seeking.
   b. I heard you have great benefits and workers get a long lunch break.

6. How did you like your last job?
   a. I had an awful boss who was always telling me to do pointless work. They didn't pay me enough either.
   b. My boss taught me the value of working hard. I learned a lot about working in a retail store.

7. What do you know about our organization?
   a. I just answered as many job openings that I could, so I'm hoping to learn more during the interview.
   b. Before the interview, I looked up your organization online to get more background information.

SPEAKER'S CORNER

Think of a company for whom you would like to work and what position you would like. Then imagine having an interview there. Write your answers to the questions in Activity A. Practice responding to each question. Then compare your answers with a partner.

Additional Interview Questions

The more questions you practice answering, the less chance there is that you will be caught off guard by an interview question. By practicing a wide variety of questions, you will also be much more confident and comfortable in an interview. Here are several more questions you might be asked during an interview.

- What did you like about your previous job experiences?
- What didn't you like about your previous job experiences?
- How do you handle conflict?
- How much money do you think this work is worth?
- When can you start?
- Do you have any questions?

The End of the Interview

When the interviewer indicates that the interview is over, shake the interviewer's hand and thank him or her for meeting with you. If the interviewer does not tell you when to expect to hear from him or her, you might ask a question such as "When will you make a decision?"

Listening Tips

Sometimes employers will begin an interview by telling you about the job and the company or organization. Listening to this information is important because it may be helpful later in answering the interviewer's questions.

Eye contact, appropriate body language, and follow-up questions are three ways in which you can show the interviewer that you are listening.

While the interviewer is speaking, make eye contact and use appropriate body language, such as nodding your head, as you listen. Looking down, crossing your arms, or slouching in your seat can signal a lack of respect or other negative qualities about how you respond to others.

Ask follow-up questions to find out more about the job and to show the interviewer that you were listening. However, wait for the right time to ask questions so that you do not interrupt the interviewer.

ACTIVITY B Read the following eight interview questions and match them with the best answer.

_____ **1.** How do you handle disagreements?

_____ **2.** What did you like about your previous job?

_____ **3.** What didn't you like about your previous job?

_____ **4.** What is something about yourself that you would like to improve?

_____ **5.** What do you know about our company?

_____ **6.** How much money do you want to earn per hour?

_____ **7.** When can you start?

_____ **8.** Why should I hire you and not someone else?

a. Let me check my calendar. My first available day would be next Monday.

b. I liked that my supervisor trusted me to take on more responsibility over time.

c. I take a deep breath and try to talk through the problem with the other person.

d. I would want to earn no less than $10.50 per hour because that's how much I was making in the final month of my previous job.

e. I disliked not being assigned as many hours as I had been promised when I started the job.

f. I am a hard worker with the experience and skills that make me a perfect fit for this position and your company.

g. People say that I am a perfectionist. I need to relax and not worry if things are not just right.

h. I did a little research before I applied for the position. I looked up your company online and also asked my neighbor about it. She orders supplies from you.

Prewriting and Drafting

Have you ever written a business letter or read a formal letter that a friend or family member wrote? Did the letter request something specific? When writing a business letter that requests a response, it is important to be as specific as possible in order to achieve what you want.

Writer's Tip It is important that the letter be written in a polite and professional tone, especially in a letter of application.

Prewriting

Before composing a letter, a writer uses prewriting techniques to identify the subject of the letter, explore ideas, and plan the letter.

 Before writing a letter of application, you can use prewriting techniques to brainstorm a job to apply for and to freewrite skills and experiences that qualify you for that particular job.

Choose a Job

Before writing a letter of application, you should know what type of job you want to apply for. You should also find out which companies are hiring in your area or think of a company that you would like to work for.

The first step is to consider your background, knowledge, and experience. What are you good at? What kind of work has given you satisfaction in the past? What talents and qualities can you bring to a job? What kind of job would allow you to use those talents and qualities? You may find it useful to brainstorm a list of jobs, then choose the one that most appeals to you.

Once a job seeker has chosen the type of job to apply for, he or she will research which companies or organizations have openings for that job. Here are a few ways to search for a job.

1. Use a job search engine on the Internet.
2. Talk to friends and family members who may have heard of job openings in their company or in the community.
3. Read the job postings in your local newspaper.

Megan, a seventh grader, decided to look for a summer job in which she could work with kids. The job listings that she found in the newspaper did not appeal to her, but a friend told her about a flyer on a park bulletin board advertising for an assistant at a summer camp for kids called Camp Tiny Tots. She decided to apply for this job.

Your Turn

Follow these steps to help you get started.

1. Make a list of your skills and interests.
2. Brainstorm a list of jobs that relate to those skills and interests.
3. Make up a job at a real or an imaginary employer where you would like to work. If you need ideas, look through newspaper listings or simply choose a nearby business to whom you could address a letter of application.

Recreational Assistant Needed

Camp Tiny Tots is looking for a dependable, energetic recreational assistant for our summer camp. Past experience and training required. If interested, please contact Camp Tiny Tots at (616) 555-1234.

Plan Your Letter of Application

Before writing a letter of application, a writer might plan it by writing down ideas, using the following steps:

1. List your positive qualities, skills, and talents. Which qualities would you emphasize in your letter? Which of these skills or talents relate to the job you want?

2. Write down ways that your previous jobs, volunteering experiences, or other activities are similar to and might help with the job you are seeking.

3. Write what you know about the company or organization, including one or two things that are particularly appealing to you.

4. Summarize the reasons why the prospective employer should hire you.

Before writing her letter of application, Megan planned her letter by following the steps listed above. At this point, she was freewriting, focusing mainly on writing down any ideas that came to mind. Here is what she wrote.

1. truthful, dependable, energetic, organized, always on time, plays the violin, good runner

2. worked as a babysitter, took first-aid course

3. brother Danny was in Camp Tiny Tots, counselors seemed nice

4. We would have a great time working together. I would do a good job.

Your Turn

Plan your own letter of application by following the steps listed.

Writer's Tip Review your ideas with a friend or family member.

Prewriting
Drafting
Content Editing
Revising
Copyediting
Proofreading
Publishing

Drafting

Megan is writing her letter of application to the person in charge of hiring recreational assistants at Camp Tiny Tots. Her friend, who works at the camp, told Megan the director's name so that she could use it in the salutation. Megan reviewed her prewriting notes and used them to help her write her first draft.

341 Orchid Street
Grandville, MI 49418
(616) 555-7864

April 30, 20–

Ms. Diane Santos
Camp Tiny Tots Program Director
Park District of Grandville
1854 Wilson Ave.
Grandville, MI 49418

Dear Ms. Santos,

I saw your job posting for a Camp tiny tots recreational assistant on a bulletin board. Ever since my brother started going there, I have been impressed by the friendly staff and how good the program is.

I recently completed the Safe Sitter course at Grandville Hospital. I babysit for many families in the community. I am also truthful, dependible, energetic, and always on time. I even play the violin!

Because of my experience and skills, I would be well-suited to this position. I can't wait to meet with you to tell you how much I want this job. You can call me and let me know when I can come in for an interview. We would have a great time working together!

Your future assistant,

Megan Bailey
Megan Bailey

Organizing Your Letter

The body of Megan's letter begins by telling how she found out about the job. The second paragraph focuses on her background and skills

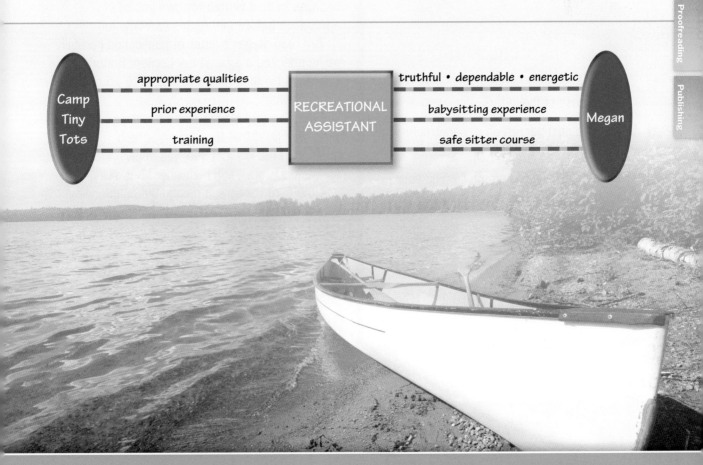 Organization

as they relate to the job. She created the graphic organizer below to help her see how her skills and background fit the job requirements. The closing paragraph expresses her desire to interview for the job. These are followed by the closing and signature.

Follow this organization when you write your letter. The opening paragraph should let the reader know that you are applying for a job. The next paragraph or paragraphs should state your qualifications and explain why you are the right person for the job. The closing paragraph should sum up the letter and ask for a response.

Your Turn

Look at your answers from the prewriting exercise on page 286 and apply them as you write your first draft. Keep in mind that this is only the first stage of the writing process, so be ready to review and revise your first draft.

Remember that you are writing for a person with the authority to decide whether or not to hire you. Keep your tone professional and polite as you persuade the employer that you are the best candidate for the job.

Writer's Tip Leave space for revisions by double-spacing your letter.

Camp Tiny Tots
- appropriate qualities
- prior experience
- training

RECREATIONAL ASSISTANT

Megan
- truthful • dependable • energetic
- babysitting experience
- safe sitter course

Prewriting

Drafting

Content Editing

Revising

Copyediting

Proofreading

Publishing

Content Editing

 Sentence Fluency Good writers revise their letters to make them better. They begin by content editing, focusing mainly on the ideas of the letter to make certain that they are clear, complete, logical, and well organized.

Many writers follow a checklist while editing their drafts. The following is an example of a checklist that writers might use to help them edit their drafts.

Content Editor's Checklist

- ☐ Does the opening paragraph clearly state the purpose of the letter?

- ☐ Does the next paragraph or paragraphs state your skills and qualifications?

- ☐ Does the closing paragraph sum up your letter and request further action?

- ☐ Does every sentence fit the topic of its paragraph?

- ☐ Have unnecessary details been removed?

- ☐ Is the tone professional, confident, and direct?

- ☐ Is there a variety in sentence length?

Writer's Tip Writers often choose to mark their changes with a colored pencil to keep their changes clear and legible.

Once writers make their own revisions, they often ask someone else to read their draft.

Megan read the letter she had written and made a few changes to the content. Then she asked her brother Tim to read it. She needed someone who already knew her skills and abilities so that she could make sure she was emphasizing the ones that related most to the job. Megan knew that her brother would give her good feedback because he had written his own letters of application before getting his part-time job.

Tim read Megan's letter of application carefully as he checked it against the Content Editor's Checklist. He then met with Megan to go over his revisions.

First, Tim told Megan about the things he liked. Tim liked that the first paragraph mentioned the job that she was applying for, the second paragraph highlighted her skills, and the third paragraph mentioned an interview as the next step.

However, he noted some things in the letter that could be improved. Here are Tim's comments.

- In the first paragraph, you need to say that you're applying for the job. Maybe you could also be more specific about where you saw the flyer.
- Your second paragraph should start with a sentence that ties together the sentences about qualities, skills, and work experience.
- I like the information about the Safe Sitter course you took, but could you be more specific about what you learned in the course? Also, I'm not sure that your reader will care that you play the violin.
- I like your closing sentence, but could you make it even more memorable?
- You should probably change your closing to a standard closing for a business letter, such as *Sincerely*.

Your Turn

Look over your first draft, using the Content Editor's Checklist. Check to make sure that you have included all the important information. Then check that every idea is in the right place and that the letter flows logically.

Trade letters of application with a partner. Refer to the Content Editor's Checklist as you read your partner's letter.

Writer's Tip When you have finished reading your partner's first draft, give your honest opinion of how you think the letter could be improved. Remember to comment on the strengths of the letter first.

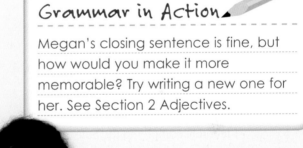

Grammar in Action

Megan's closing sentence is fine, but how would you make it more memorable? Try writing a new one for her. See Section 2 Adjectives.

Prewriting
Drafting
Content Editing
Revising
Copyediting
Proofreading
Publishing

Revising

Here are the revisions Megan made to her draft after content editing with Tim.

**341 Orchid Street
Grandville, MI 49418
(616) 555-7864**

April 30, 20–

Ms. Diane Santos
Camp Tiny Tots Program Director
Park District of Grandville
1854 Wilson Ave.
Grandville, MI 49418

Dear Ms. Santos,

am writing in response to   that I saw recently   at Springdale Park
I saw your job posting for a Camp tiny tots recreational assistant on a bulletin board.

Ever since my brother started going there, I have been impressed by the friendly staff
             the overall quality of the program. I would be proud to join the staff of Camp Tiny Tots.
and how good the program is.

                                        I was Red Cross certified in basic first aid and CPR.
I recently completed the Safe Sitter course at Grandville Hospital. I babysit for many

families in the community. I am also truthful, dependible, energetic, and always on

time. I even play the violin!

Because of my experience and skills, I would be well-suited to this position. I can't
It would be a pleasure to meet with you to discuss this opportunity. Please   at the number
wait to meet with you to tell you how much I want this job. You can call me and
above to arrange
let me know when I can come in for an interview. We would have a great time
Working with you would make this the best summer ever!
working together!

Sincerely,
Your future assistant,

Megan Bailey
Megan Bailey

Megan had taken notes on Tim's comments about her letter. She used his comments to guide her improvements.

- First, she revised the opening paragraph to make it state the purpose more clearly. What information did she add?

- Where did Megan move the first sentence in the third paragraph so that it fits better?

- She added more details about what she learned at the Safe Sitter course. What information did she take out because it is irrelevant?

- Next, how did Megan rework her closing statement so that it would have more of an impact on the reader?

- Finally, she followed Tim's suggestion about replacing her closing. What word did she use?

When Megan looked back over her draft, she realized that the tone of her letter could be changed to sound more professional. In the first paragraph, she replaced the words *how good the program is* with *the overall quality of the program*. She realized that the last paragraph also needed a more professional tone. She consulted a library book on writing letters of application to find

 **Voice** examples of good closing paragraphs. She used the examples she found to write a more direct and professional-sounding closing paragraph.

Your Turn

Now it's your turn to use your own content editor's suggestions to revise your draft. Continue to add any revisions of your own that you think will make the letter even better.

When you have finished making your revisions, go over the Content Editor's Checklist one more time.

Once you are satisfied with the content of your letter, type your revised draft.

Writer's Tip Have you addressed all the points in the checklist? If not, continue making revisions until you have.

Prewriting

Drafting

Content Editing

Revising

Copyediting

Proofreading

Publishing

Copyediting and Proofreading

Copyediting

Megan decided to wait a little while before reading her letter of application again. She wanted to read her letter with fresh eyes so that she could make it even better.

Megan returned to her draft a few hours later. She checked each sentence for logic, clarity, word choice, and grammar, using the following checklist.

Copyeditor's Checklist

- [ ] Are all words spelled correctly?
- [ ] Is the grammar accurate?
- [ ] Are any words redundant, unnecessary, or misused?
- [ ] Was the revision checked to make certain that no new errors were introduced?
- [ ] Is the structure of each sentence logical and grammatically correct?
- [ ] Is the letter written in the format of a business letter?

Megan noticed that a few of the words were redundant or unnecessary. She deleted the word *job* in the first sentence because she had mentioned that it was a posting for a recreational assistant. She also deleted the name of the program in the first sentence because Ms. Santos would know which program Megan was talking about.

 Word Choice

Megan then checked her word choice. In the second paragraph, she realized that *honest* fit more closely with her intended meaning than *truthful* did. She also replaced the phrase *always on time* with *punctual* to make it fit better in the sentence. Finally, Megan moved the heading to the left side of the paper to fit the format of a business letter.

Your Turn

Look over your own revised draft. At this stage, focus more on the sentences and your word choice than on your ideas.

Prewriting

Drafting

Content Editing

Revising

Copyediting

Proofreading

Publishing

Grammar in Action

Identify which two sentences Megan could combine using an adjective clause to show how the two ideas are connected. See Section 2.5.

Proofreading

Before printing the finished letter of application,  a good writer will proofread the draft to check for correct spelling, punctuation, capitalization, and grammar.

The following checklist is a useful aid for proofreading business letters.

Since a new pair of eyes will sometimes catch errors that the writer may have overlooked, it is a good idea to ask someone else to proofread your letter.

Megan asked her friend Claudia to proofread her letter because she knew that Claudia was a good speller and had a good eye for punctuation mistakes. Claudia followed the Proofreader's Checklist.

In the first paragraph, Claudia saw that Megan had forgotten to capitalize the title of the program, Camp Tiny Tots. She noticed that the word *dependable* was misspelled in the second paragraph. Finally, she discovered that Megan had used a comma in her salutation instead of a colon.

Your Turn

1. Read your letter of application carefully against the Proofreader's Checklist. Read it once for each item on the list.
2. When you have gone through the checklist, trade your letter with a partner. Go through your partner's letter in the same way you proofread your letter.

Proofreader's Checklist

☐ Is there a line of space before each new paragraph?

☐ Are all words spelled correctly? Use a dictionary if needed.

☐ Is the grammar accurate?

☐ Are capitalization and punctuation correct?

☐ Was the revision checked to make certain that no new errors were introduced?

Publishing

At the end of the writing process, a good writer checks the letter one more time before mailing it to a prospective employer. Megan read her letter of application once more before deciding that it was just right. Then she carefully typed her letter, read it once again, and signed her name in ink. Megan folded her letter and put it in an addressed and stamped envelope. She was ready to send her letter of application to the director of the Tiny Tots program.

341 Orchid Street
Grandville, MI 49418

April 30, 20–

Ms. Diane Santos
Camp Tiny Tots Program Director
Park District of Grandville
1854 Wilson Ave.
Grandville, MI 49418

Dear Ms. Santos:

I am writing in response to your posting for a recreational assistant that I saw recently on a bulletin board at Springdale Park. Ever since my brother started going there, I have been impressed by the friendly staff and the overall quality of the program. I would be proud to join the staff of Camp Tiny Tots.

Because of my experience and skills, I would be well-suited to this position. I recently completed the Safe Sitter course at Grandville Hospital, where I was Red Cross certified in basic first aid and CPR. In addition, I babysit for many families in the community and love spending time with young children. I am also honest, punctual, dependable, and energetic.

It would be a pleasure to meet with you to discuss this opportunity. Please call me at (616) 555-7864 to arrange an interview. Working with you will make this the best summer ever!

Sincerely,

Megan Bailey

Megan Bailey

There are many ways you can publish your letter. As a class, decide if you will publish your letters using the same publishing method or do them differently. However you choose to publish, be sure you present your best.

 Mail or e-mail your letter. If you mail it, see below how you address an envelope and fold the letter. Don't forget to sign it.

 Make a classroom newsletter. Include your letter and your classmates' in a Jobs Wanted section.

 Post your letter on a bulletin board. Label the board "Jobs Wanted" and post your letter of application along with your classmates' letters.

 Post your letter on your classroom's wiki, blog, or Web site. You can receive comments about your letter and review others' work.

 Create a job-finding portfolio to use as a model later. You may not be ready now to get a job, but you may have to refer to this letter and your classmates' letters in the future to help you write a specific letter for that perfect job.

Your Turn

Use your best handwriting or a computer to make your final copy. Then sign your name below the closing.

 Presentation

Read it once more to make sure all the necessary corrections have been made and no new errors have been introduced.

Choose one of the publishing methods. If you choose to mail your letter, follow these steps.

1. Fold it into thirds. Begin by folding the bottom third of the paper up.
2. Next, fold the top third of the paper down.
3. Finally, press the folds firmly so that the letter is flat.
4. Take a business-sized envelope and type (or write) the receiver's name and address in the center of the front of the envelope. Use the two-letter abbreviation for the state followed by the zip code. In the upper left, type your return address. Place the stamp in the upper right.

341 Orchid Street
Grandville, MI 49418

Ms. Diane Santos
Camp Tiny Tots Program Director
Park District of Grandville
1854 Wilson Ave.
Grandville, MI 49418

How-to Articles

LiNK

How to Whistle with Two Fingers

from *The Daring Book for Girls*
by Andrea J. Buchanan and Miriam Peskowitz

Make a triangle with your pinkies by putting your pinkie fingertips together, palms and fingers facing towards you. Stick out your tongue and put your pinkie-tips right on the center of it, pushing your tongue strongly against your fingers where they meet. Push your tongue back into your mouth with your fingers, so that your pinkie fingers are inside your mouth up to the first knuckles. Angle your pinkie-tips slightly down, just behind your bottom teeth, and keep your tongue pressing into your fingers. Purse your lips and blow. You may have to adjust the angle of your fingers to get that sound right, but just practice and before you know it you'll be hailing cabs with your piercing two-finger whistle!

> With its use of imperative sentences and clear steps written in chronological order, this excerpt from *The Daring Book for Girls* effectively demonstrates a how-to article.

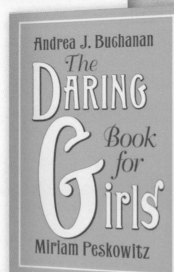

Andrea J. Buchanan
The DARING *Book for* Girls
Miriam Peskowitz

How to Eat Spaghetti

John Loftus
Room 357

We have all been there—eating spaghetti at a friend's house and making a production out of it. Sauce gets all over your face and splashes on your shirt as you suck in the spaghetti strands. You twist it up tight on your fork, but then it falls off and splashes onto the plate, or, worse yet, on your lap. Well, I'm going to tell you how to eat a plate of spaghetti without making a scene.

Since we're all familiar with twining the spaghetti on our forks, this method just adds on to that first step. Let's begin with your materials: a plateful of spaghetti with your favorite sauce, a fork, and a large spoon, such as a soup spoon. First, take your fork in one hand and the spoon in the other hand. Then put a few strands of spaghetti and sauce on your fork and hold the spoon ever so lightly under the fork. Twist your fork and it automatically twines the spaghetti around the fork. Finally, put the fork and spaghetti in your mouth. Yum! But remember not to twist too much on the fork.

More tips: lean toward the table a little to keep your clothes clean. If the spoon method takes too much time, just cut the spaghetti with the side of your fork.

Following these simple steps should help you get the spaghetti to your mouth and not on your clothes. Enjoy!

What Makes a Good How-to Article?

How-to writing is a type of expository writing, which is writing that provides information. The information in a how-to article explains how to do something in a step-by-step fashion. The instruction sheet that comes with a board game is a type of how-to writing, as is a book explaining how to do origami or other crafts.

Some how-to writing is organized as an article, with information presented in paragraph form, such as "How to Whistle with Two Fingers" on page 298. Remember these points when you write a how-to article.

LiNK

Vanishing Ball

Purpose: To demonstrate the effect of the optic nerve on vision.

Materials: white paper, pencil, ruler

Procedure: In the center of the paper, draw two, round 1/4 inch colored dots, 4 inches apart. Hold the paper at arm's length from your face. Close your right eye and look at the dot on the right side with your open eye. Slowly move the paper toward your face. Be sure to concentrate on the right dot and do not look at the one on the left. Stop moving the paper when the left dot vanishes.

Janice VanCleave

Audience

Think about your audience before you begin writing. This will affect both your tone and the type of details you give in your instructions. You can use more complex words if your audience is older or more familiar with your subject. If you're giving travel directions to your home, an audience that is unfamiliar with the area will need more detailed instructions than someone who knows the area well.

Introduction

In the introduction clearly explain what will be taught in the article. The topic of the article might be introduced in a topic sentence. As done in "How to Eat Spaghetti" on page 299, you might wish to engage readers with a sentence that gets them interested in the subject. Sometimes a how-to article will contain a heading, such as *Purpose*. Look at the excerpt on this page to see how the "Vanishing Ball" how-to article was handled.

Body

The body of your article should use chronological order in listing all the steps required to accomplish the task. Write in imperative sentences, which are sentences written in the form of commands. If necessary, list any materials or tools the reader will need. Be sure all your instructions are clear and accurate and that no steps are left out.

Conclusion

The conclusion of a how-to article should sum up what has been taught. You might also make a statement that predicts the result of following the process.

ACTIVITY A **Which of the following topics are appropriate for how-to writing? Why or why not?**

1. finding the location of the school
2. What is a blimp?
3. potential hazards in your home
4. caring for houseplants
5. making a sandwich
6. the instruments in an orchestra
7. tying a shoe
8. the Bengal tiger
9. making a paper hat
10. my favorite songs
11. doing a magic trick
12. taking care of your friend's pet bearded dragon

ACTIVITY B **Choose three topics from Activity A. For each topic write an introductory sentence that could be used if you read a how-to article on that topic.**

WRITER'S CORNER

Brainstorm a list of ideas that you think would be interesting topics for a how-to article. Share your list with a partner and check to make sure that your ideas are appropriate for how-to writing.

Grammar in Action. Identify the imperative sentences on p. 300.

The How-to Checklist

There are many points to consider when you write a how-to article. Use the checklist below to help you check your writing.

- ☐ Does the introduction explain the purpose of the article?
- ☐ Are the steps in chronological order?
- ☐ Are the steps clear?
- ☐ Are all the important steps included?
- ☐ Is there any unnecessary information?
- ☐ Is enough detail given to complete each step?
- ☐ Does the conclusion sum up what has been taught?

ACTIVITY C Evaluate the three how-to articles below, using the How-to Checklist. Answer each question in the checklist and justify your answers.

1. Guacamole is a delicious snack, and it's easy to make. First, cut two avocados in half. Scoop the avocado flesh out of the peels and put it in a bowl. Use a potato masher or fork to mash it until it is fairly smooth. Make sure you've taken out the pits! Next, finely chop a garlic clove and a tomato before adding them to the mashed avocado. The tomato is nice because it adds both taste and color. Add some lemon or lime juice, salt, and pepper, stirring the avocado mixture until all ingredients are blended. Refrigerate for at least an hour before garnishing with fresh cilantro. Serve with nachos or corn chips.

2. If you want to reproduce a miniature snow scene, here are the steps. Take boric acid crystals and put them in a glass jar. Add water to the jar. Shake the jar to mix the crystals and water. Let the jar sit still.

3. Do you want to create your own scarecrow that demonstrates your personal style? Well, grab some old clothes and let's get started! Find a solid colored T-shirt—you'll use that for the head. First, take a permanent marker and draw a funny or scary face, or you can sew on buttons for eyes and scraps of material for the nose and mouth. Add character to the face by adding a scar or some freckles. Then tie the T-shirt's arms and neck holes shut with string and finish the "head" by stuffing it with straw. Set the head aside while you stuff the body. Tie the wrists of the arms and the ankles of the pants. Fill the two halves of the body with straw. Take a long stick, such as a broom handle, and insert it into the "waist" of the pants and then take the top half of the scarecrow and place it down on the stick so that the stick goes through the torso and comes out the top. Finish off with a hat and add some straw sticking out of the hat for hair.

ACTIVITY D Put the directions below in chronological order, and then write them as a how-to paragraph.

1. Get out a big mixing bowl for the ingredients you have just gathered.
2. Let the cake cool in the pan for 10 minutes, and then take the cake out of the pan and place on a cooling rack.
3. Gather all the ingredients: the cake mix, one cup of water, one-third cup of vegetable oil, and three eggs.
4. First, preheat the oven to 350°.
5. Test the cake with a fork or toothpick near the center of the cake to see if it is done.
6. Use an electric mixer to blend the ingredients together.
7. Once the cake is room temperature, frost and decorate as you like.
8. Pour all the ingredients carefully into the bowl.
9. If the toothpick or fork comes out clean, the cake is done.
10. To make a box cake, all you have to do is follow the directions.
11. In 30 minutes check the cake to see if it looks done.
12. When the batter is smooth, pour it into a baking pan and put the pan into the oven.

ACTIVITY E Rewrite the following paragraph so that it proceeds in chronological order. Then write an introduction and a conclusion for the paragraph.

First, stick toothpicks into a foam ball so that they seem to radiate from the ball. Next, dip the ornament into the liquid starch. You should have gathered wooden toothpicks, a small plastic-foam ball, tempera spray paint, liquid starch, and gold glitter. When it is finished, you will suspend the ball from string or ribbon and hang it up where it will catch the light. While the starch is still wet, sprinkle the ornament with glitter.

WRITER'S CORNER

Find a book or a magazine article that tells how to do something. How do you know that it is how-to writing? Write the topic and list the steps for completing the process.

Tech Tip With an adult, find a how-to project online.

Relevant Details

LiNK

How to Make a Grilled Cheese Sandwich

Start with spreading softened butter on one side of each slice of bread. Lay one slice of bread, butter side down, in a frying pan. Put two slices of cheese on the bread. You may be tempted to use a lot more cheese but don't! Too much cheese oozes out as it melts and you end up with all that extra cheese in the bottom of the pan or dripping down your hand as you eat your sandwich! Now cover it with the other slice of bread with the buttered side up. Turn the stove on medium heat and place the

(continued on page 306)

A paragraph has unity when every detail relates to the topic sentence or main idea. When you write a paragraph, you must make sure that every sentence contributes important information and relates to the topic of the paragraph.

In the passage below, notice that the topic sentence is "If you experience tension in your neck, the following exercise will help you feel more relaxed and energized." Any sentence with information not directly related to the topic is a misfit sentence. Find the misfit sentence in the passage below.

Neck and Shoulder Release

If you experience tension in your neck, the following exercise will help you feel more relaxed and energized. First, sit up straight in a chair. Relax your shoulders. One side of your neck may be tighter than the other from talking on the phone. Let your arms hang from your shoulders toward the floor. Then take a deep breath. As you exhale, begin to lower your left ear toward your left shoulder. Then put your left hand on your head and use that hand to apply gentle pressure on your head to cause your head to lower even more. Finally, breathe deeply and feel your neck relax each time you exhale. Hold the stretch for 20 seconds. Return to the center and then repeat the exercise, lowering your right ear toward your right shoulder.

The misfit sentence that does not relate to the topic is "One side of your neck may be tighter than the other from talking on the phone." If the misfit sentence is taken out, the paragraph will be unified.

ACTIVITY A Find the misfit sentence in each group of sentences.

Group 1

1. First, put the oil into the pan.
2. When it starts to sizzle, put in the tortilla.
3. Have the other ingredients ready.
4. This is Pete's favorite treat.

Group 2

1. Find the smoke alarm that is chirping.
2. Remove the smoke alarm's cover and old battery.
3. When I hear a chirping noise, I always think of a cricket.
4. Insert the new battery and put the cover back on the smoke alarm.

Group 3

1. Graham crackers contain iron and calcium.
2. Roast the marshmallow on the stick so that it's hot and almost melting.
3. Quickly place the marshmallow on top of a piece of chocolate.
4. Place the marshmallow and chocolate between two graham crackers and hold together tightly until the marshmallow and chocolate melt on the crackers.

Group 4

1. Hose down the outside of the car first with a hose.
2. Soak a large sponge or cloth in the soapy water and scrub the car.
3. My favorite type of car is any sports car.
4. Be sure to rinse the car well with clean water.

ACTIVITY B Choose two topics from the following list. For each topic you choose, give three or four supporting details that relate to the topic. Be sure not to include any misfit details.

1. How to care for a new puppy (or kitten or turtle)
2. How to plan a class trip
3. How to redecorate a bedroom
4. How to make a fruit salad

WRITER'S CORNER

Refer to one set of details you gathered for Activity B. Use the details to write a short how-to article in four to five sentences.

Giving Detailed Information

While a writer should always leave out unnecessary details in a how-to article, it is just as important to include every necessary detail. Here are some important points to remember when deciding whether you have included all the relevant details.

LiNK

How to Make a Grilled Cheese Sandwich

(continued from page 304)

pan on the stove. The grilled cheese sandwich needs to cook until it's golden brown on the outside. This means peeking occasionally with a spatula. After about 2–3 minutes, it should be ready to flip. The second side will take a lot less time to turn golden brown because the pan is already heated up. You can spice up your sandwich by adding tuna salad, sliced ham or turkey, sliced tomato, or even a scrambled egg. Bon appetit!

Emma Marcic

Be Specific

Always tell your readers exactly what they need to accomplish the task. If they will need a certain sized screw, specify exactly what they should use. In a recipe, always tell how much of an ingredient to use. When giving directions, name specific streets and landmarks to make the directions clearer. In the excerpt on the left, "because the pan is already heated up" is a relevant detail.

Consider Your Audience

Think about what level of detail your audience will need. Include more details if the audience might be unfamiliar with the subject. Leave out anything that will be obvious.

Use Clear Language

In a how-to article, it is important to make certain that every instruction is clear and concise. Make sure that each step is written in the simplest way possible and that it cannot be misinterpreted. If you are unsure that a sentence is clear, ask someone else to read it.

ACTIVITY C **The instructions below do not provide enough specific information. Write any questions that the writer did not answer. Share them with the class.**

It's a rainy Saturday afternoon, and your friends are over at your house. Someone suggests to play crazy eights, but a few of you have never played the game. To play crazy eights, begin by passing out cards to each player. Place one card from the deck faceup. Each player should play a card that matches that card. If a player cannot play a card, he or she must draw cards from the top of the deck. At any time, a player may play an eight, which is a wild card. Continue the game until one player wins.

ACTIVITY D The instructions below for how to build a snowman were written for an audience that has just moved from a tropical climate and has never seen snow. Rewrite the directions by eliminating details that would be obvious to an audience that often sees snow.

Making a snowman is a great way to enjoy the winter weather. To make one, first wait for snowy weather, which usually starts in December. Make sure that there is at least a few inches of wet and sticky snow on the ground. Bundle up with a warm jacket, a scarf, a knit hat, waterproof boots, and good gloves.

Find an open space and pack a pile of snow into a ball. Roll the ball along the ground so that the snow sticks to it. Keep rolling until the ball is about two feet wide.

Next, make a second, smaller ball of snow in the same way. Stack that on top of the base. Finally, create an even smaller mound and stack it on top for the head. If you get too cold, go inside for a few minutes to warm up.

Put sticks on each side of the body for arms. Get creative by decorating the head, using stones or buttons for the face. Don't forget a nice hat on top!

ACTIVITY E Read the sentences below and decide if they use specific, clear language or if they need improvement. If they need improvement, rewrite the sentence, adding information to make it more specific.

1. The omelette recipe calls for eggs, cheese, vegetables, and butter to serve four people.

2. After smearing the glue on the ornament, sprinkle the glitter on the glue. Shake off the excess glitter.

3. When you get to the corner of Seventh and Pleasant streets, turn and you will see our house.

4. Add a little water to the base of the tree every once in a while.

5. First, lightly dampen with water the unfinished pottery that you will paint. Then paint the pottery with the background color. Before you begin, take a pencil and draw out your design on the pottery piece.

WRITER'S CORNER

Write a brief how-to article that explains to a classmate how to leave the building from the classroom. Then revise it for an audience that has never been inside your school.

Grammar in Action. Use imperative sentences in your how-to article.

Transition Words

Transition words enable the details in a piece of writing to flow smoothly. Writers use transition words to help unify a paragraph's topic and connect details in a logical order. Without transition words, sentences in a paragraph may seem hard to follow.

Transition words vary depending on the type of writing being used. For example, transition words in how-to writing are usually used to show chronological order. People writing descriptions often use transition words to show spatial order.

Transition Words That Show Chronological Order

after	next
as soon as	now
before	soon
finally	then
first, second, and so on	to begin with
later	while
meanwhile	

Transition Words That Show Spatial Order

above	in front of
across	next to
before	opposite to
behind	to the left
between	to the right
farther	under

ACTIVITY A Look back at the example paragraph "Neck and Shoulder Release" on page 304. Find the transition words and notice how each is being used. In which cases could a different transition word have been used?

ACTIVITY B The two paragraphs below need transition words to help the sentences flow from one to the next. Complete each sentence with an appropriate transition word.

Cleaning the Lights

Here's how you can clean a dusty glass light shade.

1. _____, turn off the light and carefully remove the glass shade by unscrewing it from its brackets.

2. _____, place an old towel in a sink. Fill the sink with warm water and a small amount of dishwashing liquid. Gently wash the glass shade and place it on a towel outside the sink.

3. _____, empty the sink, put another old towel in it, and run warm water. To the water, add 1/2 cup of white vinegar. Let the glass shade sit in the water-vinegar mixture for about one minute.

4. _____, remove the glass shade and lightly wipe off any moisture.

5. _____, put the dry glass shade back in place and see the light shine!

How to Write a Haiku

Following these steps can help you write your own haiku.

1. _____, brainstorm some ideas to use as your haiku's subject matter. Do this by writing down words and then narrowing them down.

2. _____, organize your thoughts into three lines. The first line should set the scene, the second should expand on it by expressing a feeling, and the third should make an observation or record an action.

3. _____, make the lines have the correct number of syllables. The first should have five, the _____ should have seven, and the _____ should have five.

4. _____, you might have to rewrite using different words to fit the criteria.

Uses of Transition Words

Transition words cannot replace good organization. They can, however, provide markers that make the organization easier to follow. They can show the logical relationship between two sentences or paragraphs. They can also show how a sentence fits into the entire piece of writing. Here are some more examples of the types of relationships that transition words can show.

More Transition Words

To Compare

like

likewise

similarly

in the same way

To Contrast

but

however

in contrast

nevertheless

instead

still

yet

otherwise

whereas

unlike

To Show Examples

for example

for instance

namely

To Show Emphasis

of course

for this reason

in fact

To Show Cause and Effect

as a result

because

so

therefore

To Conclude or Summarize

finally

last

in conclusion

in summary

To Support

additionally

again

also

besides

ACTIVITY C **Read the following paragraphs. Substitute appropriate transition words for the sentence-function labels. Do not use a particular transition word more than once.**

The Transcontinental Railroad

The Transcontinental Railroad was completed on May 10, 1869. **(1. Cause and Effect)** the world became smaller. The day after the railroad was finished, the first transcontinental freight train traveled from California to the East Coast, carrying goods including Japanese teas. **(2. Time)** on May 15, trains with passengers started moving on the tracks from coast to coast.

The Transcontinental Railroad increased the amount of trade on our continent. **(3. Cause and Effect)** there was a production boom that improved the economy. **(4. Compare)** there was an increase in people's abilities to share ideas with other people across the country. **(5. Conclude)** the Transcontinental Railroad united the country in ways that had never been possible before.

Home Theater

Watching films on DVD has far more advantages than going to the movie theater. With DVDs you are free to watch the film at your convenience, **(1. Contrast)** at the theater, movies are scheduled at definite times. **(2. Contrast)** the movie theater, DVDs are inexpensive and can be viewed as often as you wish. With DVDs you can press the pause button if you want to make a quick snack. **(3. Contrast)** at the theater you are almost forced to purchase your food before the film starts. **(4. Conclude)** with DVDs there are thousands of choices of films, **(5. Contrast)** at the theater, you are limited to what is most current or popular. No wonder DVDs are a popular choice.

ACTIVITY D **Look back over the instructions for building a snowman on page 307, Activity D. List the transition words in the paragraph. Identify other places where transition words could have been used.**

WRITER'S CORNER

Write five sentences in paragraph form comparing and contrasting two items, such as two books you have recently read or two subjects in school. Use transition words. Then go back and cross out the transition words. Do the sentences flow better when transition words are used?

Adverb Clauses

As you have learned, clauses can be used to add variety or change the meaning of your sentences. A clause can be either independent or dependent. An adverb clause is a dependent clause used as an adverb. Read the following examples of adverb clauses from a how-to paragraph about giving a speech:

Speak *confidently*.

Speak *with confidence*.

Speak *as if you were confident*.

In the first sentence, the adverb *confidently* modifies the verb *speak*. In the second sentence, the prepositional phrase *with confidence* is used as an adverb and modifies the verb *speak*. In the third sentence, the verb *speak* is modified by the adverb clause *as if you were confident*.

Adverb clauses are introduced by subordinate conjunctions.

Like an adverb, an adverb clause usually modifies a verb, though it can also modify an adjective or another adverb. It can tell when, where, why, or how something happens. It can also make a comparison or set a condition.

I can run farther *than you can throw a ball*. (The adverb clause makes a comparison.)

If Cesar doesn't get here soon, **he'll miss the first act of the play.** (The adverb clause sets a condition.)

Commonly Used Subordinate Conjunctions

after	before	since	unless
although	if	so that	until
as	in order that	than	when
as if	provided	that	wherever
because	provided that	though	while

ACTIVITY A Complete each sentence with an appropriate subordinate conjunction.

1. _____ the storm hit our town, warning was given.

2. My family and I went to a local shelter _____ we would be safe from the storm.

3. _____ the storm hit, we were all a bit frightened.

4. _____ the storm was over, people tried to return to their homes.

5. _____ many trees had been blown down, many roads were blocked.

6. The Red Cross sent rescue teams to provide emergency shelter and food _____ many people had to leave their homes.

7. _____ we finally got back to our house, we found that part of the roof had caved in.

8. Our house had less damage _____ many other houses in our neighborhood did.

ACTIVITY B Identify the adverb clauses in the following sentences and the word or words each clause modifies. Then identify the sentences that appear to be from a how-to article.

1. Stir the custard mixture constantly until it thickens.

2. When it is summer in the Northern Hemisphere, it is winter in the Southern Hemisphere.

3. Wherever Johnny Appleseed went, he planted apple trees.

4. A national park was established in northern California so that the giant redwood trees would be preserved.

5. If you want to see a secret message, put the paper under a red light.

6. Eric probably wrapped this package when he was in the basement.

7. After refrigerated boats were put into use, bananas could be exported to the United States more efficiently.

8. Before you cut the wrapping paper, determine the amount of paper you will need to wrap the item.

9. While you are typing, try not to look at the keys.

10. Because you can fall through soft ice on a pond, you need to be sure that the ice you skate on is hard.

11. Don't come until we give you the signal.

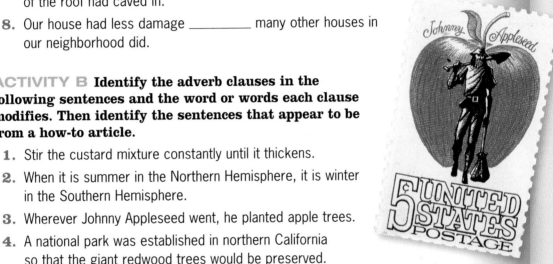

WRITER'S CORNER

Look through a book or magazine for five adverb clauses. Write each sentence that you find and underline the adverb clause. Then highlight the word or words each clause modifies.

Grammar in Action. Find the subordinate conjunction in the p. 312 excerpt.

Revising Sentences Using Adverb Clauses

You have learned that varying your sentences can make your writing more interesting. If your writing contains a series of simple sentences, one way to add variety is to combine them using an adverb clause. For example:

We visited Yellowstone National Park. We saw Old Faithful.

Instead of writing two related sentences, a writer can combine the sentences by changing one to an adverb clause and placing it before or after the verb it modifies.

When we visited Yellowstone National Park, **we saw Old Faithful.**

An adverb clause can also be used to shift the emphasis of a sentence. Rather than giving two ideas equal importance, one idea can be made less important by turning it into an adverb clause.

I went to the corner store, *where I bought an ice-cream cone.*
When I got to the corner store, **I bought an ice-cream cone.**

In the first sentence, the writer focuses on going to the corner store. In the second sentence, the focus is on buying the ice-cream cone.

ACTIVITY C **Revise each of the following pairs of sentences by making one into an adverb clause. Be sure to punctuate your sentences correctly.**

1. Determine the best position for the picture. Hammer in the nail.
2. Jugglers have to be coordinated. They must keep several objects twirling in the air at the same time.
3. I watch ice skaters. I want to learn to skate.
4. The winners of the ribbons for the best pies were being announced. Alex's heartbeat quickened.
5. Will you lend me your red pen? Mine has run out.
6. The game ended. Shane scored again.
7. The concert was over. We went to get some pizza.
8. Jillian was upset. Her new backpack had fallen in the mud.
9. Sam sneezed. He dropped his lunch tray.
10. Mrs. Pindale tightly clasped her packages. The crush of passengers got onto the bus.

ACTIVITY D Complete each sentence with an appropriate adverb clause.

1. The baby always giggles when _____.
2. We first heard the song when _____.
3. If _____, I will be allowed to go to the concert.
4. The hot pizza had just been delivered when _____.
5. Until _____, your sister won't be able to sing in choir practice.
6. The crowd went wild with cheers after _____.
7. Although _____, the lightning storm continued for hours.
8. This year's spring break will be the best if _____.
9. The girl laughed whenever _____.
10. As _____, Stella waited and watched nervously.
11. At the sight of the dog, the letter carrier looked as if _____.
12. Victor's father does not let him use the power drill because _____.

ACTIVITY E Use the adverb clauses below in sentences of your own.

1. before you buy a bike
2. if you write a letter to the store
3. because my family is trying to be more energy efficient
4. unless I am certain
5. whenever I am really hungry
6. since the TV was broken
7. after the film crew left our school
8. when the shopping bag broke
9. if I could travel anywhere
10. until I am 18

WRITER'S CORNER

Write three sentences about recent news events. Include an adverb clause in each sentence. Exchange sentences with a partner and identify the adverb clauses in your partner's sentences. For each sentence, underline the adverb clause and highlight the word or words it modifies.

Tech Tip With an adult, research news events online.

Noah Webster, early dictionary author

Dictionary

A dictionary, whether in paper form or online, is one of a writer's most valuable tools. A dictionary provides a word's meaning, part of speech, pronunciation, origin, and more. In paper dictionaries, words are organized alphabetically. To help writers find words more quickly, letter tabs and guide words are often included. Letter tabs are located on the sides of the page. They help the writer turn directly to the first letter of the word in question. Guide words, the first and last entries on each page, are found at the top of the page.

Examining an Entry

Below is a sample entry for the word *brazen*. The key on the right identifies each part of the entry. While most paper dictionaries will have this information, the appearance and location sometimes varies. Some dictionaries may have other information, such as synonyms or variant spellings. Find each part of the entry listed in the key at the bottom of the page. Then look up the word in a classroom dictionary. Does it include all these parts? Can you find any others?

Pronunciation

Pronunciations are an important part of a dictionary entry. To read the pronunciation symbols, all you need is the pronunciation key, which is usually found at the beginning of a dictionary. Many dictionaries also include a short key on the bottom of every other page.

---

bra•zen (brā´ zən) *adj.* **1.** Made of brass. **2.** Harsh and loud sounding. **3.** So bold as to be rude: *The man's brazen comments offended the woman.* *v.* To face with boldness. [<Old English *bræsen*, made of brass.] —**bra´zen•ly** adv. —**bra´zen•ness** n.

A. Syllabication
B. Pronunciation
C. Part of speech
D. Word definition
E. Sample usage
F. Etymology
G. Other forms

ACTIVITY A Refer to the sample dictionary entry on the previous page for the word *brazen* to answer the questions and follow the directions.

1. From which language does *brazen* originate?
2. Which syllable of *brazen* receives the accent?
3. How many meanings does *brazen* have in this entry?
4. How many meanings does *brazen* have as an adjective?
5. What is the adverb form for *brazen*?
6. Write a sentence for *brazen* meaning "so bold as to be rude."

ACTIVITY B Look up each italicized word in a dictionary and write the definition that best fits the context of the sentence.

1. The *quack* tried to sell us a quick remedy for the flu.
2. We used a *balance* to measure the calcium carbonate.
3. I used an iron to *press* my clothes.
4. The play received excellent *reviews*.
5. San Francisco has a *temperate* climate.
6. Paul gave two weeks' *notice* when he decided to leave his job.
7. The mechanic used a *jack* to lift up our car.

ACTIVITY C Use a dictionary to find the meanings of the following words. Write the meaning or meanings of each word. Then use the words in sentences that illustrate those meanings.

myriad   forlorn   nonpareil   gumption

WRITER'S CORNER

Find a word with three or more definitions. Write three sentences that each use the word in a different way. Exchange papers with a partner and identify the meaning of your classmate's words in each sentence.

Tech Tip With an adult, use an online dictionary.

Online Dictionaries

To use an online dictionary, you need to have only an idea of how the word is spelled. You type that spelling into the search window, and the computer will find the word for you. For this reason an online dictionary can be even easier to use than a paper dictionary.

Online dictionaries offer other useful features. They may include a feature that lets you hear the pronunciation of the word in question. Online dictionaries may also provide links to other resources such as thesauruses, encyclopedias, or other dictionaries.

Merriam-Webster's Online Dictionary

brazen
3 entries found.

> 1 brazen (adjective)
> 2 brazen (transitive verb)
> brazen-faced

Main Entry: ¹**bra·zen** 🔊
Pronunciation: \\ˈbrā-zən\\
Function: *adjective*
Etymology: Middle English *brasen*, from Old English *bræsen*, from *bræs* brass
Date: before 12th century
1 : made of brass
2a : sounding harsh and loud like struck brass **b** : of the color of polished brass
3 : marked by contemptuous boldness <a *brazen* disregard for the rules>
— **bra·zen·ly** *adverb*
— **bra·zen·ness** 🔊 \\ˈbrā-zən-(n)əs\\ *noun*

ACTIVITY D **Answer the questions about the online entry for _brazen_.**

1. What parts of speech can _brazen_ be?
2. What is the noun form of _brazen_?
3. How many syllables does _brazen_ have?
4. Where does the Middle English word _brasen_ come from?
5. From this site where could a reader link for more information about this word?
6. How many entries in this dictionary include the word _brazen_?

ACTIVITY E **Answer the following questions regarding classroom and online dictionaries. In each case decide whether a classroom dictionary, an online dictionary, or both would be a useful solution.**

1. Which kind of dictionary would you use if you wanted to hear a word pronounced?
2. Which kind of dictionary would you use if you wanted to see all the meanings of a word at one time?
3. Which kind of dictionary would you use if you wanted to learn more about the origins of a word?
4. Which kind of dictionary would you use if you were unsure of the exact spelling of the word you wanted to find?
5. Which kind of dictionary would you use if you wanted to see a word's entry and the pronunciation key at the same time?
6. Which dictionary would you use if you wanted to see the meanings of all the words that start with the letters _mag_?
7. Now that you know something about paper dictionaries and online dictionaries, which would you prefer to use? Give three reasons.

WRITER'S CORNER

Look through an article in a newspaper or magazine. Find three words about whose meaning you are uncertain. Use an online dictionary to check them. Then use each word in a new sentence.

How-to Talks

Using the library or Internet, you could likely find written directions for how to do just about anything. For many activities, however, such as baiting a fishhook, it is easier to learn by having a live person explain or even show you how to do it. When you give your own how-to talks, you have to be just as clear and logical as in your how-to writing. Here are some tips for a successful how-to presentation.

Audience

Consider the age of your audience. A five-year-old will need simpler directions than an adult will. Also think about how familiar your audience is with the topic. Showing an adult how to play a new video game may be different from showing your best friend how to play.

Introduction

Start your how-to talk by telling your audience what you will be teaching them. Then tell why someone might want to learn what you have to offer. How will your audience benefit from your talk?

Steps

Explain the steps in chronological order, making sure not to leave any out. Pause after each step to make certain that your audience understands each step. Answer questions as you go and provide more detail if your audience appears to be confused. If possible, use actual objects to demonstrate the steps. Be sure your demonstration is clearly visible and explain what you are doing as you go along.

Sometimes it is too hard to use the actual objects in your demonstrations. It may not be practical, for example, to bring in a dog to demonstrate dog grooming. In that case try to come up with some other visual aid to make your presentation clear. You can create posters, flow charts, diagrams, models, or any other kind of visual aid. Visual aids give you something to refer to as you speak, and they help your audience see the process.

Conclusion

Finish your talk by reviewing the major steps. Also be sure to leave the audience with a reminder of what you have accomplished. For a how-to talk about making a scrapbook, for example, you could say "With some string, a paper punch, and nice paper, you can keep pictures of all your friends in one eye-catching scrapbook."

ACTIVITY A **Draw the following chart. Complete the chart to develop ideas for a how-to talk.**

HOW TO . . .	FIRST STEP IN THE PROCESS	OBJECTS OR VISUAL AIDS NEEDED
1. Send an E-mail		
2. Build a Sand Castle		
3. Make a Tire Swing		
4. Play Musical Chairs		
5.		

ACTIVITY B **Choose a topic from Activity A. Write notes for the introductions of two how-to talks on the topic, one geared toward five-year-olds and one geared toward adults. How will the introductions be different?**

Tech Tip Video or podcast your presentation.

Prepare

The key to presenting a successful how-to talk is preparation. The following tips will help you make certain that you are well prepared.

- Visualize your topic and write the steps.
- Check that you haven't forgotten any steps or included unnecessary information.
- Write the steps on note cards to use during the presentation.
- Think about visual aids you could use. Can you demonstrate using actual objects, or do you need to make another type of visual aid?
- Gather or make your visual aids.
- Make sure your visual aids are large enough for everyone to see.

Practice

Practicing your how-to talk will give you a chance to get comfortable with speaking the information. Practice also lets you check whether or not your visual aids work. As you practice, keep the following questions in mind.

- Is my talk right for the age and experience level of my audience?
- Do I introduce my topic at the beginning?
- Am I speaking too fast or too slowly?
- Am I speaking clearly and loudly enough?
- Are the steps presented in the right order?
- Are my visual aids helpful and easy to see?
- Does the conclusion sum up the topic?

Present

A how-to talk is an opportunity to interact with an audience. Watch for the audience's reaction as you speak. If they are straining to hear you, speak more loudly and clearly. If they have trouble seeing your visual aid, raise it up or take it around the room. If they seem confused, repeat difficult steps by explaining them in a different way. Take time to answer questions. In a how-to talk, you have the chance to make sure that everyone understands.

Listening Tips

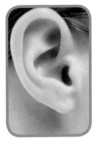

Presenting a how-to talk before an audience of good listeners can be fun for everyone involved. Follow these steps to be a good listener for a how-to talk.

- Look at the speaker and watch what he or she is doing. The speaker will know you are paying attention, and you will likely learn more from the presentation. If you miss an early step, you could become confused by later ones.
- If you are confused by a step or want to know more, ask questions, but don't interrupt the speaker. Raise your hand or wait for the speaker to ask for questions. If you are worried you will forget, write your question. Good questions are like good feedback because they let the speaker know you listened and were interested.
- If the topic is complex, you may want to write the steps and notes to go with them. These notes can help you remember what you have learned.
- Give the speaker the same kind of attention and feedback that you would appreciate.

ACTIVITY C **Using the tips on the previous page, prepare a how-to talk for one of the topics in Activity A or for a topic of your choice. Write notes on note cards and prepare any visuals that you think appropriate. Then practice your talk with a partner. Use the questions in the Practice section to check your classmate's how-to talk.**

SPEAKER'S CORNER

Give your how-to talk to a group. Be sure to speak clearly and display any visual aids so that everyone can easily see. Pause throughout the talk to ask if students have any questions. Answer the questions as you go along.

Prewriting and Drafting

Have you ever read directions to help you get somewhere? Maybe you've received an invitation that gave directions to a special event. If you did, you were reading a type of how-to article. Now you are going to create your own invitation that gives directions to a specific location. Directions are written so that they read, in order, from the starting point to the destination.

Prewriting

The prewriting stage for writing an invitation with travel directions includes choosing a route and  planning the directions. First, writers choose the route they want people to travel and then write the route out in order.

Choosing a Route

Akimi, a seventh grader, wanted to invite her friends to a skateboarding party at a new skate park. She was familiar with the location of the park since it was in her neighborhood, but she wanted to send directions to her guests. Akimi decided to give directions to the park from the junior high so that all her friends from school were familiar with the starting point. Then she took some time to choose a route from the junior high to the Tilton Skate Park. She made a list to help her choose a possible route.

Possible Routes to Tilton

- Quickest—down Dodge, across Highway 176, continue to Washington

- Most skater-friendly—Church to Gilbert, cross Washington into park

- Most hills—Circle to back of school, down Quarry Road, to Beckett and then Keaton streets, enter back side of park

- Fewest hills—Dodge, cross Highway 176, left on Hopkins, right on Addison, to Washington and the park.

Although there was a quicker route between the school and the park, Akimi decided to choose the most skater-friendly route. She chose the route involving fewer major roads because she figured that her friends would be either riding their skateboards or walking.

Writer's Tip If you can't travel the route, use a map. Maps are sometimes outdated, so check multiple sources for the accuracy of your information.

Prewriting

Drafting

Content Editing

Revising

Copyediting

Proofreading

Publishing

Your Turn

Imagine that you will be sending an invitation to friends or family who are unfamiliar with the destination. Before you can choose your route, choose a location for the event that you want to invite them to.

If you are having trouble thinking of a destination, consider these:

- a sporting or cultural event at another school
- a party at your home or a friend's home
- a swimming pool or community recreation center
- an amusement park, water park, or festival
- a new ice-cream shop

Now that you've chosen a location and event, you can choose your route. Make your school

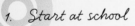 **Organization** the starting point for your

directions. When choosing a route, think about your audience. Make a list like Akimi did to help you decide which route would be the best for those invited to the event.

Planning Travel Directions

Akimi had been to the new skate park, but to make sure her directions were right, she asked her older brother, Han, to drive her on the route. She wrote the street names, directions, and landmarks in the order she saw them as her brother drove. When she got home, she rewrote her directions as a numbered list and checked a paper map to see if she had spelled the street names correctly.

Your Turn

Plan the directions for the route you chose. If your route is short enough, walk it so that you can take time to write the correct spelling of streets. While on the route, take notes about the streets, landmarks, and turns you make. Then write the directions as a numbered list. Make sure that your directions are clear and accurate.

1. Start at school
2. Turn left
3. Pass Chad's Chicken
4. Turn left onto Gilbert St.
5. Gilbert St. turns into a steep hill
6. Follow curve and go right past stop sign
7. Go two blocks and cross Washington St.
8. Cross bridge into park
9. Pass park booth and follow curve
10. Follow left fork in road to skate park

Drafting

Akimi knew that by writing a draft, she could shape her prewriting notes into travel directions. She reviewed her notes and then began to write. In her introduction she explained the purpose of the invitation. Since many of her friends hadn't been to the new skate park, she mentioned both the starting and the ending points of the trip in the introduction.

The body was easy to write. She wrote what time she had the skate park reserved so that all her friends would arrive at the same time. She also included what to bring and what not to bring.

An Invitation to My Birthday Skateboarding Party

This Saturday we'll be celebrating my birthday at the new tilton skate park. Here's all you need to know to get from Blake Jr. High to the best halfpipe and skateboarding pool in town.

The party starts at 1 p.m., and we'll have the skate park to ourselves until 3 p.m. Don't forget your pads, helmats, and boards, or you won't be skating with us. I just bought new trucks and wheels for my board so it is a smoother ride. Don't bother to bring a gift. All I want for my birthday are a good time with my friends.

When you get there the park ranger at the booth will want you to pay the entrance fee. Say you're with the Akimi skate party. You'll get a free pass. Go past the booth and follow the curve. Look for the refreshment stand on your left, and follow the left fork in the road just past it. Follow the road until you reach the skate park.

To get there begin from the front door of the school and turn left toward Chad's Chicken restaurant down the street. You pass the restaurant, go two more blocks to the stop sign. Turn right at the stop sign onto Gilbert Street, which drops down into a steep hill. Go down the hill and around the curve in the road. Go right past the stop sign at the bottom of the hill and two more blocks to the stoplight on Washington Street. You cross Washington Street and take the bridge over the river and turn right at the entrance into Tilton Park.

Don't miss my latest flatland freestyle moves. The skate park is new, so we'll just have to break it in on my birthday. And don't forget to work on some new vert tricks.

Next, she wrote her ordered list of directions in paragraph form. She tried to make the directions as detailed and precise as possible so that nobody would get lost. She also included a conclusion that she thought would get her friends excited about the party.

Writer's Tip Remember to double-space your first draft to make room for revisions.

Your Turn

Now it's your turn to begin using your notes to write a first draft.

1. Make sure to explain the purpose of the invitation and include the destination in your introduction. You may also want to use the introduction to get the reader interested in the event.

2. In the body of the invitation, write the directions in paragraph form. Make sure to write the directions in order and to mention helpful landmarks. Be sure to include every important detail and to leave out whatever will be obvious. Tell your guests any important information they will need to know about your event or the location. Do people need to bring anything special? Is there a certain time that they have to arrive?

3. The conclusion should give the reader a sense of closure as well as a reminder about the destination.

Prewriting

Drafting

Content Editing

Revising

Copyediting

Proofreading

Publishing

Editor's Workshop

How-to Articles

Content Editing

Content editors check the information in the draft for logic and completeness. When content editing, Akimi looked for the accuracy of the directions and for the necessary details needed for her guests to be able to find the skate park. Akimi used the Content Editor's Checklist when she edited her directions for content.

Content Editor's Checklist

☐ Does the introduction engage the reader and introduce the topic?

☐ Are the starting and ending locations listed in the introduction?

☐ Is each step accurate?

☐ Are the directions written in order?

☐ Are there any unnecessary details?

☐ Are there enough details, such as landmarks, to complete the task?

☐ Is the tone consistent?

☐ Does the conclusion sum up what has been taught, giving the reader a sense of closure?

Akimi checked her draft but decided she needed a fresh pair of eyes to read it over. She asked her older sister, Moriko, to edit the directions, using the checklist. Moriko enjoyed skateboarding too, and she had been to the Tilton Skate Park. She read Akimi's directions. Since Moriko was old enough to drive, she drove Akimi's route to check it for accuracy.

Moriko told Akimi what she liked about the

👓 **Voice** travel directions. She thought that the directions had an appropriate tone. They were casual and used language particular to skateboarders.

Moriko then shared with Akimi the things she thought could be improved. Here are her comments.

- I like the casual tone of the writing. The introduction doesn't have the same casualness. Maybe you can make it more engaging in order to catch your friends' attention.

- You say to go "right past" the stop sign at the

  👓 **Word Choice** bottom of the hill, but it would be more accurate to say "straight past" the stop sign.

- The directions you give are not for the quickest route. You should consider having your friends take Dodge Street across Highway 176 to the park.

Prewriting

Drafting

Content Editing

Revising

Copyediting

Proofreading

Publishing

- I think it would be better to explain how to get to the park before explaining to your reader how to find the halfpipe within the park.
- You have some landmarks, like Chad's Chicken, but others would be helpful.
- Maybe you should remind the readers at the conclusion where and when the party is. If you do, keep the same casual tone.

Akimi trusted her older sister's feedback so she decided to work on fixing the things Moriko mentioned.

Grammar in Action

Make sure you use the imperative mood for your directions. Make sure the verb agrees with the subject, which is almost always in the second person. Refer to Section 4.7.

Your Turn

Using the Content Editor's Checklist, look for ways to improve your own draft.

Trade your travel directions with those of a classmate. Read your classmate's directions several times and check it against the Content Editor's Checklist.

Writer's Tip After you finish reading your partner's draft, tell your partner the good things that you read. Then explain how you think the travel directions might be improved.

Revising

Here are the revisions Akimi made to her draft after content editing with Moriko.

An Invitation to My Birthday Skateboarding Party

Forget the cake and punch for my birthday this year.   in style with a party

This Saturday we'll be celebrating ~~my birthday~~ at the new tilton skate park. Here's all you need to know to get from Blake Jr. High to the best halfpipe and skateboarding pool in town.

The party starts at 1 p.m., and we'll have the skate park to ourselves until 3 p.m. Don't forget your pads, helmats, and boards, or you won't be skating with us. ~~I just bought new trucks and wheels for my board so it is a smoother ride.~~ Don't bother to bring a gift. All I want for my birthday are a good time with my friends.

On your left will be a steel sculpture of a hawk and on your right will be a small booth.

When you get there the park ranger at the booth will want you to pay the entrance fee. Say you're with the Akimi skate party. You'll get a free pass. Go past the booth and follow the curve. Look for the refreshment stand on your left, and follow the left fork in the road just past it.

Look for the gray halfpipe and

Follow the road until you reach the skate park.

                                                        onto Church Street,

~~To get there~~ begin from the front door of the school and turn left toward Chad's Chicken restaurant down the street. You pass the restaurant, go two more blocks to the stop sign. Turn right at the stop sign onto Gilbert Street, which drops down into a steep hill. Go down the hill and around the curve in the road. Go ~~right~~ straight past the stop sign at the bottom of the hill and two more blocks to the stoplight on Washington Street. You cross Washington Street and take the bridge over the river and turn right at the entrance into Tilton Park.

Prewriting

Drafting

Content Editing

Revising

Copyediting

Proofreading

Publishing

Don't forget to be at the Tilton Skate Park on Saturday by 1 p.m., or else your going to

~~Don't~~ miss my latest flatland freestyle moves. The skate park is new, so

we'll just have to break it in on my birthday. And don't forget to work on

This Saturday will be the prime time to show your stuff!

some new vert tricks.

Look at the revisions that Akimi made to her draft. She used Moriko's suggestions as well as another way she found to improve her travel directions.

- Akimi agreed that her introduction didn't have the same "feel" as the rest of her piece. What did she add that would engage her friends and introduce the topic?

- She changed *right* to *straight*. She originally meant to have people go past the stop sign. She didn't realize that this made it sound like people should turn right at the stop sign.

- She decided to leave the route the same. Moriko's route was quicker, but Akimi knew that it was difficult to cross Highway 176 on a skateboard.

- Akimi also agreed that the piece should be in order. Which paragraphs did she switch to make the piece flow from starting point to destination?

- Which landmarks did she add that everyone would notice?

- She had trouble thinking of a conclusion. How did she restate the information regarding time and place while keeping the tone of her piece? How did she use the information in sentences that also mentioned her new moves?

After Akimi incorporated Moriko's suggestions, she read her revised draft. She noticed that there was an unnecessary detail that did not add to the directions. She deleted the reference to the new trucks and wheels for her skateboard.

Your Turn

Use the ideas from your classmate that you feel make the content of your directions better. Write your changes as neatly as you can next to the text being changed so you can read them when you rewrite your invitation.

Writer's Tip When you have finished adding the revisions, use the Content Editor's Checklist again to be sure that you didn't miss anything.

Copyediting and Proofreading

Copyediting

Akimi knew that the content was greatly improved thanks to her and Moriko's edits. But she wanted to make sure that all the sentences were clear, logical, and grammatically correct. Akimi used this Copyeditor's Checklist to copyedit her invitation.

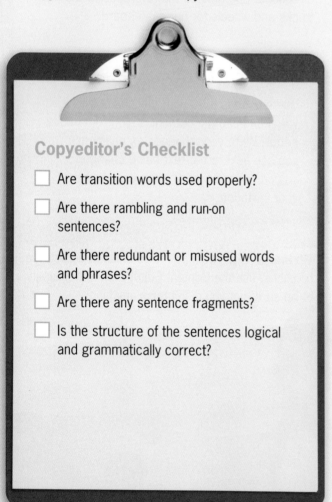

Copyeditor's Checklist

- [ ] Are transition words used properly?
- [ ] Are there rambling and run-on sentences?
- [ ] Are there redundant or misused words and phrases?
- [ ] Are there any sentence fragments?
- [ ] Is the structure of the sentences logical and grammatically correct?

Akimi knew that transition words were helpful when writing directions. She noticed that her directions seemed choppy and hard to follow in places. She decided to fix this problem by using more transition words such as *then* and *after*. For example, she added the word *After* in two places in the new third paragraph, to the beginning of the sentences about passing the stop sign and crossing Washington Street.

Akimi also was having difficulty with the flow of the new fourth paragraph. The sentences seemed choppy and made the directions difficult to read.

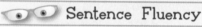 **Sentence Fluency** She fixed the problem by using an adverb clause. She combined the two sentences that explained how to receive a free pass.

Akimi realized that her new sentence places more of an emphasis on how to get the free pass. It also adds variety to the paragraph.

Your Turn

Look over your revised draft and use the Copyeditor's Checklist. Would more transition words help the flow of your travel directions? Do you have any sentences that can be improved by using adverb clauses?

Writer's Tip When you copyedit your work, remember that it is helpful to look for only one type of error at a time.

Proofreading

Before writing the finished invitation, Akimi wanted to proofread the latest version of her draft to

 Conventions

check the spelling, punctuation, capitalization, and grammar. She wanted to make certain that no new errors had been introduced during the revising stage.

Akimi asked her friend Madison to read her invitation. Akimi figured that since Madison had never been to the Tilton Skate Park, she would focus on the items in the Proofreader's Checklist rather than the travel directions. Madison found one error in capitalization. She also found that Akimi had misspelled the word *helmets.*

After Madison had finished proofreading the directions, Akimi looked over her invitation one more time. She discovered that a new error had been introduced in the copyediting stage. The last sentence of the third paragraph was grammatically incorrect with the added transition word *After.* She then fixed that sentence.

Your Turn

Trade your invitation with a classmate and proofread each other's work. Use the Proofreader's Checklist and check one item at a time. Then check your own work against the checklist.

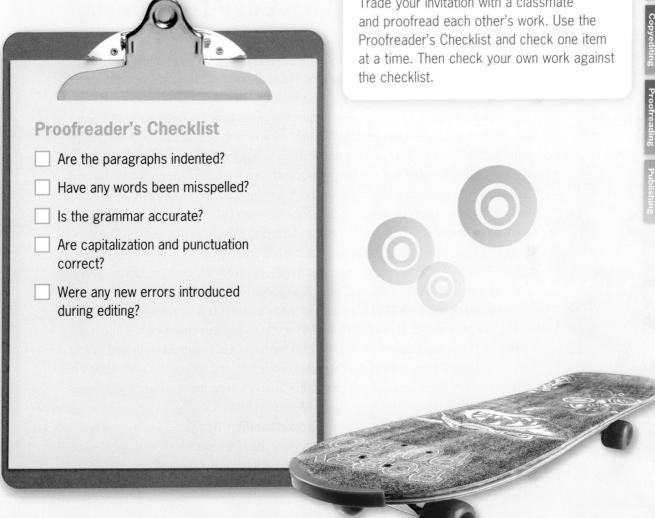

Proofreader's Checklist

☐ Are the paragraphs indented?

☐ Have any words been misspelled?

☐ Is the grammar accurate?

☐ Are capitalization and punctuation correct?

☐ Were any new errors introduced during editing?

Prewriting
Drafting
Content Editing
Revising
Copyediting
Proofreading
Publishing

Publishing

When publishing an invitation, you might mail it to the people who are being invited, post it on a bulletin board, or send it via e-mail. As Akimi prepared to publish her invitation, she read her draft again to make certain that she had written all the necessary revisions and corrections. She used a computer to type her finished piece. Then she made copies for all her friends and made sure that they had the invitations a week before the party.

An Invitation to My Birthday Skateboarding Party

Forget the cake and punch for my birthday this year. This Saturday we'll be celebrating in style with a party at the new Tilton Skate Park. Here's all you need to know to get from Blake Jr. High to the best halfpipe and skateboarding pool in town.

The party starts at 1 p.m., and we'll have the skate park to ourselves until 3 p.m. Don't forget your pads, helmets, and boards, or you won't be skating with us. Don't bother to bring a gift. All I want for my birthday is a good time with my friends.

Begin from the front door of the school and turn left onto Church Street, toward Chad's Chicken restaurant down the street. After you pass the restaurant, go two more blocks to the stop sign. Turn right at the stop sign onto Gilbert Street, which drops down into a steep hill. Go down the hill and around the curve in the road. Then go straight past the stop sign at the bottom of the hill and two more blocks to the stoplight on Washington Street. After you cross Washington Street, take the bridge over the river and turn right at the entrance into Tilton Park.

On your left will be a steel sculpture of a hawk, and on your right will be a small booth. The park ranger at the booth will want you to pay the entrance fee. You'll get a free pass if you say you're with the Akimi skate party. Go past the booth and follow the curve. Look for the refreshment stand on your left, and follow the left fork in the road just past it. Then look for the gray halfpipe and follow the road until you reach the skate park.

Don't forget to be at the Tilton Skate Park on Saturday by 1 p.m., or else you're going to miss my latest flatland freestyle moves. The skate park is new, so we'll just have to break it in on my birthday. And don't forget to work on some new vert tricks. This Saturday will be the prime time to show your stuff!

There are many ways you can publish your article. As a class, decide how you will Presentation publish them. You might even choose different methods, depending on your topic.

 Create a class book. It can be a directory for places to go for people your age. Place everyone's directions in categories (such as parks or stores), numbering the pages, and creating a table of contents that lists the featured locations. Then make a cover, choosing a snappy title such as "How to Get to There from Here." Decorate the cover and bind the book in a three-ring binder or a report cover.

Do a PowerPoint presentation and show your map. Try using a software program to help you design your map or add clip art for certain things, such as a compass rose.

 Post it to your classroom's blog, wiki, or Web site. You can also include images. Add a photo or other visual of the location.

 Mail it to your friends. If you made a "real" invitation, send it to them. Create a design, such as a border, to make your directions more noticeable and attractive. Add art to illustrate what the final destination looks like or what activity will happen at the destination.

 Film it. Add background music as you walk your route, following the directions in your invitation. You might ask some friends to help you.

Writer's Tip After you print out a final copy, read it one more time to check that there are no errors. If there are errors in the steps of the directions, someone could get lost.

Your Turn

Choose one of the publishing options. Before you publish your invitation, you need to make revisions from the proofreading stage and check your directions a final time. Use your best handwriting or print out a final copy.

You might want to add a design or art to your invitation. Add a map to your directions to help your readers if the route is complicated or covers a long distance. When you are finished adding visuals, your invitation is ready.

Prewriting

Drafting

Content Editing

Revising

Copyediting

Proofreading

Publishing

Descriptions

LiNK

The Reptile Room
by Lemony Snicket

Klaus shivered. He hadn't been thinking of Olaf's assistants. Besides scheming to get his hands on the Baudelaire fortune, Olaf was the leader of a terrible theater troupe, and his fellow actors were always ready to help him with his plans. They were a gruesome crew, each more terrifying than the next. There was a bald man with a long nose, who always wore a black robe. There were two women who always had ghostly white powder on their faces. There was a person so large and blank-looking that you couldn't tell if it was a man or a woman. And there was a skinny man with two hooks where his hands should have been. Any of these people could be lurking outside Uncle Monty's house, waiting to catch them if they tried to escape.

> *The Reptile Room, Book the Second* of *A Series of Unfortunate Events*, written by Lemony Snicket, tells the story of three sibling orphans and their unusual adventures. This excerpt is an excellent example of descriptive writing, creating an image of the characters and setting a suspenseful mood.

Eleanor Russo
Room 307

Down Clark Street

I walked onto the bus with a heavy backpack and an even heavier heart, for I knew that my night was going to be full of homework. The bus driver was scruffy with a huge beard and glasses thick and yellowed like big toenails. He growled and gave me a nasty look as if to say "What are you lookin' at?" I quickly flashed my pass and grabbed a seat near the door in the middle of the bus. At the next stop, a man in a formal suit all made out of red velvet got on. He had snowy white hair and wore dark sunglasses even though it was overcast and gray. Something about him made me feel uncomfortable. Maybe it was the way he studied the other passengers through those strange triangular spectacles.

Next onboard was a woman, worn and ragged, who looked older than she probably was, teetering down the aisle wearing a large silver whistle draped around her neck. She held on to it protectively as if it was a precious medal, and not the horrible, dingy thing that it looked like to me. "Bleeep, bleeeeep, bleep, bleep!" She blew it over and over. And that's when I saw that the whistle was shaped like a pig. "Where am I?" I wondered. Is this bus only picking up the oddest people in Chicago?

Then I noticed what I should have been paying attention to all along—my stop. I realized I had missed my stop. I had to walk an extra three blocks to get back to my house. Though I felt silly for getting off the bus so late, I also felt relieved to escape into the freshness of the rainy day.

What Makes a Good Description?

Descriptive writing uses vivid words to portray a person, place, or thing. A good description will capture a reader's senses and imagination in such a way that the reader experiences the smell, taste, sound, or feeling being conveyed by the writer. To do this effectively, you must think carefully about your subject.

Creating an Image

When describing a scene, begin by taking a moment to picture it in your mind. When you've developed a clear picture, use precise language to describe your scene to a reader. For example, if you were to write about the beach, you would probably want to describe how the water looked. If the water was blue, specify what kind of blue. Was it blue like the afternoon sky? Blue-green? Blue like faded blue jeans? By being specific and using words creatively, a writer makes descriptive writing interesting.

Setting a Mood

Mood is the overall feeling a writer creates. The language used in a description might set a mood that is bright, gloomy, frantic, and so on. "Down Clark Street" on page 337 sets a mood of uneasiness, while the excerpt on the left sets a mood of nostalgia. The character is sharing a happy memory. What mood does the description below set?

> **LiNK**
>
> ## Under the Royal Palms
>
> In the summer months, rain would often pour unannounced, pounding furiously on the treetops, the roof, and the soil. These summer rains provided wonderful fun for my mother and me. Together we would run outside in our bathing suits to play. It was wonderful to feel the strong drops on my bare back...
>
> Alma Flor Ada

The glorious sun burst through my window. I heard the birds outside chirping merrily and smelled fresh bacon wafting up from the kitchen. I was ready for the first day of summer.

ACTIVITY A Read the description below from *The Red Pony* by John Steinbeck and answer the questions that follow.

The afternoon was green and gold with spring. Underneath the spread branches of the oaks the plants grew pale and tall, and on the hills the feed was smooth and thick. The sagebrushes shone with new silver leaves and the oaks wore hoods of golden green. Over the hills there hung such a green odor that the horses on the flats galloped madly, and then stopped, wondering; lambs, and even old sheep, jumped in the air unexpectedly and landed on stiff legs, and went on eating; young clumsy calves butted their heads together and drew back and butted again.

1. What color words does the author use in the description?
2. What animals does the author describe? How does he describe each kind of animal?
3. What words does the author use to describe particular senses?
4. What vivid adjectives, verbs, and adverbs does the author use?

ACTIVITY B Choose one of the following ideas and freewrite any details that come to mind about the scene you have chosen. Try to write several vivid words that could describe the scene.

A. It is a hot summer day, and you are spending it at the local pool with some friends. Explain how you feel when you are in the water, and describe the sights and sounds around you.
B. You are riding down a country road in a car. You pass a small farmhouse. A man, woman, and child are in the yard. Describe the scene in detail.
C. Your family moved, and you had to change schools. You arrive for your first day in the new school. Describe how you feel and what you see and hear around you.

WRITER'S CORNER

Think about something exciting or surprising that happened to you. Write a four-sentence paragraph describing the event, creating an image and setting the mood for the reader.

Choosing the Right Words

The purpose of a good description is to create a strong image in the reader's mind. A writer must choose words carefully to create strong images and evoke the senses.

The more exact and specific the words you choose, the clearer the picture will be to the reader. Notice how adding more specific details clarifies the picture being described.

The puppy chewed up my sock.

The brown and white puppy chewed my striped green sock to shreds.

A good writer also uses words that appeal to the senses. Concentrate on the smell, taste, touch, sight, or sound of the picture you're trying to create. Include any sensory details that are relevant to the description.

The fluffy, pink cotton candy put a sweet taste in my mouth and a sticky coating on my face.

ACTIVITY C **Look over the descriptions used in** *The Reptile Room* **on page 336 and "Down Clark Street," the student model, on page 337. Answer the following questions about the descriptions.**

The Reptile Room

1. Identify words or phrases that the author uses to describe the theater troupe.

2. Which description uses words that make the troupe seem scary?

3. Which descriptive verb is used to describe what these people might be doing?

4. Which descriptive verb is used to describe what Olaf is doing to get the fortune? Can the root of this word be used only as a verb?

5. Why do you think the writer chose these words to describe the mood?

6. What mood is felt from reading this excerpt?

Down Clark Street

1. Identify words that the writer uses to describe the bus driver.

2. How is the man in the formal suit described?

3. What mood is felt from reading this excerpt?

4. How does the writer feel about the rainy day?

ACTIVITY D Below are example sentences that use the senses of sight, sound, touch, taste, and smell. After reading each sentence, choose one of the suggestions below it and write a descriptive sentence of your own. Be sure to use exact words in your writing.

1. **Sight:** *The fireworks sprinkled sequins of color across the dark sky.*

   Try describing:
   a sunrise   a racehorse   an abandoned house

2. **Sound:** *The old train chugged, coughed, and choked going up the steep hill.*

   Try describing:
   a song on the radio   a school cafeteria   a traffic accident

3. **Touch:** *The damp, chilly night seeped into my aching body.*

   Try describing:
   the veins on a leaf   a piece of sandpaper   a cold wind

4. **Taste:** *The sour grapes left a bitter taste in my mouth.*

   Try describing:
   chocolate ice cream   pizza   a lemon

5. **Smell:** *The scent of honeysuckle filled the meadow with heavy sweetness.*

   Try describing:
   a bakery   perfume   a farm

ACTIVITY E Pick five topics you did not choose in Activity D. Write a sentence describing each topic, focusing on creating a mood with your words, such as cheerful, suspenseful, excited, or amazed.

ACTIVITY F The following sentences lack detailed descriptions. By using as many sense impressions as possible, make each sentence come alive. (You may want to change the structure of the sentence.)

1. It rained.
2. Alonzo ate the cookies.
3. The milk smelled bad.
4. The music was loud.
5. The fall festival was crowded.

WRITER'S CORNER

Choose a topic below and develop it into a brief description. Use as many senses as you can in your description.

a. a snake shedding its skin
b. the first bite of your favorite meal
c. watching a sunset
d. the final moments of a race
e. a springtime walk in the woods

Organization

When writing a description, it helps to organize your details so that one detail flows logically into the next. For example, in describing your bedroom, you might focus first on the floor, then your bed and desk, and conclude by describing the walls and ceiling. Generally how you arrange your description depends on what you are describing.

Spatial Order

Spatial order is often used to describe a person or place. Imagine how your eyes might scan a room when you're looking for something. You can go from left to right, right to left, up to down, or down to up.

> **I gazed in wonder at the ancient tree's lofty green branches, its thick gnarled trunk, and the tangle of roots that disappeared beneath my feet.**

Chronological Order

Use chronological order if your description is leading the reader through a particular scene or experience.

> **At first I felt the slightest rumble, as if a train were passing nearby. Then the entire kitchen started to quake. Cups and dishes went crashing to the floor, and the room was enveloped in a cloud of dust.**

Comparing and Contrasting

Use a comparing and contrasting organization when you want to tell how two things are alike or different. You may describe one item and then another, giving equal weight to each item, or compare and contrast parts of each item.

> **When the scientist emerged from the time machine, he appeared almost as a different person. Where smooth skin once covered his face and hands, there were now deep wrinkles and gray spots. His pearly white teeth had turned a shade of yellow. Instead of bright, excited eyes, the scientist's tired eyes gazed at me through wire-rim bifocals.**

ACTIVITY A **How would you organize each of the following descriptions? Discuss your answers.**

1. how the new school is better than the old school
2. the view from the top of a mountain
3. the mess inside my locker
4. a butterfly emerging from a cocoon
5. a new dance routine
6. the difference between the city and the suburbs
7. a journey to the bottom of the ocean
8. a scientist's laboratory
9. a movie you have recently seen
10. your new neighbor

ACTIVITY B **Rewrite the descriptive paragraph below in spatial order.**

Cobwebs lined the top of the walls. Everything on the floor was covered in a thick coat of dust. Wallpaper sporting an ancient floral pattern was slowly peeling from the wall. Bits of insulation drooped from the attic's ceiling. All over the floor were ancient objects, children's toys, boxes of clothes, and a pile of old suitcases. One black spider hung from its web, seemingly indifferent to our arrival. There must have been a leak in the ceiling at one point because a brown stain was in the corner. One wall was covered with mirrored tiles, some of them broken or chipped.

ACTIVITY C **Rewrite the descriptive paragraph below in chronological order.**

From the top comes the hint of a flower, sheathed in a protective covering. The gardener plants the seeds and waits. The stem grows higher and higher. Finally, the beautiful flower emerges to greet the day. With the help of nutrients from the soil and water, a tiny sprout emerges from the seed. Soon bright green leaves begin to grow from the sprout.

WRITER'S CORNER

Write a five-sentence description of what you did last Saturday or Sunday. Use chronological order.

Grammar in Action. Use transition words in your Writer's Corner description. See Chapter 3, Lesson 3.

Venn Diagrams

When writing a description organized by comparison and contrast, writers often use a Venn diagram. The purpose of a Venn diagram, like that of other graphic organizers such as a word web and a time line, is to organize a writer's ideas before writing them in paragraph form.

Here are the steps for making a Venn diagram that compares and contrasts two items.

1. Draw two large, overlapping circles.
2. Write the name of one item at the top of each circle.
3. Write "Both" where the circles overlap.
4. Write the ideas that are true of only that item under its name in the outer section of its circle.
5. Write the ideas that are true of both items in the middle where the circles overlap.

Once you're ready to write a complete description, you will use the ideas in the middle of the Venn diagram to compare the pair of items and use the ideas on the outer edges to contrast the pair. Look at the example below of a writer's comparison and contrast of cats and dogs.

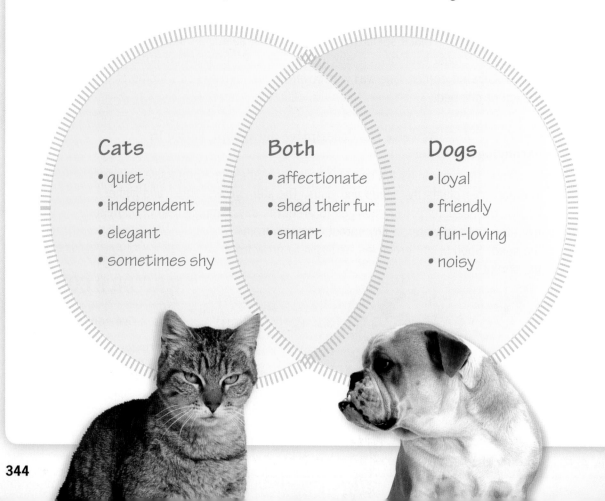

Cats
- quiet
- independent
- elegant
- sometimes shy

Both
- affectionate
- shed their fur
- smart

Dogs
- loyal
- friendly
- fun-loving
- noisy

Words That Compare and Contrast

When you write a compare-and-contrast description, certain words can help you. Words that indicate two items are being compared include *like, likewise, similarly,* and *in the same way.* Contrasting is showing how things are different. Words that indicate things are being contrasted include *but, however, in contrast, nevertheless, on the other hand,* and *yet.*

ACTIVITY D Choose three pairs of topics below. Make a Venn diagram to organize details that make each topic alike and different.

1. flowers and trees
2. camping in a tent and staying in a hotel
3. monkeys and apes
4. soccer and baseball
5. in-line skating and ice skating
6. spring and fall
7. the city and the country
8. Italian food and Greek food
9. your bedroom and your brother's or sister's bedroom
10. swimming in a pool and swimming in a lake

ACTIVITY E Choose a Venn diagram you created in Activity D to help you write a short paragraph comparing or contrasting the two topics. Be sure to use the comparing and contrasting words at the top of this page.

ACTIVITY F Write a brief description comparing and contrasting dogs and cats, using the ideas in the example Venn diagram on page 344. Use words such as *like, similarly, but,* and *however* in your description.

Grammar in Action Use the comparative degree in your Writer's Corner sentences. See Adjectives, Section 2.3.

Noun Clauses

You learned in Chapters 2 and 3 about ways adjective and adverb clauses can make your writing more interesting. Another useful clause is the noun clause, which is a dependent clause used as a noun. Here are some ways a noun clause can act in a sentence.

As a Subject

Whichever flowers you choose to plant **will be an improvement over the weeds.**

As a Subject Complement

The taller weeds are *what you'd pull out first*.

As a Direct Object

I like *how flowers can brighten up a yard*.

As an Object of a Preposition

Our planting will return the garden to *what it used to be*.

As an Appositive

The knowledge *that the flowers will bloom* **makes me smile.**

A noun clause may begin with an introductory word such as *that, what, who, whose, which, when, where, why, how, whatever, whoever,* or *whichever*. In some cases, though, the introductory word is understood and may be omitted. In the second example below, the introductory word *that* has been omitted.

Lucy says *that the prettiest flowers in a garden are tulips*.

Lucy says *the prettiest flowers in a garden are tulips*.

Using Noun Clauses

One way a noun clause can add variety and interest to your sentences is by clarifying information or expanding on a thought. In the examples below, a simple noun is expanded into a noun clause that gives more information.

Raul did not know the plan.

Raul did not know *that we planned to open a restaurant*.

A noun clause can replace a noun when the writer wants to express an idea in a more elaborate, descriptive, or poetic way. For example:

I'll give you anything.

I'll give you *whatever your heart desires*.

Finally, a writer may use a noun clause to shift the emphasis of a sentence. In the examples below, the writer uses a noun clause to rearrange the sentence and shift the focus.

I have obviously failed you.

That I have failed you **is obvious.**

In the second sentence, the writer has chosen to emphasize not the failure itself, but the fact that the failure was obvious.

As you examine your own writing, think of ways you could use noun clauses to clarify, elaborate on, or shift the focus of your sentences.

ACTIVITY A Use a noun clause to replace or expand on the underlined words in each sentence below. The new sentence should provide clarity or additional information to the original sentence.

1. Everyone was excited by the idea.
2. We could go anywhere for our vacation.
3. Everyone was surprised by Todd's actions.
4. When you get inside, talk to that man.
5. We were relieved to arrive at the destination.
6. That thought is ridiculous.
7. The world would be a better place if we realized my dream.
8. Gardening is a hobby that many enjoy.
9. Alex did not know the recipe.
10. The colors you pick for your bedroom will complement your comforter.

WRITER'S CORNER

Using the Venn diagram you created on page 345, write a short paragraph on that topic. Be sure to use a noun clause in one of your sentences. Then circle the word or words that the noun clause modifies.

Grammar in Action. Find the first noun clause in the p. 336 excerpt.

Varying Sentences with Noun Clauses

Knowing when to use a noun clause can help you vary your sentences. A noun clause can shorten a sentence or expand it. A well-placed noun clause can add interest by breaking up monotonous sentences.

In the following examples, a noun clause is used to shorten a sentence:

> **These woods belong to someone, and I think I know who.**
> *Whose woods these are* **I think I know.**

The second sentence is the opening line of Robert Frost's poem "Stopping by Woods on a Snowy Evening."

A writer may choose to combine two sentences into one if it will improve the rhythm. Look at how the writer revised the following paragraph to break up a series of simple sentences:

> **They could not see it. They could not hear it. A moose was in these woods, however. That could not be denied.**
> **They could not see it. They could not hear it.** *That a moose was in these woods*, **however, could not be denied.**

A noun clause will not always improve a sentence. Sometimes noun clauses just add clutter. In the example below, eliminating the noun clause improves the sentence.

> **A DVD player is** *what people often use to record movies*.
> **People often use a DVD player to record movies.**

ACTIVITY B Rewrite the sentences below, using noun clauses.

1. I know who she is; it cannot be denied.
2. He did not reply, but that may not mean anything.
3. He got in here, but I do not know how.
4. Henry was surprised to hear what we wanted. We wanted to fly to Spain.
5. I wanted to get rid of the blue table.
6. America needs innovators like her.
7. His research topic is unknown.
8. The Chicago fans hope the Cubs will win.

ACTIVITY C Find the noun clauses in the paragraph below. Choose at least two sentences with noun clauses and rewrite them. Discuss how your revisions changed the sentences.

In the desert plains of Peru lie vast line drawings that can only be seen from an airplane. No one knows who drew them, and no one knows why they were drawn. What is known is that there are approximately 300 drawings of various animals, plants, and shapes in an area of about 400 square miles. Some experts believe that the drawings were made by an ancient civilization called the Nazca between 300 BC and AD 800. Others think that space aliens may have drawn them. Regardless of who drew the lines, many people wonder how this feat could have been accomplished before the invention of modern machines, including airplanes.

ACTIVITY D Complete the answers to the questions below. Use noun clauses in your sentences.

1. Who's that man wearing a cowboy hat?
   I don't know _____.

2. When is the first day of class?
   I believe _____.

3. What is Gabriela talking about?
   I don't understand _____.

4. What do you remember about your last birthday?
   I remember _____.

5. Will the test be difficult?
   I can tell you _____.

6. What did you see at the art museum?
   _____ were paintings by Picasso and van Gogh.

7. Why is that hammer helpful?
   The hammer is helpful _____.

8. What didn't Sara's friends know about him?
   They didn't know _____.

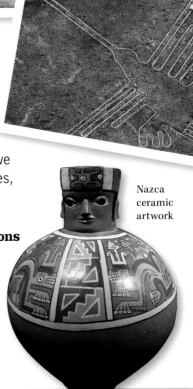

Nazca ceramic artwork

WRITER'S CORNER

Write three sentences about recent news events. Include a noun clause in each sentence. For each sentence, underline the noun clause and write how it is used in the sentence, such as a subject or a direct object.

Tech Tip With an adult, research news events online.

Adjective and Adverb Suffixes

LiNK

Under the Royal Palms

On both previous occasions, the crowds had been like the full and gentle swelling of the river after the summer rains. Now the mob was like the flood after a hurricane: uncontrollable, turbulent, sweeping away everything in its path.

Alma Flor Ada

A suffix is a syllable or syllables added to the end of a word. A suffix can change the function, or use, of the word. Suffixes added to nouns or verbs can create adjectives, nouns, or adverbs. A suffix that creates an adjective is an adjective suffix. A suffix that creates an adverb is an adverb suffix.

If the suffix *-ous* is added to the noun *poison*, for example, the adjective *poisonous* results. The adjective means "full of poison," as in "People once thought that tomatoes were poisonous."

The suffix *-ly* changes adjectives to adverbs. Adding *-ly* to *angry*, for example, creates *angrily*, which means "in an angry way."

The suffixes below create adjectives when added to base words. Sometimes adding a suffix changes the spelling of its base word.

SUFFIX	MEANING	EXAMPLE(S)
-able, -ible	capable of being	readable, divisible
-al	relating to	fictional
-ant, -ent	having the quality of	pleasant, obedient
-ive	having the quality of	talkative
-less	without	useless
-ous	full of	joyous

Since the function of an adjective is to describe, adjective suffixes are particularly useful in descriptive writing.

ACTIVITY A Add a suffix from the list on page 350 to complete each sentence.

1. Nocturnal animals are act_____ at night.
2. The deer stood motion_____ at the edge of the forest.
3. Farmland in Nebraska is highly product_____.
4. It seems point_____ to argue about which river is longest when we could look up the answer in an encyclopedia.
5. The clay pot was too por_____ to hold water.
6. The fabric of the couch is treated with a water-resist_____ chemical.
7. My boots are made from extremely dur_____ material.
8. The apartment, which was advertised as spac_____, was actually the size of a large closet.
9. We visited the center for psychologic_____ testing at the university.
10. Tania's gull_____ nature sometimes gets her into trouble.
11. The firefighters felt help_____ when the blaze went out of control.
12. The moment_____ occasion was captured on film.

ACTIVITY B Write a new word by adding an adjective suffix to each base word below. Consult a dictionary if you need help spelling the new word correctly.

1. courtesy
2. manage
3. speech
4. attract
5. excel
6. access
7. cranium
8. harmony
9. agriculture
10. effect

WRITER'S CORNER

Skim through a book of fiction for five adjectives containing a suffix from the list on page 350. Write the name of the book, and list the adjectives and the words they modify.

More Adjective Suffixes

Here are more adjective suffixes and their meanings.

SUFFIX	MEANING	EXAMPLE
-en	made of, like	golden
-ful	full of	thankful
-ic	characterized by	metallic
-ish	like, preoccupied with	childish
-some	characterized by	tiresome
-y	inclined to, suggesting	itchy

ACTIVITY C **For each definition below, use a suffix from the list above to make an adjective that fits the definition. Use a dictionary for help with spelling.**

1. characterized by poetry
2. characterized by a lonely feeling
3. full of sorrow
4. inclined to shine
5. preoccupied with oneself
6. made of wood
7. full of fear
8. characterized by adventure
9. suggesting cream
10. characterized by majesty

ACTIVITY D Put each base word and suffix together to make a word. Then use the word in a sentence. Use a dictionary for help.

Base Word	Suffix
1. appreciate	-ive
2. loathe	-some
3. relent	-less
4. wealth	-y
5. comic	-al
6. bounty	-ful

ACTIVITY E Complete each sentence below with a word containing the suffix indicated. Use the list of base words for clues.

adventure	luxury
descend	pain
grace	rely
hero	renew
invent	sun

1. **-ic** Mrs. Hill made a _____ effort to save the toddler from danger.

2. **-some** Only _____ people have interest in climbing Mount Everest.

3. **-al** I received a magazine subscription _____ notice in the mail.

4. **-able** Kendra gets a lot of babysitting jobs because she is quite _____.

5. **-y** I love to play softball on _____ days.

6. **-ful** I'm not _____ enough to be a ballet dancer.

7. **-ous** The rooms at highly rated hotels are usually quite _____.

8. **-less** Some medical tests are considered _____.

9. **-ant** Paul claims to be a _____ of George Washington.

10. **-ive** Benjamin Franklin was known for being quite _____.

WRITER'S CORNER

What is the suffix that *wholesome*, *bothersome*, and *fearsome* have in common? Knowing what the suffix means, how would you define the three words? Look up the words in a dictionary to check if you are right.

Tech Tip With an adult, use an online dictionary.

Thesaurus

Whether you're writing a description, a personal narrative, or a letter to a friend, it can sometimes be hard to think of just the right words. One book that can help is a thesaurus, a reference tool that gives synonyms for words. A thesaurus can help when you want to replace a word with a synonym that fits better. For example, suppose you wrote the following sentence describing a circus act:

The trapeze artist surprised the audience by completing a triple somersault in midair.

Because the word *surprised* doesn't seem strong enough, you look up *surprise* in a thesaurus and find *astonish* and *amaze* listed as synonyms. Both words suggest a stronger feeling of surprise. Either word could replace *surprised* in this sentence.

LiNK

Smoky Night

Outside, the sky is hazy orange. Flames pounce up the side of our building.

Three fire engines scream to a stop. Fire fighters jump out, running, pulling hoses. I see our window where Mama and I had stood. The fire hasn't reached it yet.

Eve Bunting

Looking Up a Word

When you look up a word in a thesaurus, first check to see what type of thesaurus it is. A dictionary thesaurus lists the words in alphabetical order, so you can flip to the correct letter and use the guide words at the top of each page to find your word. An index thesaurus groups words into categories, each of which is assigned a number. The easiest way to locate a word is to look it up in the index, find the number assigned to it, and then find the word by using the numbers listed at the top of each page.

Some thesauruses give the definitions of the synonyms they list. If your thesaurus does not give definitions and you are unsure of the exact meaning of a word, look it up in a dictionary before you use it in your writing.

ACTIVITY A Using a thesaurus, write two synonyms for each word below. Then use one of the synonyms in a sentence.

1. speak
2. excited
3. bad
4. surprised
5. rough

6. cold
7. destroy
8. walk
9. request
10. create

ACTIVITY B Read the sample thesaurus entries for the words *look* and *annoy*. Then choose which synonym fits best in each sentence that follows. You may consult a dictionary if you are unsure which word fits best.

look *verb* glance, glare, observe, peek, stare; *noun* view, inspection, appearance, manner

1. Benicio tiptoed to the closet and _____ at the wrapped gifts.

2. When Alicia saw her sister wearing Alicia's favorite sweater, she _____ at her.

3. The students enjoyed the _____ out the window.

4. The rhino just stood and _____ at the people.

5. Had you _____ the team at practice before you decided to try out?

annoy *verb* bother, bug, disturb, provoke, fret, tease, plague, torment, irk, irritate, worry *noun* anger, irritation, nuisance

6. Salma _____ her older brother as he worked on his homework.

7. His _____ grew as the carpenter hammered nail after nail so early in the morning.

8. It was such a _____ to pick up the toys after she had told the children to put their things away.

9. The idea of not being able to find a solution to the problem _____ him night after night.

WRITER'S CORNER

Choose an object in your home and imagine that you have to sell it. Write two sentences about it, using descriptive and enticing language. Use a thesaurus to help you choose vivid words.

Hamlet

To be, or not to be, that is the
question:
Whether 'tis nobler in the mind
to suffer
The slings and arrows of
outrageous fortune,
Or to take arms against a sea
of troubles,
And by opposing end them.

William Shakespeare

Replacing Words

A thesaurus is particularly useful when you find that a word is vague, imprecise, or repeated too frequently. When you find a word that should be replaced, look it up in a thesaurus and find a synonym to replace it.

In the example below, the word *shook* seemed imprecise, while the word *cold* did not seem strong enough. The writer used a thesaurus to replace these words with words that seemed more specific and precise.

> **The explorer shook as a cold wind blew in from the north.**
> **The explorer *shuddered* as a *frigid* wind blew in from the north.**

In this example the word *went* is both vague and repeated, so the writer replaced it with more precise and varied words.

> **Pedro went down the driveway as the car went away.**
> **Pedro *raced* down the driveway as the car *sped* away.**

ACTIVITY C For each sentence use a thesaurus to find synonyms for the underlined vague or imprecise word. Choose a synonym that fits well in the sentence and rewrite the sentence with that word.

1. Morgan <u>talked</u> on the phone with her friend for two hours.
2. The librarian was really <u>nice</u> about showing me how to use some of the reference books.
3. The view from the rim of the Grand Canyon is <u>beautiful</u>.
4. I found the noise from the electric drill really <u>annoying</u>.
5. The contractors did a <u>poor</u> job of fixing the roof.
6. It was <u>kind</u> of you to give a donation for our band trip.
7. Sometimes it's better to be <u>slow</u> than to be hasty.
8. What sights do you plan to <u>see</u> on your trip?
9. Diego was <u>happy</u> to hear his sister won the student election.
10. The chef tasted her assistant's soup and thought it was <u>good</u>.

11. Because of the gusty winds, Sasha's homework papers <u>flew</u> through the air.

12. Josh <u>made</u> his science project by adding sodium bicarbonate to the existing formula.

ACTIVITY D **Choose the best word to replace the underlined word in each sentence. If you do not know the meaning of the word, look it up in a dictionary.**

1. The famous leader's speech <u>encouraged</u> me to work harder. (advanced, inspired, fostered, stimulated)

2. Our teacher congratulated us for all that we <u>finished</u> this year. (accomplished, completed, concluded, ended)

3. I believe it is our <u>job</u> as citizens to vote. (assignment, chore, duty, employment)

4. The <u>ordinary</u> American watches several hours of TV every day. (average, normal, standard, common)

5. It is <u>plain</u> from the look on your face that you disagree. (distinct, obvious, honest, straightforward)

ACTIVITY E **The following paragraph contains several vague, imprecise, or repeated words that could be replaced with synonyms. Choose at least five words to replace and find the appropriate synonyms in a thesaurus. Then rewrite the paragraph with the replacement words.**

The Hike Against Asthma took place this morning. It was a good day for the many people who took part in it. The weather was good, and everyone seemed happy to be there. Some people ran the entire course. Others were happy just to walk the course and enjoy a good conversation. Oscar Garza got to the end of the route first, so he got a free plane ticket.

Oral Descriptions

Have you ever described a person, a place, or an object to a friend or family member? If you have, then you've given an oral description. When describing something, the speaker often creates sensory images with vivid words or phrases to make the listener feel involved in the description.

Giving an oral description to a small group of classmates is similar to describing an experience to a friend or family member. Follow these steps as you plan your oral description.

Choose a Topic

Choose any topic that you can describe with plenty of sensory details. Your topic should be something that has personal significance to you. You might choose a place, such as your grandmother's house; a person, such as your older sister; or a treasured object, such as your charm bracelet.

Marmot

Consider Your Audience

Think about how much your audience (in this case your classmates) know about your topic. If you're describing your dog, you probably don't need to describe what a dog looks like. If you're describing your pet marmot, you might need to add a more detailed physical description.

Jot Down Details

Once you have chosen your topic, jot down whatever details come to mind. Pick out the most interesting details or the ones that your audience will understand or relate to. Then think of the most vivid way of describing each detail. You may want to consult a thesaurus to help you choose just the right words. Your details should combine to create an overall feeling about whatever you are describing.

Organize Your Description

Use a graphic organizer or make an outline to help you organize your description. You will begin your oral description with an introduction that draws in your audience and makes them want to hear more. Then organize your description in a logical order, such as spatial order, sequential order, or another way that makes sense for your topic. Conclude your description with a sentence that sums up your feelings.

Prepare Note Cards

Once you have selected the details you will use and settled on a way to organize your talk, write your notes on note cards. Use one card each for your introduction and conclusion. Use a note card for each main idea, writing words and phrases that will create an image in the listener's mind.

Consider Your Tone

Consider the tone of voice you will use in your oral description. The tone will depend on your topic. If you're describing a spooky swamp, you might use an ominous tone. If you're describing a sleek, new sports car, you might use an enthusiastic tone.

ACTIVITY A **Choose a common classroom object to describe. Write five or six details about the object. Describe the details to a partner one by one and see how quickly he or she can guess what you are describing. Then see how quickly you can guess what your partner is describing.**

SPEAKER'S CORNER

Use the steps in this lesson to prepare a three-minute oral description. Choose a topic, jot down details, organize your description, and prepare note cards to use in a talk to your class. With a small group, practice delivering your opening sentence, using different tones of voice.

Practice

Practicing your oral description will help you feel prepared when it is time to present it to your audience. The more you practice, the more familiar you will be with your description and the less time you will spend looking at your note cards. As you practice, ask yourself the following questions:

- Will my introduction catch the audience's attention?
- Do I describe things in a logical order?
- Do I speak clearly and carefully so that the listener will understand every detail?
- Do I make frequent eye contact with the listeners?
- Do I speak with an appropriate tone of voice?
- Do I use vivid words in my description?
- Have I provided details that describe sound, touch, smell, or taste if appropriate?
- Does my last sentence clearly indicate that it is the conclusion?

Listening Tips

Here are some tips to consider when you are listening to someone give an oral description.

- Look at the speaker as you listen so that he or she knows you are listening.
- At times, though, you may want to close your eyes to help you imagine what the speaker is describing. Try to picture the person, place, or object being described. Make it clear through your posture that you are still engaged and interested in what the speaker is saying.
- Don't interrupt the speaker. When the speaker is finished, you may wish to provide feedback on what details were the most vivid or which parts of the description you did not understand.

ACTIVITY B Review your note cards from the Speaker's Corner on page 359 and share some of your details with a partner. Give each other feedback about which details are the most interesting and vivid. Use your partner's suggestions to revise some of your details. Use the questions below to help you evaluate each detail.

1. Is the detail described vividly, using sensory words?
2. Are there any general words that can be replaced with more specific ones?
3. Does the detail contribute to an overall feeling about what is being described?
4. Does the detail seem irrelevant or distracting?
5. Is the detail expressed clearly and concisely?

ACTIVITY C Meet with a partner to practice your oral description. Use your note cards to help you recall key points. Focus on making eye contact and speaking in an appropriate tone of voice. Ask your partner if your description seemed well organized. Offer ideas for reorganizing your partner's description.

SPEAKER'S CORNER

Present your oral description to your classmates. Make frequent eye contact and use an expressive tone of voice. When your description is done, ask your classmates for feedback. Could the class visualize what you described? Were all the details vivid and interesting?

Tech Tip Videotape or podcast your presentation.

Writer's Workshop

Prewriting and Drafting

Have you ever been to a place that made you feel especially excited, frightened, or content? Have you ever wished you could make others feel as if they had been there too? When you write a description, you can take your readers anywhere you want by creating a strong image in their minds.

Prewriting

Before writing a description, good writers prepare by generating ideas and planning out  the description. They begin by choosing a topic that is familiar and rewarding to write about. Then they freewrite details and organize them, often with the help of a graphic organizer.

Choosing a Topic

Michael, a seventh grader, was assigned to write a description for class. He wanted to think of a place that was important to him, but also one that he could picture clearly in his mind. He brainstormed ideas for his description by asking himself the following questions:

- Where do I like to go with friends?
- Where do I like to go by myself?
- Where would I take a visitor?
- What are the most beautiful or unusual places I've ever seen?
- Where do I feel especially comfortable or relaxed?

Michael considered writing about his bedroom, but he couldn't think of enough vivid details. Next, he thought about his family's summer cottage, but there seemed to be too much to describe. Finally, he decided to write about one room in the cottage, the attic where he loved to hide out with his cousins.

Your Turn

Select a special place to write about. Use the questions under Choosing a Topic to brainstorm ideas for an interesting topic.

After listing several topics, think about each one. Have you asked yourself the questions and listed possible topics but still can't decide?

To help you generate ideas, try

- looking through an album of family photographs
- talking to a friend or a family member
- reviewing a personal journal

Writer's Tip If your topic is so broad that it overwhelms you, don't give up. Imagine that you are a photographer looking through a zoom lens, which can zoom in from far away to close up. Picture in your mind your special place. Keep zooming in until you arrive at a topic that you can manage.

Using a Graphic Organizer

Recalling, selecting, and organizing details are at the heart of any good piece of descriptive writing. You might simply freewrite to generate details about your topic. In many cases, however, you might also use a graphic organizer to help you think of ideas. If your description will be organized in chronological order, creating a time line might help you think of each event. If you are comparing and contrasting, you might use a Venn diagram.

Michael spent a few minutes freewriting, jotting down many visual details about his attic. However, he found he was missing many sensory details. He decided to use a word web to help him think of details related to all five senses. Read the word web that Michael started.

Organization

Prewriting
Drafting
Content Editing
Revising
Copyediting
Proofreading
Publishing

Your Turn

Freewrite as many details as you can related to the place you will describe. Create a graphic organizer similar to the one Michael made. Write on it some of the important sensory details you recall about your topic. To help you generate ideas, ask yourself the following questions:

- What can you see in your special place?
- What sounds can you hear?
- What do you smell?
- Can you taste anything there?
- What can you touch?

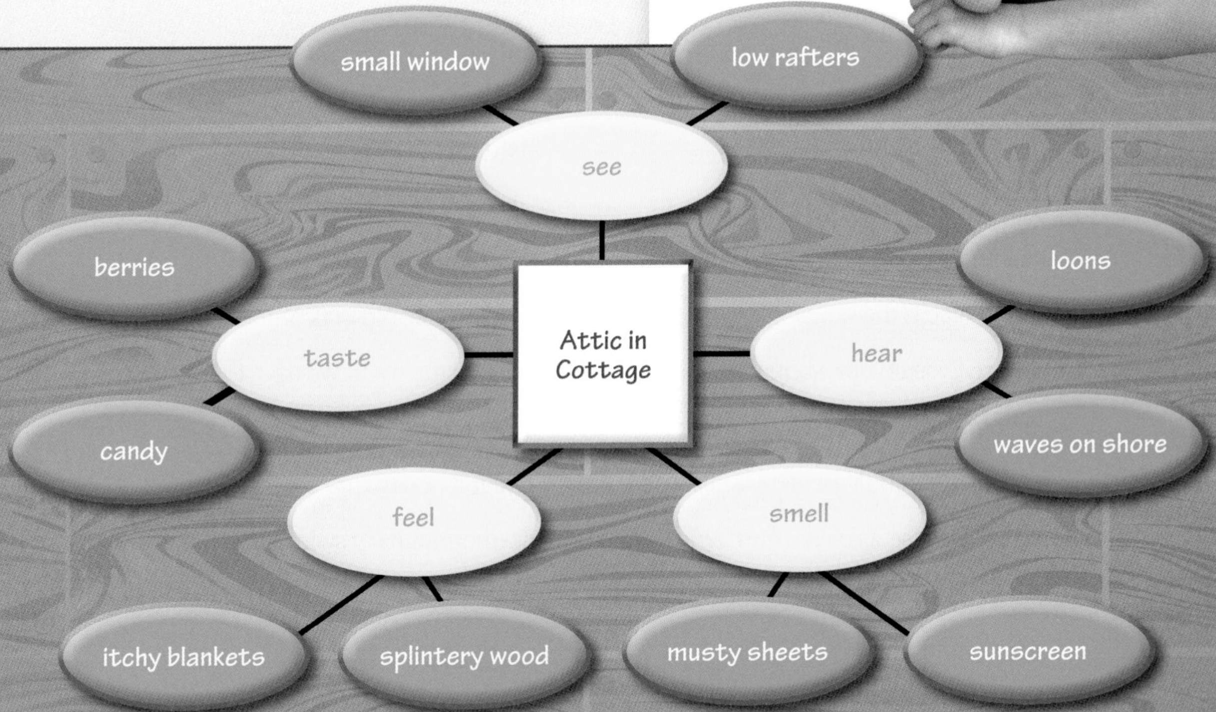

small window

low rafters

see

berries

loons

taste

Attic in Cottage

hear

candy

waves on shore

feel

smell

itchy blankets

splintery wood

musty sheets

sunscreen

Drafting

After collecting and organizing his details, Michael began to develop them into a draft. He knew before he started writing that he would describe the attic fondly. He hoped that readers would feel as if they had been there too. After studying the details he had written, he decided to organize the description mainly in spatial order.

Our Attic Hideaway

The best part of every summer is the month we spend at our family's cottage on Lake Minnetonka. The cottage is like an old sweatshirt worn but comfortable. And it does have indoor plumbing—finally! The attic is where all the cousins sleep. It's our hideaway.

To reach the attic, you climb up a ladder and push open the trap door. It takes a moment for your eyes to adjust to the room. It's dark because there's no electricity. You'll probably notice the smell first. It's the smell that all attics seem to have, combined with a smell of insect reppelent and sunscreen. If your're more than five feet tall, be careful not to bang your head on the attics low, slanted beams. Or get a splinter from the wood.

The entrance is surrounded by odds and ends. In the corner are several scary figures. Don't be scared! They're just dressmakers' dummies. There are lots of other things you might use at a cottage. You can poke through all kinds of interesting odds and ends in the boxes and suitcases, which is always fun on a rainy day. At the far end of the attic is the sleeping area, which has four comfortable old cots. You might even notice Everest, our ancient terrier, curled up on one of the beds. We have to carry Ev up ourselves. But he likes to hang out with the guys, maybe because he's one too?

In the middle of the attic is our play area. Old milk crates are scattered about, which we use as chairs and tables. We also have mountains of swimming trunks and towels, books and magazines and snacks like berries and candy that we smuggle up. It's a wonderful mess!

You'd love to fall asleep in the attic to the sound of waves lapping on the beach. You can hear loons calling, crickets chirping, and sometimes even wolves. That is, if you can hear anything over the sound of my cousins snoring like buzz saws!

Michael introduced the topic and explained its significance in the first paragraph. Then he 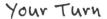 described his special place in spatial order, moving from one part of the attic to another, as if someone was climbing the ladder and walking across the attic.

Because sounds and smells did not fit in any particular order spatially, Michael added them wherever they seemed to fit logically. He described the smells at the beginning because a visitor would notice them first. He described the sounds after describing the cots because he usually heard the sounds when he was going to sleep.

Your Turn

Review the details in your freewriting and in your graphic organizer. Decide on the best way to organize your essay. Then write your draft.

- Begin with an introduction that introduces the topic and engages the reader.
- Continue the draft by describing the details in a logical order.
- Finish with a conclusion that sums up the description and leaves a lasting impression.

Writer's Tip Remember to double-space your draft so that you can revise easily.

Grammar in Action

What is the noun clause in Michael's first paragraph where the introductory word is understood and omitted?

Using Transition Words

Even when ideas are put in a logical order, they will not always form a clear and well-worded essay. You may find that some sentences don't flow well together. Remember that transition words can help you tie your sentences together. They can give a clearer sense of how the details fit together logically. Use some of the transition words below when organizing a description in spatial order.

above	behind	in front of	to the left
across	below	next to	to the right
before	farther	opposite of	under

Prewriting
Drafting
Content Editing
Revising
Copyediting
Proofreading
Publishing

Editor's Workshop

Content Editing

After completing the first draft of a description, writers take a second look at the ideas in their drafts to find areas that need improvement. Often, writers will take a break of at least a few hours and often much longer before they begin content editing.

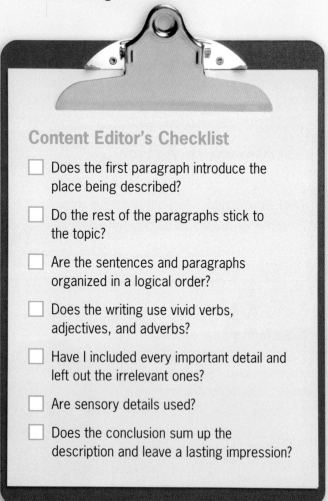

Content Editor's Checklist

☐ Does the first paragraph introduce the place being described?

☐ Do the rest of the paragraphs stick to the topic?

☐ Are the sentences and paragraphs organized in a logical order?

☐ Does the writing use vivid verbs, adjectives, and adverbs?

☐ Have I included every important detail and left out the irrelevant ones?

☐ Are sensory details used?

☐ Does the conclusion sum up the description and leave a lasting impression?

When Michael returned to "Our Attic Hideaway" the next day, he could review it more objectively. He looked for details that were unnecessary and for important details that he should add. He also looked for sections that could be revised to make them clearer, more logical, and better-organized. Michael used the Content Editor's Checklist to help him remember all the ways to improve a draft of a description.

After Michael revised his description, he traded papers with his classmate Julia so that they could edit each other's drafts. Michael wondered whether he had described the attic clearly enough so that a reader who had never seen his special place could picture it. He wondered whether some sentences in his essay strayed too far from the topic. Julia would be able to answer these questions.

Julia read Michael's draft once to get an overall impression about it. She wrote question marks next to the parts that confused her. Then she reread the draft, checking it item-by-item against the Content Editor's Checklist.

Julia discussed her suggestions with Michael. She started with positive points. Overall, Julia said that Michael's draft was excellent. She thought there were plenty of sensory details. She also said the description formed a clear picture of what the attic was like and why it was special. Julia did have the following suggestions for improving Michael's essay.

- Since the topic of the essay is the attic, maybe you should make that clearer in the first paragraph. Also, the sentence about the plumbing doesn't seem related.
- Look for more places to add vivid words. Could you describe the ladder, the cots, or the smell of the attic more clearly?
- Could you make some of the details clearer? I don't get a good idea of what the dressmakers' dummies look like. And what are the "other things you might use at a cottage"?
- In the third paragraph, I like that you mentioned the dog, but I think you go on too much about him. He's not that important to the description of the attic.
- I like how you conclude by describing the sounds you hear when you go to sleep in the attic. But is there something else you could say to sum up the description?

Michael asked Julia to clarify a few of her comments. He thanked Juia for her suggestions and decided to make most of the changes she suggested.

Your Turn

Reread your draft before you begin to revise it. Review your draft with the help of the Content Editor's Checklist.

Trade papers with a classmate. Make suggestions to help your partner improve his or her draft and ask your partner to do the same for you.

When your partner offers suggestions for your description, try to be receptive to his or her comments. Be sure you understand your partner's recommendations. Remember to listen carefully, discuss the suggestions, and follow the ones that you believe will improve your essay.

Writer's Tip Be clear and constructive in your comments. Be sure to provide positive feedback as well as constructive criticism.

Prewriting

Drafting

Content Editing

Revising

Copyediting

Proofreading

Publishing

Writer's Workshop

Revising

Here are the revisions Michael made to his draft after content editing with Julia.

Our Attic Hideaway

The best part of every summer is the month we spend at our family's cottage on Lake Minnetonka. The cottage is like an old sweatshirt worn but comfortable. ~~And it does~~ *My favorite room in the cottage is the attic.* ~~have indoor plumbing—finally!~~ The attic is where all the cousins sleep. It's our hideaway.

To reach the attic, you climb up a *rickety* ladder and push open the trap door. It takes a moment for your eyes to adjust to the room. It's dark because there's no electricity. You'll probably notice the smell first. It's the *musty* smell that all attics seem to have, combined with a smell of insect reppelent and sunscreen. If your're more than five feet tall, be careful not to bang your head on the attics low, slanted beams. Or get a splinter from the wood.

The entrance is surrounded by odds and ends. In the corner are several scary figures. *that look like headless monsters.* Don't be scared! They're just dressmakers' dummies. *Beside them are* ~~There are lots of other~~ *water skis, beach toys, and rafts.* ~~things you might use at a cottage.~~ You can poke through all kinds of interesting odds and ends in the boxes and suitcases, which is always fun on a rainy day. At the far end of the attic is the sleeping area, which has four comfortable old cots. You might even notice Everest, our ancient terrier, curled up on one of the beds. ~~We have to carry Ev up ourselves. But he likes to hang out with the guys, maybe because he's one too?~~

In the middle of the attic is our play area. Old milk crates are scattered about, which we use as chairs and tables. We also have mountains of swimming trunks and towels, books and magazines and snacks like berries and candy that we smuggle up. It's a wonderful mess!

You'd love to fall asleep in the attic to the sound of waves lapping on the beach. You can hear loons calling, crickets chirping, and sometimes even wolves. That is, if you can hear anything over the sound of my cousins snoring like buzz saws! *In any case our attic hideaway is the best room in my favorite place in the world.*

Look at the revisions Michael made to his draft. He used most of the ideas Julia offered and looked for other ways to improve his description.

- Michael agreed that the topic needed to be made clearer in the first paragraph. He emphasized the attic by saying it was his favorite part of the cottage. Should he take out the sentence about the plumbing?

- He added vivid adjectives in two places. He described the smell of the attic as "musty" and the ladder as "rickety."

 Word Choice

Since he'd already written that the cots were comfortable and old, does he need to add more description?

- He came up with better ways to describe a few details. He compared the dummies to headless monsters and specifically mentioned water skis, beach toys, and rafts.

- Michael agreed that he'd added too much about the dog. The information about carrying him up and why he liked to spend time upstairs didn't seem relevant to the attic's description. Which sentence should he keep, and which ones should he take out?

- Finally, he decided to revise the last paragraph. What could he do to sum up the description?

After reviewing his draft again, Michael found that one part of his description was out of place. Because the cots were placed against the far wall, he realized their description should come after the description of the play area, which was in the middle of the attic. He moved the last two sentences of the third paragraph to make them fit better.

Your Turn

- Use your own and your classmate's ideas to revise your description.
- Choose only the changes that you think will improve the description and then mark them neatly on your draft.
- When you have finished inserting changes, review the revised draft again, using the Content Editor's Checklist.

Copyediting and Proofreading

Copyediting

After revising his draft with Julia's help, Michael felt much better about his description. He liked the content, organization, and style of his essay. He felt that the description would create a clear picture of the attic in his readers' minds. He knew

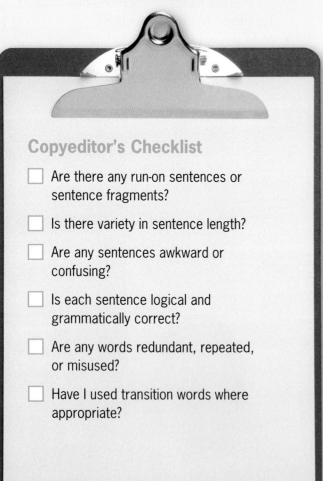

Copyeditor's Checklist

- [ ] Are there any run-on sentences or sentence fragments?

- [ ] Is there variety in sentence length?

- [ ] Are any sentences awkward or confusing?

- [ ] Is each sentence logical and grammatically correct?

- [ ] Are any words redundant, repeated, or misused?

- [ ] Have I used transition words where appropriate?

he could make it even better, however, if he revised it again. He decided to copyedit his draft, using the Copyeditor's Checklist.

To get a feel for the flow of the sentences, Michael read his essay aloud. Some of his

Sentence Fluency sentences were short

and choppy. Other sentences did not seem to flow logically. Reading aloud also helped him find some words that were repeated too many times.

After reviewing his draft, Michael made several corrections. He noticed that the second paragraph concluded with a sentence fragment, so he combined it with the previous sentence. He thought there were too many short, choppy sentences in the second paragraph, so he combined the second and third sentences, using a noun clause. In the last paragraph, he added the word *howling* after *wolves* to make the sentence flow better.

Michael also noticed that he had repeated the word *smell* a few times. He looked in a thesaurus and found the word *whiff*, which refers to a light odor. He used this word for the smell of the insect repellent and sunscreen, which was not as strong as the musty smell of the attic.

Finally, Michael added a transition word to explain that the water skis, beach toys, and rafts were next to the dummies.

Prewriting

Drafting

Content Editing

Revising

Copyediting

Proofreading

Publishing

Proofreading

Proofreading is the final step that writers take before publishing a finished piece. Writers

 Conventions

proofread their manuscript for errors in spelling, capitalization, punctuation, and grammar. Proofreading is not difficult, but it's easy to miss mistakes. Using the Proofreader's Checklist below will help you catch errors.

Proofreader's Checklist

- ☐ Are the paragraphs indented?
- ☐ Have any words been misspelled?
- ☐ Are there errors in grammar?
- ☐ Are capitalization and punctuation correct?
- ☐ Were new errors introduced during the editing process?

Michael asked Mrs. Margolies, a teacher's aide in his class, to proofread "Our Attic Hideaway." He knew that she might catch errors in his draft that he missed because he had already read it so many times.

Mrs. Margolies found several mistakes in Michael's essay. For example, she found a few errors in punctuation. She added a dash to the second sentence to make it grammatically correct. She also added a comma after *books* and *magazines* in the fourth paragraph so that it would make more sense. What other mistakes can you find in Michael's draft?

Publishing

Michael corrected the mistakes that Mrs. Margolies found in his essay, made some last-minute changes of his own, and then printed it out. He looked forward to sharing "Our Attic Hideaway" with his class and his family.

Our Attic Hideaway

by Michael Murray

The best part of every summer is the month we spend at our family's cottage on Lake Minnetonka. The cottage is like an old sweatshirt—worn but comfortable. My favorite room in the cottage is the attic, where all the cousins sleep. It's our hideaway.

To reach the attic, you climb up a rickety ladder and push open the trap door. It takes a moment for your eyes to adjust to the room, which is dark because there's no electricity. What you'll probably notice first is the musty smell that all attics seem to have, combined with a whiff of insect repellent and sunscreen. If you're more than five feet tall, be careful not to bang your head on the attic's low, slanted beams, or get a splinter from the rough wood.

The entrance is surrounded by odds and ends. In the corner are several figures that look like headless monsters. Don't be scared! They're just dressmakers' dummies. Beside them are water skis, beach toys, and rafts. You can poke through all kinds of interesting odds and ends in the boxes and suitcases, which is always fun on a rainy day.

In the middle of the attic is our play area. Old milk crates are scattered about, which we use as chairs and tables. We also have mountains of swimming trunks and towels, books and magazines, and snacks like berries and candy that we smuggle up. It's a wonderful mess! At the far end is the sleeping area, which has four comfortable old cots. You might even notice Everest, our ancient terrier, curled up on one of the beds.

You'd love to fall asleep in the attic to the sound of waves lapping on the beach. You can hear loons calling, crickets chirping, and sometimes even wolves howling. That is, if you can hear anything over the sound of my cousins snoring like buzz saws! In any case our attic hideaway is the best room in my favorite place in the world.

As a class, decide how you will publish your descriptions. You might even choose different

 Presentation publishing methods, depending on your topic. Give these ideas a try. Whichever way you choose to publish, be sure you are presenting your best material.

 Post it on your classroom's wiki, blog, or Web site. Have classmates read one another's descriptions and comment on them.

 Create a class magazine. Decorate the margins with small pictures of things representing the descriptions.

 Film it. If your description is of a place nearby, film it and add music that lends itself to the mood of your description. You can also narrate it with your descriptive writing.

 Create a class book for a younger grade. Decorate the margins with small pictures of things representing the descriptions.

 Does your school have a literary magazine or a newspaper? If so, you may be able to submit your essay for publication. Find out what the requirements for submission are and follow them exactly.

Writer's Tip If you used a computer to input corrections, use a spell-checker to check the spelling one last time. Note that a spell-checker will not catch homophones. If you copied over your essay by hand, make sure you didn't leave out any words.

Prewriting
Drafting
Content Editing
Revising
Copyediting
Proofreading
Publishing

Your Turn

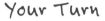

Choose one of the publishing options. Use your best handwriting or a computer to make your final copy. Take a last glance before you publish your description.

- Make sure the title of your finished description stands out by printing it in boldface or by underlining it.
- Write or type your name underneath the title.
- If your description is more than one page long, be sure to number each page.
- If you include pictures, make certain that your pictures match your descriptions.

Descriptions • 373

Book Reviews

LiNK

Because of Winn-Dixie
by Kate DiCamillo
Kirkus Reviews, April 1, 2000. www.kirkusreviews.com

A 10-year old girl learns to adjust to a strange town, makes some fascinating friends, and fills the empty space in her heart thanks to a big old stray dog in this lyrical, moving, and enchanting book by a fresh new voice. India Opal's mama left when she was only three. . . . Enter Winn-Dixie, a dog who "looked like a big piece of old brown carpet that had been left out in the rain." But, this dog had a grin "so big that it made him sneeze." . . . Because of Winn-Dixie, Opal meets Miss Franny Block, an elderly lady whose papa built her a library of her own when she was just a little girl and she's been the librarian ever since. . . . And, Otis, oh yes, Otis, whose music charms the gerbils, rabbits, snakes and lizards he's let out of their cages in the pet store. Brush strokes of magical realism elevate this beyond a simple story of friendship to a well-crafted tale of community and fellowship, of sweetness, sorrow and hope. And, it's funny, too. A real gem.

> The introduction of the *Because of Winn-Dixie* review uses descriptive phrases to explain the book's main themes. Sentence variety and quotes from the book capture the reader's interest. The body of the review describes the scene and the characters while the conclusion expresses the reviewer's opinion of the book.

CHAPTER 5

A Review of Island of the Blue Dolphins

by José Ramirez

Island of the Blue Dolphins, by Scott O'Dell, is an inspiring account of courage and ingenuity. This work of historical fiction tells the story of Karana, a Native American girl, and Ramo, her younger brother.

Alone on a deserted island, Karana and Ramo battle starvation, a pack of wild dogs, and their own fear as they await the return of the "big ship" that left them behind.

When Ramo is killed by the dog pack, Karana swears revenge. She uses her anger to become determined and resourceful. For 18 years she leads a solitary life. Her only friends are the creatures she manages to tame.

Karana learns a surprising life lesson when she befriends the target of her hatred, Rontu, the leader of the dog pack. This friendship helps her fight her loneliness and better understand herself.

This book constantly reminds the reader of the incredible power of human beings to survive and to overcome life's hardships. Karana's mastery of the wilderness is admirable, and her courage and determination are truly inspirational. In Island of the Blue Dolphins, O'Dell has written a story of adventure that celebrates the strength of the human spirit. Readers will never forget the island or the girl who was so brave.

What Makes a Good Book Review?

A book review gives information about a book and tells what the reviewer liked and disliked about it. Unlike a book report, a book review is an evaluation, not just a summary. It is designed to persuade someone to read or not to read the book. How do the reviewers of *Because of Winn-Dixie* and *Island of the Blue Dolphins* feel about the books?

Think of these things when you write a book review.

Audience

Good book reviewers consider the age and knowledge of their audience. They adjust their language and tone to fit the audience. For example, a reviewer might use a more formal tone when writing for adults than when writing for children.

Introduction

The introduction of a book review should give readers a general idea of what the book is about and how the reviewer responded to it. You want to catch the readers' attention right away so that they will finish reading the review.

Body

The body of a review details the plot, setting, characters, and theme of the book. Can you identify the theme in the *Owl Moon* review on page 377? The body should provide just enough information to give readers a strong impression of the book. However, you should never give away the ending.

Conclusion

The conclusion of a book review gives the reviewer's evaluation, offering reasons and examples to support the opinion, and tells whether he or she recommends the book.

ACTIVITY A Read each introduction. What general impression of the book does the reviewer convey?

1. *Johnny Tremain,* a novel by Esther Forbes, is the inspiring story of a young boy living in Boston at the time of the American Revolution. It gives an exciting account of the famous men of the time and of the events that led up to the Boston Tea Party.

2. In *Julie of the Wolves,* Jean Craighead George tells an exciting and moving story of hardship, survival, and making difficult choices. I lived every moment with Julie, a young Inuit girl, as she battled incredible odds trying to find her place in the world.

3. *Julie of the Wolves,* by Jean Craighead George, probably appeals to people who love adventure, but more sensitive readers like me may find it too much to bear. I found this story of an Inuit girl's trek across the Arctic tundra, the loss of her wolf friend Amaroq, and her relationship with her father to be very, very sad.

ACTIVITY B Read each conclusion. What are the reviewer's recommendations about reading the book?

1. *Johnny Tremain* held my interest from beginning to end. It showed me the struggle for American liberty through the eyes of a clever, courageous, and patriotic boy of 14. Johnny Tremain is a teenager of yesterday, but he will appeal to teenagers today.

2. *The Secret Garden* is a book for anyone who has ever felt lonely and sad. Its story of friendship and discovery cheers the heart. Frances Hodgson Burnett has created characters that will live in my mind forever, and they'll live in yours too.

3. I enjoyed most of *Johnny Tremain,* and I learned a lot about the events that led up to the American Revolution. However, I thought the ending was unbelievable—just too good to be true. If you like realistic endings, you'll be disappointed just as I was.

LINK

Owl Moon by Jane Yolen

reviewed by Marya Jansen-Gruber

It was a snowy, still night and the moon was bright in the sky when a little girl and her father went towards the woods to look for owls. . . .

In this extraordinary title, Jane Yolen captures the magical moment when two people come face to face with a wild creature, a beautiful owl in its natural habitat. She also explores, in simple words packed with imagery, the bond that connects the little girl and her father as they take a special journey under an Owl Moon.

The illustrations in this special book beautifully compliment the text. . .

WRITER'S CORNER

Choose a book that you had a strong reaction to. Write a three- or four-sentence conclusion for a review of that book. Tell your readers whether or not you recommend the book and why.

Grammar in Action. Be sure to have pronoun and verb agreement in your conclusion. See Section 3.

Planning a Book Review

Before writing a book review, a writer should recall all the important information to include. The review should name the title, the author, and the type of book, such as fantasy or historical fiction. It should also mention the main characters and the setting, as well as summarize the plot. Finally, it should discuss the book's theme and describe the reviewer's reaction to the book.

As you plan your book review, you may find it helpful to list this information on a sheet of paper. Below is a list that one writer made before reviewing *Out of the Dust* by Karen Hesse.

Title and Author:
<u>Out of the Dust</u>, Karen Hesse

Type of Book:
Historical fiction

Main Characters:
Billie Jo, a resourceful 15-year-old girl, her mother and father

Setting:
Oklahoma during the Dust Bowl in the 1930s

Plot's Main Events:
1. Billie Jo and her family are struggling on the farm.
2. Their neighbors start leaving for California.
3. Her mother dies in an accident.
4. Billie Jo runs away from home.

Theme:
The struggle to survive during a difficult time

My Evaluation:
This book is a realistic, poetic story that reminded me to keep going forward when life gets hard.

ACTIVITY C Review the information from the list on page 378 and answer the following questions. Then write an introduction and a conclusion for a review of this book.

1. What information from this list might be included in the introduction of a review of *Out of the Dust*?
2. What might be included in a conclusion?

ACTIVITY D Read the book review on page 375 and answer these questions.

1. Who is the author of *Island of the Blue Dolphins*?
2. What type of book is it?
3. Who are the main characters of the book?
4. What is the setting of the book?
5. What are the main events of the book's plot?
6. What is the theme of the book?
7. What is the reviewer's evaluation of this book?

ACTIVITY E Think of a book that you have recently read. Using the questions from Activity D, make a list similar to the one on page 378. Then write a brief introduction for a review of the book.

A farm family braves an Oklahoma dust storm in 1936.

With an adult, look up a book review online.

WRITER'S CORNER

Read a book review in a magazine or a newspaper. In paragraph form, answer the following questions about the book.

1. Who are the main characters of the book?
2. What is the setting of the book?
3. How long is the plot summary in the review?
4. What is the theme of the book?
5. What is the reviewer's evaluation of the book?
6. Does the review make you want to read the book? Why or why not?

Tech Tip

Writing a Book Review

Palace of Mirrors by Margaret Peterson Haddix

reviewed by Sandi Pedersen

Cecilia is not really just a peasant girl who lives in a small hut in a small village outside the palace. She is a princess in hiding until the traitors who killed her parents are found and she can return to the palace. Cecilia dreams of the day when she can wear silk instead of rags and when she can give orders instead of cleaning up after the cow. Cecilia and her best friend Harper set out to the palace to face whatever danger awaits. Instead, they find that things aren't always as they seem.

Once you have identified all the information that will go into a book review, the next step is to craft the information in an engaging and persuasive way. The important information about the characters, setting, and plot should be sketched concisely, giving a clear impression of the characters and events in the book. The review should also identify the theme and, most importantly, give your evaluation of the book.

Character and Setting

A good book review sets the scene of the story by describing the important characters and the setting. How much time you spend on each depends on how important they are to the story. You could write as little as a few words, or as much as several sentences, on each. For the setting tell where and when the action takes place. In a character sketch, you might give information on a character's age, background, and personality.

Here is an example of a paragraph that describes the setting and main character of *Johnny Tremain*. What is the setting of the story? What do you know about the main character?

Johnny Tremain is a confident young man living in Boston before the American Revolution. He works capably as a silversmith's apprentice until a tragic accident changes his life forever.

Plot Summary

Much of the body of a book review summarizes the plot of the book. A plot summary might begin by describing the characters' situation at the beginning of the story. It then tells, in paragraph form, the problem or conflict that the characters face. It might describe the climax of the story, but it should never tell how the story ends.

When you summarize the plot, be sure to include only the most important details. Leave out any information that is not related to the main conflict of the story.

ACTIVITY A **Think of a real person whom you admire. Ask yourself the following questions. Then write a brief character sketch of that person.**

1. What are the age and gender of this person?

2. What activities, such as a job, is this person involved in?

3. What are three adjectives you might use to describe the personality of this person?

4. What other important information would help someone understand this person?

ACTIVITY B **Read these personal narratives. Write a brief summary of what happened in each one.**

1. There it was. My brother had challenged me to take a shortcut home from school. When in a moment of weakness I accepted his foolish suggestion, the journey resulted in a cross-country race. Streets were taboo. Only the wide-open spaces and the narrow wooded trails were considered. Hurdling fences, crawling beneath bridges, groping through fields thick with weeds, on and on my brother traveled, followed by breathless me. Finally, on reaching our destination, I sank exhausted to the ground, vowing that never again would I permit my brother to entice me into taking a shortcut home.

2. Some days working at the Burger Bay are just amazing. Last Saturday I went in at 11:30 to work the lunch shift. Everything was a mess. The people who had worked breakfast had been too busy to get the place cleaned up. By the time the lunch crowd hit, all five of us were in a frenzy. We couldn't find anything. A customer came up and ordered a medium drink, and we were out of cups. It took 10 minutes for the manager to bring the new cups up from the basement. By that time the customer had finished yelling at me, but a line seven customers long had formed behind him. They were all upset because they had to wait so long. Then the grill caught fire. Eventually, the fire department arrived—after we had put out the fire, but just in time to eat the leftover hamburgers. The customers had decided that trying to get food at Burger Bay was too much work.

WRITER'S CORNER

In a five-sentence paragraph, describe the main characters and setting of a story you like. Then summarize the plot.

Grammar in Action. Use vivid adjectives in your paragraph. See Section 2.

Theme

A theme is an overall idea that a book develops. A theme could be summed up in a sentence, such as *Love conquers all;* a phrase, such as *the importance of family;* or simply a word, such as *restlessness* or *faith.* A book might have one theme or many themes.

In a book review, the book's themes can be summed up wherever they fit logically. Where are the themes described in the review on page 375?

Evaluation

The reviewer's evaluation of the book is the most important part of a book review. It gives the reviewer's opinion of the book and reasons to support those opinions.

The reviewer's evaluation usually comes after the character sketch and plot summary. However, it can make important use of those components. It can tell readers whether the characters are believable or likeable, or whether the plot is interesting enough to keep readers engaged. The reviewer might also tell readers whether the themes of the story are clear.

A good reviewer gives an honest opinion of a book, whether it is positive or negative. The only rule is that the opinions should be supported with reasons and examples from the book.

A reviewer should also keep in mind the audience's perspective and tastes. For example, don't give a rave review to a mystery just because you love mysteries. Instead, tell whether this mystery is particularly well written or enjoyable.

ACTIVITY C Think of a book that you have read or a movie that you have seen that features one of the themes below. Then write a brief summary of how this theme is shown in the plot or other components of the book or movie you have chosen.

   A. Good conquers evil.

   B. Overcoming hardship can make you a stronger person.

   C. Family is the most important thing.

   D. Money can't buy everything.

   E. Good deeds will be rewarded.

Former South Korean President Kim Dae Jung was awarded the Nobel Peace Prize in 2000 for his good deeds, including securing peace with North Korea.

ACTIVITY D Read each evaluation below. Determine which evaluations use reasons and examples to support the reviewers' opinions. Which evaluations are the most persuasive? Why?

1. From the first page on, this book gives the reader too many useless details, which really slowed down the plot. It spent half a page, for example, describing a barn door. The end of this book couldn't come soon enough.

2. John was an excellent character. I could really relate to him because he was my age, and he played the trumpet, as I do. I also like that he played basketball, which is my favorite sport.

3. Lensey Namioka's *The Samurai and the Long-Nosed Devils* always kept me guessing. Zenta and Matsuzo's adventures in feudal Japan not only moved quickly from one climax to the next but also taught me a few things along the way.

4. This book was great. I would recommend it to anyone who asks me about it. It was also fairly short, so it won't take up too much time even if you don't like it.

5. I liked the story of *Julie of the Wolves* very much. The characters were good, and so was the plot. I particularly liked the ending, but you'll have to read it to see for yourself.

6. If you enjoy adventure stories, you should read this book. The author's vivid descriptions made me feel as if I were traveling through the mountain passes and fighting for survival. It didn't make me want to become an explorer, but it sure did keep me reading.

ACTIVITY E A new book has just come out. You've read an ad for the book in your favorite magazine, you've read a review of the book on the Internet, and you've gone to the library and read the blurb on the back cover of the book. Which one would influence you most about whether to read the book? Give reasons for your answer.

WRITER'S CORNER

Think of a book you have read recently. Write three or four sentences evaluating it. Be sure to use reasoning and examples in your evaluation.

Expanding and Combining Sentences

Good writers use a variety of sentences to keep the reader focused and interested. One way to make sentences more interesting is to add descriptive words, phrases, or clauses. Another is to combine short sentences into compound sentences.

Expanding Sentences

You can use a variety of parts of speech to expand sentences. Adjectives, adverbs, and prepositional phrases are especially good choices for expanding sentences. Notice how the addition of different parts of speech expands the following sentence and gives a clearer picture of what happened.

> **The horse trotted home.**
> **The *well-groomed* horse trotted home.** (adjective added)
> **The well-groomed horse trotted *briskly* home.** (adverb added)
> **The well-groomed horse trotted briskly home *across the snowy field*.** (prepositional phrase added)

Be selective in expanding sentences. Don't add words just to make a sentence longer. Always have a reason for adding that extra detail.

ACTIVITY A Expand each sentence by adding an extra word, phrase, or clause at each ^ mark.

1. The ^ house was on a ^ moor.
2. A ^ ball was caught by the ^ player.
3. The ^ girl walked ^ down the ^ path.
4. That ^ photographer took ^ pictures.
5. A ^ cardinal sang ^.
6. ^ canoes went down the ^ river.
7. She found a ^ garden ^.
8. He ^ sang the ^ ballad.
9. The ^ children cared for the ^ plants ^.
10. ^, the hikers packed up their backpacks and continued ^.

ACTIVITY B Expand these sentences as you choose. Use your imagination.

1. The storm approaches.
2. The clouds gather.
3. The sails fill.
4. The waves heighten.
5. The boats race.
6. The girl watched the wolves.
7. The wolves hunted.
8. The girl followed.
9. Snow fell.
10. The wolves shared the food.
11. The girl built shelter.
12. Friends visited the house.
13. Dinner is served.
14. Everyone went for a walk.
15. She took a nap.

WRITER'S CORNER

Write a simple sentence on a sheet of paper. On another sheet expand your sentence using words, phrases, or clauses. Then trade your original sentence with a partner and expand your partner's sentence. Compare your sentences and discuss how each revision changed the meaning of the sentences.

Combining Sentences

Good writers try to avoid having many short sentences one after the other. Combining those sentences into longer compound sentences can make your writing seem less "choppy." Sentences can be combined by using the coordinate conjunctions *and, but, or, so, yet,* and *nor.*

It is important to choose a conjunction based on the relationship between the sentences you are combining.

and	connects ideas that are alike and equal in importance Pilar is going swimming, and Connor is going too.
but	connects opposite or contrasting ideas Pilar is going swimming, but Connor is not.
yet	connects opposite or contrasting ideas Pilar is going swimming, yet she's afraid of the water.
or	connects alternative ideas (or choices) Connor may go swimming, or he may just fish.
nor	connects ideas that are alike and equal in importance Pilar is not going swimming, nor is Connor.
so	connects opposite or contrasting ideas Pilar is not going swimming, so Connor decided not to go either.

ACTIVITY C The conjunctions in the following sentences are used incorrectly. Replace them with appropriate conjunctions.

1. I know I should drink milk, and it makes me sick.
2. Ava ran to the train station, or she missed the train anyway.
3. My mother works for the city, yet so does my father.
4. I do not put butter on pancakes, but I do put syrup on them.
5. Do you want to go to the symphony, nor do you want to go to the theater?
6. The pouring rain got her books wet, and her folders were dry.
7. Neither rain or shine will keep me from riding my bike to school.
8. At the movie theater, I like to snack on nachos, yet I ask for the jalapeño peppers on the side.
9. Andrew will go to Memphis State University, and he will go to the University of Tennessee.
10. Sam was itchy because of the poison ivy on his legs, or he applied a special cream.

ACTIVITY D Combine each pair of sentences into one compound sentence. Be sure to use a comma and an appropriate conjunction.

1. Bats have furry bodies. Their wings are smooth and flexible.

2. The weather may be sunny tomorrow. It may rain.

3. John cannot go to the movies. John cannot go to the game.

4. Maribel cannot go to the movies. Maribel does not want to go.

5. Raul cannot go to the movies. Raul really wants to go.

6. I oppose Caroline's views. We remain friends.

7. Beethoven had great musical talent. The viola and piano were his special instruments.

8. Spencer lost a five-dollar bill. He can't find it anywhere.

9. With the introduction of TV, people thought radio would disappear. Radio remains a source of entertainment and information.

10. Molly makes paper flowers with special colored paper. Molly gives the flowers to her friends as gifts.

Beethoven

ACTIVITY E Rewrite these paragraphs, combining sentences with conjunctions to make the writing more interesting.

Across Five Aprils, by Irene Hunt, tells the story of Jethro Creighton, a nine-year-old boy, during the Civil War. Jethro has to grow up faster than most boys. He learns to take on huge responsibilities.

The story is set in Illinois. Many members of Jethro's family go to fight for the Union. His favorite brother joins the Confederate army. Neighbors are angry with Jethro's family. The neighbors cause trouble for the family. The Creighton family is devastated. They find a way through their hardships.

Will Jethro's brother come home? Will he die in the war? Read the book to find out.

WRITER'S CORNER

Look over what you wrote for the Writer's Corners on pages 381 and 383. Do you see any sentences that you can combine by using conjunctions? Rewrite those sentences to make them more interesting.

Outlines

An outline is a plan for a piece of writing that helps you organize your ideas. It helps you make sure that each paragraph focuses on one idea and that every detail in the paragraph supports that idea. An outline follows a specific format, dividing ideas into three categories: main ideas, subtopics, and details.

Creating an Outline

To create an outline, begin by deciding on the main ideas of your writing. You

Frances Hodgson Burnett

might list the introduction as one idea, the body as one or more main ideas, and the conclusion as one main idea. Label each main idea with a Roman numeral followed by a period.

If you plan to divide the main idea into subtopics in your writing, list the subtopics under the main idea. Subtopics are two or more parts of a main idea. Each subtopic should be indented and labeled with a capital letter followed by a period.

If a subtopic can be further divided into two or more details, list the details below the subtopic. Indent the details under the subtopic. Label each detail with a number followed by a period.

The main idea, subtopics, and details in an outline might be listed as words, phrases, or sentences. Just be sure each level is consistent throughout your outline.

On page 389 is an example of an outline one student created before writing a book review of *The Secret Garden*.

ACTIVITY A **Review the outline on the following page. Then answer the questions and follow the instructions below.**

1. Which main ideas are likely to include more than one paragraph?
2. Which subtopics summarize the plot?
3. Which subtopics include the reviewer's evaluation?
4. Use the outline to write an introduction for a review of *The Secret Garden*.

The Secret Garden, by Frances Hodgson Burnett

I. Introduction
   A. This is a story of friendship and discovery set in a manor on the Yorkshire moors of England.
   B. It is a moving story that you will never forget.

II. Body
   A. Mary, Colin, and Master Craven are all lonely, sad, and afraid.
      1. Mary is sent to live with her uncle after her parents die.
      2. Colin is sick and believes he will die.
      3. Master Craven avoids his son because Colin reminds him of his deceased wife.
   B. A secret garden helps them all.
      1. A bird helps Mary find the garden.
      2. She tells Colin and Dickon her secret.
      3. Mary, Colin, and Master Craven all learn to be happier.

III. Conclusion
   A. This book teaches life lessons.
      1. It's never too late to change.
      2. You should face your problems instead of hiding from them.
   B. Everyone who has ever felt sad or lonely should read this book.

Revising Outlines

Creating an outline can not only help you organize your ideas, but also help you see which ideas may need to be revised. After you have completed an outline, look it over carefully. Do some subtopics have many details, while others have none? If so, you might consider adding or deleting details to make your writing more balanced. If you have few details, think of more to add. Try to keep your outline balanced by making sure that the items at each level of the outline are of equal importance. Outlines can help you find details that are out of place or don't belong. Does each detail fit under its subtopic? If not, move it to a subtopic where it fits better. If a detail does not fit under any subtopic, leave it out. Try to arrange your details in a logical order.

ACTIVITY B **Evaluate the outline below. Decide what sections of the outline need to be revised and revise it with your class.**

Going Camping

I. Recreational vehicles
  A. Kinds
      1. Van
      2. Pickup camper
      3. Some recreational vehicles have electricity.
  B. Other features
      1. Built-in gas stove
      2. Plumbing
II. Tents
  A. Lots of kinds, including family-sized and two-person
  B. Sleeping
      1. Sleeping bag
      2. Air mattress
  C. Cooking
      1. Wood fire or grill
      2. Be sure to bring bug spray.

ACTIVITY C Choose one of the main ideas of your revised outline from Activity B. Write a paragraph based on the outline. How did the outline help you?

ACTIVITY D Two different writers freewrote the following ideas for an essay. Choose one of the series of notes. Review the notes and organize them into an outline. Feel free to add subtopics or eliminate details that do not fit.

Why I Love Summer

- Lots of things to do inside or outside
- Reading books
- Camping—having campfires, exploring the woods
- Watching TV and videos
- Playing outside with friends
- Swimming at the beach
- Playing beach volleyball
- Staying up late
- Playing family games, like cards or board games
- Being with my friends and family
- Wish it would last forever

Winter Sports Offer So Much

- Getting exercise during the cold, snowy months
- Ice-skating indoors and outdoors
- Downhill skiing
- Cross-country skiing
- Winter sports requirements
- Different clothes
- Great reason to drink hot chocolate
- Excellent activity to do with friends
- Playing ice hockey
- Field hockey differs from ice hockey
- Wearing sunscreen and sunglasses as part of gear
- Being with friends
- Gets you out and enjoying the winter

WRITER'S CORNER

Complete the outline you began in the Writer's Corner on page 389 by adding details. Then evaluate your outline. Are there subtopics or details that need to be added, moved, or deleted? Revise your outline if necessary.

Prehistoric monsters attack a submarine in *The Land That Time Forgot* by Edgar Rice Burroughs.

Prefixes

A prefix is a syllable or syllables added to the beginning of a word. The word to which the prefix is added is called the base word. A prefix changes the meaning of the word to which it is added.

Study the prefix chart below. Which prefixes do you think you read most often?

PREFIX	MEANING	EXAMPLE
anti-	against	antibiotic
mis-	badly, wrongly	misunderstood
post-	after	postmodern
pre-	earlier, before	preteen
sub-	under	submarine
(also *sup-* or *sus-*)		

When you write, be sure to use the correct prefix for each base word. Remember that a prefix changes the meaning of a word and that the wrong prefix will create a word with the wrong meaning.

ACTIVITY A **Write five sentences, each using one of the example words above. Use a dictionary if you are unsure of a word's meaning.**

ACTIVITY B **Make a chart like the one below. Write each word, its meaning, and other words that begin with the same prefix. Use the example to get started. Use a dictionary if you need help.**

PREFIX	BASE WORD	WORD	MEANING	OTHER WORDS
anti-	war	antiwar	against war	antismoking, antitheft
mis-	inform			
post-	election			
pre-	paid			
sub-	zero			

ACTIVITY C Use a word that begins with the prefix at the top of each set to complete each sentence.

anti-

1. Every winter my dad puts _____ in our car.
2. A person who never associates with others is considered _____.

mis-

3. I _____ the number of students in our field trip, and I thought one of us was lost.
4. Francis _____ the instructions for caring for the begonia, and so he had to spend 10 minutes looking for them.

pre-

5. Ellen's six brothers and sisters always gather in the living room to watch the football _____.
6. The triceratops, like all dinosaurs, is a _____ animal.

post-

7. When we have completed a chapter, we take a _____.
8. I added a _____ to the letter to Anita because I had forgotten to mention that I had a new kitten.

sub-

9. Washington, D.C., has a very modern _____ system.
10. Under each topic in my outline, there are three _____.

ACTIVITY D Add an appropriate prefix from the list on page 392 to each of the following words. Then give the meaning of the new word and use it in a sentence.

1. view
2. total
3. flight
4. trust
5. print
6. behave
7. slavery
8. committee
9. judge
10. standard

WRITER'S CORNER

Look at a book you have read recently. Read a few paragraphs and identify at least five words that have prefixes. Name the book and list the five words. Write a sentence of your own using each of those words.

More Common Prefixes

Here are a few more commonly used prefixes. What other examples can you think of for each prefix?

PREFIX	MEANING	EXAMPLE
extra-	beyond	extraterrestrial
in- (also *im-*, *il-*, *ir-*)	not	inaccurate
inter-	between	interact
super-	more than, over	supernatural
trans-	across	transnational

ACTIVITY E Below are definitions of words that begin with one of the prefixes listed above. Name each word that is being defined. Use a dictionary if you need help.

1. not yet fully developed or mature
2. not possible
3. to plant in another place
4. between continents
5. not legal
6. a man with more than human powers
7. casual or not formal
8. moving faster than the speed of sound
9. something from beyond Earth
10. across the Atlantic Ocean
11. action between people
12. not reversible

ACTIVITY F Choose eight words with prefixes that you wrote in Activity E. Write a sentence to illustrate the correct use of each word.

ACTIVITY G Identify the words in the following paragraph that have prefixes you have studied. Then give a definition for each word.

This work of science fiction chronicles an imaginary space flight, the first interplanetary trip for the new supership *Helix*. The purpose of the flight is to transplant people to a new colony on a distant planet. Everything goes smoothly until the power generator malfunctions. It's impossible for the ship to receive signals. The preflight training pays off, and no one panics. The chief engineer, showing extraordinary control, goes to work with a flashlight and soon finds the source of the problem. Incredibly, a mouse has gotten into the main power source. With the mouse now in a place of honor in a cage on the control panel, the ship continues its journey.

ACTIVITY H Add an appropriate prefix to each word. Then give the meaning of the new word and use it in a sentence. It's possible to add different prefixes to some base words.

1. ordinary
2. efficient
3. logical
4. state
5. sensory
6. humane
7. structure
8. human
9. reverent
10. national

WRITER'S CORNER

Use a dictionary to find five more words that have prefixes used in this lesson. Use each word in a sentence.

Tech Tip With an adult, use an online dictionary.

Oral Movie Reviews

Critics on television often give oral reviews of movies. You do the same thing when you tell your friends about a movie you loved—or hated. Here are some tips for giving an oral movie review.

Audience

Consider your audience as you plan your review. What type of movies might your listeners like? While you might prefer movies with great characters, some people might like movies with lots of action. Make your review appeal to your entire audience.

Introduction

Begin your review by stating the name of the movie, the lead actors, and the director. Give the listeners a general idea of what the movie is about and a brief reaction to it.

Body

Briefly describe the characters and summarize the plot, giving important details. Don't give away the ending. Include a few words or sentences about the movie's theme or message.

Conclusion

End your review with your evaluation of the movie. You might discuss whether the characters were believable or the special effects convincing. You might note if the movie dragged on for too long. Do you recommend it? Why or why not?

Voice

Let your tone of voice show your opinion of the movie. Speak with enthusiasm if you really liked the movie. Use a more neutral tone if you did not.

Preparing an Oral Movie Review

For an oral review, it's best to select a movie that you had strong feelings about—one that you really liked or really disliked.

Use note cards to help you remember the important information for your review. Write your notes in words or phrases. You should not read the cards word for word. Follow these tips to prepare for your oral movie review.

1. Write the introductory information on your first card. Include the name of the movie, the actors, the director, and what type of movie it is.
2. Write each main point or event on a separate card, followed by keywords that will help you remember details.
3. Consider researching and sharing some background information that will help your audience understand the characters, setting, or plot.

ACTIVITY A **Meet with a partner and select a movie that you both have seen. Write notes about what you liked or didn't like about the movie, giving reasons and examples. Discuss your notes with your partner. What similarities and differences did you find in your opinions?**

SPEAKER'S CORNER

Choose a movie you have watched recently to review orally for the class. Freewrite notes about the characters, setting, and plot.

Practice

The more you prepare and practice, the more comfortable you'll feel on the day of your oral movie review. Write out your notes a day or two ahead of time.

When everything is ready, practice giving your review in front of a mirror or for a friend or family member. As you practice, ask yourself the following questions:

- Do I have an informative and interesting introduction?
- Do I summarize the plot in a logical order?
- Do I speak clearly and carefully so the listener will understand?
- Do I speak with emotion or emphasis so the audience understands my feelings?
- Does my conclusion clearly state my opinion of the movie and tell whether I recommend it?
- Do I give reasons and examples to support my opinion?

Listening Tips

When you listen to someone else give an oral movie review, keep the following points in mind:

- Don't interrupt. If you have questions about the characters, setting, or plot of the story, jot them down on a sheet of paper and ask them at the end of the review.
- Listen for details that support the speaker's points.
- Decide whether you would like to see the movie that was reviewed. If the speaker liked the movie, the best feedback you can give is to watch it yourself and share your ideas.

ACTIVITY B Use the freewriting notes you took for the Speaker's Corner on page 397 to create an outline of your movie review. Decide what information to include in your introduction, body, and conclusion. Use the outline below as a guide or create your own. When you have finished, create note cards for your presentation, writing a few important words or phrases on each note card.

I. Introduction
   A. director and actors
   B. what this movie is about
   C. my reaction
II. Body
   A. characters and setting
   B. plot summary
      1. first main event
      2. second main event
      3. third main event
   C. theme of the movie
III. Conclusion
   A. first thing I liked or didn't like
   B. second thing I liked or didn't like
   C. summary of my reaction

ACTIVITY C Use the library or the Internet to find some background information that you can share about the movie you chose for your oral review. This could be information about films the director or stars were previously involved in or some aspect of the setting or plot. Make notes on the information to use in your review.

SPEAKER'S CORNER

Prepare to give your oral movie review to your class, following the tips in this lesson. Remember that you want to persuade your classmates to see or not to see the movie, so make sure your opinions come through loud and clear.

Tech Tip Videotape your oral movie review.

Prewriting and Drafting

Have you ever read a terrific book, one that had an impact on you? Did you want to tell your friends about it? Have you ever read a book that was so disappointing that you'd never recommend it? Books such as these make perfect subjects for book reviews. Book reviews combine expository writing, giving information about a book, and persuasive writing, influencing others to read or not to read the book.

Prewriting

Before writing a review, writers should select a book that they have read recently and to which  they had a strong reaction. They then follow other prewriting steps, including writing down the ideas and information they will include, and organizing the review, often using a graphic organizer.

Choosing a Book

Before writing a book review, a writer must carefully choose a book to review. Sara, a seventh grader, thought of two books that she recently had read. The book she had just finished was a fantasy novel. Though she liked it, she didn't think it was particularly memorable. She decided to choose another book she had read recently, *Lily's Ghosts* by Laura Ruby. Even though she had not read it as recently, the characters and story still seemed fresh in her mind.

Getting the Facts

Sara began making a list of the information she would use in her review. She flipped through her copy of the book to refresh her memory, then took the following notes on important information to include in her review.

> Book: <u>Lily's Ghosts</u> by Laura Ruby
>
> Type of Book: mystery
>
> Setting: Cape May, New Jersey
>
> Characters: Lily, Vaz, Lily's mom, Uncle Wesley, ghosts
>
> Plot points:
>
> 1. Lily and mom move in to Uncle Wesley's house.
> 2. Lily discovers ghosts that live in the house.
> 2. Lily meets Vaz. They discover Wesley's evil plot.
> 3. Uncle Wesley tries to get the treasure for himself.
> 4. Vaz and the ghosts help Lily solve the mystery.
>
> Themes: getting used to new places, facing your fears
>
> My Reaction: Good. A thrilling mystery with a twist

Your Turn

Select a book to review that you have recently read. A good book to choose is one that you had a strong feeling about, either positive or negative. You should remember what happened in the book.

Next, flip through your book and make a list like the one Sara made. Write notes about the type of book, setting, characters, plot, theme, and your reaction.

Organizing Your Ideas

Once Sara had chosen a book to review and written the important information to include, she **Organization** began to organize her review. She considered using a word web or a time line, but finally decided that an outline would be the most useful tool for organizing her review. Here is the outline she made for her review of *Lily's Ghosts*.

Your Turn

Plan your book review by turning the list of information you wrote into an outline. Remember to make each main idea equally important. Give your subtopics equal importance with each other as well. Make sure all your details fit the subtopic they are grouped under and that no misfit details have been added.

Lily's Ghosts by Laura Ruby

I. Introduction
  - A. This book is a mystery set in Cape May, New Jersey.
  - B. It is an exciting and fun novel.

II. Plot
  - A. Lily and her mother move in with her mother's rich uncle Wesley.
  - B. Lilly discovers ghosts that live in the house.
  - C. Lily becomes friends with Vaz.
  - D. They begin to solve a mystery.
    1. They find a treasure map.
    2. Uncle Wesley finds out about the map.
    3. He kidnaps them and makes them find the treasure.
    4. Uncle Max tells Lily everything.

III. My Reaction
  - A. The story is exciting and funny.
  - B. The characters seemed real, especially Lily.
  - C. I would recommend this book to anyone.

Prewriting

Drafting

Content Editing

Revising

Copyediting

Proofreading

Publishing

Drafting

Sara was writing her review for an Internet review site, so she knew that she was writing for a general audience. She had to give people enough information to make them want to read the book, and she had to write it in a somewhat formal style.

Sara reviewed her outline and wrote a first draft, adding information and details as she went.

Lily's Ghosts, by first-time author Laura Ruby, is a mystery and a ghost story wrapped into one. This story is set in the seaside town of Cape May, New Jersey, after all the tourists have gone home.

Lily and her mother, Arden are down on their luck. They are forced to rely on the generosity of Arden's rich uncle Wesley and move into his waterfront beach house. Lily is furious to be moving again after her mother's breakup with her latest boyfriend. Strange things keep happening, from objects mysteriously moving to strange phone calls.

Lily discovers that several ghosts, including the ghost of her mother's uncle Max are haunting her. She becomes friends with Vaz, and with the help of the ghosts, they begin solving a mystery together.

Uncle Max helps Lily to find a treasure map that uncle Wesley has been looking for. As they learn more, they discover that uncle Wesley is planning an evil plan. Uncle Wesley hears that Lily has found the map inside a kewpie doll. He decides to kidnap Lily, Arden, and Vaz. He decides to force them to find the treasure for him.

Just before opening the treasure, the main characters struggle with their kidnappers, and Lily gets hit on the head and faints. While she is passed out, she is visited by uncle Max and learns everything.

Right up to the surprise ending, this book kept me guessing. While the story is sometimes exciting or scary, it is also funny.

The characters are also memorable. Everyone seems interesting and real. Even the ghosts! Lily's personality makes her a perfect heroine to bridge the real world with that of the ghosts. I would recommend this book to anyone.

Your Turn

Look at your outline and write your first draft. Be sure to include important information such as characters, setting, and plot. Include your opinion in the introduction and expand on it in the conclusion, which might be more than one paragraph long.

Remember that you are writing for a general audience. Be sure to summarize the plot clearly and to include enough information to give readers a good idea of the book. Think of reasons that the average reader might enjoy this book.

Writer's Tip Double-space your review to make room for revisions later.

Plot Summary: What to Include?

When you summarize the plot of your book, be sure not to include too much or too little information. You want to give the readers a good idea of what the book is about, but not so much that they find out the whole story.

A plot summary should begin by telling the characters' situation and what is happening when the book opens. This is sometimes called the setup because it sets up the conflict of the book. The summary then describes the conflict and the main events that build up to the climax.

The climax of a book is the dramatic moment that the rest of the plot builds toward. While you can hint at the climax of the story in your plot summary, don't tell how it is resolved. Leave enough out so that your audience wants to know more.

You can find plot summaries in many places. The back cover of a book or DVD box usually includes a plot summary of the book or movie. You can read book and movie reviews in newspapers and magazines. It might be helpful to look in some of these places to find examples of concise plot summaries.

Prewriting

Drafting

Content Editing

Revising

Copyediting

Proofreading

Publishing

Editor's Workshop

Content Editing

Sara wanted her review to be the best it could be. First, she read her draft aloud to herself before sharing it with an editor. She wanted to catch as many mistakes as she could herself so that it would be as clean as she could make it before handing it to a content editor. She went over her draft, using the following Content Editor's Checklist.

Sara did a first revision of her book review. Then she asked a friend to read it. She needed someone who had not read the book so she could be sure that she had included everything a reader would want to know.

Ben sat behind Sara in English class. They often traded papers and did peer conferences. Sara knew that Ben would give her solid feedback that was expressed respectfully. Sara would do the same for Ben.

Ben read Sara's review carefully and checked it against the Content Editor's Checklist. Then he and Sara had a conference.

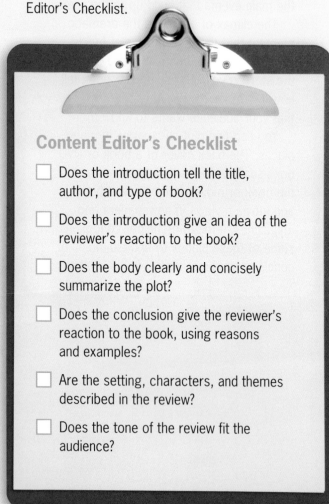

Content Editor's Checklist

- [ ] Does the introduction tell the title, author, and type of book?

- [ ] Does the introduction give an idea of the reviewer's reaction to the book?

- [ ] Does the body clearly and concisely summarize the plot?

- [ ] Does the conclusion give the reviewer's reaction to the book, using reasons and examples?

- [ ] Are the setting, characters, and themes described in the review?

- [ ] Does the tone of the review fit the audience?

First, Ben told Sara about the things that he liked. Ben understood the plot of the book and even wanted to read it to find out how the story ended. But there were some things in the review that could be improved. Here are Ben's comments.

- In the introduction can you add a few words that give an idea of your reaction to the book? You might also mention the ghosts, since they seem to be the most important part of the book.

- Can you tell me a little more about Lily?

- The last sentence of the second paragraph doesn't seem to fit in that paragraph. I think you should move it to another paragraph.

- Who is Vaz? You make it sound like I should already know who he (or she) is.

- I think you tell a bit too much about the climax of the story in the fifth paragraph. I don't want you to tell me everything.

- I don't think you have said anything about the theme in this review. Is there anything about the theme that you could add?

Sara knew that Ben's ideas were good ones, so she decided to add the information he requested and follow most of his other suggestions.

Your Turn

Look for ways to improve your first draft. Trade book reviews with a classmate. Read your classmate's draft and use the Content Editor's Checklist to help you make suggestions.

Give your honest opinion of how you think the review could be improved. Be sure to comment on the strong points too. Your partner will do the same for you.

Grammar in Action

Reread your book review so that you've correctly used any troublesome adverbs or prepositions. See Sections 6.4 and 7.2.

Writer's Workshop

Book Reviews

Revising

Lily's Ghosts, by first-time author Laura Ruby, is a [thrilling] mystery and a [spooky] ghost story wrapped into one. This [fun] story is set in the seaside town of Cape May, New Jersey, after all the tourists have gone home. [The town's many ghosts, however, remain.] [13-year-old] Lily and her mother, Arden are down on their luck. They are forced to rely on the generosity of Arden's rich uncle Wesley and move into his waterfront beach house. Lily is furious to be moving again after her mother's breakup with her latest boyfriend. [She's not happy about her new home, either—] Strange things keep happening, from objects mysteriously moving to strange phone calls.

Lily discovers that several ghosts, including the ghost of her mother's uncle Max are haunting her. She becomes friends with [a local boy named] Vaz, and with the help of the ghosts, they begin solving a mystery together.

Uncle Max helps Lily to find a treasure map that uncle Wesley has been looking for. As they learn more, they discover that uncle Wesley is planning an evil plan. Uncle Wesley hears that Lily has found the map inside a kewpie doll. He decides to kidnap Lily, Arden, and Vaz. He decides to force them to find the treasure for him.

~~Just before opening the treasure, the main characters struggle with their kidnappers, and Lily gets hit on the head and faints. While she is passed out, she is visited by uncle Max and learns everything.~~

Right up to the surprise ending, this book kept me guessing. While the story is sometimes exciting or scary, it is also funny. [It also taught me something about facing your fears and learning to like a new home.]

The characters are also memorable. Everyone seems interesting and real. Even the ghosts! Lily's [matter-of-fact] personality makes her a perfect heroine to bridge the real world with that of the ghosts. I would recommend this book to anyone [who likes a mystery with a twist].

406 • **Chapter 5**

Notice the revisions that Sara made to her draft. She used most of the suggestions Ben made and

 **Voice** looked for other ways that she could improve her book review. She really wanted to express how she felt about the book.

- She added the adjectives *thrilling*, *spooky*, and *fun* to give readers an idea of what she thought of the book. What did she add to tell more of what the book was about?

- Sara found two places to add information about Lily's character. She wrote Lily's age and described her as "matter-of-fact." Where did she add this information?

- Sara understood Ben's comment about the last sentence in the second paragraph, but she decided not to move it. What did she do to make the sentence fit better in the paragraph?

- She added a phrase to tell more about the character of Vaz. What phrase did she add?

- Sara agreed that she told a bit too much about the plot. What did she delete?

- Sara looked back at her prewriting notes to see what she could add about the theme. Where did she add a sentence about the theme?

Finally, Sara looked back over her draft for any other revisions she should make. She realized that her recommendation was a little too broad for a general audience. What if a reader didn't like mysteries? She revised her last sentence to fit a general audience.

Your Turn

Use your ideas and the ideas you got from your content editor to revise your book review. When you have finished, go over the Content Editor's Checklist again. Can you answer yes to each question?

Writer's Tip You might want to set your draft aside overnight and then look at it again the next day. That way you will be looking at it with fresh eyes and fresh ideas. Things you didn't notice when you were writing your first draft may jump out at you when you come back to it.

Prewriting

Drafting

Content Editing

Revising

Copyediting

Proofreading

Publishing

Copyediting and Proofreading

Copyediting

After revising her draft, Sara felt that she had a strong book review. She liked how the plot was summarized, giving just enough information to entice the reader to want to read the book. She also felt that she had offered good reasons for liking the book. She decided to set her draft aside overnight so she could read it again with fresh eyes. When she returned to her book review, she decided to copyedit it, using this Copyeditor's Checklist.

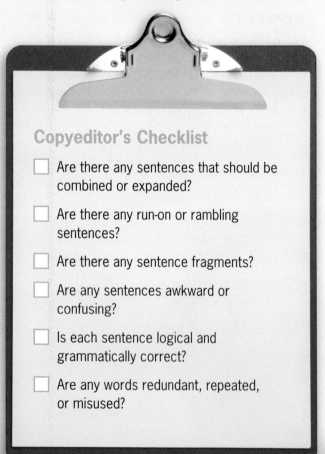

Copyeditor's Checklist

- ☐ Are there any sentences that should be combined or expanded?

- ☐ Are there any run-on or rambling sentences?

- ☐ Are there any sentence fragments?

- ☐ Are any sentences awkward or confusing?

- ☐ Is each sentence logical and grammatically correct?

- ☐ Are any words redundant, repeated, or misused?

Sara decided that she should describe the opening of the book as soon as possible, so she **Sentence Fluency** combined the first two sentences of the second paragraph. In the fourth paragraph, she decided to combine the last two sentences to make the summary more concise.

Next, Sara realized that she had a sentence fragment—*Even the ghosts!*—in her last paragraph. First, she considered making the fragment into a complete sentence, but that seemed to make the review too wordy. Instead, she used a dash to link the fragment to the end of the previous sentence, which made a more interesting sentence.

Finally, Sara noticed that she used the words *planning* and *plan* in the fourth paragraph. To avoid the repetition, **Word Choice** she tried to think of another word for *planning*. She looked up the word in her thesaurus and found the word *hatching,* which means "to devise or plan, especially in secret." She thought that would be the perfect word to use.

Prewriting

Drafting

Content Editing

Revising

Copyediting

Proofreading

Publishing

Your Turn

Look over your review, using the Copyeditor's Checklist. Next, look carefully at your word choice to make sure you have chosen the right words. Are there any words of whose meanings you are uncertain? If so, look them up in a dictionary.

Proofreading

Before publishing a finished review, a good writer proofreads his or her draft to check for errors in  spelling, grammar, capitalization, and punctuation. The errors an editor finds in the proofreading stage may be small, but they are important. An editor might use a Proofreader's Checklist like the one below to help find any remaining errors.

Proofreader's Checklist

☐ Are the paragraphs indented?

☐ Have any words been misspelled?

☐ Are there errors in grammar?

☐ Are capitalization and punctuation correct?

☐ Were new errors introduced during the editing stage?

Sara knew that her classmate Alexandra had a good eye for details, so Sara asked her to proofread her draft. In exchange she agreed to proofread Alexandra's draft.

Alexandra commented that she enjoyed reading Sara's draft, but she also noticed a few mistakes.

First, Alexandra noted that there was a comma missing in the third paragraph after the name *Max*. She explained that since the phrase *including the ghost of her mother's uncle Max* was set off by a comma at the beginning, it also needed a comma at the end.

Finally, Alexandra noticed an error in capitalization that occurred throughout the review. She explained that when a word like *Uncle* is used as part of a name, as in *Uncle Wesley* or *Uncle Max,* it should be capitalized.

Sara incorporated Alexandra's suggestions and looked over her draft one more time. She realized that she had repeated the word *also* in her revision of the fifth paragraph. To avoid the repetition, she deleted the word and began the sentence with the phrase *In addition.* She also noticed one other error in punctuation that Alexandra missed. Can you find it?

Your Turn

Read your review carefully, using the Proofreader's Checklist.

After you have proofread your own draft, trade book reviews with a partner. Go through your partner's review in the same way, using the Proofreader's Checklist.

Publishing

Sara read her book review again, making sure it was just as she wanted it. Then she added a catchy title and uploaded her review onto an Internet review site.

A Great Mystery and More!

Reviewer: Sara from Philadelphia

Lily's Ghosts, by first-time author Laura Ruby, is a thrilling mystery and a spooky ghost story wrapped into one. This fun story is set in the seaside town of Cape May, New Jersey, after all the tourists have gone home. The town's many ghosts, however, remain.

Down on their luck, 13-year-old Lily and her mother, Arden, are forced to rely on the generosity of Arden's rich Uncle Wesley and move into his waterfront beach house. Lily is furious to be moving again after her mother's breakup with her latest boyfriend. She's not happy about her new home, either—strange things keep happening, from objects mysteriously moving to strange phone calls.

Lily discovers that several ghosts, including the ghost of her mother's Uncle Max, are haunting her. She also becomes friends with a local boy named Vaz, and with the help of the ghosts, they begin solving a mystery together.

Uncle Max helps Lily to find a treasure map that Uncle Wesley has been looking for. As they learn more, they discover that Uncle Wesley is hatching an evil plan. Uncle Wesley hears that Lily has found the map inside a kewpie doll. He decides to kidnap Lily, Arden, and Vaz, and force them to find the treasure for him.

Right up to the surprise ending, this book kept me guessing. While the story is sometimes exciting or scary, it is also funny. In addition, it taught me something about facing your fears and learning to like a new home.

The characters are also memorable. Everyone seems interesting and real—even the ghosts! Lily's matter-of-fact personality makes her a perfect heroine to bridge the real world with that of the ghosts. I would recommend this book to anyone who likes a mystery with a twist.

There are many ways you can publish your review.

 Post your article to a Web site that publishes children's book reviews. Work with an adult to find an appropriate site and share your article with the world.

 Make a classroom newsletter. Include all of the students' book reviews so that the class can learn about new books that they might be interested in.

 Mail or e-mail your review to a local newspaper or to a children's magazine. If it gets printed, be sure to save a copy or two for your scrapbook.

 Submit your review to the school newspaper. Perhaps include a survey for students to voice their opinions about a book.

Whenever you publish your work, your goal is to share your thoughts and experiences with other people.

Your Turn

Look over your book review one final time before you publish it. You might want to use your computer's spell-checker to check the spelling. Add a catchy title. Use your best handwriting or a computer to make your final copy.

Choose one of the publishing options. If you choose to post your review online, don't  **Presentation** use your full name. You might choose a good screen name instead. You may want to use the same screen name if you post additional reviews. If your review is a good one, readers will look forward to reading your opinions about other books.

After you have posted your review, be sure to tell others about the site and your screen name. You may want to send friends and family an e-mail with a link to the review. They will enjoy reading your work in cyberspace.

Creative Writing

LiNK

The Lion, the Witch and the Wardrobe

by C. S. Lewis

Aslan stood at the center of the crowd of creatures who had grouped themselves round him the shape of a half-moon. There were Tree-Women there and Well-Women (Dryads and Naiads as they used to be called in our world) who had stringed instruments; it was they who had made the music. There were four great centaurs. . . . There was also a unicorn, and a bull with the head of a man, and a pelican, and an eagle, and a great Dog. And next to Aslan stood two leopards of whom one carried his crown and the other his standard.

But as for Aslan himself, the Beavers and the children didn't know what to do or say when they saw him. People who have not been in Narnia sometimes think that a thing cannot be good and terrible at the same time. . . .

> With magical characters, a fascinating setting, and clear heroes, *The Lion, the Witch and the Wardrobe* is a great example of a fantasy book.

Facing the Dragon

by Lilly Jonas
Room 213

"I don't like the looks of this," seven-year-old Madeline muttered to her big sister Hannah as they stepped off the local amusement park's Dragon Quest ride. Suddenly, they were in a village of cobblestone streets and grassy huts. The only evidence of the amusement park was the box of popcorn in Madeline's hand.

Madeline and Hannah gazed in wonder as dozens of odd creatures hurried past. A huge ogre lumbered by, ordering all villagers off the streets. An old wizard stroked his beard, lost in thought. Hannah grabbed her sister's hand and approached the wizard.

"Excuse me, sir, but I think we're lost," she said, explaining what had happened. "Can you help us?"

"Perhaps. But these villagers need help too," the wizard said.

The wizard explained that the only way home was through a distant cave. Guarding it was a fierce dragon who ate nothing but villagers. The girls were frightened, but they needed to get home.

Madeline and Hannah crossed a cornfield on the way to the cave. There they found the dragon, who was licking his lips as he thought of his next meal of grilled villager.

Seeing the girls, the dragon let out a fiery roar. Madeline jumped back, tossing her popcorn at the dragon as a distraction. The dragon stopped a moment, examined the popcorn, and gobbled it up. He grinned briefly before going after the girls again.

Hannah had an idea. She grabbed Madeline and raced back into the cornfield. The dragon chased them, breathing fire all the way. Suddenly, they heard a popping noise. The dragon's breath was popping the corn! The dragon took one look at the popcorn falling off the cobs and sat down to eat, forgetting about the girls.

"There are other things to eat besides villagers," Madeline shouted as they raced toward the cave and their home on the other side. The dragon, thrilled at his new discovery, seemed to agree.

What Makes Good Fantasy Fiction?

Fantasy fiction takes readers to places they've never experienced. Fantasy stories often take place in a world filled with magical characters and mythical beasts. In this world the line between good and evil is clear—readers know which characters to root for.

Writers of fantasy fiction draw in their audience by using original word choices and a lively, suspenseful voice so readers can escape into the story. *The Lion, the Witch and the Wardrobe* by C. S. Lewis and *Alice in Wonderland* by Lewis Carroll are examples of fantasy books.

Like most narratives, a fantasy story has a beginning, a middle, and an end that provide an organized pattern of events, usually told in chronological order. Here are some things to remember when you write a fantasy-fiction story.

Beginning

Many fantasy stories begin by introducing a main character and the setting. A good beginning also introduces a problem, a conflict, or a goal.

Middle

The middle of a fantasy story develops the plot. The main character often must confront obstacles in trying to reach a goal or overcome a problem. These obstacles are part of a story's rising action, a series of spiraling events. The rising action leads to an exciting defining moment known as a climax. The plot moves along through literary techniques and dialogue.

End

At the end of a story, the conflict or problem is resolved or the goal is achieved. The resolution often leads to a conclusion that might answer remaining questions and bring the story to a close.

ACTIVITY A Read the list of story ideas and decide which ideas could be made into fantasy stories. How do you know?

1. A girl goes into a closet that opens up into an outside trail leading her to a rainbow.
2. A boy who is deaf plays baseball really well and makes new friends.
3. A young boy beats the champion at chess.
4. An elf must confront the evil giant who has wrecked his village.
5. Two girls face challenges starting a business knitting scarves and selling them.
6. A girl rides a horse that flies up in the sky along with the birds.
7. A boy stumbles into a town where nobody ever gets old.
8. Two boys build a doghouse that's too small for their dog.
9. A girl has trouble making friends at her new school.
10. A talking rabbit leads two children to a secret playground.
11. Three sisters plant a flower garden in their yard, and one early morning they find a fairy sitting on a peony petal.
12. Two friends decide to become kid detectives in their neighborhood.

ACTIVITY B Choose one of the ideas from Activity A that could be made into a fantasy story. Imagine a story you could write using this idea. Write a brief description of what might happen in the beginning, middle, and end of this story.

LiNK

The Lion, the Witch and the Wardrobe

Once there were four children whose names were Peter, Susan, Edmund and Lucy. This story is about something that happened to them when they were sent away from London during the war because of the air-raids. They were sent to the house of an old Professor who lived in the heart of the country...

C. S. Lewis

WRITER'S CORNER

Write a brief review of a fantasy story you have read, explaining how you know it is fantasy fiction. Then explain what happens at the beginning and the middle, but don't reveal the end.

Tech Tip Post your review on a class blog.

Setting

Before planning a story, a writer imagines the setting, or time and place, of a story. In fantasy fiction the setting is often a time and place that are far different from the real world. When choosing a setting for your story, ask yourself questions to develop the setting. Is the setting similar to the real world? In what ways is it different? Will the action take place in a city, town, or countryside?

A fantasy story might take place in more than one setting, such as when characters go on a long journey. The settings of a story can help set up the problems a character will face.

Character

A character is a person, an animal, or another living creature who takes part in a story. In fantasy fiction some characters might be imaginary, such as talking animals or mythological beasts, while others might be more realistic. A story usually focuses on one main character or sometimes a few characters. Secondary characters can be introduced as the plot develops, but usually do not drive the story from beginning to end.

Character traits are the qualities that define a character. Writers often decide on the main characters' traits before writing a story. Then they can use the information to decide how the characters will react to different situations as the writers write their story.

Appearance and Background

Begin developing a character by imagining what he or she looks like. Is your hero tall or short, strong or weak, attractive or ugly? Does your villain have green skin, three eyes, or wings?

Imagine your character's background, such as age and experiences before the story begins. Does your young hero work as a tailor or a hunter? Does your ogre live underground or on a mountain?

Personality and Motivation

The most important aspect to consider is a character's personality. What are the character's good and bad qualities? Is she brave or cowardly, smart or foolish, idealistic or practical?

Your main character should always do things for a reason, whether big or small. Is your character trying to save the city or simply get by in life? Does your villain plan to take over the world or just make life miserable for one person? Consider your characters' motivations as you decide how they will react to the conflict in your story.

ACTIVITY C Look back at the story "Facing the Dragon" on page 413 and answer the following questions.

1. What is the setting of the story?
2. How does the setting affect the plot?
3. Who are the main characters?
4. Who are the secondary characters?
5. What information does the author give about the characters?
6. What is the motivation of the main characters?
7. What other information could be given to further develop the characters?

ACTIVITY D Choose one of the settings below and write a description of it. Include the use of the senses, such as sights, sounds, and smells.

A. a county fair
B. a cave
C. a moving train
D. an outdoor market
E. the moon
F. a magical garden

ACTIVITY E Think of a main character from a book you have read or a movie you have seen. Answer the questions below about this character.

1. What does the character look like?
2. What is the character's age?
3. What is the character's background?
4. What is the character's personality like?
5. What motivates the character to act in the story?

LiNK

The Lion, the Witch and the Wardrobe

Lucy felt a little frightened, but she felt very inquisitive and excited as well. She looked back over her shoulder and there, between the dark tree-trunks, she could still see the open doorway of the wardrobe and even catch a glimpse of the empty room from which she had set out.

C. S. Lewis

WRITER'S CORNER

Imagine a setting and a main character for a fantasy story you would like to write. Jot down words and phrases to describe this setting and character. Then write the first two beginning sentences that introduce this setting and character.

Grammar in Action. Use vivid adjectives when describing your fantasy setting and main character. See Section 2.

Plot Development

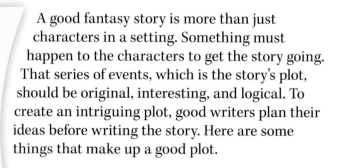

A good fantasy story is more than just characters in a setting. Something must happen to the characters to get the story going. That series of events, which is the story's plot, should be original, interesting, and logical. To create an intriguing plot, good writers plan their ideas before writing the story. Here are some things that make up a good plot.

Conflict

The first step in developing a plot is to establish a conflict or problem for the main character to face or a goal to achieve. The plot doesn't begin to develop until something actually happens to the main character to change his or her life. It could be a magic shoe that a boy finds or news that an evil genie has captured the king's palace.

Rising Action

As the plot develops, life should get more complicated for the main character. A series of obstacles might be thrown in her way to keep her from accomplishing her goal. Perhaps the hero will solve the original problem, only to find that a new problem has been created. The rising action may include surprising twists, but it should also be logical.

Climax

The climax of a story is the dramatic moment that the story builds toward. It might be the final confrontation between the main character and the villain or the last test the hero might face in a quest.

Resolution

The resolution of a story comes after the problem has been resolved or the goal accomplished. The resolution ties up any loose ends, shows how the characters have been affected by the events of the story, and may hint at the future of the characters.

ACTIVITY A Rearrange the plot events below in a logical order. Then identify the problem, the events that make up the rising action, the climax, and the resolution.

1. Marcus wrestles and slays the alligator.
2. An evil alligator comes to destroy the gnomes.
3. Marcus falls into a sewer on the way to school.
4. The gnomes make Marcus their leader.
5. The gnomes help Marcus find his way home.
6. Marcus encounters a society of tiny gnomes.

ACTIVITY B Copy the following chart for a fantasy story's plan about a giant tarantula. Fill in the blanks, and some events in the rising action that lead to the given climax. Then write a satisfying resolution to the story.

Characters: _____

Setting: _____

Conflict or Problem: _____

Rising Action:

1. _____
2. _____
3. _____
4. _____

Climax: The main character says the magic words that cause the giant tarantula to scurry away, leaving the magic locket lying on the ground.

Resolution: _____

WRITER'S CORNER

Look back at the setting and character you wrote about in the previous Writer's Corner. Freewrite a problem or conflict the main character might face and the rising action that might lead to a climax. Write in four or five sentences to explain the climax to this story.

Fine-tuning Your Plot

Writing a good story is like taking a journey without quite knowing how you'll get there. While you may begin with one idea, your story may completely change by the time you reach the end. Here are some tips for writing an interesting and compelling story.

Make It Logical

Find ways to set up each event with earlier information. In the story on page 413, for example, the writer set up the climax by including the box of popcorn in Madeline's hand at the beginning. Also make sure that your characters' actions make sense based on the personalities and motivations you have given them.

Work Backward

If you have trouble thinking of action for your story, you might plan the climax first. Write a draft of the climax, and then imagine what events might lead to it. As you write, the climax may change, but sketching it out in the beginning can help you develop your plot.

Foreshadow the Climax

Another useful technique is foreshadowing. When you foreshadow an event, you give hints to what will happen with an earlier, smaller incident. For example, a character might be startled by bumping into a spider web and say how much he hates spiders. This incident could foreshadow a showdown with a giant spider during the story's climax.

Use Flashbacks

While your story will probably be told in chronological order, you can use the technique of flashbacks to tell something that happened before the beginning of the story. In a flashback, an earlier part of the story may be told as part of a character's memory or dream. The character's memory may be jogged by seeing a familiar object or hearing a familiar sound. Look at this example.

> Peter knew he couldn't relax in this cave for long. The storm would let up soon, and his pursuers were not far behind. For now he sat back and let the rain take him back to his country cottage.
>
> "One cup of piping tea," Mother said, handing him a warm mug. They stared out the window for a moment, watching the rain drench the crops. "They say that in the midst of a summer rain, the sprites come out from within the trees," Mother said.
>
> Peter sprang up. The sprites! Perhaps they could help him!

ACTIVITY C Match each situation in the first column with one of the characters in the second column. Then describe what each character might logically do in the situation.

Character

A wise, old man

A strong and fearless warrior

A cautious but clever child

Situation

A raging river must be crossed.

A dragon is sleeping on the magic ring.

A knight challenges the character to a sword fight.

ACTIVITY D Choose three of the following events. Think of an incident that might be used earlier in the story to foreshadow each event.

1. Peter jumps from treetop to treetop in pursuit of an evil elf.
2. Tanya calms a monster by playing a game of cards with him.
3. Keisha throws a magic pearl back into the ocean.
4. Tyler gathers an army of walking vegetables to defeat King Candy.
5. A talking dog leads Chloe back home.

ACTIVITY E The following scene is written in chronological order. Rewrite it, using a flashback.

When she was a child, Arianna's father gave her a silver bracelet. She loved her bracelet, but one day when she was playing in the woods, she slipped from a tree and was knocked unconscious. When she awoke, she was home in bed, and the bracelet was gone.

Years later, Arianna was walking in the same woods. She stumbled on a tree root and found herself flat on the ground. Lifting her face, she spied a shiny bracelet under a pile of leaves. Suddenly she remembered everything.

WRITER'S CORNER

Look over a story you have read recently and answer these questions. Is the plot logical? Do the characters make the choices you would expect? Can you find any times where flashbacks or foreshadowing are used? Are they effective?

Dialogue

Dialogue is written conversation. Using dialogue can add interest to a story and help develop the characters. With good dialogue, characters come to life, and readers feel as if they are there as the story unfolds. How does using dialogue in the following example help enliven the story?

After an hour of walking the trail, Lucy and her father seemed to be lost. Dad looked at his map one last time.

Dad thought that the map showed they should turn right at the sign. Lucy didn't think turning right made sense, since they had already been turning right a lot. She suggested that they turn left. Dad said that the map doesn't lie and ordered Lucy to follow him.

After about 10 minutes of reluctantly following Dad, Lucy saw a sign that said that the parking lot where they had started was only one mile away. Lucy had to admit that Dad's directions had been right. Dad replied that he was usually right. Then they arrived back at the parking lot, sore but happy.

After an hour of walking the trail, Lucy and her father seemed to be lost. Dad looked at his map one last time.

"According to my map, we should turn right here," he said.

"That doesn't make sense," Lucy replied. "We've been turning right a lot already. I think we should turn left."

"The map doesn't lie, Lucy. Follow me," Dad said.

After 10 minutes of walking, they came to a fork in the trail. "Look!" Lucy shouted. "This sign says the parking lot is ahead only one mile away. I guess you were right, Dad."

"As usual," Dad replied with a grin. And before they knew it, they were back at the parking lot, sore but happy.

Rules for Writing Dialogue

The dialogue in the passage on page 422 follows certain rules. Keep these rules in mind when you write dialogue in your stories:

- Start a new paragraph every time you change speakers. If your characters are trading one-line comments, your paragraphs may be very short. That's fine.
- Always place any punctuation marks, such as periods, commas, or exclamation points, before the closing quotation marks. Use a comma, not a period, to set off a statement from its speaker.
- Generally, identify the speaker at the end of the quotation. If the quotation is long, you might break it up by identifying the speaker in the middle. If you do, break the quotation in a logical place, such as at the end of a clause or sentence.
- For variety, use words such as *cried, explained, barked,* and *called.* Make sure the word you choose fits the action. For a quiet conversation, use *murmured,* not *screamed.*

LiNK

The Lion, the Witch and the Wardrobe

"Sh. Look!" said Susan.

"What?" said Peter.

"There's something among the trees over there to the left."

They all stared as hard as they could, and no one felt very comfortable.

"There it goes again." said Susan presently.

"I saw it that time too," said Peter. "It's still there. It's just gone behind that big tree."

"What is it?" asked Lucy, trying very hard not to sound nervous.

C. S. Lewis

ACTIVITY A Discuss the dialogue in the story on page 413. Where did the writer use dialogue? When did the writer summarize what was said? Why do you think the writer used these techniques?

ACTIVITY B Revise this dialogue by adding punctuation and paragraph indentations where needed.

On a spring day like this, I love to take a long walk said Annie. Really? said Melissa I like to sit on the back porch and read. Brianna laughed at them. How can you even think of doing anything as quiet as sitting on the porch or taking a walk? I want to have a huge party, with music and dancing! I guess everybody just likes different things Michael responded. If I had my choice, I would go for a long bike ride.

WRITER'S CORNER

Think of a conversation you have had today and write it as a short dialogue. Keep in mind the rules for writing dialogue.

Tech Tip With an adult, use an online thesaurus for word variety.

Using Dialogue Colorfully

Good dialogue makes a story more colorful. It can break up dull passages, exhibit the personality of the characters, and bring readers into the action as it unfolds. A good writer chooses dialogue carefully, using it only when it adds to a story. Here are some tips for when to use dialogue.

Showing Character Traits

Use dialogue that shows the personality of the characters. If the character is a nervous person, have him show it in what he says. Colorful dialogue can reveals a character's background or personality. A character might also reveal something about another character's personality by saying something about him or her.

Conveying Emotions

Dialogue can be a great way to show emotion. Short spoken lines can convey strong emotions in a character.

> **"Look out!"**
> **"Where do you think you're going?"**
> **"You're alive!"**

Revealing Conflicts

Another use of dialogue is to show conflict between characters. If two characters don't trust each other or have differing viewpoints, it can be revealed through dialogue.

Advancing Plot

Sometimes dialogue can be used to advance a plot, such as when a character tells something that the other character doesn't know. A character might tell where a secret passage is hidden or announce that help is on the way.

Paraphrasing

Dialogue is useful when it adds something meaningful or revealing to a story. Sometimes, however, you might choose to paraphrase, or give the information yourself. Paraphrase a character's speech when he or she gives a long, drawn-out explanation or repeats something the reader already knows. Save your dialogue for the times when it can improve the story.

ACTIVITY C Revise the following narrative paragraph, using dialogue. Keep in mind the rules for writing dialogue.

Ruby and Liam go hiking in the park. They have been hiking for an hour when they find an injured squirrel on the path. It is a baby and seems to have fallen from a tree. They try to decide what to do. Ruby isn't sure whether they should touch it; she has heard that baby animals that have been touched by humans will be abandoned by their parents. Liam agrees but doesn't think that the little squirrel, which is hardly moving, will live if they don't help it. They make a sling out of Liam's shirt, roll the squirrel into it, and carry it carefully to the closest telephone. They call the park ranger, who comes to take care of the animal.

ACTIVITY D Select one of the following situations. Write a brief dialogue to show what you think might happen between the people involved.

A. An ice-cream truck goes slowly down the street, playing a catchy tune. Peter and Julio hear it and chase after it in order to buy ice-cream sandwiches.

B. Ava is surprised when she pushes a button on a vending machine and sees a girl who is as small as a doll come out. The girl, whose name is Grace, talks to Ava about being one of several little people who want to escape from the machine.

C. Colin was listening to the radio on his way to school when the announcer said that the station would give a free baseball cap to everyone who came by the station before five o'clock that afternoon. Colin is supposed to go straight home after school. He calls home to see if he can get permission to go to the radio station.

D. A baby robin asks the other animals it encounters— a squirrel, a chipmunk, a rabbit, and an adult robin—how to fly.

E. A friend asks you to go to a movie on Saturday afternoon. You want to go, but you have previously agreed to play soccer.

WRITER'S CORNER

Make up a situation that might happen at school as the basis for a dialogue. Write a sentence explaining that situation. Then write a short dialogue to fit your explanation.

Grammar in Action Refer to Section 8 to help you write your sentence.

Figurative Language

When describing something in a story, even a vivid verb, adjective, or adverb sometimes does not seem strong enough. Instead, a writer might choose figurative language that compares the subject being described to another familiar subject.

When using figurative language, a writer often emphasizes one quality of a subject by making an exaggerated comparison. It is important to choose carefully when selecting figurative language to use. Inexact or excessive figurative language can lessen the impact of the description. When chosen carefully, however, figures of speech can add impact and interest to a story.

Figurative language includes figures of speech such as simile, metaphor, personification, and hyperbole. Each one describes something in a different way.

Similes

A simile compares two different things by linking them using the word *like* or *as*. Similes can describe people, places, things, emotions, and actions. The simile makes clear a quality that the two things have in common. For example, an unheated car and the North Pole can both be cold, and a pile of books and a mountain can both seem very high.

Our car is as cold as the North Pole.
This pile of books I have to read is like a mountain.

Metaphors

Like a simile, a metaphor compares two subjects, but without using the words *like* or *as*. Metaphors state that one thing *is* another thing, while similes say one thing is *like* another thing. The similes above, for example, might be written as metaphors instead.

Our car is an iceberg on wheels.
I have to read a mountain of books.

Clichés

Many similes and metaphors are so well known that they are overused. Overused expressions are called clichés. Similes can be clichés, such as *sleep like a baby, as slow as a turtle,* and *as quiet as a mouse.* So can metaphors, such as *it's a piece of cake.* Good writers try to avoid clichés by replacing an overused expression with a more original one. Read the following sentences. The first one uses a cliché, while the second one replaces the cliché with something more original.

> **Henry is as cool as a cucumber.**
>
> **Henry is as cool as a slice of watermelon.**

ACTIVITY A **Complete each sentence below with words that create a simile. Be creative and avoid using clichés.**

1. This new blanket is as soft as _____.
2. Greg cleans his room as fast as _____.
3. The people getting off the train rushed like _____.
4. The clown's nose looked like _____.
5. Your backpack is as heavy as _____.
6. Now that my brother is on the wrestling team, he eats like _____.

ACTIVITY B **Write sentences containing metaphors to describe the following subjects. Avoid clichés.**

1. a birthday party
2. rain
3. a cat's fur
4. muddy boots
5. a darkened room
6. an enemy's glare
7. a crying baby
8. directions to a house
9. a bird's song
10. a giant's footprint

LiNK

The Lion, the Witch and the Wardrobe

With these words he handed to Peter a shield and a sword. The shield was the color of silver and across it there ramped a red lion, as bright as a ripe strawberry at the moment when you pick it. The hilt of the sword was of gold and it had a sheath and a sword belt and everything it needed, and it was just the right size for Peter to use.

C. S. Lewis

WRITER'S CORNER

Using your home as the source of inspiration, write two similes and two metaphors. You may refer to family members or objects in your home.

Personification

Personification compares an idea, an inanimate object, or an animal to a person by giving it human qualities. A writer might personify an object by describing it as having human emotions, exercising free will, or doing something that a person might do, such as walking, talking, or crying.

The tired shoes ached and groaned for one last mile.

The impatient fire engine screamed a warning as it raced through the streets.

Hyperbole

Hyperbole is a figure of speech that makes deliberate exaggerations. The word *hyperbole* comes from a Greek word meaning "excess." The purpose of hyperbole may be to give a dramatic effect or to add humor.

It's so hot outside that the roads are melting!

Matthew will have a million reasons for being late.

ACTIVITY C Determine whether each of the following statements contains a simile, a metaphor, personification, or hyperbole.

1. The car came screaming out of the parking lot.
2. It will take me a hundred years to read that book.
3. Tony was shaking like a jackhammer.
4. Winter could boast of another snow storm.
5. I spent the day wading through a sea of paperwork.
6. Paige cackled like a witch.
7. "You're just a puppy who's lost his way," Armando said to his friend.
8. The children thought that the story would never end.
9. My favorite chair was waiting patiently for me when I got home.
10. The broken-down car crawled on the gravel road for one more mile.
11. When I climbed out of bed that winter morning, the floorboards were as cold as ice.
12. You are the light of my life.

ACTIVITY D Answer the following questions by imagining what each object would say or do if it were alive. Then use your answer to help you write a sentence that uses personification to describe the object.

1. How might a library book encourage someone to check it out?
2. How might an airplane feel as it flies through the air?
3. Might a pencil ever think that no one appreciates it?
4. How might an old car feel when it drives up a hill?
5. What might a chain saw think as it tears into a stump?

ACTIVITY E Create your own hyperbole by completing the following with exaggerations.

1. It snowed so much that _____.
2. The basketball players are so tall that _____.
3. The sound of the thunder could _____.
4. I'm so tired I could _____.
5. Jane's coat is so warm that _____.
6. We had to wait so long for the train that _____.
7. She had eyes that could _____.
8. My uncle is so smart that _____.
9. He has a list of excuses so long that _____.
10. My mother bakes cookies so delicious that _____.

ACTIVITY F Rewrite the paragraph below, using at least two figures of speech.

Though she was very tired, Misha dragged herself out of bed. The sun was shining through her window. As she walked downstairs, the smell of breakfast cooking seemed very nice. The only thing to spoil the morning was the sound of her brothers arguing noisily. "Be quiet!" she whispered with irritation.

WRITER'S CORNER

Using the same theme as in the previous Writer's Corner, write two examples of personification and two of hyperbole. Trade your examples of figurative language with a partner and identify each other's figures of speech.

Limericks

A limerick's a lighthearted verse
Whose second line rhymes with its first.
  The third and fourth line
  Are much shorter, but rhyme,
While the fifth line goes back to the first.

Edward Lear, 1857

Limericks are one of the most commonly used poetic forms, partly because they are short, fun, and easy to remember. Some of the most familiar limericks are silly rhymes that tell stories about fictional people to whom strange or nonsensical things happen.

Like writers of fantasy stories, limerick writers can use their imaginations to come up with fantastic characters and surprising situations. Consider the following example by Edward Lear, who is often considered the father of the limerick:

There was a Young Lady whose chin
Resembled the point of a pin;
  So she had it made sharp,
  And purchased a harp,
And played several tunes with her chin.

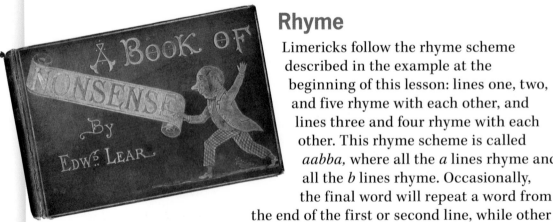

Rhyme

Limericks follow the rhyme scheme described in the example at the beginning of this lesson: lines one, two, and five rhyme with each other, and lines three and four rhyme with each other. This rhyme scheme is called *aabba*, where all the *a* lines rhyme and all the *b* lines rhyme. Occasionally, the final word will repeat a word from the end of the first or second line, while other times the writer will think of a new rhyming word.

The rhyme scheme often helps a limerick tell a story. The first two rhyming lines, the *a* lines, might introduce a character and the situation. The next two rhyming lines might tell what the character does or what happens to him or her. The final line gives a satisfying (and often humorous) conclusion by relating back to the first two lines, both in content and rhyme. Does the previous Edward Lear limerick follow this pattern?

Rhythm

The rhythm of a poem is determined by which syllables are given greater stress. To determine the rhythm of a poem, you might read it aloud and listen for the words to which you give greater stress. As you read, you might mark each unstressed syllable with a ⌣ and each stressed syllable with a ⁄.

There was a Young Lady whose chin

The rhythm in a limerick is anapestic rhythm. An anapest is a series of three syllables in which the first two syllables are unstressed and the third syllable is stressed. Lines one, two, and five contain three anapests, while lines three and four each contain two.

Occasionally (as in the Edward Lear limerick), one of the first unstressed syllables in a line may be omitted. One or two unstressed syllables may also be added at the end of a line. Which syllables are stressed in the Edward Lear limerick?

ACTIVITY A Copy the limerick at the top of page 430 and add marks to indicate the stressed and unstressed syllables.

ACTIVITY B Rewrite the following opening lines to limericks. The lines should rhyme and use anapestic rhythm.

1. Once there was a young man who came from New York.
   Pork was the one thing that he feasted on.

2. I once knew an old doctor.
   Her feet were buried in blocks of concrete.

3. A yo-yo is a pretty curious item.
   It's a toy that is circular, and it comes on a string.

Writing a Limerick

Every poet writes a limerick in a different way. Some people think of a complete idea for their limerick first, while others develop their ideas as they write. One poet might write the first lines first, while another might start from the middle or even the end. When you write a limerick, you might try several approaches and choose the one that is most comfortable for you. Here are some suggestions to get you started writing a limerick.

1. Think of an idea for your limerick. Will it be about a person with a strange personality, ideas, or features? Will it be about a real-life subject?

2. Think of rhyming words that could be useful in your limerick. You could use a rhyming dictionary or brainstorm lists of words. In a limerick you might rhyme a word with the name of a person or a place. As you think of words you could use, you may decide to change what your limerick is about.

3. Write one line of your limerick, making sure it follows anapestic rhythm. You might start with the first line, which could introduce the subject, or with another line. For example, you might begin with the third line because it is a shorter line, or the last line if you already have in mind how the limerick will end.

4. If you have written the first or third line, write the line that follows it. End the line with a word that rhymes with the end of the previous line. It may take several tries to get the line just right. If you get stuck, try using another rhyming word. You might even decide to change the idea for your limerick as you try out different lines.

5. Write the rest of the limerick. Use a rhyming dictionary or brainstorming to help you come up with rhymes for the rest of the poem. Make sure that each line has the correct rhythm. Try to think of a clever or funny ending for your limerick.

6. Read your limerick aloud, listening for the rhythm. You might even mark the stressed and unstressed syllables to see if each line follows anapestic rhythm. If some of your lines don't, find ways to add, delete, or move words to improve the rhythm.

ACTIVITY C Complete the following limericks by filling in the missing lines or words. Be sure to follow the *aabba* rhyme scheme and anapestic rhythm of a limerick.

1. There was an Old Man with a beard,
   Who said, "It is just as I _____.
      Two Owls and a Hen,
      Four Larks and a Wren,
   Have all built their nests in my _____."
   —*Edward Lear*

2. There was an Old Man who said, "Hush!
   I perceive a young bird _____."
      When they said, "Is it small?"
      He replied, "_____."
   It is four times as big as the bush!"
   —*Edward Lear*

3. A talented sculptor _____
   Once sculpted a woman from snow.
      He said that he loved her,
      And always thought _____,
   But he knew in the spring she would _____.
   —*Joe Thompson*

Character from an Edward Lear limerick, painted by Frances Broomfield, 1994

ACTIVITY D Choose one pair of opening lines below and complete the limerick. Be sure to follow the rhythm and rhyme scheme of a limerick.

A. A young man from Kalamazoo
   Decided to paint himself blue.

B. My brother's a curious boy
   He thinks everything is a toy.

C. On top of the roof of my house
   Lives a tiny but hardworking mouse.

WRITER'S CORNER

Complete your limerick that you began in the previous Writer's Corner using the tips on page 432. Make sure your limerick follows the correct rhythm and rhyme scheme. When you have finished, share your limerick with the class.

Storytelling

Good stories, when told by good storytellers, can be delightful to hear. A good storyteller speaks in a dramatic voice, building suspense and interest as he or she reaches the climax. The listeners may be kept at the edge of their seats, anxious to hear what happens at the end of the story.

Have you ever told a story? It could have been a well-known story that you retold to someone. It could have been a story that you made up. If you have ever heard a story or have told one yourself, you already know something about storytelling. In this lesson you will learn some techniques for becoming a better storyteller.

Beginning, Middle, and End

Begin your story by introducing the characters and setting. Set up the plot by telling the conflict that the characters must face.

In the middle of the story, develop the plot by detailing the rising action that leads to the climax. Use dialogue frequently to help develop the characters. Avoid long explanations and unnecessary details. Focus on the most dramatic moments to keep your listeners' attention. Make the climax the most dramatic moment of your story.

End your story by showing how the conflict or problem was resolved or how the goal was reached. Give a satisfying resolution that answers any remaining questions and brings the story to a close.

Voice and Dialogue

The way you use your voice can draw in your listeners and keep their attention. Vary the tone of your voice to match the story. You might use a pleasant voice to describe the setting at the beginning or the resolution at the end, but a more dramatic voice to describe moments of conflict. Pause at key moments to add suspense.

The way you speak dialogue can help bring your characters to life. Vary your pitch to show which character is speaking. Use a deeper voice for a giant or a shaky voice for a frightened child. Use the emotion that the character might be feeling as you speak your dialogue.

Sound Effects

You may find it helpful to use other sounds to enliven the story in your listeners' minds. Stomp your feet to re-create the approaching footsteps of the enemy, or crinkle cellophane to reproduce the sound of a crackling fire. Make sounds, such as the whooshing of wind or the ticking of a clock, with your mouth.

ACTIVITY A Practice speaking each of the following lines of dialogue, using the tone of voice you think the character would use.

1. "Watch out for those rocks!" the skipper cried as the boat tossed in the waves.

2. "Maybe I have what you're looking for," the woman said with a sly grin. "But then again, maybe I don't."

3. "Wait! You're going . . . too fast . . . for me," the tortoise sputtered as he found himself falling farther behind.

4. "You say you can show me the way out of here," the troll said skeptically, "but why should I trust you?"

ACTIVITY B Imagine you are going to retell "Facing the Dragon" on page 413. Write the important points and key details of the story. Then think of where you would change the tone of your voice or use sound effects to add drama. Compare your notes with a partner's. Did you both choose the same important points and details to write about?

SPEAKER'S CORNER

Choose a story to tell to your classmates. It can be a story you wrote or a familiar story that you enjoy. If you have a written version of this story, read it aloud. Practice varying your tone and pace and speaking dialogue in the characters' voices. Take notes on what parts of the story to include and what parts to leave out.

Tech Tip Videotape yourself telling the story you chose.

Prepare

Before you tell a story to an audience, it's important to prepare. Use the following suggestions as you prepare to tell your story:

- Choose a story that you enjoy. You may tell a story that you wrote or retell one that you have heard or read. Remember that even if you are retelling someone else's story, you will be using your own words.
- Use note cards to write important events. Write keywords and phrases rather than complete sentences. You may write some information, such as direct quotations, word for word.
- Look through your notes to make sure you have included all the important parts of a good story. Introduce the characters and setting vividly. Be sure that you have included rising action, a climax, and a resolution.
- Plan when and how to change your voice during your telling of the story.
- Think of times to use sound effects to enhance your story. Try out the sound effects to see if they are effective.

Practice

Practice is one of the keys to good storytelling. The more you practice your story, the more at ease you will feel when you tell the story to an audience.

Practice telling your story in front of a mirror or another person. Then ask yourself the following questions:

- Do I describe the characters and setting vividly?
- Do I include all the main points and key details needed for the audience to understand the story?
- Do I speak clearly so that the listeners will understand everything in the story?
- Do I vary the pace of my speaking to fit the story?
- Do I speak with the right tone and emotions as I speak the part of each character?
- Are my characters' voices easy to distinguish?

- Do I use sound effects when appropriate?
- Do I make my story interesting by using vivid words and figures of speech?

Listening Tips

A good story needs good listeners. Here are some tips to make you a better listener.

- When a character is described, try to create a picture of the character in your mind. Do the same with the setting.
- Listen to the dialogue—not only what the storyteller is having the characters say, but also how they're saying it. This may give you a stronger sense of the characters' personalities.
- Listen for details. Perhaps you can predict how the story will end if you pay attention to the details.
- Feel free to laugh during funny parts in the story.
- Listen for sound effects to help you imagine the scene.
- When the storyteller has finished, give him or her some helpful feedback. Ask questions or say things such as "I liked the way you made the characters come to life in their dialogue."

ACTIVITY C **Prepare to tell the story that you chose in the previous Speaker's Corner, using the tips on page 436. Rewrite onto note cards the notes you have taken. Think of ways to engage your audience by using your voice and sound effects.**

ACTIVITY D **Practice telling the story you selected to a partner. Use the Practice tips on page 436 to help you identify what you still need to work on. Give your partner feedback on how to improve his or her story and listen to your partner's feedback for your story.**

SPEAKER'S CORNER

Tell the story that you have prepared and practiced in this lesson. Be sure to speak clearly and confidently and to use the storytelling techniques described to engage your audience. When you listen to your classmates tell their stories, use the Listening Tips to help you get the most out of the stories.

Writer's Workshop

Prewriting and Drafting

Have you ever read a story or seen a movie filled with imaginary creatures or strange worlds? Was the setting fascinating, the characters intriguing, or the plot exciting? Good fantasy fiction often includes all of these. It takes work to make a good fantasy story, but it can also be lots of fun. In this workshop you will move step-by-step through the writing process as you create your own fantasy story.

Prewriting

Before settling down to write, writers take time to think about the story they will write and to jot down ideas. First, they brainstorm story ideas, coming up with a setting, characters, and plot. Then they expand on their ideas, thinking of character traits and outlining a plot for their fantasy story.

Brainstorming

Some writers begin to think of ideas by brainstorming different settings for their story to take place in, while others first come up with ideas for conflicts that could lead to an interesting plot. Maria decided to begin by thinking of characters. She listed all kinds of fantastic creatures, such as genies and flying horses, but finally decided to make her main character a mermaid.

Because her main character was a mermaid, she didn't have to spend much time on the setting. She knew her story would take place in the ocean.

Next, she thought of ideas for a plot. She thought of having her character find a sunken treasure but couldn't think of a conflict that would make the story interesting. Finally, she decided to have the mermaid face an evil creature. Because her story took place in the sea, she decided to make the creature a sea monster.

Your Turn

Spend a few minutes brainstorming ideas for your story. Begin by listing possible settings, characters, or plots. Continue writing until you have thought of ideas for all three aspects of your story. For ideas, you might write settings, characters, and plots of fantasy stories or movies you have enjoyed. If you get stuck, you might ask yourself the following questions:

- What setting would be fun to write about? A big city or a small village? Up in the clouds or underground? In the desert or on a mountain? Which places could lead to interesting characters and plots?
- What characters would you enjoy creating? Will there be realistic people or fantastic creatures? Will any characters have magical abilities? Will animals or objects talk and move?
- What will happen in your story? Will the characters go on a long journey? Will they discover something magical? Will the climax include a fight or a chase?

Planning Your Story

Maria had a good idea in mind for her fantasy story. Though she was anxious to start writing, she knew her story would turn out better if she **Organization** planned it out beforehand. Maria plotted her story on a sheet of paper, writing more ideas about her characters, setting, and plot. She made sure to include some specific traits for each character and to describe the conflict, rising action, climax, and resolution to her story. Here is the plan she made.

> Setting: In the ocean, then in a cave
>
> Characters: Sandy—independent teenager, likes adventure
>
>   Mom—caring, gets nervous a lot
>
>   Sea monster—big, purple, mean, hungry
>
> Conflict: Sandy has to save her friends from the sea monster.
>
> Rising Action:
>
> 1. Sandy's friends go to explore a cave.
>
> 2. The sea monster heads for the cave.
>
> 3. Sandy goes to warn them.
>
> 4. The sea monster chases Sandy through the cave.
>
> Climax: The cave collapses on the sea monster, and Sandy escapes.
>
> Resolution: Everyone cheers for Sandy for saving the day.

Your Turn

Develop the ideas you brainstormed for your story by creating a plan like the one Maria made. Write the setting of your story first, including any settings the character might travel through in the course of the story. Next, flesh out the characters, giving them names and some character traits. The traits you write may describe their appearance, background, age, personality, and motivations.

Describe the plot next. Begin by noting a conflict, which might be a problem the characters face or a goal they must achieve. Next, describe the rising action that makes the characters' lives more complicated. Describe the climax, the dramatic moment that the story builds up to.

Finally, describe the resolution, which might tie up loose ends, show how the characters have been affected by events in the story, and perhaps hint at the future of the characters.

As you plan your story, feel free to revise your previous ideas. Be prepared to change the setting if it seems dull, add or subtract characters if needed, or alter the plot if you think it might be improved.

Writer's Tip The more care you take with planning your story, the more likely your story will be a memorable one.

Prewriting
Drafting
Content Editing
Revising
Copyediting
Proofreading
Publishing

Drafting

Because she had made a detailed plan, Maria found it easy to write her draft. She had fun  introducing her main character and setting, imagining what a mermaid might do. She added some dialogue to bring her characters to life.

She even included a line of dialogue that foreshadowed the climax.

Maria focused most of her attention on the plot, which she thought was quite exciting. Finally, she added a resolution that showed how everything worked out in the end.

Into the Cave

At the bottom of the ocean lived a teenage mermaid named Sandy. She loved adventures, but her mother always got in the way.

"Don't you dare" her mother said when her friends invited her to explore a weird cave. "That place is too dangerous."

Her friends went off to explore. Sandy sat around the house. She listened to music and ate her lunch of seaweed and clams. She was bored, so she went off to do some flips in the backyard.

Suddenly, there was a rumbling sound, and all the water started to swirl. "What's that sound?" her mother asked. Then she saw a huge beast passing overhead. It was a purple sea monster.

"Quick! Hide in the basement with me!" her mother shouted. Sandy looked out the window and watched the monster go by. It was headed strait for the cave!

Ignoring her mother, Sandy swum outside and headed for the cave to warn her friends. But when she arrived, they were gone.

She called out to her friends and swam slowly inside. Then the whole place went pitch-black. The sea monster was coming into the cave behind her.

Sandy wished she'd listened to her mother, but she didn't have time to worry about that now. She swam deeper into the cave, with the sea monster close behind. As she swam, the passageways got smaller and smaller.

Prewriting

Drafting

Content Editing

Revising

Copyediting

Proofreading

Publishing

Finally, she reached a dead end, and the ugly sea monster was right behind her, staring at her with glowing green eyes. At the last second, the part of the cave that the sea monster was in collapsed, and Sandy was saved!

She came out of the cave, where her friends were waiting for her. They cheered! The sea monster had been killed by the collapsing cave.

"You did it! You saved us!" her friends shouted. Sandy just smiled as she looked back at the cave. Her mother was right. The cave was dangerous. For sea monsters!

Your Turn

Use the plan you created to write the first draft of your fantasy story. Add details as you go, giving more information about your setting and characters as the story moves along. As you write, include dialogue to bring your characters to life or to advance the plot.

You might want to use literary devices such as foreshadowing or flashbacks to add interest to your story.

Remember to make certain that every sentence of your story serves a purpose, such as describing the scene, making the characters more interesting, or advancing the plot.

Make sure your story is written in a logical way. It will most likely be written in chronological order, except for any flashbacks you might add. Rather than filling your story with strange coincidences, try to make each event follow logically from what came before it.

Following the Characters

Remember to let your characters drive the action of the story. The choices your characters make will depend on their personalities and motivations. If you have a clear idea of your characters in your mind, the choices they make will seem perfectly natural.

In Maria's story, for example, each character did what could be expected based on the character traits Maria had given them. Sandy's mother was naturally nervous and she cared for her daughter, so she told Sandy to stay away from the cave and to hide in the basement when the sea monster came.

Sandy loved adventure, so she ignored her mother's warnings and rushed out to warn her friends. The sea monster behaved according to his motivations too—he chased after Sandy because he was hungry.

Content Editing

Maria was happy with her story. She enjoyed writing about her characters and the underwater setting. She thought her plot was fast-moving and exciting.

Maria knew, however, that with editing, she could make her story even better. She set it aside for a day and returned to it with fresh eyes. She checked to make certain that it included all the characteristics of a good fantasy story and that the narrative was creative, logical, and clear. She used this Content Editor's Checklist to help her.

After she had gone through her story herself, she decided to give her draft to a content editor to help improve it even more. She gave it to her best friend, Elizabeth, whom she knew would not only enjoy her story but also have ideas for making it even better.

Elizabeth read Maria's story once all the way through. Then she checked it over more carefully, answering each question in the Content Editor's Checklist.

Content Editor's Checklist

- ☐ Does the beginning of the story introduce the characters and setting and set up the conflict?

- ☐ Does the middle of the story develop the plot, including rising action and a climax?

- ☐ Does the end of the story include a resolution of the conflict that answers remaining questions?

- ☐ Do the characters have clear traits, including personality and motivations?

- ☐ Is dialogue used to develop the characters or advance the plot?

- ☐ Are literary devices such as foreshadowing and flashbacks used when appropriate?

- ☐ Does the story use a lively voice and original word choice, including figurative language?

- ☐ Is the story logical and clear?

After jotting down some of her comments, Elizabeth went over the draft with Maria. First, Elizabeth told Maria how much she enjoyed the story. She thought the character of Sandy was great and the plot was exciting. She particularly enjoyed the foreshadowing Maria used at the beginning of the story. Next, Elizabeth made the following suggestions for improvement:

- Could you tell a little more about the setting, like what kind of houses they live in?

- I like the details you give about Sandy's boring day at the beginning, but it doesn't add much to the story. Why don't you cut some of that and get to the conflict faster?

- You could probably also take out the dialogue where her mother asks about the sound. It doesn't add much.

- Maybe you could use dialogue in the section where Sandy calls out to her friends in the cave.

- In lots of fantasy stories, somebody finds something magical. Is there anything magical you could add to this story?

- The climax seems like too much of a coincidence. It would be better if you could make the ending more logical.

Maria thanked Elizabeth for reading her story and offering suggestions. She asked Elizabeth for more details about some of her comments. Then Maria decided to go through the story again to decide which of Elizabeth's suggestions to use.

Your Turn

Before you begin revising, reread your draft. Use the Content Editor's Checklist to help you.

Trade papers with a classmate. Make suggestions on your partner's draft and listen carefully as your partner makes comments on yours.

Take your partner's suggestions seriously. If you are unsure about any suggestion, ask your partner to clarify. Use the suggestions that you agree will improve your draft.

Writer's Tip Remember to give positive feedback as well as helpful suggestions. Be specific in your comments.

Prewriting

Drafting

Content Editing

Revising

Copyediting

Proofreading

Publishing

Revising

Here are the revisions Maria made to her draft after her conference with Elizabeth.

Into the Cave

in a coral village

At the bottom of the ocean lived a teenage mermaid named Sandy. She loved adventures, but her mother always got in the way.

"Don't you dare" her mother said when her friends invited her to explore a weird cave. "That place is too dangerous."

Her friends went off to explore. Sandy sat around the house. She listened to music and ate her lunch of seaweed and clams. ~~She was bored, so she went off to do some flips in the backyard.~~

Suddenly, there was a rumbling sound, and all the water started to swirl. ~~"What's that sound?" her mother asked.~~ Then she saw a huge beast passing overhead. It was a purple sea monster, *and it looked big enough to swallow a house.*

"Quick! Hide in the basement with me!" her mother shouted. Sandy looked out the window and watched the monster go by. It was headed strait for the cave!

Ignoring her mother, Sandy swum outside and headed for the cave to warn her friends. But when she arrived, they were gone. *"Helloooo," she called nervously, "anybody in there?"* She called out to her friends and swam slowly inside. Then the whole place went pitch-black. The sea monster was coming into the cave behind her.

Sandy wished she'd listened to her mother, but she didn't have time to worry about that now. She swam deeper into the cave, with the sea monster close behind. As she swam, the passageways got smaller and smaller.

Prewriting

Drafting

Content Editing

Revising

Copyediting

Proofreading

Publishing

Finally, she reached a dead end, and the ugly sea monster was right behind her,
she squirmed into a narrow hole.
staring at her with glowing green eyes. At the last second, ~~the part of the cave that~~

~~the sea monster was in collapsed, and Sandy was saved!~~
through the hole to another opening,
She came ~~out of the cave,~~ where her friends were waiting for her. They cheered!
was so big that he had
The sea monster ~~had been killed by the collapsing cave!~~ *gotten stuck inside the cave.*

"You did it! You saved us!" her friends shouted. Sandy just smiled as she looked

back at the cave. Her mother was right. The cave was dangerous. For sea monsters!

Notice the revisions Maria made to her draft. She used most of Elizabeth's suggestions and found other ways to improve her story.

- Maria added a bit more description of the setting. How did she describe the area?
- She agreed that she could cut some information about what happened before the sea monster came. She kept the part about the lunch of seaweed and clams, but what sentence did cut?
- Since she had mentioned the sound in the previous sentence, what did Maria decide to cut?
- Maria decided to try writing dialogue for the part where Sandy calls into the cave. Why do you think she added it?
- Maria didn't think her story needed anything magical to make it interesting, so she decided not to use that idea.
- Finally, Maria agreed that the climax seemed like a coincidence. It would be better if the climax was the result of something logical happening. How did Maria change the climax?

After looking over her draft, Maria realized that she could describe the size of the sea monster

 Word Choice

more strongly. She decided to use hyperbole, saying that the monster looked big enough to eat a house.

Your Turn

Use the ideas that you and your partner thought of to revise your story. Select the ideas that you think will improve your story. Mark them neatly on your draft. When you have finished, look over your draft one more time and check it against the Content Editor's Checklist. Can you answer yes to each question?

Grammar in Action

Identify the simple sentence that Maria changed into a compound sentence.

Copyediting and Proofreading

Copyediting

Maria felt that the story she had written had been improved by her revisions. She liked the characters and the plot of her story. She especially liked the new ending, where the sea monster's size caused him to get stuck in the cave.

She knew from experience, however, that there were probably mistakes that she had made along the way. She decided to copyedit her draft to make sure it was clear, logical, and grammatically correct. She also checked her sentence structures and word choice. She used this Copyeditor's Checklist.

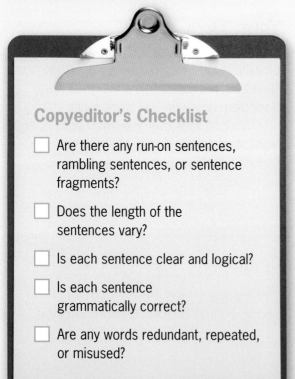

Copyeditor's Checklist

- ☐ Are there any run-on sentences, rambling sentences, or sentence fragments?

- ☐ Does the length of the sentences vary?

- ☐ Is each sentence clear and logical?

- ☐ Is each sentence grammatically correct?

- ☐ Are any words redundant, repeated, or misused?

Maria began the copyediting step by reading her story aloud. By reading aloud, she noticed 👓 **Sentence Fluency** that the sentences in the third paragraph seemed choppy, so she combined two of them.

Next, she realized that the word *weird* didn't fit the description of the cave, so she changed it to *mysterious.*

Sandy also noticed that she had used the word *swam* in most cases, but in the sixth paragraph she had used *swum.* She checked with her teacher, who told her that *swam* is the past tense, while *swum* is the past participle. In this case the correct word was *swam.*

Finally, she noticed that her last sentence was actually a fragment. To make the sentence grammatically correct, she added a dash between the two sentences, which still gave the final phrase a strong impact.

Your Turn

Read your draft again and check it over once more, using the Copyeditor's Checklist.

Writer's Tip You may want to read your description aloud as you copyedit.

Proofreading

When Maria had finished copyediting, her draft was nearly complete. She was confident that the content editing and copyediting had made her story better.

The only editing step that remained was the proofreading step, where she would ask a partner to check her draft once more for errors. She gave her draft to her classmate William, who checked it against this Proofreader's Checklist.

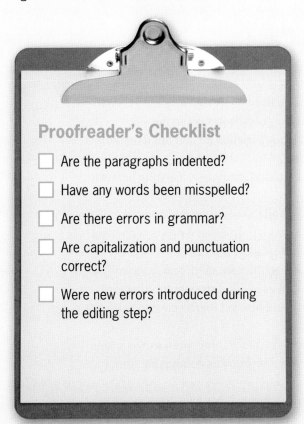

Proofreader's Checklist

- ☐ Are the paragraphs indented?
- ☐ Have any words been misspelled?
- ☐ Are there errors in grammar?
- ☐ Are capitalization and punctuation correct?
- ☐ Were new errors introduced during the editing step?

William found a few mistakes in Maria's story. He noted that the word *straight* had been misspelled in the fifth paragraph.

Next, he noticed an error in punctuation. He knew that the mother's statement in the second

 Conventions

paragraph should end with a punctuation mark, either a comma or an exclamation point. Since she already had used a lot of exclamation points in her draft, Maria decided to add a comma.

Finally, William found a mistake that had been made in the content-editing step. Her new line of dialogue, where Sandy calls into the cave, was really two sentences. She would have to change the comma to a period after *nervously* and begin the next word with a capital letter.

Your Turn

Look over your draft, using the Proofreader's Checklist to help you.

Next, trade drafts with a partner and proofread each other's story. Use the Proofreader's Checklist to make suggestions on your partner's story.

Prewriting

Drafting

Content Editing

Revising

Copyediting

Proofreading

Publishing

Writer's Workshop

Publishing

Maria corrected the mistakes that William had found in her story before printing it out. She looked forward to sharing her fantasy story with the class.

Into the Cave

by Maria Nolan

At the bottom of the ocean in a coral village lived a teenage mermaid named Sandy. She loved adventures, but her nervous mother always got in the way.

"Don't you dare," her mother said when Sandy's friends invited her to explore a mysterious cave. "That place is too dangerous."

Her friends went off to explore. Sandy sat around the house, listening to music and eating her lunch of seaweed and clams.

Suddenly, there was a rumbling sound, and all the water started to swirl. Then she saw something passing overhead. It was a purple sea monster with giant flippers and scales, and it looked big enough to swallow a house.

"Quick! Hide in the basement with me," her mother shouted. Sandy looked out the window and watched the monster go by. It was headed straight for the cave!

Ignoring her mother, Sandy swam outside and headed for the cave to warn her friends. But when she arrived, they were gone.

"Helloooo," she called nervously. "Anybody in there?" She swam slowly inside. Then the whole place went pitch-black. The sea monster was coming into the cave behind her.

Sandy wished she'd listened to her mother, but she didn't have time to worry about that now. She swam deeper into the cave, with the sea monster close behind. As she swam, the passageways got smaller and smaller.

Finally, she reached a dead end, and the ugly sea monster was right behind her, staring at her with glowing green eyes. At the last second, she squirmed into a narrow hole.

She came through the hole to another opening, where her friends were waiting for her. They cheered! The sea monster was so big that he had gotten stuck inside the cave. "You did it! You saved us!" her friends shouted. Sandy just smiled as she looked back at the cave. Her mother was right. The cave was dangerous—for sea monsters!

Whenever you publish your work, your goal is to share your thoughts and experiences with other people. There are many ways you can publish your story. Be sure you have a catchy title for your story before you publish.

 Presentation

 Post it on your classroom's wiki, blog, or Web site. Have classmates read one another's fantasy stories and comment on them.

 Film it. Enlist the help of friends to take parts and paint scenery. Add music. Do the narration as you film it.

 Create a book for a younger grade. Decorate the margins with small pictures to illustrate the story. You might choose to print the title and your name on a separate cover page and illustrate it with a scene from your story. Number each page and put the pages together using staples or a binder. Display your book in the hallway or library of your school.

 Does your school have a literary magazine or a newspaper? If so, you may be able to submit your story for publication. Find out what the requirements for submission are and follow them exactly.

Your Turn

Choose one of the publishing options. Look over your story one more time before you publish it.

- You might use a spell-checker to search for spelling errors if you used a computer.
- Make certain that you have not made any new mistakes along the way.
- Add your name below the story's title.
- Use your best handwriting or a computer to make your final copy.

If you enjoyed writing this story, you might consider writing more on your own. There's no limit to the number of interesting settings, characters, and stories you can create.

Fantasy Fiction

Read about the narrow escape of a mermaid named Sandy. Her encounter with a sea-dwelling sea monster is worthwhile reading. Check it out at our own school library.

Prewriting

Drafting

Content Editing

Revising

Copyediting

Proofreading

Publishing

Expository Writing

LiNK **Paul Gauguin and the South Pacific**

by Andrea J. Buchanan and Miriam Peskowitz

Perhaps you have seen French artist Paul Gauguin's vivid paintings of village scenes, huts, and the spiritual life of South Sea Island people, in his trademark oranges and lush greens. Gauguin (1848–1903) embraced these islands. On his

Self-portrait

last legs as a failed businessman, he left . . . and boarded a ship for the South Pacific. There he dreamt, he could escape the conventions of European life and the Impressionist school of art, which he found confining.

In Tahiti and the Marquesas Islands, where Gauguin lived the rest of his days, he painted his now renowned images of island life. . . . he died of illness at the young age of 54, before he could serve his time. Gauguin is buried on the Marquesas Islands, and his work earned fame and fortune only after his death.

> This article demonstrates characteristics of expository writing, such as an introduction that tells what the article is about, contains facts not opinions, and concludes with a memorable statement.

CHAPTER 7

Bridget F.
Room 7B

Stephanie Wilson as Astronaut

Imagine traveling in space is what you do for a living! This adventure is Stephanie Wilson's career—a NASA astronaut. Stephanie Wilson is the second African American woman to travel in space. She has already been a part of two space mission crews and logged 28 days in space.

Stephanie Diana Wilson was born in 1966 in Boston, Massachusetts. Stephanie is married to Julius "BJ" McCurdy and has no children. In 1988 she graduated from Harvard University with a Bachelor of Science degree in Engineering. After two years of working at Martin Marietta Astronautics Group in Denver, Colorado, Wilson went back to graduate school at the University of Texas. In 1992 Stephanie earned a Master of Science degree in Aerospace Engineering.

After being selected by NASA in 1996, Stephanie reported to the Johnson Space Center to start training. Following her work in Mission Control, Stephanie was assigned to Astronaut Office Shuttle Operations Branch, where she worked on the Space Shuttle's Main Engines, External Tank, and Rocket Boosters. In 2006 Stephanie was assigned to the crew of STS-121. The mission of the crew was to fly to the International Space Station, or ISS, to test new equipment. While on the ISS, the crew of STS-121 repaired a rail car. Almost a year later, on October 23, 2007, Stephanie was assigned to her next mission, the crew of STS-120. This crew delivered a module to the ISS and then relocated a solar array. During the relocation, the panels were snagged and damaged. The crew repaired the panel in 238 orbits, traveling 6.2 million miles in 15 days.

Stephanie is a remarkable astronaut and woman. She has inspired women that no dream is impossible. She is an inspiration for all women to reach for their dreams.

What Makes Good Expository Writing?

Have you ever read a fascinating article about insects or a news report about the latest basketball game? Each of these is an example of expository writing. Expository writing provides factual information to the reader. Its purpose is to inform, explain, or define something to its audience. One kind of expository writing is the expository article.

Introduction

The introduction of an expository article tells what the article is about. It includes a topic sentence, which concisely states the main idea, telling the reader what he or she will learn about the topic. In the introduction below, the final sentence is the topic sentence.

> **Have you ever wanted to learn how a dollar bill is printed or see the House of Representatives in action? Look no further than Washington, D.C. Whether it's to view the city's many monuments, to visit historic sites, or to enjoy museums, people flock from around the country to visit the nation's capital.**

Body

In the body of an expository article, the writer provides details to support the main idea. The writer relies on facts, not opinions, and offers research or personal experiences to back up the information. The body might include several subtopics related to the main idea. The subtopics should be organized in a logical way. For example, an article on plant photosynthesis might explain the process from beginning to end, while an article about the latest fashions might move from one type of clothing to the next.

Conclusion

In expository writing the conclusion summarizes the article. The conclusion leaves readers thinking about the topic by making a memorable statement, such as the one used in the excerpt on page 453, or giving a thought-provoking insight.

ACTIVITY A **Which of the following ideas would make good expository articles? Which ones would not? Explain your answers.**

1. an essay on why my father is the best father in the world
2. an explanation of the theories of why the dinosaurs became extinct
3. an article explaining how Orson Welles's film *Citizen Kane* influenced filmmakers
4. a story about two boys becoming friends
5. an essay about why the mayor should be reelected
6. a biography of Sojourner Truth
7. a review of the latest hit movie
8. an informational article on planning balanced meals
9. an article on the history of the steam engine
10. a description of my dream house

ACTIVITY B **Identify the topic of each article title below. Then write a topic sentence that might identify the main idea of the article.**

1. Why People Need Exercise
2. What Is an Armadillo?
3. The New Models at the Auto Show
4. Freedom Is . . .
5. Hobbies Are Important

ACTIVITY C **Choose a title from Activity B and create an outline. Refer to Chapter 5, Lesson 5 for helpful tips.**

WRITER'S CORNER

Choose a piece of expository writing you have read. Find and write the topic sentence from the piece. Then write a list of facts or examples that support the main idea.

Main Idea and Details

Details are specific information and examples that give substance to a piece of expository writing. The more details you supply to support your main idea, the more interesting and informative your writing will be. However, make sure all your details are relevant to your main idea. Here are some tips for gathering details.

- Think about any details you already know about a topic and write them.
- List any personal experiences you have had with the topic that are relevant to the main idea.
    - Record more details from newspapers, magazines, books, and the Internet.
    - Interview people who can give more details, such as friends, parents, teachers, or experts.

The chart below is one writer's way of preparing to write about the volcanic eruption of Mount St. Helens.

You will probably have a main idea in mind before you begin gathering details. However, your main idea may change as you learn more details. You may find that your details support a different main idea that seems more interesting. You might even discover that your details contradict your main idea.

Main Idea:

The Mount St. Helens catastrophic eruption was more destructive than any on record in the United States.

Details:

- erupted May 18, 1980, 8:32 a.m.
- located in Cascade Mountains in Washington, fifth-highest mountain in the state
- Hot ash and gases blew into air and slid down mountain, burning everything along the way.
- More than 50 people were killed plus animals and plants within 70 square miles (181 square kilometers).
- Ash made nearby cities dark, covering everything.

For example, you might begin with the main idea that children like the same types of food that their parents like, based on personal experience. What if you found research showing that children don't like the same foods that their parents like? In this case you might alter your main idea to fit your research-based details.

ACTIVITY D Read each list of details. Then write a topic sentence whose main idea fits the details.

1. **a.** The Saami, who live in Finland, stay in villages in valleys during the cold winters.

   b. They live in mountains the rest of the year.

   c. They move from one mountain home to the next, so the reindeer they herd can find fresh food.

2. **a.** Some people like going to the movies on a rainy day.

   b. Other people prefer staying home and reading a book.

   c. Still others enjoy going out and splashing around in the rain.

3. **a.** Scientists once thought atoms were the smallest things in the universe.

   b. Later, it was discovered that atoms contain protons, neutrons, and electrons.

   c. Even smaller particles called quarks were eventually discovered inside protons and neutrons.

ACTIVITY E Choose one of the following topics. Then write a main idea and two details that could support the main idea.

   A. types of music on several radio stations

   B. a historical figure I'd like to meet

   C. why recycling is important

   D. what life in a spaceship is like

WRITER'S CORNER

Write a topic sentence on either a natural disaster or an endangered species that interests you. Use the tips on page 454 to find details about the topic. Record five facts that might be used in an expository article.

Tech Tip With an adult, research your topic online.

Fact and Opinion

Facts

Most of the details in expository writing are facts. A fact is a statement that can be proved true or false. Often you can prove a fact by checking a reliable source such as an encyclopedia, an almanac, or a textbook. Sometimes you can check a fact by personally observing a situation. Consider the following statements of fact.

> **There are nine justices on the U.S. Supreme Court.**
>
> **The Supreme Court Building is located at One First Street in Washington, D.C.**
>
> **The Supreme Court Building has two statues in front.**

Each of these facts can be proved in a different way. You could prove the first fact by looking in a book about the Supreme Court. The second fact could be proved by looking in a telephone directory of Washington, D.C. You could prove the third fact by checking a photograph of the Supreme Court Building or by viewing the building yourself.

Lady Justice

Opinions

An opinion is a statement that tells what someone believes. Opinions are often based on the person's likes and dislikes or on ideas that cannot be proved. For expository articles intended to inform not persuade, good writers avoid including their own opinions in their writing. The opinions of experts, however, may sometimes be included.

When you hear or read a piece of expository writing, pay attention to words or phrases that signal that a speaker's statement might be an opinion, not a fact. Consider these opinions:

> **I think the Supreme Court is very fair.**
> **The phrase *I think* signals the speaker's opinion.**
>
> **A Supreme Court justice has a great job.**
> **The word *great* reflects a judgment that can't be proved.**

ACTIVITY A With a partner take turns reading aloud each fact and telling how you could prove whether it is true or not.

1. A Supreme Court justice's salary is over $200,000 a year.
2. The Supreme Court Building is kept at a temperature of 68°F.
3. The Supreme Court currently has more male justices than female justices.
4. The word *supreme* means "highest in rank or power."
5. The Supreme Court was formed in 1790.
6. The Supreme Court Building has pillars outside.
7. Some newspapers publish Supreme Court decisions.
8. The Supreme Court Building had over 500,000 visitors last year.

ACTIVITY B Read each statement and determine whether it is a fact or an opinion.

1. I feel the Supreme Court needs more female justices.
2. The Supreme Court is too powerful.
3. The Supreme Court is composed of a chief justice and eight associate justices.
4. I think the Supreme Court works too slowly.
5. A Supreme Court justice has a very difficult job.
6. The Supreme Court receives about 7,000 petitions per term.
7. Some lawyers become Supreme Court justices.
8. The Supreme Court makes fair and wise decisions.
9. The Supreme Court decision *Brown v. Board of Education* helped eliminate segregation in schools.
10. The Supreme Court is an important institution.

LiNK

Dinosaur Detectives

In 1978, a paleontologist named Jack Horner was visiting a fossil shop in Montana, U.S.A. He found the bones of a baby dinosaur. This was an important discovery. Few baby dinosaurs had ever been found!

Horner traced the fossil back to the rocky hillside where it had been discovered, and began to dig. Soon he had discovered a huge nest. . . .

Peter Chrisp

WRITER'S CORNER

Find more information about the Supreme Court. Then write a new fact and an opinion about it. For the fact tell how it can be proved. For the opinion identify the clue words that signal it is an opinion.

Using Facts in Your Writing

In most types of expository writing, you will need to use more than one fact to support your topic sentence. Here is a list of tips to follow when using facts as details in your writing:

- Check for the accuracy of your facts by using a reliable source such as a textbook, an encyclopedia, or a reputable Web site.
- Provide enough facts to support your topic sentence and make your writing believable. Make sure each statement is supported by a fact or an example; otherwise, the statement will sound like an opinion.
- If you have collected so many facts that you will probably not be able to fit them all in the piece you are writing, choose the facts that are the most relevant. Omit the ones that repeat the same points.
- Leave out facts that are unrelated to the subject of your writing. Such facts will sidetrack the reader, making the main idea of the piece difficult to understand.

ACTIVITY C **Read the list of facts about antibiotics. Imagine you are going to write an essay whose topic sentence is "Antibiotics should be used with caution." Which facts would be the most relevant to the essay? Which would be the least relevant?**

1. Bacteria can become resistant to an antibiotic.
2. Alexander Fleming discovered the uses of penicillin, one of the most important antibiotics, in 1928.
3. Antibiotics are substances produced by microorganisms that kill or inhibit other microorganisms.
4. Antibiotics may cause side effects.
5. Many of the antibiotics in use today are members of the genus *Streptomyces*.
6. Antibiotics work only against infections that are caused by bacteria.
7. Some antibiotics are effective against only certain types of bacteria.
8. Doctors say antibiotics should never be saved and reused.
9. The word *antibiotic* comes from words meaning "against life" because antibiotics kill living microorganisms.

ACTIVITY D Rewrite the following expository essay, omitting any words or sentences that are opinions.

These days, technology is everywhere. In fact, it's in too many places! People walk the streets and ride trains listening to MP3 players or have cell phones to their ears, chatting away. Cell phones are so popular that the number of them in use has doubled in the past three years. Why people can't just wait to get home before they call someone is beyond me.

Another popular technology is laptop computers. People can be seen using these annoying laptops in coffee shops, restaurants, or even on park benches. Part of the reason for the popularity of laptops is because they have become smaller and less expensive, with some costing as little as a few hundred dollars. That's still too expensive if you ask me.

Adding yet another layer of technology are video displays that pop up everywhere. No longer confined to sports stadiums, huge monitors show commercials from the tops of buildings. Some people find this technology fun and convenient, while others find it to be a distraction. I definitely fall into the latter category.

ACTIVITY E Read the essay you rewrote in Activity D. Answer the following questions about your essay.

1. What is the topic of the essay?
2. What is the main idea of the essay?
3. How is the essay organized?
4. What are three facts the author might have added to make the essay stronger?
5. What resources could you use to check those facts?

ACTIVITY F Read the sentences about X-rays. Identify which are facts and which are opinions. Rewrite the opinions to make them into facts.

1. X-rays were discovered by W. C. Röntgen in 1895.
2. X-rays are the best invention ever made.
3. Radiation is released each time an X-ray is taken.
4. Patients should be nervous when receiving an X-ray.
5. Doctors enjoy reviewing X-rays.

WRITER'S CORNER

Think of a main idea for an expository article. Then write, in random order, three facts and three opinions about your main idea. Exchange your facts and opinions with a partner and identify which are facts and which are opinions. How could you check your partner's facts?

Noun and Verb Suffixes

Give us independence

Noun Suffixes

A suffix is a syllable or syllables added to the end of a word to change its meaning. The suffixes below all create nouns when added to verbs, adjectives, or other nouns.

Study the suffix chart. Some examples required spelling changes when their suffixes were added.

SUFFIX	MEANING	EXAMPLE
-ance, -ancy, -ion, -ity, -ment, -ness, -ship, -ty	state of being	vigilance, infancy, convention, generosity, assignment, kindness, kinship, modesty
-ant, -ent, -er, -ist, -or	one who	attendant, resident, hitter, chemist, juror

Be sure to use the correct suffix. An incorrect suffix may convey the wrong meaning. Know which base word takes each suffix, or look up the base word and find the entry for the word with a suffix.

ACTIVITY A **Make a chart like the one below. Write each word and two other words that end with the same suffix. Use a dictionary for help.**

SUFFIX	BASE WORD	NEW WORD	OTHER WORDS
-ion	elect	election	celebration, omission
-ity	agile		
-ance	govern		
-ness	happy		
-ist	moral		

ACTIVITY B Add a noun suffix to the word in parentheses to complete each sentence. Use a dictionary if you need help.

1. The teacher granted everyone (permit) to spend 15 more minutes outside.
2. The (quick) with which the storm came up took us by surprise.
3. The (distract) caused by the accident created a traffic nightmare.
4. My brother got a (promote) and a raise in salary.
5. Pete's cooking (able) always wins him praise.
6. When she writes poems, Marge's (creative) comes through.
7. My sister can make a beautiful floral (arrange).
8. To gain (citizen), a person must live in the United States for five years.
9. In fables the fox is famous for its (clever).
10. Some dogs have a (compel) to chew on slippers.

ACTIVITY C For each definition below, use a suffix from this lesson to make a noun that fits the definition.

1. one who acts
2. state of being loyal
3. state of being a citizen
4. one who operates a machine
5. state of being hesitant
6. one who creates art
7. one who curates
8. state of being committed
9. one who works with flowers
10. state of repenting

WRITER'S CORNER

Read a page of an expository article and identify five words with noun suffixes. Use each word in a sentence. Include the name of your source.

Grammar in Action
Identify the first word that contains a suffix from the list on p. 460 that is used in the excerpt on p. 450.

Verb Suffixes

Some suffixes can be added to words to create verbs. Notice that the spelling of a base word can change when a suffix is added. Here are a few examples.

SUFFIX	MEANING	BASE WORD	EXAMPLE
-ate	make	motive	motivate
-en	cause to be	soft	soften
-ify	make	beauty	beautify
-ize	cause to be	personal	personalize

ACTIVITY D **Add a verb suffix from the chart above to the word in parentheses to complete each sentence. Use a dictionary for help with spelling.**

1. Samuel tried to (light) his friend's load by taking some of the supplies from his backpack.

2. When they got together, all the singers tried to (harmony).

3. Before a test always be sure to (sharp) your pencil.

4. The new club decided to (regular) its rules by voting on them.

5. To become a good speller, you need to (internal) the correct spellings by memorizing them.

6. The criminal tried to (just) his actions by claiming that nobody was hurt by his crime.

7. As the sun goes down, the sky will (dark).

8. When you cook, you need to (active) spices by heating them in butter or oil.

9. I didn't (real) a profit when I sold my old bike.

10. Did you see Matthew's face (red) when the class discovered his secret?

ACTIVITY E **Add an appropriate verb suffix from the chart above. Then use the new word in a sentence. Use a dictionary for help with spelling.**

1. sympathy
2. deep
3. color
4. simple
5. familiar
6. moist
7. fright
8. wide
9. real
10. oblige

ACTIVITY F Write a word to fit each definition. Each word should end with a noun suffix or a verb suffix from the lesson.

1. something that is required
2. one who plays the piano
3. state of being sharp
4. cause to be sweeter
5. act of placing
6. make into a mummy
7. state of being novel
8. one who does carpentry
9. state of being friends

ACTIVITY G Find the words in the following expository paragraph that have the noun and verb suffixes you have studied in this lesson. Then give a definition of each word.

Can you identify the first producers of peanuts? There were the Indians in South America in about 1500 BC. In the 1500s Spanish and Portuguese explorers sent shipments of peanuts from South America to Europe, Asia, and Africa. In 1925 the scientist George Washington Carver familiarized farmers in the United States with the usefulness of peanuts and how easy they were to grow. Today the popularity of peanuts is especially evident at baseball games, where total consumption each summer amounts to more than one million bags. However, there has been a sudden rise in peanut allergies in children. Scientists have yet to identify the cause.

George Washington Carver

Grammar in Action. Use one coordinating or correlative conjunction in your paragraph. See Sections 9.1 and 9.2.

Quotations

Direct quotations are a person's exact words, either spoken or in print, that are incorporated into your own writing. When gathering facts for an expository piece, you might come across a written or spoken quotation that eloquently, colorfully, or concisely sums up a point you want to make. You might discover a quotation that leaves a strong impact, driving home an important point. These types of quotations can be especially useful to include in an expository article. For example:

> **John F. Kennedy, our 35th president, once said, "Ask not what your country can do for you—ask what you can do for your country." Have you ever asked yourself what you can do for your country? The possibilities are endless if you make a conscious effort to make the world a better place.**

In this paragraph the writer uses a famous quotation to introduce a topic about making a positive impact on the world. When using a quotation, a writer quotes exactly what a person said. The source, or the person who said or wrote the words, is identified at the beginning or end of the quotation.

In reports of actual events, such as in newspapers or magazines, quotations made by ordinary people often help the report come to life. One way to add more interest to the article on page 451 would be to add a quotation. How does the quotation at the end of the paragraph below affect your impression of the article?

> **Stephanie is a remarkable astronaut and woman. She has inspired women that no dream is impossible. Her father commented, "Her seventh-grade teacher said that Stephanie has what it takes to succeed. She's going to go far." She is an inspiration for all women to reach for their dreams.**

President John F. Kennedy and his wife, Jacqueline

ACTIVITY A **Read the following paragraphs from two different expository school reports. For each paragraph tell whether or not the quotation is effective and explain why.**

1. Sacagawea was a Native American woman who helped Meriwether Lewis and William Clark explore our country. She was their guide and interpreter of several Indian languages. Clark indicated her value to him when he wrote the following on June 13, 1805: "I found the Indian woman extremely ill. This gave me some concern, as well as for the poor object herself, then with a young child in her arms, as from her condition of being our only dependence for a friendly negotiation with the Snake Indians, on whom we depend for horses to assist us in our travel from the Missouri River to the Columbia River." Sacagawea recovered and guided the explorers until August 17, 1806.

2. Captain Clark wrote, "I saw at a distance several Indians on horseback coming towards me. Charbonneau and Sacagawea who were before me at some distance danced for the joyful sight." Lewis and Clark met with a Shoshoni chief to ask for horses to take them across the mountains. First, they gave their message in English to someone who spoke French. He relayed the information to Charbonneau in French. Charbonneau translated the message into Hidatsa, and Sacagawea translated from Hidatsa into Shoshoni.

ACTIVITY B **Read the following quotations. Which would add the most impact to an article about playing the guitar? Which would you be least likely to use? Explain your answers.**

1. "Playing the guitar is as easy as breathing, once you get started," said guitar teacher Julia Sperling.

2. "Playing the trumpet is easier than playing the guitar," my father told me, "but you need much stronger lungs to play the trumpet!"

3. "The first evidence of guitars comes from Spain in the 15th century," writes Margo Masterson in *The History of Guitars*.

WRITER'S CORNER

Look through newspaper or magazine articles for three effective quotations. Write a sentence for each, explaining why the quotation is effective.

Detail of map from Lewis and Clark expedition

Collecting Quotations

Have you ever read something in a book, newspaper, magazine, or online that made an impact on you? It is a good idea to copy that quotation onto a note card exactly as it is written. Include the source of the quotation and the title, publisher, and copyright information of the written source material. You never know when you may be able to incorporate that quotation into a report or a piece of writing.

Sometimes you will hear spoken words that catch your attention. When this occurs, take notes by writing exactly what you hear.

Punctuating Quotations

In most cases quotations should be punctuated the same as dialogue. Here are some more rules to remember when writing quotations.

- Generally, use a comma to introduce a quotation or to introduce its source. Capitalize the beginning of the quotation and use quotation marks.

  Helen Keller once said, "One can never consent to creep when one feels an impulse to soar."

- If the quotation is preceded by an introductory word such as *that,* or if the quotation is the subject or object of a sentence, use no punctuation to introduce the quotation and do not capitalize it.

  Albert Einstein claimed *that* "imagination is more important than knowledge."

- Use quotation marks before and after every part of a divided quotation.

  "I believe," Columbus said, "the earth is round."

- Sometimes a quotation includes another quotation. The included quotation is known as a quotation within a quotation and is marked with single quotation marks.

  Marsela asked, "Was it Lincoln who said, 'With malice toward none; with charity for all'?"

Christopher Columbus sailed the *Santa Maria* to America.

- When writing a long quotation, you might punctuate it by using a colon. If you do so, use an introductory phrase such as *these words* or *the following.*

> **Martin Luther King Jr. spoke these words: "I have a dream that one day in the red hills of Georgia, the sons of former slaves and the sons of former slave-owners will be able to sit down together at the table of brotherhood."**

ACTIVITY C Revise each of the following sentences, using the appropriate punctuation and capitalization.

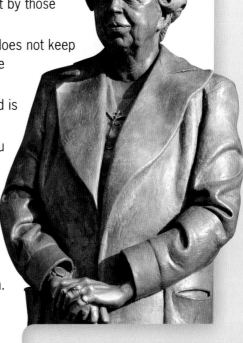

Eleanor Roosevelt

1. There never was a good war wrote Benjamin Franklin or a bad peace.

2. Emily Dickinson wrote success is counted sweetest by those who ne'er succeed.

3. Henry David Thoreau wrote the following if a man does not keep pace with his companions, perhaps it is because he hears a different drummer.

4. The teacher said explain the proverb a penny saved is a penny earned.

5. Laugh and the world laughs with you; weep and you weep alone proclaimed Ella Wheeler Wilcox.

6. Mark Twain wrote I never let my schooling interfere with my education.

7. Eleanor Roosevelt said these words I believe that anyone can conquer fear by doing the things he fears to do, provided he keeps doing them until he gets a record of successful experiences behind him.

8. We cannot always build the future for our youth said Franklin D. Roosevelt but we can build our youth for the future.

9. Connor asked me the meaning of this quote by Heraclitus much learning does not teach understanding.

10. I'm not happy when I'm writing wrote Fannie Hurst but I'm more unhappy when I'm not.

11. Nobody ever drowned in his own sweat wrote Ann Landers.

12. Charles Lamb said that newspapers always excite curiosity. No one ever lays one down without a feeling of disappointment.

WRITER'S CORNER

Write three sentences about a topic related to one of the quotations in this lesson or another quotation you find somewhere else. Include the quotation in the paragraph.

Library and Internet Sources

Information is everywhere. When researching information, you might look in newspapers or magazines. You might watch a television program or film, or interview a friend or expert. In this lesson you will consider two of the most efficient ways of finding information: using references from the library and gathering information on the Internet.

Library Sources

Some of a library's best sources are not available to check out. The chart below lists some common library reference sources you might have to read while you're there.

REFERENCE	INFORMATION
almanac/yearbook	annual facts, statistics, news articles
atlas	maps and other geographic information
encyclopedia	articles on specific topics
articles and periodicals	periodic publications such as magazines
Reader's Guide to Periodical Literature	listings of magazine articles

The Catalog

The resources in a library, including books, DVDs, and CDs, are listed in the catalog. Most libraries have their catalog on computer. A few libraries might still use a card catalog, which consists of printed cards inside small drawers in a cabinet.

Books are listed in the catalog in three ways: by author, by title, and by subject. To find a book in the computer catalog, type in the author, title, or subject. If you don't have a specific book in mind, type a keyword, which is a word related to the topic.

Each listing in the catalog contains key information besides the title, author, and subject, such as the publication date. The listing might also tell you if the book is checked out and which of the library's branches have the book.

Finding a Nonfiction Book

Once you find the nonfiction book you're looking for in the catalog, write the call number and locate that number on the library shelves. Nonfiction books are organized in numerical order, usually using the Dewey Decimal System. Once you have found your book, browse through the books in that area. You will find other books about the same subject. If possible, use books with the most current publication dates; these books will have the most up-to-date information available.

Women Olympic Champions

By Aaseng, Nathan/Lucent Books, 2001

Call No.:	796.082 AAS
Subjects	• Women athletes—Juvenile literature.
	• Olympics—History—Juvenile literature.
Description:	112 p.: ill.; 24 cm.
Contents:	The struggle for acceptance—Sonja Henie—Babe Didrikson—Nadia Comaneci—Jackie Joyner-Kersee.

Location	Section	Call No.	Status
Nichols Library	Juvenile	796.082 AAS	IN
Wood St. Library	Juvenile	796.082 AAS	Due: 04 APR

ACTIVITY A **Use the sample computer catalog entry above to answer the questions.**

1. Who is the author of *Women Olympic Champions*?
2. What keywords might bring up a listing of this book?
3. What is the date of publication of the book?
4. Where is a copy of this book available?
5. What women athletes are featured in the book?

WRITER'S CORNER

Choose a topic and look up three or four books about it at your school or local library. Write the book titles, authors, and library call numbers. Briefly describe the content of each book.

Internet Sources

The Internet can seem like the easiest place to find sources for an article. There is a Web site dedicated to nearly every subject, and in some cases, dozens of sites. In addition, Web sites sometimes have more up-to-date information than library books.

To conduct sound research on the Internet, it is important to look critically at each Web site you visit to be sure it is reliable. Because nearly anyone can be published on the Internet, it can be difficult to tell if a site's information is accurate and unbiased. Internet sites also change frequently, and some of them disappear completely.

Conducting Web Searches

To conduct a Web search, visit a search engine and type in keywords for the topic you are considering. To find the best Web sites, type several specific keywords in the search field, leaving out words such as *of* or *the*. For example, to find out how long a chickadee lives, type "chickadee lifespan" in the search field.

Evaluating Web Sites

The best way to evaluate the accuracy of a Web site is to find out who created it. If it was created by an organization you are familiar with or by an educational or a government source, there's a good chance the information is reliable. If it was created by an individual without any specific credentials or by somebody hoping to sell something, look at the site more critically before you trust its information.

Another hint of a Web site's reliability can be found in the extension at the end of a Web address. These are a few examples:

.com	**commercial sites**
.edu	**sites developed by schools**
.gov	**government sites**
.mil	**military sites**
.org	**sites developed by organizations**

Other extensions indicate that a Web site originated in another country. For example, .uk sites were created in the United Kingdom, while .mx sites were created in Mexico.

Be wary of sites that end in .com if you are looking for unbiased information. The makers of those sites may be more interested in selling you something than in teaching you something.

ACTIVITY B **What keywords would you type to conduct a search for the following topics? Give at least two examples for each topic.**

1. the life of inventor Alexander Graham Bell
2. where Canada geese fly in the winter
3. how rock music has evolved since the 1960s
4. the best home-run hitters of the last 20 years
5. why it's important to get a good night's sleep

ACTIVITY C **Imagine that you are writing an article about the efforts to improve the fuel efficiency of cars. Which of the following sites would you expect to offer the most reliable, unbiased information? Which sites are likely to be less reliable or more biased? Explain your answers.**

1. a .com site telling why Ford has the best, most fuel-efficient line of cars on the market today
2. an .edu site detailing the history of fuel efficiency in cars
3. the site of a man who believes that all cars should be run on solar power
4. a site from a lobbying group that works to convince Congress to raise fuel-efficiency standards
5. a United States Department of Energy site about fuel efficiency

ACTIVITY D **Conduct a search on the following topics. Identify two keywords and list two sources for each topic.**

1. how bats see in the dark
2. the most recent space shuttle
3. the history of the Statue of Liberty

WRITER'S CORNER

Choose a topic to research. Go to the library or search the Internet for information. Then describe how you searched and what results you found.

Destination Guides

A destination guide is a report about a place. In an oral destination guide, a speaker explains what a place is like, tells some of its history, and gives an unbiased report of some of the good and bad aspects of the place. In this lesson you will learn what makes an effective destination guide and then deliver an oral report to your classmates.

Choosing a Topic

A good topic is one that will interest your audience. You might choose an exotic location that is very different from your home, or you might choose a place with an interesting history. You might choose a famous (or infamous) place, or you might choose an obscure place that your audience might like to know about.

Narrow your topic so that you can cover all your information in a brief talk. If you choose a large and diverse place such as New York City, focus on one aspect of it, such as sights you could visit in one day. If you choose a specific place such as Monument Valley, you could include several aspects, such as how it was formed, different ways to explore it, and other interesting facts.

When you have chosen a place to talk about, think of a main idea that might sum up your destination, such as "Albuquerque is a city with a rich culture and history" or "Vermont is a state known for its natural beauty." You might change your main idea as you gather details, but it helps to have one in mind as you begin.

Gathering Details

Gather your details in the same way you would collect information for an expository article. Begin by writing everything you know about the place, including personal experiences and information you have heard from other people.

You might interview someone who has visited the place and insert a colorful or an insightful quotation from the person.

Research your place, using library or Internet sources. An almanac can tell you basic facts about a country, state, or city, including its size, population, and geography. An encyclopedia entry can also give basic facts. A guidebook can give up-to-date information on sights to see and helpful travel tips.

Using a Visual

As you research, keep an eye out for visuals you could use in your talk. You might use a map or globe to show the location, or display a photograph of the place. If you have visited the place, you might share photos. If you plan to display an image to the class, make sure that it is large enough for everyone to see.

ACTIVITY A Evaluate each of the following guide topics. Which topics are too broad? If a topic is too broad, rewrite the topic to narrow its focus.

1. the historic past of Jamestown, Virginia
2. sights to see in Toronto
3. things to see and do in Mexico
4. walking in California's Muir Woods
5. the history, culture, and geography of Sydney, Australia
6. visiting New Hampshire's White Mountains

ACTIVITY B Choose one topic from Activity A that you think would make a good destination guide and research it. Using the library or the Internet, find three sources of information on that subject. Write several facts that you learn about the topic. Then write a topic sentence that could sum up a guide about the topic.

SPEAKER'S CORNER

Expand the research you did for Activity B. Use your topic sentence to develop at least one paragraph for your destination guide. Make sure you properly cite your information sources.

Tech Tip Use an online tool to help you organize your details.

Organizing Your Destination Guide

Once you have gathered all your details, you can use an outline or jot down notes to help you create an informative and engaging talk. Open with an introduction that engages your audience and states the main idea of your talk, using a topic sentence.

In the body present your details in an organized way. For example, you might include separate sections on the history, geography, and culture of the place you choose. Or you might focus on one aspect of the place, such as its history or geography, and give details in chronological or spacial order.

In the conclusion summarize what you have said about the place. End with a memorable statement.

Preparing

When you have organized your talk, write your notes on note cards and prepare your visual. When you write notes, remember to use words and phrases rather than sentences for most of the information. If you use a quotation, however, write it word for word so that you get the person's words exactly right.

Use a separate note card for each section of your talk. Here is an example of one student's note cards for the body of a talk about Bodie State Historic Park in California.

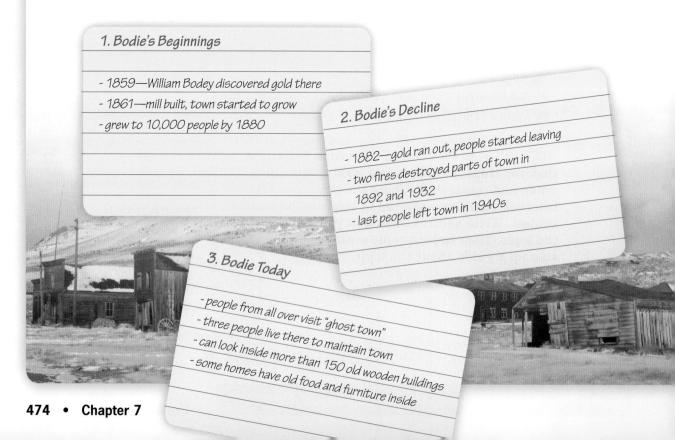

1. Bodie's Beginnings

- 1859—William Bodey discovered gold there
- 1861—mill built, town started to grow
- grew to 10,000 people by 1880

2. Bodie's Decline

- 1882—gold ran out, people started leaving
- two fires destroyed parts of town in 1892 and 1932
- last people left town in 1940s

3. Bodie Today

- people from all over visit "ghost town"
- three people live there to maintain town
- can look inside more than 150 old wooden buildings
- some homes have old food and furniture inside

Presenting and Listening

When you present your destination guide, remember to speak in a clear, engaging voice, making eye contact with your audience as you go. Identify your visual clearly when you display it. Keep handy a list of basic facts you could use to answer any questions at the end of your talk. You might have available a list of resources your audience could consult if they have any further questions.

When you listen to another student's talk, remember to listen actively. Listen for the topic sentence as a clue of what's to come. When the speaker has finished, provide him or her with some feedback. You might offer any interesting personal experiences you have had about the place or ask questions that came to mind during the talk.

ACTIVITY C The notes below are details for a guide to sights in Boston, Massachusetts. Organize the details in a logical order. Then write a topic sentence for this talk. Delete any details that don't fit your topic sentence.

- Children's Museum
- Battle of Bunker Hill site
- Freedom Trail shows historic sites
- can be confusing to drive around
- Museum of Science
- Faneuil Hall has lots of food and shops
- Museum of Fine Arts
- Harvard Square fun to walk around
- *U.S.S. Constitution*—ship used in many battles
- Haymarket—outdoor food market
- famous for its clam chowder

Prewriting and Drafting

Have you ever learned about something so interesting that you wanted to share what you knew with others? Writing an expository article allows you to do just that.

Prewriting

Before beginning to write an expository article, a writer must choose a topic and a main idea to

focus the article. Then the writer researches the topic and plans the article, organizing it in a logical order and selecting the details that fit the plan.

Choosing a Topic

Javier is a seventh grader who likes animals, and he enjoys learning about them. He knew that the expository article he wrote for his class would be about an animal.

He remembered a whale-watching trip he took in Monterey Bay. He thought his class would be interested in hearing how the humpback whale he saw showed off for the people in the boat. He could also tell the class about the whales' habits and appearance. He decided that with a little research, he could write an interesting and informative article on humpback whales.

Your Turn

Choose a topic for an article. Nearly anything that interests you could be a good article topic. Try thinking of topics that you already know a little about. Plan to do some research to learn more about your topic.

Gathering Details

Before he began researching humpback whales, Javier thought about what he might like to learn. First, he wrote what he already knew about humpback whales. Then he wrote what he wanted to know.

What do they eat?
How fast do they swim?
How big are they?
Why do they spout water?
Do they jump up out of the water?
Why are they endangered?

Next, Javier began his research. He searched the Internet, using keywords such as *humpback whales*, *diet*, and *endangered*. Then he searched the library, looking in the catalog for books about humpback whales.

When Javier had found a few interesting books about whales, he browsed that section of the library for more books. He wrote the interesting facts he learned.

Prewriting

Drafting

Content Editing

Revising

Copyediting

Proofreading

Publishing

Subtopic 1: Watching humpbacks

- whale watching at Monterey Bay

- They like to do tricks.

- 50-foot body

- big white flippers and long flukes

Subtopic 2: Humpback habits

- swim in large groups

- go up to 15 miles per hour

- breathe through their blowholes

- 10,000 humpbacks today

Subtopic 3: Endangered species

- Whalers used to kill them.

- nearly extinct in 1960s

- laws passed to protect them

Subtopic 4: Dangers today

- water pollution

- fishing nets

- whaling by some countries

Your Turn

Gather details about the topic you have chosen. Begin by writing what you already know about the subject. Then list any questions you would like to answer. Research your topic, using the Internet, library, and other sources. As you research, write the facts you learn and document the sources.

Organizing Your Details

Once Javier had completed his research, he began to organize his details into subtopics. He Organization decided to keep all his details about his whale-watching trip together. Because he would be explaining what he saw, Javier decided to describe what the humpback whale looks like under that subtopic.

Javier decided to include a second subtopic about the humpback's habits. There he listed facts about its breathing, swimming, and eating. In the third subtopic, he listed details about the dangers to humpback whales. He listed on note cards the details and their subtopics.

After Javier had organized his details into subtopics, he put his subtopics in order. He decided to begin with the whale-watching trip because that seemed the most interesting. He put the whale's habits next, followed by the two subtopics about dangers to humpbacks.

Your Turn

Organize your details into subtopics, listing each subtopic with its details either on note cards or in an outline on a sheet of paper. Arrange your subtopics in a logical order. Save any details that do not fit your subtopics; you might be able to use them in your introduction or conclusion.

Drafting

After he had organized his ideas, Javier was ready to write a first draft. He looked at his subtopics and details and wrote a topic sentence that fit his main idea: "Humpback whales are friendly animals that need our help in order to survive." From there he wrote an introduction that engaged the reader and mentioned each of his subtopics.

Javier found it easy to write the body of his article because it was already organized. He wrote one paragraph for each subtopic. He wrote a concluding paragraph that summed up what he had written. He included a quotation he had found in his research because he felt it would make an impression on the reader.

The Friendly Humpback Whale

If you go whale watching, you'll see humpback whales showing off for the crowd. However, life isn't easy for them. Humpback whales are friendly animals than need our help in order to survive.

The best way to see a humpback whale is on a whale-watching trip. I took a trip to watch the whales, and a whale came right up to our boat. You could clearly see its 50 foot long body, huge white flippers, and fluke. The humpback we saw performed several tricks for us, rubbing up against the boat, rolling onto it's side, and breaching.

Humpback whales like eating and swimming together. They go in large groups. They swim up to 15 miles-per-hour. Once or twice every minute, they go to the surface and breathe. To do this, they spout water and air out of their blowholes and breathe air in. Humpbacks feed on a diet of small fish and tiny creatures called krill and plankton. There are about 10,000 humpbacks alive today.

Unfortunately, people have not always been friendly to humpback whales. At one time there were many whalers who hunted whales for food and oil. By the 1960s the humpback whale was nearly extinct. Then in 1966 many countries adopted laws to protect whales from whalers. However, the humpback is still an endangered species.

The dangers that remain to humpbacks include water pollution, fishing nets catching them, and whaling allowed by a few countries.

Franklin D. Roosevelt once said "Men and nature must work hand in hand. The throwing out of balance of the resources of nature throws out of balance also the lives of men." That statement is just as true today.

Your Turn

Use the subtopics and details you have organized to create a first draft. Focus your article by writing a topic sentence stating the main idea of your article.

- Write an introduction that includes the topic sentence and introduces the subtopics of the article. Be sure to engage the reader with your opening sentence.

- In the body of the article, write a separate paragraph for each subtopic and its details. You might open each paragraph with a sentence that introduces the subtopic.

- In the conclusion sum up the main idea of the article. End with a memorable statement or an insight that leaves the reader thinking about the topic.

- Consider including a quotation that will make an impression on the reader.

Using Quotations

When correctly used, a good quotation can make your article livelier and more interesting. Quotations can make a point in an eloquent, colorful, or concise way.

When choosing a quotation to use, make sure the point the source is making fits the main idea of the article. If the quotation is long, choose the most insightful or memorable portion for your article. Remember to identify the source directly before or after the quotation.

The introduction or conclusion of an article is a good place for a strong quotation. In an introduction a quotation can eloquently introduce an idea that will be explored in the article. As in Javier's article, a quotation can also provide a memorable insight to conclude the article.

Content Editing

Javier had enjoyed writing his article. He had learned more about humpback whales and thought  Voice they were interesting animals. He hoped that his readers would find his article interesting too.

Javier knew that he could make his article more interesting and enjoyable with good editing. The day after writing his draft, he looked at it critically, checking to make sure it was factual, focused, and well organized. He used this Content Editor's Checklist to help him edit.

Javier found a few places where his article could be improved, but he decided to give it to a content editor before making any changes. He gave it to his friend John, who knew little about humpback whales, because Javier wanted to see if he would understand everything in his article.

John read through the article twice. He read it the first time to see what it was about. The second time he studied it more carefully, using the Content Editor's Checklist.

Content Editor's Checklist

- [ ] Is the article clearly focused on a main idea about a topic?

- [ ] Does the introduction engage the reader and include a topic sentence?

- [ ] Do the body paragraphs include subtopics that support the main idea?

- [ ] Is the body organized in a logical order?

- [ ] Do the details of each paragraph support the paragraph's subtopic?

- [ ] Does the conclusion summarize the main idea and leave readers with a thought-provoking insight?

- [ ] Is the article written using formal language and a confident voice?

- [ ] Does the article inform readers, using methods such as explanations, statistics, examples, and quotations?

When he sat down with Javier, John began by noting some of the good things about Javier's article. John thought the information was interesting and the article was well organized overall. He made the following suggestions for improvement:

- I think you should start the introduction with a more general sentence about humpback whales.
- Can you tell us where you went whale watching?
- I don't understand some of the terms you use. What is a fluke? What about breaching?
- Is there a way you could make a better transition from the second paragraph to the third paragraph?
- The last detail in the third paragraph doesn't seem to fit, so you should probably just take it out.
- I like the closing quotation, but I don't think you explain it well enough. How is that statement true today?

Javier asked John to clarify a few of his comments and thanked him for his help. Javier decided to go through his draft again and decide which of John's suggestions to use.

Your Turn

Reread your draft and evaluate it, using the Content Editor's Checklist.

Trade papers with a classmate. Read your partner's article and use the Content Editor's Checklist to check it over. Note some things you like about the draft and make specific suggestions for improvement. Listen carefully to your partner's suggestions for revision. Make any changes that you agree will improve your draft.

Writer's Tip Make sure that the introduction is engaging and includes a topic sentence, that the body includes supporting details, and that the conclusion leaves a lasting impression.

Prewriting

Drafting

Content Editing

Revising

Copyediting

Proofreading

Publishing

Revising

Here are the revisions Javier made after his conference with John.

The Friendly Humpback Whale

Have you ever wondered what life is like for a humpback whale?
If you go whale watching, you'll see humpback whales showing off for the crowd.
as an endangered species,
However, life isn't easy for them. Humpback whales are friendly animals than need

our help in order to survive.

The best way to see a humpback whale is on a whale-watching trip. I took a trip
to Monterey Bay
to watch the whales, and a whale came right up to our boat. You could clearly see its
long tail, or
50 foot long body, huge white flippers, and fluke. The humpback we saw performed
, or coming high out of the water and splashing as it came back
several tricks for us, rubbing up against the boat, rolling onto it's side, and breaching.
down.
Humpback whales like eating and swimming together. They go in large groups.
When they aren't showing off,
They swim up to 15 miles-per-hour. Once or twice every minute, they go to the

surface and breathe. To do this, they spout water and air out of their blowholes and

breathe air in. Humpbacks feed on a diet of small fish and tiny creatures called krill

and plankton. ~~There are about 10,000 humpbacks alive today.~~

Unfortunately, people have not always been friendly to humpback whales. At one

time there were many whalers who hunted whales for food and oil. By the 1960s the

humpback whale was nearly extinct. Then in 1966 many countries adopted laws to

protect whales from whalers. However, the humpback is still an endangered species.

The dangers that remain to humpbacks include water pollution, fishing nets

catching them, and whaling allowed by a few countries.

Franklin D. Roosevelt once said "Men and nature must work hand in hand. The

throwing out of balance of the resources of nature throws out of balance also the
Maybe as more people get to know these friendly creatures, they will be inspired to help
lives of men." ~~That statement is just as true today.~~ *humpback whales instead of hurting them.*

Look at the revisions Javier made to his article. He took several of John's suggestions and made some of his own to improve his article.

- How did Javier change the introduction to engage the reader?
- Where did Javier add the name of the place he went whale watching?
- He looked over his notes and added definitions of what two words?
- He agreed that the second and third paragraphs didn't flow together well. What did he add to the beginning of the third paragraph to create a transition?
- Although he agreed that the information about the number of whales did not seem to fit, he thought the information was too important to leave out. Where did Javier find a logical place to include the information?
- Javier agreed that the quotation in the final paragraph needed more explanation. How did he explain how the quotation related to his article?

Grammar in Action

What punctuation mark is missing from Javier's last paragraph? See Section 10.1.

Javier looked over his draft once more after making his corrections. He thought his fifth paragraph was too short, but he didn't want to expand it. He realized that the information was related to the fourth paragraph, so he moved it to the end of that paragraph.

Your Turn

Revise your draft, using your partner's suggestions and your own ideas. Use the suggestions that you think will improve your article. When you have finished, go over the draft again, using the Content Editor's Checklist. Make sure you can answer yes to each question.

Copyediting and Proofreading

Copyediting

Javier felt that the changes he had made improved his article. The revised draft was more informative, flowed better, and had a better introduction and conclusion.

Javier knew that his draft could still be improved, however. He needed to copyedit his draft, checking for logic, grammar, clarity, and other aspects of the article. He used this Copyeditor's Checklist.

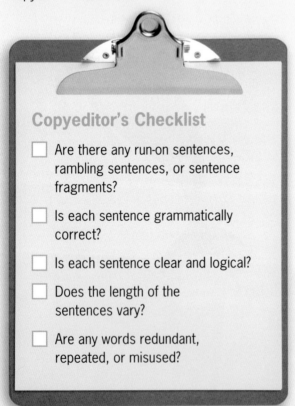

Copyeditor's Checklist

- [ ] Are there any run-on sentences, rambling sentences, or sentence fragments?

- [ ] Is each sentence grammatically correct?

- [ ] Is each sentence clear and logical?

- [ ] Does the length of the sentences vary?

- [ ] Are any words redundant, repeated, or misused?

Javier began copyediting by reading his draft aloud, listening for awkward sentences or repeated words. The first thing he noticed was that, in his new opening, he had used the words *humpback whales* too many times in the first paragraph. He changed the words in one place to *these gentle animals*.

He also realized that the last sentence of his first paragraph didn't make sense, so he changed the word *than* to *that*.

Next, Javier realized that the explanation of breaching he had added in the second paragraph made the final **Sentence Fluency** sentence very long. To make it easier to read, he broke it into two sentences.

Finally, Javier found that his sentence about humpbacks swimming in groups sounded **Word Choice** awkward. He used a thesaurus to help him choose another word for *go*. He replaced it with *travel* to make it more precise.

Your Turn

Reread your revised draft and edit it with the help of the Copyeditor's Checklist. Reading your draft aloud can help you identify changes to make.

Prewriting

Drafting

Content Editing

Revising

Copyediting

Proofreading

Publishing

Proofreading

Javier's draft was nearly complete. He knew, however, that there could be mistakes he had not caught in the previous editing stages. He asked his classmate Claire to proofread his draft. She used this Proofreader's Checklist.

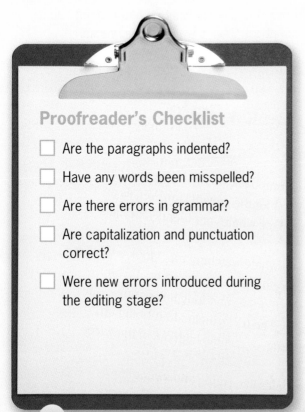

Proofreader's Checklist

☐ Are the paragraphs indented?

☐ Have any words been misspelled?

☐ Are there errors in grammar?

☐ Are capitalization and punctuation correct?

☐ Were new errors introduced during the editing stage?

Claire discovered a few mistakes in Javier's draft. First, she noticed that the word *its* had been misspelled in the second paragraph. She reminded Javier that the contraction *it's* should be used when it could be replaced with the words *it is*. In this

 Conventions

case substituting *it is* did not make sense in the sentence, so she knew the possessive adjective *its* was the correct word to use.

Next, she found two errors Javier made about when to use hyphens. In the second paragraph, she realized that he should have hyphenated the phrase *50-foot-long*, because the phrase was modifying the noun *body*. In the third paragraph, she saw that the phrase *miles per hour* should not have been hyphenated, because it was not modifying anything.

Finally, Claire discovered a mistake in the way Javier had punctuated his quotation. She noted that before the quotation, the word *said* should be followed by a comma.

Your Turn

Review your draft, using the Proofreader's Checklist to help you. Look for any new errors that may have been made along the way.

Exchange your draft with a partner and proofread your partner's article. Be receptive to the corrections your partner suggests and make suggestions on your partner's article. Remember to thank your partner for his or her suggestions.

Publishing

Javier made the corrections Claire had suggested before he printed out his article. He looked forward to sharing what he had learned about humpback whales with his classmates.

The Friendly Humpback Whale

by Javier Ramos

Have you ever wondered what life is like for a humpback whale? If you go whale watching, you'll see these gentle animals showing off for the crowd. However, as an endangered species, life isn't easy for them. Humpback whales are friendly animals that need our help in order to survive.

The best way to see a humpback whale is on a whale-watching trip. I took a trip to Monterey Bay to watch the whales, and a whale came right up to our boat. You could clearly see its 50-foot-long body, huge white flippers, and long tail, or fluke. The humpback we saw performed several tricks for us. The tricks included rubbing up against our boat, rolling onto its side, and breaching, or coming high out of the water and splashing the water as it came back down.

When they aren't showing off, humpback whales like eating and swimming together. They travel in large groups, swimming up to 15 miles per hour. Once or twice every minute, they go to the surface and breathe. To do this, they spout water and air out of their blowholes and breathe air in. Humpbacks feed on a diet of small fish and tiny creatures called krill and plankton.

Unfortunately, people have not always been friendly to humpback whales. At one time there were many whalers who hunted whales for food and oil. By the 1960s the humpback whale was nearly extinct. Then in 1966 many countries adopted laws to protect whales from whalers. Today there are about 10,000 humpbacks. However, the humpback is still an endangered species. The dangers that remain include water pollution, fishing nets catching them, and whaling allowed by a few countries.

Franklin D. Roosevelt once said, "Men and nature must work hand in hand. The throwing out of balance of the resources of nature throws out of balance also the lives of men." Maybe as more people get to know these friendly creatures, they will be inspired to help humpback whales instead of hurting them.

Whenever you publish your work, your goal is to share your thoughts and experiences with other Presentation people. This is your chance to teach others about a topic that interests you. There are many ways you can publish your expository article.

 Create a class book. Your classmates may have photographs, illustrations, or other souvenirs of their experiences. These are interesting items to attach to the articles.

 Have your class book on hand for Parents' Night. You might wish to present it as a PowerPoint presentation or a video.

 Film it. Make your own documentary. Narrate your article with a backdrop of photographs, music, illustrations, or interview someone who can add information to your topic.

 Make a classroom newsletter or magazine. Collect your classmates' articles and add photographs or illustrations to create an eye-catching newsletter or magazine.

Your Turn

Look over your article one more time before you publish it. Check that any mistakes have been corrected and that no new errors were introduced in the final editing stages. Print out or write a final copy. Now you are ready to choose one of the publishing options.

Writer's Tip Think of an intriguing title for your article and put it at the top of the page. Include your name below the title.

Prewriting

Drafting

Content Editing

Revising

Copyediting

Proofreading

Publishing

Research Reports

LiNK

Elements of Successful Educational Television

Deborah K. Wainwright, Children's Media Center

The only way a television program can inform its viewers is by capturing and maintaining their attention throughout the show. Since most educational television has its sights set on teaching the youngest of viewers, considerable research has been aimed at determining the elements of a program's content that not only attracts kids but engages them cognitively as well (Campbell, Wright & Huston, 1987; Crawley et al., 2002; Lorch & Castle, 1997; Rolandelli, Wright, Huston & Eakins, 1991). . . . It seems reasonable to conclude, therefore, that a program can guide the amount of mental effort a viewer invests by increasing the viewer's attention to the television screen. But, to capture children's attention, the program simply must appeal to them. To create programming that educates even while it entertains, both the formal features of the medium and the instructional content must be taken into consideration.

> This excerpt contains important components of a research report: an engaging introduction, a thesis statement, parenthetical information, and a conclusion that summarizes.

CHAPTER 8

Teens and Smoking

by Taylor Gray

Room 202

Teenage cigarette addiction is one of the most serious and pervasive health problems in the United States today and the single most preventable cause of death. Teenagers begin smoking for a variety of reasons, but once they begin, it can be very difficult to stop. As this fact sheet illustrates, smoking is a dangerous habit that teens should avoid in order to live a long and disease-free life.

Why do teens smoke?

Most teenage smokers start smoking to be like their friends or adults who smoke, according to psychiatrist Margaret Bell. However, many teens smoke to rebel against their nonsmoking parents. In fact, Bell said in an interview, "Teens may be smoking both to rebel against their parents and authority and to conform to their peers."

What are the dangers of cigarette smoking?

Rudi Philips's *Fact Book on Nicotine Addiction* cites the dangers of smoking. In 1964 the United States Surgeon General first warned that smoking causes lung cancer. Scientists at the time concluded that smoking causes heart and lung diseases. Smoking causes 87 percent of lung cancer deaths and is responsible for cancers of the larynx, esophagus, and oral cavity (Philips 243). Every year, smoking kills more than 400,000 people (250).

What do cigarettes contain?

Cigarettes contain more than 4,000 chemical agents, including tar and nicotine. Almost 90 percent of these poisons stay in a smoker's lungs after smoking a cigarette. Nicotine is what causes cigarette addiction. The quick addiction to cigarettes at a young age, according to Philips, is what makes it difficult to quit smoking later in life (102).

What Makes a Good Research Report?

A research report explores a specific idea about a topic. Facts are gathered by researching sources such as interviews, books, encyclopedias, almanacs, magazines, newspapers, maps, and documents on the Internet. The information is presented using formal language, avoiding the use of the pronoun *I*.

Introduction

A good research report begins with an introduction that engages the reader in the topic and previews the information to be presented. The most important sentence of the introduction is the thesis statement, which states the thesis, or the main point explored in the report. Examples of strong thesis statements include "Space exploration brings many benefits on Earth" or "The aid of France was crucial to winning the American Revolution." Can you find the thesis statement in the excerpt on page 491?

Body

The body of a research report presents details that support the thesis statement. The details are often grouped into main ideas, which can be further divided into subtopics. Each paragraph in a report often focuses on one subtopic and begins with a sentence introducing the subtopic. If a detail has been drawn from research, the source of the research is cited in the text. The body might also include graphics or other images that illustrate the ideas presented.

Conclusion

The conclusion summarizes the thesis of the report. It might sum up the research. It might also draw conclusions that are supported by the research, as was done in the excerpt on page 488. The conclusion is followed by a Works Cited page that lists the sources used in the report.

ACTIVITY A Look back at the excerpt from "Teens and Smoking" on page 489. Find the answers to these questions.

1. What is the thesis statement of this research report?
2. What main ideas does the report discuss?
3. What are three facts that the author presents?
4. What conclusion does the author want readers to draw?
5. What types of sources did the author use?

ACTIVITY B Read the following sets of main ideas to be explored in a research report. For each set write a thesis statement that is supported by the three main ideas. Then think of two kinds of sources to which you could refer in researching the report.

1. a. College graduates have more satisfying careers than people who do not attend college.
   b. College graduates earn more money than high school graduates.
   c. High school graduates are more likely to be laid off from their jobs than college graduates.

2. a. The average global temperature is increasing.
   b. Global warming threatens marine and other animal life.
   c. Lowering emissions of greenhouse gases can reduce the effects of global warming.

3. a. The Maya civilization had an elaborate system of writing.
   b. Maya art reflected their lifestyle and culture.
   c. Maya society was a complex system based on class.

LiNK

Pediatric Private Practice After Hurricane Katrina

Hurricane Katrina brought unprecedented devastation to the U.S. Gulf Coast. Since August 29, 2005, there has been slow progress toward recovery. This recovery has involved an uneven, and often bumpy, collaboration between individuals, businesses, state governments, federal agencies, and private organizations.

Scott Needle
American Academy
of Pediatrics

WRITER'S CORNER

Choose a familiar topic, such as a favorite sport, hobby, or style of music, and write three or four facts you know about that topic. Then write a thesis statement that might be supported by the facts you have written.

Creating Resilient Habitats: Native Fish Recover in a Time of Climate Change

A warming climate is predicted to change freshwater flows, particularly in snow-dominated regions such as the northern Rockies, where up to 80% of annual precipitation has traditionally fallen as snow. Spring runoff is predicted to begin a month earlier resulting in low water flows during the summer and fall months (Brick, et al. 2008). This could have severe effects on bull trout...

Sierra Club

Choosing a Topic

The topic you choose to research should interest you so that you will want to learn more about it. A good topic will have several sources to use for research.

Keep in mind that a topic that is too broad will be difficult to research in depth. However, you might choose a broad topic and narrow it as you research. Examples of good research topics include child labor in the 1800s or how climate change affects fish, as shown in the excerpt here.

When you have selected a topic, it may be helpful to write several questions that you would like to answer. Having these questions in mind will help you guide your research.

Conducting Research

Good research reports use information from several sources. For a report on solar power, a writer might read through a book about solar power, type "solar power" into a Web search engine, and interview someone whose home uses solar panels.

When researching, you don't have to read entire books on your subject. Instead, browse through the book and look for sections that most closely relate to your topic. The table of contents at the beginning of the book and the index at the end can help you find the parts of a book to read for your paper.

The sources you choose should always be reliable. If you interview someone, make sure the person is knowledgeable about the topic you're researching. If you search the Internet, make sure the Web site sites you access are accurate and reliable.

Writing a Thesis Statement

After you complete your research, think of a main point that is supported by the research you conducted. It could be a summary of the information you have gathered, or it could make an argument that is supported by the research. Develop this main point into a thesis statement. Once you have written your final thesis statement, you can begin organizing your facts in a way that supports your thesis.

ACTIVITY C **Consider each topic as if you were preparing to write a research report. Would the topic be appropriate for a five-page research report? If the topic is too broad, think of a way to narrow it.**

1. the civil rights movement in the United States
2. the effects of westward expansion on a community of Native American families
3. how immigration has influenced one state
4. how all jobs have changed over the years
5. changes to the environment over the last three centuries

ACTIVITY D **Read the following list of chapters from a book about the Pilgrims. Answer the questions.**

Contents

1. Which chapters would you read while researching a report about the Pilgrims' arrival in their new land?
2. Which chapter might tell about the political structure of the Pilgrim community?
3. Which chapter might you read for a report about the diet of the Pilgrims?
4. At which chapter would you begin when researching why the Pilgrims left their homes in England?
5. Which chapter might you read for a report about the marriage customs of early settlers in the New World?

WRITER'S CORNER

Choose a topic that would be appropriate for a research report and find information about it. Write three details and a possible thesis statement.

Grammar in Action. Use an adjective clause or an adverb clause in your thesis statement and identify it.

Gathering and Organizing Information

Researching a topic can seem overwhelming. Sources are so full of information that it is sometimes hard to know what information to include in a paper and what to leave out. By taking careful notes and organizing them logically, you can make the writing process easier.

Taking Notes

Once you have located several sources for your research report, you can begin taking notes. If you have narrowed your topic, you won't find it necessary to read entire books on your subject. Remember to use the index or table of contents to find the location of specific chapters or sections of the book.

One of the most effective ways of taking notes is to use note cards. When you find an important detail about your topic, write it on a note card. The detail can restate a fact or an idea in your own words, or it can be a direct quotation. If you quote a source, include quotation marks to remind you that you are using the source's words, not your own.

At the bottom of the note card, identify the source and the page number on which the information was found. Be sure to write just one fact on each note card. This will make it easier to rearrange your facts when you organize your report. Here are two note cards the author of the report on page 489 created.

kills more than 400,000 people each year

Philips p. 250

"Teens may be smoking both to rebel against their parents and authority and to conform to their peers."

Margaret Bell, interview

Brain coral

ACTIVITY A **Read these sources about coral reefs. Follow the instructions at the end.**

A. Page 199 of the book *Coral Extinction* by Walter Krane

Human development represents the greatest threats to reefs. The encroachment of human populations can introduce pollutants and outside sediments that disrupt the ecosystem of the reefs. In addition, rising populations lead to more fishing, which depletes the number of reef fish. This further upsets the balance of coral ecosystems. Most of the coral from the Great Barrier Reef, to name the most dramatic example, could be destroyed by 2050.

B. An article from the magazine *Nature Today*, issue 7, page 12

We headed out to the Great Barrier Reef, a 1,000-mile series of reefs along Australia's northeast coast that's as beautiful as any work of art. To newcomers like us, the dazzling array of colors and shapes can take one's breath away.

"You can't understand how beautiful it is until you actually see it," said Margaret Weir, our guide.

C. The Web site www.coralreef.net.

Coral reefs are integrated organic communities that form when the skeletons of marine organisms accumulate underwater, leaving buildups of calcium carbonate, or limestone.

There are three types of coral reefs: fringing reefs, barrier reefs, and atolls. A fringing reef is found close to sea level near a newly exposed shoreline. Barrier reefs, such as the Great Barrier Reef, are formed farther from the shore along a receding shoreline. Atolls are ring-shaped reefs that surround lagoons whose land has sunk beneath the water.

1. Create two note cards with information for a report about types of coral reefs.

2. Create three note cards, including at least one from each source, with information for a report on the Great Barrier Reef.

3. Create three note cards for a report with this thesis statement: "Coral reefs are a beautiful treasure whose existence is in danger."

4. Create one note card with information for a report about the dangers of too much fishing.

WRITER'S CORNER

Using the topic you chose for the previous Writer's Corner, find two new sources about the topic. Write two note cards from each source.

Tech Tip With an adult, find one source online.

Organizing Your Notes

When you have finished taking your notes, you can begin shaping them into an organized structure. Follow these steps as you organize your report:

- Use your thesis statement to arrange and revise your notes. Begin by removing any note cards that do not fit your thesis. Even if the detail is fascinating or the quotation is eloquent, eliminate it if it will steer your paper away from your thesis.
- Arrange your notes into main ideas, creating one stack of note cards for each main idea. You might further divide your main idea into subtopics. If a note card does not fit into any main idea, consider whether it will fit in your introduction or conclusion as part of an overall summary. If not, leave the note card out.
- Finally, arrange your main ideas in a logical order. You might organize them in order of importance, moving from the least important to the most important. You might place related main ideas near each other.
- To help visualize your report, create an outline from your note cards. Give a heading to each main idea and list the related details under each main idea. Use what you learned in Chapter 5 to help you create your outline.

ACTIVITY B The following notes were written on note cards for a report with the following thesis statement: "Nelson Mandela was an instrumental figure in ending apartheid in South Africa." Decide which notes are related to the thesis statement. Explain your reasoning.

- Apartheid: legalized segregation of different races
- Mandela began fighting apartheid policies as a member of the African National Congress in 1948.
- Mandela was arrested in 1962 for work with ANC.
- Mandela was married three times.
  - While in prison, Mandela's reputation as a South African leader grew.
  - "I dream of an Africa which is in peace with itself." —*Mandela*
  - Population of South Africa is about 43 million.
  - Mandela became 1st black president of S. Africa in 1994, presided over end of apartheid.
  - Some say apartheid created to give ruling party control over social and economic institutions.
  - S. Africa climate mild, similar to San Francisco Bay area.

Nelson Mandela

ACTIVITY C The following notes were written on note cards for a research report about the Indus Valley civilization. Organize the notes into three main ideas. Eliminate any notes that do not fit your main ideas. Then think of a thesis statement that fits the main ideas.

- built planned cities with straight streets
- houses built around courtyards
- civilization discovered in 1920s
- also traded with distant civilizations such as Mesopotamia
- religious objects such as charms used to ward off evil spirits
- made statues of the gods
- nearby mountains among world's tallest
- worshiped natural things such as sun or trees
- traded by ship with at least nearby civilizations of Makkan and Meluha
- sewer system built that drained into river
- trade often involved copper or grains

ACTIVITY D Create an outline from the main ideas and details in Activity C. The introduction should identify the main ideas, and the details should be listed under each main idea.

Excavated Indus Valley homes and streets

WRITER'S CORNER

Select one set of notes you organized for Activity B or Activity C. Use them to write in paragraph form part of a research report about the subject.

Citing Sources

When researching a subject, it is important to keep track of the sources of your information. The reason to do this is to give credit to the source of each fact, idea, or quotation that you collect. By citing your sources, you show your readers that your information is well researched and credible. You also give your readers places to look for more information about your topic.

Works Cited

The complete list of your sources appears at the end of your research report in the Works Cited page. The Works Cited page includes entries for each source. Each entry includes all the key information from the source, such as the publisher of a book or the magazine the article appeared in. The information always follows a specified format. Here are some examples of common Works Cited entries. For each entry follow the order, punctuation, and indentation shown below.

Books

An entry for a book includes the author, title, location of the publisher, publisher, and the year the book was published. This information can be found on the title page and the copyright page at the beginning of the book. Here is an example of how the entry is written and formatted.

> O'Shea, Gloria. <u>Here Come the Pheasants.</u> Cambridge, MA:
> Northeast Books, 2010.

Periodicals

An entry for a periodical, such as a newspaper or a magazine, should include the author's name, the title of the article and periodical, the date of the periodical, and the pages on which the article appears.

> Jackson, Monty. "Carefree Vacations." <u>Travel Times</u>
> 10 July 2005: 35–39.

For an article in a scholarly journal that does not give an exact date, include the volume number and the publication year instead of the date of the publication.

> **Mostel, Harmon. "Socializing Gibbons." Primate Journal 13 (2009): 201–211.**

Encyclopedias

An entry for an encyclopedia article includes the title of the article, the title of the encyclopedia, and the edition of the encyclopedia.

> **"Burma." World Book. 2007 ed.**

Web Sites

A Web site entry should include the author (if available), the title of the article, the date you looked at the site, and the Web address.

> **Desai, Vinod. "Arms and Armor in the Middle Ages." 17 Nov. 2004 <www.virtualbb.net/middleage/armor23>.**

ACTIVITY A Use the information in each item to write a Works Cited page entry for the source. Use the format and punctuation from this lesson.

1. Michael Johnson's book *Into the Day*, which was published in 2009 by Mainline Books, located in San Francisco, California.

2. Sandra Cleary's article "In Stars, Scientists See Echoes of the Past," which appeared on page A12 of *The Ottawa Star* on April 18, 2008.

3. The Web page at www.streetcopy.net/barnaby, where the article "A Man Named Barnaby" is located. You read the article by Anthony Perez on October 13, 2006.

4. The article "Improved Energy Policy" by Peter Zinger. The article was published on pages 78–80 of volume 13 of the periodical *National Affairs* in 2010.

5. The encyclopedia entry "Whippoorwill," which appears in the 2007 edition of the *Encyclopedia of Nocturnal Birds*.

WRITER'S CORNER

Pick a topic and collect three sources in the classroom or library, including at least one Web site, related to that topic. Write a Works Cited entry for each source.

Parenthetical Notations

The Works Cited page tells your readers what sources you used in your research report. It is also important, however, to tell readers what information came from which source. By using parenthetical notations, you can cite the source of each piece of information.

In parenthetical notations, the source of the information in a sentence is identified in parentheses at the end of the sentence. This should be done each time you use a note card to write a sentence.

When possible, include the author's last name and the page number in the parentheses. If the author is not available, as often occurs in an encyclopedia entry or on a Web page, list the title of the article or Web page and, if possible, the page number.

In the examples below, the first sentence includes information from an anonymous Web site, while the second cites a page from a book by Stephen Edwards. Notice how the parenthetical notations are followed by a period.

> **A meteor becomes visible when it enters Earth's atmosphere and burns up ("Meteor Facts").**
>
> **The best place to view a meteor shower is under a dark sky, far from city or suburban lights (Edwards 101).**

Leonid meteor shower, 1870

If a source is cited more than once in a paragraph, list only the page number after the first notation. If you list the author's name within the text of a sentence, you may also cite only the page number. For example:

> **The Leonid, one of the most spectacular meteor showers, appears in the night sky once every 33 years (Edwards 14). The meteors from this shower are produced by the comet Tempel-Tuttle (17). Amy Alderson notes that the Leonid meteor shower's path comes as close as 33,000 miles to Earth (25).**

If you use information from more than one source in a sentence, cite each source directly after the fact, not at the end of the sentence. For example:

> **Astronomer Mario Villa has called the Leonid "a dazzling display of beauty" (27), while others have called it "breathtaking" and "stunning" (Atwood 101).**

Plagiarism

Failure to cite the source of information or ideas gathered through research is called plagiarism. Plagiarism is stealing another person's ideas or information and pretending that it is your own. Refer to page 281 for more about plagiarism.

ACTIVITY B Write an entry for the Works Cited page for each of the following sources. Then write the parenthetical notation that would go at the end of a sentence citing that source.

1. A quote from page 13 of Henry Stoltz's article "Uncovering the Mammoths," which appeared on pages 11 through 15 of the June 14, 2009, issue of *Modern Science*.

2. A fact from page 23 of the anonymous entry titled "Woolly Mammoth" in the 2007 *Scholar's Encyclopedia*.

3. An idea taken from pages 129–130 of Enrique Cabrera's book *Ancient Beasts*, which was published in 2008 by Topeka Press in Topeka, Kansas.

4. A fact from the Web page titled "Mammoth Facts" at www.sidewinder.net/mammoth, written by Peter Cruz, which was visited on March 3, 2010.

5. An idea taken from page 99 of the article "Thawed Beast" by Louise Cox, which appeared on pages 95–101 of the *Archaeology Journal*, volume 3, issue number 5, published in 2009.

ACTIVITY C Correct each of the following parenthetical notations.

1. As Nathan Sellers noted, the earliest recorded woolly mammoths walked Earth about 150,000 years ago (Sellers 28).

2. Mammoths sported thick coats of fur to protect them from the cold ("About Mammoths," www.mammoths.net).

3. The woolly mammoth has been described as a "fearsome beast" (Wilcox 49) that must have "earned the grudging respect of early man" (Wilcox 101).

WRITER'S CORNER

Take the sources you collected in the previous Writer's Corner or collect at least three sources about a new topic. Write in paragraph form four or five sentences about the topic, using information from each source. Cite the source of each fact, quotation, or idea, using parenthetical notations.

Varied Sentences

As you have learned in previous lessons, variety is one key to crafting engaging writing with an original voice. You can create variety by changing the length of your sentences. You can also create variety by changing the type and structure of your sentences.

Natural and Inverted Order

The most common sentence type is where the sentence's subject is followed by its predicate. The sentences in the paragraph below use this structure, which is called natural order.

> **Dozens of excited guests sat in a darkened room, listening for the sound of the car pulling in. Nobody said a word. Finally, Jared walked in, flicking on the lights. We all jumped out of our seats with a shout of "Surprise!" The confetti came down, and the party began.**

This sentence type is often the best one to use, particularly in formal writing such as research reports. When writing creatively, however, you might sometimes use a different structure. Inverted order, or reversing the order of the subject and predicate, can add interest and drama to your writing. The first, third, and fifth sentences below use inverted order.

> **In a darkened room sat dozens of excited guests, listening for the sound of the car pulling in. Nobody said a word. Finally, in walked Jared, flicking on the lights. We all jumped out of our seats with a shout of "Surprise!" Down came the confetti, and the party began.**

Varying Sentence Types

Another way to vary sentences is to use different types of sentences. Most of the sentences in a research report will be declarative, stating a fact and ending with a period. However, an occasional interrogative sentence or exclamatory sentence will get the reader's attention.

Declarative: **Dolphins communicate with one another.**
Interrogative: **Did you know that dolphins communicate with one another?**
Exclamatory: **How smart dolphins must be to communicate with one another!**

Opening with Modifiers

Many sentences often begin with the subject. To add variety, the sentence can be revised by beginning with a single-word modifier, a phrase, or a clause.

Single-word modifier: Recently, I had a surprising experience.
Phrase: To get my present, I was ordered to sing a song.
Clause: After I sang a silly song, I could open my gift.

ACTIVITY A Tell whether each sentence is in natural order or inverted order. Think of another way to write each sentence.

1. Along the streets of New York City are many skyscrapers.
2. The city's streets stretch out like stone-and-glass canyons.
3. The sight amazes many visitors to the city.
4. Towering over the nearby buildings stands the Empire State Building.
5. On the streets during rush hour are hordes of people.

ACTIVITY B Each sentence begins with a noun as the subject. Revise each sentence so that it begins with the opening suggested in parentheses.

1. Jennifer was lucky to know the way home. (Begin with an adverb.)
2. The runners crossed the finish line, hungry and tired. (Begin with two adjectives connected by *and*.)
3. Ben's favorite trucks are in the toy box. (Begin with a phrase.)
4. Some athletes listen to their favorite music to relax before the game. (Begin with a phrase starting with *to*.)
5. The band marched down Main Street, playing "The Stars and Stripes Forever." (Begin with a phrase starting with an *ing* word.)

WRITER'S CORNER

Write three sentences about one thing you did this week. Use simple sentences that begin with the word *I*. Then rewrite the sentences, adding variety by inverting the order, beginning sentences with modifiers, or using exclamatory or interrogative sentences.

Grammar in Action To add variety to your paragraph, refer to Section 8, Sentences.

Rhythm and Voice

Have you ever examined a favorite piece of writing to figure out what you like about the writing? It can be hard to tell what makes good writing. One thing is certain, however—most good writers use a variety of sentence types, shifting between long and short sentences, simple and compound sentences.

You have learned many ways of varying your sentences. You can expand them by adding words, phrases, or clauses; by changing the sentence structure; or by combining sentences with conjunctions or punctuation.

As you vary your sentence lengths, you may develop a rhythm. A good rhythm avoids placing too many long or short sentences together, which can be dull. It also avoids always switching between long and short sentences, which can be predictable.

Try to create a rhythm that fits the content of the writing. For example, you might build up suspense in a paragraph with several short sentences, then make the most important sentence a longer one. For example:

The quarterback stepped back to pass, and time stood still. He looked from one receiver to the next. Nobody was open. He edged to the right. The opposing team was closing in. Then he raised his arm and let the ball fly, up, up over the gasping players, floating in a perfect spiral, until it came plunking right into the hands of Number 22, who stood all alone in the end zone.

There are no set rules for interesting writing. Just keep experimenting. As you experiment with different ways of writing sentences, you will begin to develop a unique voice, or style of writing.

ACTIVITY C Imagine that each declarative sentence is in a research report. To make the sentence stand out more, change it to either an interrogative sentence or an exclamatory sentence.

1. There may have been life on Mars.
2. The first birds appeared during the Jurassic Period.
3. The hottest city in the United States is Key West, Florida.
4. The French high-speed train known as TGV can travel at a speed of 186 miles per hour.
5. The biggest thrill for a mountain climber is to climb Mount Everest.

ACTIVITY D Rewrite each paragraph, using strategies you have learned. You might expand sentences by adding words, phrases, or clauses, or combine them, using conjunctions or punctuation. Share your new paragraphs with the class.

1. It was raining heavily. We came out of the subway. Deep puddles were forming everywhere. We decided to run home. We went leaping over puddles. We went racing across the streets. We made it home. We were soaked but happy.

2. The world seems to be getting smaller. Information travels across continents in seconds. People fly from one country to another. They don't even think about it. We know much more about our world than we ever did before.

3. The astronauts strapped themselves into their seats. They checked the controls. "We're all clear," said the captain. He punched a code into the computer panel. The rockets ignited. They made a deafening rumbling sound. Then the ship began to take off into the air.

4. Your heart is like a big pump. It sends blood to every part of your body. The blood travels through blood vessels. Blood brings oxygen and nutrients to your body. The oxygen and nutrients are used up. The lungs return oxygen to the blood. Then the heart sends the blood out again.

5. We gazed up at the mountain. It seemed to be daring us to climb it. The peak was hidden behind a cloud. The upper half was covered in snow. I looked at my fellow climbers. I adjusted my pack. I took a deep breath. I knew it was time to start climbing.

ACTIVITY E Exchange the paragraphs you wrote in Activity D with a partner. Study the different choices you made for each paragraph. Then revise your own paragraphs again, incorporating revisions that were inspired by your partner's paragraphs.

WRITER'S CORNER

Read a paragraph from a book you enjoyed. Study the sentence lengths and structures. Does the writer use variety? Is there a rhythm to the writing? Rewrite the paragraph, using different sentence structures. Did the rhythm change?

Tech Tip Record your reading. Do you hear variety and rhythm?

Denotation and Connotation

All words have denotations, and many have connotations. A denotation is the core, or primary, meaning of a word found in a dictionary. A connotation is an implied meaning of a word.

A connotation might stretch a word's meaning. Often it suggests a positive or negative value to a word. It is important to know a word's connotation to understand when it is appropriate to use the word. Here are a few words with the same denotations but different connotations.

WORD	DENOTATION	CONNOTATION
famous notorious	well-known	positive negative
thrifty stingy	inclined not to spend	positive negative
slender skinny	thin	positive negative
adventure ordeal	experience	positive negative

Not all words have a positive or negative connotation. Instead of *famous* or *notorious*, a writer could simply use *well-known*, which has a neutral connotation.

Words with positive or negative connotations often reveal the writer's opinion about a subject. In a research report, the writer's opinion should be supported by facts drawn from research. Therefore, it is generally best to use words that have a neutral connotation.

Al Capone was a *notorious* gangster.

Eliot Ness was a *famous* law enforcement agent who captured Capone.

ACTIVITY A **Read each sentence. Decide if the underlined word has a positive connotation or a negative connotation. Consult a dictionary if you are unsure of a word's exact meaning.**

1. I can be <u>stubborn</u> sometimes.
2. Henry takes <u>pride</u> in making the honor roll.
3. My little brother was <u>whining</u> about his injury.
4. Rita is <u>dedicated</u> to her work.
5. My dad is <u>confident</u> in his abilities.
6. Mr. Hall is a <u>workaholic</u>.
7. Carrie is <u>generous</u> to all her friends.
8. The story he wrote was sometimes <u>repetitious</u>.
9. That man was <u>arrogant</u> when he talked down to us.
10. Oscar is a <u>careful</u> worker.

ACTIVITY B **Find the word in each sentence that has a connotation that is not appropriate for a research report. Rewrite the sentence, using words that avoid a positive or negative connotation.**

1. The orangutan is generally dumber than its cousin, the chimpanzee.
2. Many people enjoy spending their vacations loafing at the beach.
3. One economist proclaimed that the nation's unemployment rate will decline over the next decade.
4. Studies show that excessive racket can damage a person's ears.
5. Dolphins are among the most brilliant of sea animals.
6. For years the mayor has been grappling with the problem of too many vagrants on the street.
7. "The rain forests have been disappearing at an accelerated pace in the last several years," complained naturalist Myra Hansen.

WRITER'S CORNER

Think of three words that have negative connotations and write sentences using those words. Exchange your paper with a partner. Rewrite your partner's sentences, replacing each negative word with a word with a neutral connotation.

Choosing Proper Connotations

The connotation of some words is not always positive or negative. It can also give a more exact definition for a word. Connotations might tell a specific situation for an action or a specific type of an object. Here are some words whose connotations define the word more specifically.

WORD	DENOTATION	CONNOTATION
diagnosis	identification	especially of a disease
elude	avoid or escape from	by daring or skill
smirk	smile	in a self-satisfied way

Connotations are important to know when you choose synonyms from a thesaurus. Though two words may have the same denotation according to the thesaurus, it is always useful to check the word in a dictionary if you are unsure of the specific connotation.

For example, in an article on the virtues of smiling, a writer might want to vary the word *smile*. She might find that the word *smirk* is a synonym for smile and write the following sentence: "A pleasant smirk will liven up any room." If the writer knew the connotation of the word *smirk*, she would know that the word was not appropriate for the sentence.

ACTIVITY C For each sentence choose the word in parentheses whose connotation best fits the context of the sentence. Consult a dictionary if you need help.

1. The detectives were called in to (investigate   explore   study) the crime.

2. On a summer evening, sitting alone by the lake gives me a wonderful feeling of (loneliness   solitude   isolation).

3. Cameron's mother (promised   threatened   pledged) to ground him if he came home late again.

4. Mara decided to (summon   invite   request) everyone in her class to her birthday party.

5. The teacher asked the students to take out two (empty   bare   blank) sheets of paper for the test.

ACTIVITY D Each sentence contains a word with the correct denotation, but the wrong connotation. Find the inappropriate word and replace it with a word with the correct connotation.

1. Moles squat almost completely underground.
2. They have a freakish appearance, with no ears and tiny eyes.
3. Though they are blind, moles are able to wander underground with ease because of their sensitive noses.
4. For food, moles mainly devour earthworms and grubs.
5. They burrow through the ground in tunnels in random quests for food.
6. As they search for food, moles sometimes injure garden plants that come into their path.
7. The tunnels they dig can also assist the soil by aerating it, which means bringing air into it.

ACTIVITY E The passage contains several words with connotations that do not fit the context or are not appropriate for a formal research report. Identify the words with the wrong connotations and replace them with more appropriate words.

In the past 50 years, the growth of the suburbs has ruined the nation's landscape. Many families who once lived in cities have fled to the suburbs, where they built gaudy homes with wide lawns and gardens. As a result, land that was once graced by forests and farmland is now littered with highways, houses, and businesses geared to the new residents.

Many of those who escape to the suburbs still wander back to the cities for work. As the suburbs expand, commuters have begun journeying greater distances, in some cases driving two hours in each direction. Many have begun rummaging for job opportunities closer to home.

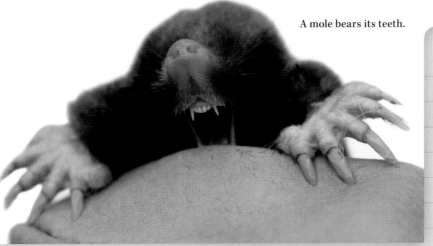
A mole bears its teeth.

WRITER'S CORNER

Choose five words that you did not use to complete the sentences in Activity C. Write new sentences using the words you chose.

Oral Science Reports

Have you ever wondered how some part of nature works? Have you wondered what an atom looks like, or how many stars are in the sky, or how fish get oxygen? Each of these topics can be a good starting point for an oral science report. In an oral science report, you choose one interesting aspect of the natural world, however big or small, and bring it to life with your presentation and visuals.

Choosing a Topic

A good topic for an oral science report is a narrow topic that you find interesting but don't know much about. You might choose some aspect of life science, such as the life cycle of a frog; earth science, such as why volcanoes erupt; or physical science, such as the phase changes of gases, liquids, and solids. Choose a topic that will also interest your audience. A strong topic might be one that you can demonstrate or illustrate in some way.

Make certain that your topic is narrow enough to cover in a brief speech. If you begin with a broader topic, narrow it as you conduct your research. Choose one aspect of the topic that you find particularly interesting.

Conducting Research

When you have chosen a narrow science topic for your report, begin researching using library and Internet sources. Write each piece of information on a separate note card and cite the source on the card. Be sure to note whether you are quoting a source or using your own words.

Create a separate note card for each source, using what you learned in Lesson 3. Though you will not be creating a Works Cited page, you should have your sources available to support your research and to provide to members of your audience who want to learn more.

As you research, keep in mind possibilities for visuals. Note which pages have diagrams or pictures that you might want to use in your oral report.

Organizing Your Report

Begin organizing your report once you are satisfied you have enough information. First, think of subtopics that fit your notes. Next, organize your note cards, creating a separate pile for each subtopic. Discard any note cards that don't fit any subtopic.

When you have organized your notes, think of a thesis statement. For a brief oral report, your thesis statement could be a general statement that summarizes your research, such as "Birds sing for many reasons, from showing they're hungry to attracting a mate."

To prepare your report, rewrite your notes on new cards. Write a card for the introduction, for each subtopic, and for the conclusion. Include an engaging opening and your thesis statement in your introduction. On each subtopic card, write words and phrases for each idea related to that subtopic. On the conclusion card, summarize the report. Think of an intriguing concluding statement.

ACTIVITY A **Read the following notes for a science report. Write each note on a note card and organize the notes into subtopics. Arrange the subtopics in a logical order and eliminate notes that do not fit your subtopics. Write a thesis statement that fits the notes.**

- under earth's surface are about 20 plates
- sudden vibration of earth is an earthquake
- seismographs measure strength of earthquakes
- melted rock moves in circular pattern, moving plates
- plates fit together like a puzzle
- plates move 2–15 centimeters per year
- plates usually slide smoothly past each other
- when plates snag, they sometimes jolt forward
- jolting causes earth to vibrate
- plates float on melted rock
- melted rock rises to surface in volcanoes

SPEAKER'S CORNER

Research a type of natural disaster, such as a wildfire, a tsunami, or an ice storm, for an oral science report. Find at least five facts, using two sources. Follow the steps in the Organizing Your Report section to prepare your presentation.

Tech Tip With an adult, explore a weather Web site.

Diatryma,
a prehistoric
flightless
bird

Engaging with Visuals

For any oral presentation, and particularly for presentations about complicated ideas, visuals can be the key to engaging and educating the audience. In an oral science report, a visual can illustrate a concept or show a process, often more effectively than words alone.

After you have researched your report, look through it for ideas that could be illustrated through visuals. Use the suggestions below to help you.

Demonstrations

A demonstration is an excellent way to show how something happens. For a report about the properties of acids, you could demonstrate how an acid such as vinegar can make a dull penny shiny. For a report on the properties of heat, you might demonstrate how running hot water over a lid can make it expand and thus open more easily. After your demonstration, be sure to explain what happened and the principles involved.

Diagrams

A diagram is particularly useful in illustrating complex ideas and processes. Diagrams can be drawn on large poster boards, using one picture or several to show steps in the process. In a report showing how dinosaurs might have evolved into birds, you might show different possible steps in the evolution. A report on black holes might illustrate the different steps in the formation of a black hole.

When you use a diagram, point to each section as you refer to it. Be sure that the diagram is visible to everyone in your audience.

Samples

A sample can vividly illustrate aspects of the natural world. You might pass out colorful autumn leaves to your audience while you discuss how leaves change colors. A report on minerals might be more engaging if you pass around samples of the rocks you are discussing.

Other Visuals

Photographs, drawings, maps, videos, and other visuals can make any oral report more interesting. The key is to find the visual that best illustrates the ideas in your report. Try to be creative, but be sure that the visual you choose educates your audience and sticks to the topic of your report.

Practicing and Presenting

After you have prepared your report and decided on a visual, practice your report with a classmate or family member. Speak confidently and slowly. Make eye contact with your audience to be sure that they are absorbing all the information.

Canada goose

Focus particularly on your visuals as you practice. If you have a demonstration, try it at least once to make certain that it works. Remember to point to each portion of your diagram during your report. If you pass around samples, keep a sample for yourself so you can refer to it during the report. Be sure that any visual you create is clearly visible to your audience.

When you present your report to the class, be prepared to answer questions at the end. Have a list of your sources available if anyone in your audience would like to learn more.

ACTIVITY B Think of a visual you could use for each topic. Decide whether a demonstration, a diagram, or another visual would be the most appropriate. Describe the visual you would use.

1. the flight path of a comet
2. how a car engine works
3. why we have reflexes
4. single-celled organisms
5. why metals rust
6. the migration of Canada geese
7. how mirrors work

ACTIVITY C Review the notes you took and organized in the previous Speaker's Corner. Think of a visual that would make your report more engaging. Prepare your visual and decide when to present it.

SPEAKER'S CORNER

Practice and present your oral science report. At the end of your report, invite your audience to ask questions. Answer the questions if you can. If you cannot, refer your audience to the sources you found.

Prewriting and Drafting

What ideas interest you? Are you intrigued by accounts of distant battles and strange cultures? Or are you fascinated by various theories of nature and the universe? In a research report, you can learn all about whatever topic interests you and share it with your audience.

Prewriting

The first steps in writing a research report are to choose a narrow topic and to research it, taking notes on note cards. A writer then organizes the notes and creates an outline from them.

Choosing a Topic

For his seventh-grade social studies report, Bayani wasn't sure what to write. He was interested in  stories about early settlers to the New World and the difficulties they faced. Covering all the early settlers, however, would have been too much for a four-page report.

    After a brief library search, he began browsing a book on early settlements. He came across a chapter about the lost colony of Roanoke, an early British colony that mysteriously disappeared. Because he enjoyed a good mystery, he thought it might be an interesting topic to learn and write about.

Your Turn

Think of a topic that interests you. You might decide on a general field, such as physical sciences or world cultures. Then narrow your topic, either by brainstorming what you know or by using library or Internet research to help you.

Researching

Before he began researching, Bayani wrote what he had already learned. Next, he focused his research by writing the following list of questions:

> How many people were part of the colony?
>
> What Native Americans lived nearby?
>
> What was life like for the colonists?
>
> What theories have been suggested to explain their disappearance?
>
> Which is the most likely theory?

    Bayani circled the final question because he thought the answer to that question might become his thesis statement.

    Next, Bayani began his research. He looked up a few books about early settlements, using their indexes to find references about Roanoke. He thought that he should know about the most recent theories on the colony, so he searched the Internet and the periodical index.

He typed "lost colony Roanoke" into a search engine and browsed a few of the Web sites that he found. He also found two articles on the topic by searching the *Reader's Guide to Periodical Literature*, which lists published articles by subject.

As he researched, Bayani made a note card for each fact or idea and listed the source. He made a separate note card for each source's entry on his Works Cited page.

Your Turn

1. Before you begin your research, stop to consider what you already know about the topic and write it on a sheet of paper.
2. Make a list of questions that you would like to answer. Think of which question might lead to a thesis statement and circle it.
3. Find several sources and research your topic, taking notes on note cards and citing your sources. Make separate cards for each source's Works Cited page entry.

Organizing Your Information

After researching his topic, Bayani began organizing his stack of cards. He made one pile with basic information about the colony, such  as who was in the colony and for how long. He made another pile about the colony's disappearance. Then he made separate piles for each theory about what could have happened to the colonists.

Bayani looked back at his list of questions. He found that all of them had been answered except for the last one. He evaluated his research and found that experts could not agree on which theory was the most likely. As a result, he wrote this thesis statement: "Though some theories are more likely than others, we may never know what happened to the lost colony of Roanoke."

Finally, Bayani wrote an outline. He divided his report into several main ideas, including the introduction, a description of the settlers' arrival, the problems the settlers encountered, their disappearance, and each theory of what might have happened.

Your Turn

Begin organizing your ideas by sorting your note cards into main ideas and subtopics. Discard any notes that do not fit.

Next, create an outline for your report. Use a Roman numeral for each main idea and a capital letter for each subtopic. Use an Arabic number for each detail that falls under a subtopic.

John White's drawing of a Roanoke Island Indian community

Drafting

Bayani used his outline and his note cards to write a first draft. He wrote an introduction that introduced the topic and included a thesis statement. In the body he explored his main ideas in a logical order. In the conclusion  he summed up his thesis and left the reader with a final thought.

Here is what Bayani wrote for the first and last pages of his report.

What Happened to the Lost Colony of Roanoke?

The lost colony of Roanoke is one of history's greatest mysteries. The settlers, who were among the first English colonists, arrived at the island of Roanoke in 1587. Three years later, they disappeared. Some believe that they married into one Native American tribe or that they were killed by another tribe. Others say that something else happened to them. Though some theories are more likely than others, we may never know what happened to the lost colony of Roanoke.

The colony of Roanoke was settled in 1587 (Delillo 24) It was not the first group of Europeans to settle there. In 1585 the first colony had been set up. A year later it was mostly abandoned, and the 15 people who stayed behind were killed by a nearby tribe (Delillo 21). The second settlement included more than 100 people, who were probably scared to settle there because of what happened to the first group. This included their leader John White, his pregnant daughter, Eleanor Dare, and her husband. Eleanor gave birth to the first English child born in the New World (Johnson 105).

A month after landing with the settlers, White decided to go back to England for supplies. When he arrived, however, he had to stay because England was in the middle of a war with Spain. He did not return to Roanoke until 1590 (Johnson 109). When he got there, he found that everyone had disappeared. As Brad Pauley wrote in the _Virginia Monthly:_ "All that remained was one fence and a tree carved with one word: CROATOAN" (Pauley 43).

All these theories are possible. Many experts agree that two theories are the most likely. The theory that they were killed by a hostile tribe is considered likely (Johnson 107). The other most likely theory is that they married into the tribe at Croatoan island. This would explain the carving that John White found (109). Other theories, such as that they were killed by disease or a storm, are ridiculous ("Uncovered History" 1).

We may never know what happened to the lost colony of Roanoke. Historians are always looking for new clues about what happened. New theories are sometimes brought up. Whatever happened to them, they will always be remembered for risking their lives in an unfamiliar land.

Your Turn

Use your note cards and outline to write the first draft of your report.

- Write an introduction that lists each main idea and states the thesis of your report.
- You might further divide your main ideas into subtopics, writing a paragraph for each subtopic. Be certain that your report as a whole supports the thesis. If it does not, change your thesis to fit the information you found.
- Create a Works Cited page to document your sources. Use the guidelines from Lesson 3 to help you write each entry.

Writer's Tip Make sure that all your information is related to your thesis.

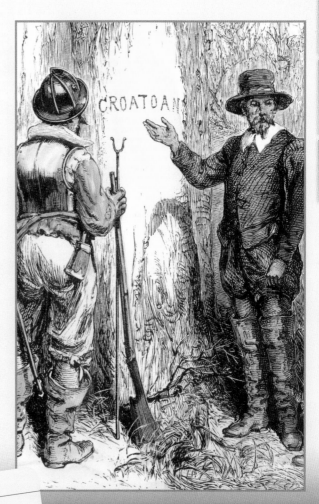

Content Editing

Bayani thought his research report was interesting and informative. It told the story of the settlers at Roanoke, explored the theories of their disappearance, and used research to evaluate the various theories.

To improve his report, Bayani decided to begin editing. First, he read it over to himself, making sure that the report was focused, organized, and complete. He used the Content Editor's Checklist to help him.

Next, he gave his draft to his classmate Luke to read. Since Luke did not know much about the Roanoke colony, he would be able to tell Bayani if more information was needed. With the help of the Content Editor's Checklist, Luke could check if the draft was based on facts and used formal language.

Content Editor's Checklist

- [ ] Does the introduction identify the topic and main ideas and include a thesis statement?

- [ ] Does each main idea support the thesis?

- [ ] Does the body include information from several sources?

- [ ] Is the source of each researched fact or idea documented?

- [ ] Does the conclusion sum up the research and restate the thesis?

- [ ] Does the report use formal language and a confident tone?

- [ ] Is information about each source included in the Works Cited page?

Roanoke settlers baptize the first baby of the colony, born to Eleanor Dare.

When Luke had finished going through the report, he made several comments. He thought that the topic was interesting and that the report was filled with fascinating information. He had several suggestions for improving the report, including these notes about the first and last pages:

- In the introduction, can you mention a few more theories you talk about in the report?
- The part in the second paragraph about the settlers being scared doesn't seem to come from your research. Is this just your opinion?
- I would be interested in knowing the name of Eleanor Dare's child.
- On the last page, I think you need more information to support your thesis. Why is the theory that they were killed by a hostile tribe considered likely?
- Maybe you should end the report with a final sentence that is more closely related to the thesis.

Bayani asked Luke a few questions about his comments, then thanked him for his help. Bayani decided to go through his draft and decide which of Luke's suggestions to use.

Grammar in Action

What is the subject and subject complement in the first sentence of Bayani's report? Refer to Section 1.3.

Your Turn

Look over your entire draft, using the Content Editor's Checklist. Be sure to eliminate any statements not supported by research.

Trade drafts with a partner and review each other's drafts, using the Content Editor's Checklist.

- Take note of the things you like about your partner's draft and make suggestions for improvement.
- Listen carefully to your partner's suggestions and be open to making changes to your draft.

Writer's Tip Organize your report logically, following your outline.

Prewriting

Drafting

Content Editing

Revising

Copyediting

Proofreading

Publishing

Revising

Cap from Virginia Dare soda pop

Bayani made many revisions after his conference with Luke. Here are examples of the changes he made to the first and last pages.

What Happened to the Lost Colony of Roanoke?

The lost colony of Roanoke is one of history's greatest mysteries. The settlers, who were among the first English colonists, arrived at the island of Roanoke in 1587. Three years later, they disappeared. Some believe that they married into one Native American tribe or that they were killed by another tribe. Others say ~~that something else happened to them.~~ they were taken hostage by the Spanish or that they simply moved inland. Though some theories are more likely than others, we may never know what happened to the lost colony of Roanoke.

The colony of Roanoke was settled in 1587 (Delillo 24) It was not the first group of Europeans to settle there. In 1585 the first colony had been set up. A year later it was mostly abandoned, and the 15 people who stayed behind were killed by a nearby tribe (Delillo 21). The second settlement included more than 100 people, ~~who were probably scared to settle there because of what happened to the first group.~~ This included their leader John White, his pregnant daughter, Eleanor Dare, and her husband. Eleanor gave birth to the first English child born in the New World, Virginia Dare (Johnson 105).

The last that was known of the settlers came from John White. A month after landing with the settlers, White decided to go back to England for supplies. When he arrived, however, he had to stay because England was in the middle of a war with Spain. He did not return to Roanoke until 1590 (Johnson 109). When he got there, he found that everyone had disappeared. As Brad Pauley wrote in the <u>Virginia Monthly</u>: "All that remained was one fence and a tree carved with one word: CROATOAN" (Pauley 43).

Prewriting

Drafting

Content Editing

Revising

Copyediting

Proofreading

Publishing

All these theories are possible. Many experts agree that two theories are the most likely. The theory that they were killed by a hostile tribe is considered likely
This is because the same thing happened to the first settlement at Roanoke.
(Johnson 107). The other most likely theory is that they married into the tribe at Croatoan island. This would explain the carving that John White found (109).
because there was nothing left of their settlement
Other theories, such as that they were killed by disease or a storm, are ridiculous ("Uncovered History" 1).

We may never know what happened to the lost colony of Roanoke. Historians are always looking for new clues about what happened. New theories are sometimes brought up. Whatever happened to them, they will always be remembered for risking their lives in an unfamiliar land.

Look at the revisions that Bayani incorporated into his draft. He used some of Luke's suggestions for the first and last pages of his report.

- How many theories did Bayani add to his introduction?
- Which opinion did he delete?
- He added the child's name, Virginia Dare.
- Where did he give a reason that the first theory was considered likely?
- Bayani liked the final sentence of his report and decided not to change it.

Bayani made other changes to his report. He also found two additional changes to be made on the first and last page. He opened the third paragraph with a topic sentence that introduced the paragraph's main idea. He also added a reason why some of the other theories were considered less likely.

Your Turn

Revise your draft, using your partner's suggestions and any ideas for changes that you found when rereading the draft. Make any changes that you think will improve the report. When you have finished, reread your draft a final time. Make sure you can answer yes to each question on the Content Editor's Checklist.

Sheet music for the song
Hello Virginia (Sweet Virginia Dare)

Copyediting and Proofreading

Copyediting

Bayani knew that his revisions had made his draft much stronger. The report was better focused, better organized, and more complete. With copyediting, however, he knew his report would be even better. He checked his draft for logic, grammar, and clarity, using the following Copyeditor's Checklist.

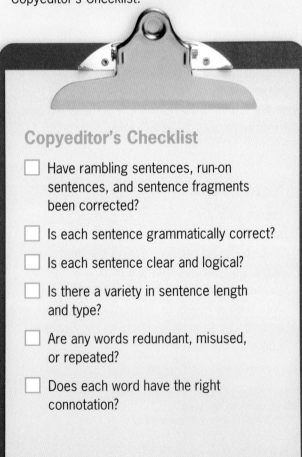

Copyeditor's Checklist

☐ Have rambling sentences, run-on sentences, and sentence fragments been corrected?

☐ Is each sentence grammatically correct?

☐ Is each sentence clear and logical?

☐ Is there a variety in sentence length and type?

☐ Are any words redundant, misused, or repeated?

☐ Does each word have the right connotation?

Bayani went through his entire draft a few times, checking for each point on the checklist. He found several areas where his writing could be made clearer or more correct.

On the first page, for example, he found several mistakes. In the first sentence, he realized that it **Word Choice** would be better to say that the *story* of the lost colony, not the colony itself, was a great mystery. In the third sentence, he changed the tense of the verb *disappeared* to show that the colony could have disappeared any time before three years had passed.

On the last page, he also made a few corrections. In the next to last paragraph, he thought that there were too many simple sentences. For variety he combined the first two sentences, turning the first one into a clause. **Sentence Fluency** He also realized that the word *ridiculous* at the end of the paragraph had a negative connotation. He replaced it with the words *less likely,* which have a more neutral connotation.

Your Turn

Reread your draft and copyedit it with the help of the Copyeditor's Checklist.

Proofreading

Bayani was almost ready to create his final draft. He still had one final step to take before publishing: proofreading. He gave his draft to his classmate Ellie, who checked the draft for spelling, punctuation, format, and grammar. She used this Proofreader's Checklist.

Proofreader's Checklist

- ☐ Are the paragraphs indented?
- ☐ Have any words been misspelled?
- ☐ Are there errors in grammar?
- ☐ Are capitalization and punctuation correct?
- ☐ Is each citation written correctly?
- ☐ Were any new errors introduced during the editing stage?

Map of the Carolina Coast, 1600s

Ellie discovered mistakes on each page of Bayani's draft. Here are some examples she found on the first and last pages.

In the second paragraph, she found that Bayani had forgotten to add a period after his first citation. She also reminded him that his second citation did not need to include the name *Delillo* because this name was the last one cited.

She also found that the name *John White* in the second paragraph needed to be set off with commas because White was the only leader, and therefore his name was nonrestrictive. Finally, in the third paragraph, she noted that he did not need to cite the name *Pauley* because he had stated the source's name in the sentence.

Finally, Ellie discovered a spelling error. She saw that he had misspelled the word *disappeared* in the third paragraph.

Ellie shared what she had found with Bayani. He thanked Ellie for her help and made the corrections.

Your Turn

Look over your draft, using the Proofreader's Checklist, before giving it to a proofreader. Use what you learned in Lesson 3 to help you cite sources.

Trade drafts with a partner. Read your partner's draft with the help of the Proofreader's Checklist. Make corrections to your partner's draft. Listen carefully to the comments your partner makes about your draft. Thank your partner for his or her suggestions.

Prewriting

Drafting

Content Editing

Revising

Copyediting

Proofreading

Publishing

Publishing

After Bayani had made the corrections that he and Ellie had found in the proofreading stage, he typed his final report on his computer and printed it out.

He included a cover page with his name and the title at the front and a Works Cited page at the end.

What Happened to the Lost Colony of Roanoke?

by Bayani Tan

The story of the lost colony of Roanoke is one of history's greatest mysteries. The settlers, who were among the first English colonists, arrived at the island of Roanoke in 1587. Three years later, they had disappeared. Some believe that they married into one Native American tribe or that they were killed by another tribe. Others say that they were taken hostage by the Spanish or that they simply moved inland. Though some theories are more likely than others, we may never know what happened to the lost colony of Roanoke.

The colony of Roanoke was settled in 1587 (Delillo 24). It was not the first group of Europeans to settle there. In 1585 the first colony had been set up. A year later it was mostly abandoned, and the 15 people who stayed behind were killed by a nearby tribe (21). The second settlement included more than 100 people. This included their leader, John White, his pregnant daughter, Eleanor Dare, and her husband. Eleanor gave birth to the first English child born in the New World, Virginia Dare (Johnson 105).

The last that was known of the settlers came from John White. A month after landing with the settlers, White decided to go back to England for supplies. When he arrived, however, he had to stay because England was in the middle of a war with Spain. He did not return to Roanoke until 1590 (Johnson 109). When he got there, he found that everyone had disappeared. As Brad Pauley wrote in the *Virginia Monthly*: "All that remained was one fence and a tree carved with one word: CROATOAN" (43).

Though all these theories are possible, many experts agree that two theories are the most likely. The theory that they were killed by a hostile tribe is considered likely. This is because the same thing had happened to the first settlement at Roanoke (Johnson 107). The other most likely theory is that they married into the tribe at Croatoan island. This would explain the carving that John White found (Johnson 109). Other theories, such as that they were killed by disease or a storm, seem to be less likely because there was nothing left of their settlement ("Uncovered History" 1–2).

We may never know what happened to the lost colony of Roanoke. Historians are always looking for new clues about what happened. New theories are sometimes brought up. Whatever happened to these settlers, they will always be remembered for risking their lives in an unfamiliar land.

Works Cited

Delillo, John. <u>The Early Settlers</u>. Olympia, WA: Fountain Books, 2001.

Johnson, Nadia. <u>Mysteries in Time</u>. New York, NY: Underdog Press, 1998.

Pauley, Brad. "Searching for the Lost Colony." <u>Virginia Monthly</u> 23 (2002): 42–47.

"Uncovered History." 11 February 2005 <www.historypages22.org/Roanoke>.

 Presentation

Whenever you publish your work, your goal is to share your thoughts and experiences with other people. There are many ways you can publish your report.

 Create a classroom book. Include visuals, such as charts, graphs, and photographs of your research topic. These are interesting items to attach to the research reports.

 Post the reports on your classroom's wiki, blog, or Web site. You can receive comments about your report and review others' work.

 Create a class journal of research by combining everyone's research report under a single cover. Arrange the reports in alphabetical order and create a table of contents.

 Film it. Make your own documentary. Narrate the report with a backdrop of photographs, music, and illustrations, or interview someone who can add information to your topic.

 Have your class journal on hand for Parents' Night. You might wish to present it as a PowerPoint presentation.

Your Turn

Look over your draft once more before publishing. Print out or write a final copy. Create a cover page for your report, including the title of your report, your name, and any other information your teacher requests. Include the Works Cited page at the end. Then choose one of the publishing options.

Common Proofreading Marks

Use these proofreading marks to mark changes when you proofread. Remember to use a colored pencil to make your changes.

Symbol	Meaning	Example
¶	begin new paragraph	over. ¶Begin a new
◡◠	close up space	close u p space
∧	insert	students think ^should^
⟋	delete, omit	that the ~~the~~ book
/	make lowercase	Mathematics
∼	reverse letters	reve(sr)e letters
≡	capitalize	washington
⌄⌄	add quotation marks	I am, I said.
⊙	add period	Marta drank tea ⊙

A Frustrating and Rewarding Day

Have you ever had a day that was really frustrating. I have, but fortunately everything turned out OK in the end.

It was a hot day in July when our neighborhood held a fare to raise money for a girl who was ill with leukemia. We were surprised at the medical treatments for a child who was sick in the hospital. the concession stand to hundreds big number of people who came to eat food and play games like water balloon my cousins from across town came.

in a popcorn popper and to se... ..it, however, retriever, got so

Grammar and Mechanics Handbook

Grammar

Adjectives

An adjective points out or describes a noun.

> **That** dog is **hungry**.

Adjective Clauses

An adjective clause is a dependent clause used as an adjective. See CLAUSES.

Adjective Phrases

An infinitive phrase can be used as an adjective. See INFINITIVES.

A participial phrase can be used as an adjective. See PARTICIPLES.

A prepositional phrase can be used as an adjective. See PREPOSITIONS.

Articles

An article points out a noun. See ARTICLES.

Common Adjectives

A common adjective expresses an ordinary quality of a noun or a pronoun: *tall* ship, *majestic* mountains.

Comparison of Adjectives

Most adjectives have three degrees of comparison: positive, comparative, and superlative.

The positive degree of an adjective shows a quality of a noun or a pronoun.

> My grandmother is a **tall** woman.
> The dancer is **famous**.
> LaTonya is a **careful** worker.

The comparative degree is used to compare two items or two sets of items. This form is often followed by *than*.

> My grandfather is **taller** than my grandmother.
> The singer is **more famous** than the actor.
> James is a **less careful** worker than LaTonya.

The superlative degree is used to compare three or more items or sets of items.

> My uncle Jack is the **tallest** member of the family.
> The singer is the **most famous** person here.
> Gloria is the **least careful** worker of them all.

The adjectives *few, fewer,* and *fewest* are used to compare concrete nouns. Note that the nouns are plural in form.

> Lorna made **few** free throws.
> Gail made **fewer** free throws than Lorna.
> Mary Pat made the **fewest** free throws of all.

The adjectives *little, less,* and *least* are used to compare abstract nouns. Note that the nouns are singular in form.

> I have **little** time to practice free throws.
> My brother has **less** time to practice than I do.
> Of us all, my sister has the **least** time to practice.

Demonstrative Adjectives

A demonstrative adjective points out a definite person, place, thing, or idea. The demonstrative adjectives are *this, that, these,* and *those. This* and *that* are singular; *these* and *those* are plural. *This* and *these* refer to things or people that are near; *that* and *those* refer to things or people that are farther away.

> **This** dog is very friendly. (singular and near)
> **Those** cats are more skittish. (plural and far)

Descriptive Adjectives

A descriptive adjective gives information about a noun or pronoun. It tells about age, size, shape, color, origin, or another quality.

> I have a **sweet**, **little**, **gray**, **Persian** kitten.

Indefinite Adjectives

An indefinite adjective refers to all or any of a group of people, places, or things. Some of the most common indefinite adjectives are *all, another, any, both, each, either, every, few, many, more, most, neither, no, one, other, several,* and *some*. Note that *another, each, every, either, neither, no, one,* and *other* are always singular, and the others are plural.

> **Each** player has a glove.
> **Several** players have bats.

Interrogative Adjectives

An interrogative adjective is used in asking a question. The interrogative adjectives are *what, which,* and *whose.*

Which is usually used to ask about one or more of a specific set of people or things. *What* is used to ask about people or things but is not limited to a specific group or set. *Whose* asks about possession.

> **Which** position do you play?
> **What** time is the game?
> **Whose** equipment will you borrow?

Numerical Adjectives

A numerical adjective tells an exact number: *twenty-five children, eighth grade.*

Participial Adjectives

A participle is a verb form that is used as an adjective. A participial adjective stands alone before or after the word it modifies. See PARTICIPLES.

Position of Adjectives

Most adjectives go before the words they describe.

> **Mexican** pottery comes in many shapes.

Adjectives may also directly follow nouns.

> The vase, **ancient** and **cracked**, was found nearby.

An adjective can follow a linking verb (as a subject complement), or it can follow a direct object (as an object complement).

> The archaeologist was **excited**.
> She considered the vase **extraordinary**.

Possessive Adjectives

A possessive adjective shows possession or ownership. Possessive adjectives have antecedents. A possessive adjective must agree with its antecedent in person, number, and gender.

> John has a skateboard. **His** skateboard is silver.
> Jo and Luis have bikes. **Their** bikes are new.

Possessive adjectives change form depending on person and number. Third person singular possessive adjectives change form depending on gender.

	Singular	Plural
First Person	my	our
Second Person	your	your
Third Person	his, her, its	their

Proper Adjectives

A proper adjective is formed from a proper noun: *Brazilian* rain forest, *Chinese* emperors.

Subject Complements

An adjective may be used as a subject complement. See SUBJECT COMPLEMENTS.

Adverbs

An adverb is a word that modifies a verb, an adjective, or another adverb. Adverbs indicate *time, place, manner, degree, affirmation,* or *negation.*

> ***Sometimes*** my family goes to the zoo. (time)
> We like to watch the animals ***there***. (place)
> We stroll ***slowly*** along the paths. (manner)
> Watching the animals can be ***quite*** entertaining. (degree)
> We'll ***undoubtedly*** go to the zoo next week. (affirmation)
> We ***never*** miss an opportunity to see the animals. (negation)

Adverb Clauses

A dependent clause can be used as an adverb. See CLAUSES.

Adverb Phrases

A prepositional phrase can be used as an adverb. See PREPOSITIONS.

Adverbial Nouns

An adverbial noun is a noun that acts as an adverb. Adverbial nouns usually express *time, distance, measure, value,* or *direction.*

The trip took a few **hours**. (time)
We traveled about a hundred **miles**. (distance)
The temperature was about 70 **degrees**. (measure)
The bus fare was 30 **dollars**. (value)
It was the farthest **north** I've ever been. (direction)

Comparison of Adverbs

Most adverbs have three degrees of comparison: positive, comparative, and superlative.

Grace works **carefully**.
Zach works **less carefully** than Grace.
Meagen works **most carefully** of anyone in class.

Wiley ate **rapidly**.
David ate **less rapidly** than Wiley.
Matt ate **least rapidly** of all.

Carly walks **fast**.
Maggie walks **faster** than Carly.
Ryoko walks **fastest** of us all.

Conjunctive Adverbs

A conjunctive adverb connects independent clauses. A semicolon is used before a conjunctive adverb, and a comma is used after it. Common conjunctive adverbs include *also, besides, consequently, finally, furthermore, hence, however, indeed, instead, later, likewise, moreover, nevertheless, nonetheless, otherwise, still, therefore,* and *thus.*

Ryoko walked fastest; **therefore**, he arrived first.

Interrogative Adverbs

An interrogative adverb is used to ask a question. The interrogative adverbs are *how, when, where,* and *why.*

When did Ryoko arrive?

Antecedents

The noun to which a pronoun or a possessive adjective refers is its antecedent. A pronoun or a possessive adjective must agree with its antecedent in person and number. Third person singular personal, possessive, intensive, and reflexive pronouns and possessive adjectives must also agree in gender. See GENDER, NUMBER, PERSON.

Appositives

An appositive is a word (or words) that follows a noun and helps identify it or adds more information about it. An appositive names the same person, place, thing, or idea as the noun it explains. An appositive phrase is an appositive and its modifiers.

An appositive is restrictive if it is necessary to understand the sentence. It is nonrestrictive if it is not necessary. A nonrestrictive appositive is set off by commas.

The Italian sailor **John Cabot** explored Canada.
Magellan, **a Spanish navigator**, sailed around the world.

Articles

An article points out a noun. *The* is the definite article. It refers to a specific item or specific items in a group. *The* may be used with either singular or plural concrete nouns and with abstract nouns.

We went to **the** park yesterday.
The parks in our area are very well kept.
The grass is always mowed.

A and *an* are the indefinite articles. Each is used to refer to a single member of a general group. *A* and *an* are used only with singular concrete nouns. The article *an* is used before a vowel sound. The article *a* is used before a consonant sound.

I ate **a** sandwich and **an** apple.

Clauses

A clause is a group of words that has a subject and a predicate. An independent clause expresses a complete thought and can stand alone as a sentence. A dependent clause does not express a complete thought and cannot stand alone as a sentence.

Adjective Clauses

A dependent clause can describe a noun or a pronoun. An adjective clause usually begins with a relative pronoun *(who, whom, whose, which, that)* or a subordinate conjunction *(when, where)*. These words connect the dependent clause to the noun it modifies.

> I read a book **that was fascinating**.
> I'll never forget the place **where we met**.

A restrictive adjective clause is necessary to the meaning of the sentence. A nonrestrictive adjective clause is not necessary to the meaning. Nonrestrictive clauses are set off by commas. As a general rule, the relative pronoun *that* is used in restrictive clauses and *which* in nonrestrictive clauses.

> Chicago, **which has many tourist attractions**, is located on Lake Michigan.
> The attraction **that we liked most** was Navy Pier.

Adverb Clauses

A dependent clause can describe or give information about a verb, an adjective, or other adverb. An adverb clause can tell *where, when, why, in what way, to what extent (degree),* or *under what condition.* An adverb clause begins with a subordinate conjunction.

> We'll go **wherever you'd like**.
> We can leave **after you finish your homework**.
> **Because it's late**, we'll take a taxi.

Noun Clauses

Dependent clauses can be used as nouns. These clauses can function as subjects, complements, appositives, direct objects, indirect objects, and objects of prepositions. Most noun clauses begin with one of these introductory words: *that, who, whom, whoever, whomever, how, why, when, whether, what, where,* and *whatever.*

That rabbits make good pets was a surprise to me. (subject)
The fact is *that chinchillas make good pets too*. (subject complement)
The idea *that I could like a ferret* seems strange. (appositive)
My parents will buy me *whatever I choose*. (direct object)
I am interested in *how guinea pigs are raised*. (object of preposition)

Conjunctions

A conjunction is a word used to join two words or groups of words in a sentence.

Coordinating Conjunctions

A coordinating conjunction joins words or groups of words that are similar. The coordinating conjunctions are *and, but, nor, or, so,* and *yet.*

The boys *and* girls ran into the park. (nouns)
They played on the swings *or* in the sandbox. (prepositional phrases)
They sailed boats, *but* they didn't go swimming. (independent clauses)

Correlative Conjunctions

Correlative conjunctions are used in pairs to connect words or groups of words that have equal importance in a sentence. The most common correlative conjunctions are *both . . . and, either . . . or, neither . . . nor, not only . . . but also,* and *whether . . . or.*

Each correlative conjunction appears immediately in front of one of the words or groups of words that are connected. In sentences with *neither . . . nor,* the verb agrees with the subject closest to it.

Both my mother *and* my father like dogs.
Neither my brothers *nor* my sister likes cats.

Subordinate Conjunctions

A subordinate conjunction is used to join a dependent and an independent clause. Common subordinate conjunctions include *after, although, as, as if, as long as, because, before, even though, if, in order that, since, so that, than, though, unless, until, when, whenever, where, wherever,* and *while.*

Unless you help me, I won't finish this today.
I can't help you *until* I've completed my own project.

Direct Objects

The direct object of a sentence answers the question *whom* or *what* after the verb. A noun or an object pronoun can be used as a direct object.

> Consuela made **cookies**.
> The children ate **them**.

Gender

Third person singular personal, possessive, intensive, and reflexive pronouns and possessive adjectives change form depending on gender—whether the antecedent is masculine *(he, him, his, himself)*, feminine *(she, her, hers, herself)*, or neuter *(it, its, itself)*.

Gerunds

A gerund is a verb form ending in *ing* that is used as a noun. A gerund can be used in a sentence as a subject, an object, a subject complement, or an appositive.

> **Reading** is his favorite pastime. (subject)
> People from many cultures enjoy **dancing**. (direct object)
> My dad likes to relax by **cooking**. (object of a preposition)
> My favorite hobby is **skateboarding**. (subject complement)
> Her hobby, **hiking**, requires little equipment. (appositive)

A gerund phrase consists of a gerund, its object or complement, and any descriptive words or phrases. The entire phrase acts as a noun.

> **Reading mysteries** is a relaxing form of recreation. (subject)
> Linda's hobby is **riding her bike**. (subject complement)
> People around the world enjoy **watching fireworks**. (direct object)
> Americans celebrate the Fourth of July by **attending firework shows**.
>   (object of a preposition)
> His job, **creating fireworks displays**, can be very dangerous.
>   (appositive)

Indirect Objects

An indirect object tells *to whom* or *for whom,* or *to what* or *for what,* an action is done. A noun or an object pronoun can be used as an indirect object

I gave **Sven** a present.
I gave **him** a birthday card too.

Infinitives

An infinitive is a verb form, usually preceded by *to,* that is used as a noun, an adjective, or an adverb.

To study is your present job. (noun)
I have a history report **to do**. (adjective)
I went **to study** in the library. (adverb)

An infinitive phrase consists of an infinitive, its object or complement, and any descriptive words or phrases.

To finish the science report was my goal. (noun)
I made a decision **to write about bears**. (adjective)
I arrived too late **to finish it today**. (adverb)

Hidden Infinitives

A hidden infinitive is an infinitive without *to.* Hidden infinitives occur after verbs of perception such as *hear, see, know,* and *feel* and after verbs such as *let, make, dare, need,* and *help.*

I heard the birds **sing** this morning.
I'll help **build** a birdhouse.

The word *to* is also omitted after the prepositions *but* and *except* and the conjunction *than.*

I'll do anything but **mow** the lawn.
I'd rather help out than **do** nothing.

Split Infinitives

An adverb placed between *to* and the verb results in a split infinitive. Good writers try to avoid split infinitives.

Subjects of Infinitives

An infinitive used as a direct object can have a subject. The subject tells the doer of the infinitive. If the subject is a pronoun, it is always in the object form.

We wanted *her* to clean the garage.

Interjections

An interjection is a word or phrase that expresses a strong or sudden emotion, such as happiness, delight, anger, disgust, surprise, impatience, pain, or wonder.

Ouch! I stubbed my toe.
Wow, that's amazing!

Mood

Mood shows the manner in which the action or state of being of a verb is expressed.

Indicative Mood

The indicative mood is used to state a fact or ask a question. The simple tenses, the progressive tenses, and the perfect tenses are all part of the indicative mood.

I *bought* a new cell phone.
Have you ever *sent* pictures with a cell phone?
The pictures *are* amazing!

Imperative Mood

The imperative mood is used to express a command or a request. The imperative mood uses the base form of a verb. The subject of an imperative sentence is usually understood to be the second person pronoun, *you.*

Follow the directions carefully.
Watch out!

A command can be given in the first person by using *let's* before the base form of a verb.

Let's go.

Emphatic Mood

The emphatic mood gives special force to a simple present or past tense verb. To make an emphatic mood, use *do, does,* or *did* before the base form of the verb.

> I ***do like*** to use cell phones.
> I ***did use*** my cell phone last night.

Subjunctive Mood

The subjunctive mood is used to express a wish or a desire; to express a command, a recommendation, or a necessity after *that;* or to express something that is contrary to fact.

The past tense of a verb is used to state present wishes or desires or contrary-to-fact conditions. *Were* is used instead of *was,* and *would* is used instead of *will.*

> I wish you ***were*** here. (a wish or desire)
> If we ***had*** enough money, we ***would*** go to the movies.
>   (a contrary-to-fact condition)

The base form of a verb is used in a clause after *that.*

> The coach insisted that Laura ***be*** on time. (command after *that*)
> It's imperative that she ***call*** him tonight. (necessity after *that*)

Nouns

A noun is a name word. A singular noun names one person, place, thing, or idea: *girl, park, ball, memory.* A plural noun names more than one person, place, thing, or idea: *girls, parks, balls, memories.*

Abstract Nouns

An abstract noun names something that cannot be seen or touched. It expresses a quality or a condition: *morality, sadness, idea, duration.*

Appositives

An appositive is a word (or words) that follows a noun and helps identify it or adds more information about it. See APPOSITIVES.

Collective Nouns

A collective noun names a group of people, animals, or things considered as one: *team, herd, bunch.*

Common Nouns

A common noun names any one of a class of people, places, or things: *reader, province, star.*

Concrete Nouns

A concrete noun names something that can be seen or touched: *table, hammer, artist, Ohio River.*

Gerunds

A gerund is a verb form ending in *ing* that is used as a noun. A gerund or a gerund phrase can be a subject, an object, a subject complement, or an appositive. See GERUNDS.

Infinitives Used as Nouns

An infinitive is a verb form, usually preceded by *to.* An infinitive or infinitive phrase used as a noun can be a subject, a subject complement, an object, or an appositive. See INFINITIVES.

Noun Clauses

A dependent clause can be used as a noun. See CLAUSES.

Noun Phrases

A gerund phrase can be used as a noun. See GERUNDS.

A prepositional phrase can be used as a noun. See PREPOSITIONS.

Possessive Nouns

A possessive noun expresses possession or ownership.

To form the singular possessive, add *-'s* to the singular form of the noun.

    student   student**'s**   Heather   Heather**'s**

To form the possessive of a plural noun ending in *s,* add the apostrophe only. If the plural form of a noun does not end in *s,* add *-'s.*

    cowboys   cowboys**'**   children   children**'s**

The singular possessive of a proper name ending in *s* is usually formed by adding *-'s.*

    James   James**'s**   Mrs. Williams   Mrs. Williams**'s**

The plural possessive of a proper name is formed by adding an apostrophe to the plural of the name.

Mr. and Mrs. Adams   the Adamses**'** children

The possessive of compound nouns is formed by adding *-'s* to the end of the term.

commander in chief   commander in chief**'s**
brothers-in-law   brothers-in-law**'s**

Separate possession occurs when two or more people own things independently of one another. To show separate possession, use *-'s* after each noun.

Diane**'s** and Peter**'s** murals are colorful.

Joint possession occurs when two or more people own something together. To show joint possession, use *-'s* after the last noun only.

Marta and Ryan**'s** mural is colorful.

Proper Nouns

A proper noun names a particular person, place, or thing: *Meryl Streep, Hollywood, Academy Award.*

Number

The number of a noun or pronoun indicates whether it refers to one person, place, thing, or idea (singular) or more than one person, place, thing, or idea (plural).

Object Complements

An object complement follows the direct object of a sentence. A noun used as an object complement follows the direct object and renames it. An adjective used as an object complement follows the direct object and describes it.

We elected Yoko **president**.
We found her leadership **inspiring**.

Participles

A participle is a verb form that is used as an adjective. A present participle always ends in *ing*. A past participle generally ends in *ed*.

Participial Adjectives

A participial adjective stands alone before or after the word it modifies.

> The **sobbing** child clung to her mother.
> The child, **sobbing**, clung to her mother.

A participle has voice and tense. The present participle shows a relationship between the time of the action of the participle and of the main verb. Past and perfect forms show action that was completed at some time before the action indicated by the main verb.

> The project **being started** now is supposed to end today.
>   (present passive)
> The project **started** yesterday is important. (past passive)
> Their group, **having started** late, rushed to finish. (present
>   perfect active)
> **Having been delayed** twice, the project is behind schedule.
>   (present perfect passive)

A participle that is essential to the meaning of a sentence is restrictive and is not set off by commas. A participle that is not essential to the meaning of the sentence is nonrestrictive and is set off by commas.

> The project **started on Monday** ran into terrible snags.
> The other project, **started a day later**, finished first.

Dangling Participles

A dangling participle is a participial phrase that does not modify a noun or pronoun. Dangling participles should be corrected.

> **Working hard**, the doghouse was soon finished. (incorrect)
> **Working hard**, the girls soon finished the doghouse. (correct)

Participial Phrases

A participial phrase consists of the participle and an object or a complement and any descriptive words or phrases. A participial phrase can come before or after the word it modifies.

> **Kissing the child gently**, the mother tried to soothe him.
> The child, **sobbing loudly**, refused to quiet down.

Person

Personal, possessive, intensive, and reflexive pronouns and possessive adjectives change form according to person—whether the antecedent is the person speaking (first person), being spoken to (second person), or being spoken about (third person).

Phrases

A phrase is a group of words that is used as a single part of speech.

Gerund Phrases

A gerund phrase consists of a gerund, its object or complement, and any descriptive words or phrases. See GERUNDS.

Infinitive Phrases

An infinitive phrase consists of an infinitive, its object or complement, and any descriptive words or phrases. See INFINITIVES.

Participial Phrases

A participial phrase consists of the participle, its object or complement, and any descriptive words or phrases. See PARTICIPLES.

Prepositional Phrases

A prepositional phrase is made up of a preposition, the object of the preposition, and any modifiers of the object. See PREPOSITIONS.

Verb Phrases

A verb phrase is two or more verbs that work together as a unit. A verb phrase may have one or more auxiliary verbs and a main verb.

> The boy **is studying**.
> He **has been studying** for an hour.

Predicates

The predicate of a sentence names an action or a state of being.

> The horses **jumped**.
> They **were** beautiful.

Complete Predicates

The complete predicate is the verb with all its modifiers and objects or complements.

The horses **jumped all the hurdles well**.

Compound Predicates

A compound predicate contains more than one verb joined by a coordinating conjunction.

The horses **ran swiftly and jumped** over the fence.

Simple Predicates

The simple predicate is the verb or verb phrase.

The horses **have been running** for a long time.

Prepositions

A preposition is a word that shows the relationship between a noun or pronoun (the object of the preposition) and some other word in a sentence.

Prepositional Phrases

A prepositional phrase is made up of a preposition, the object of the preposition, and any modifiers of the object. A prepositional phrase may be used as an adjective, an adverb, or a noun.

She was the winner **of the game**. (adjective)
She threw her hat **into the air**. (adverb)
On the podium is where she stood. (noun)

Pronouns

A pronoun is a word used in place of a noun. The noun to which a pronoun refers is its antecedent. A pronoun must agree with its antecedent in person and number. Third person personal, possessive, intensive, and reflexive pronouns must also agree in gender. See GENDER, NUMBER, PERSON.

Demonstrative Pronouns

A demonstrative pronoun points out a particular person, place, or thing. The demonstrative pronouns are *this, that, these,* and *those.*

This and *that* are singular; *these* and *those* are plural. *This* and *these* point out things that are near; *that* and *those* point out things that are farther away.

> **This** is my bike. (singular and near)
> **Those** are my skates. (plural and far)

Indefinite Pronouns

An indefinite pronoun refers to any or all of a group of people, places, or things. Indefinite pronouns can be used as subjects or objects.

> **Many** had heard about the strange old house.
> The loud noises were heard by **everyone**.

Most indefinite pronouns are singular, but some are plural. Singular indefinite pronouns include *another, anybody, anyone, anything, each, either, everybody, everyone, everything, much, neither, nobody, no one, nothing, one, other, somebody, someone,* and *something.* Plural indefinite pronouns include *both, few, many, others,* and *several.*

> **Everyone** is busy.
> **Nobody** wants to make a mistake.
> **Several** are drawing posters.
> **Others** want to use the computer.

The indefinite pronouns *all, any, more, most, none,* and *some* can be singular or plural, depending on how each is used in a sentence. These pronouns are singular and take a singular verb when they are followed by a phrase with a singular noun or an abstract noun. They are plural and take a plural verb when they are followed by a phrase with a plural noun.

> **Most** of the work was completed.
> **Most** of the projects were completed.

The indefinite pronouns *no one, nobody, none,* and *nothing* are negative words. They should never be used in sentences with other negative words such as *no, not,* or *never.*

Intensive Pronouns

Intensive pronouns end in *self* or *selves.* An intensive pronoun emphasizes a preceding noun or pronoun. It must agree with its antecedent in person, number, and gender.

> My sister paid for the car **herself**.
> I **myself** can't afford to buy a car.

Intensive pronouns change form depending on person and number. Third person singular intensive pronouns change form depending on gender.

	Singular	**Plural**
First Person	myself	ourselves
Second Person	yourself	yourselves
Third Person	himself	themselves
	herself	
	itself	

Interrogative Pronouns

An interrogative pronoun is used to ask a question. The interrogative pronouns are *who, whom, whose, which,* and *what.*

Who refers to people. It is often the subject of a question. *Whom* also refers to people. It is the object of a verb or a preposition.

Who is the captain of the hockey team?
Whom did he meet at the rink?
To **whom** will they sell their old skates?

Whose is used to ask about possession. *Which* is used when asking about a group or class. *What* is used for asking about things or seeking information.

Whose are those skates?
Which of the teams will be the toughest opponent?
What did you buy at the refreshment counter?
What is the date of the first game?

Object Pronouns

An object pronoun can be used as a direct or an indirect object of a verb or as the object of a preposition. The object pronouns are *me, you, him, her, it, us,* and *them.*

Tom met **her** at the video store. (direct object)
Gina wrote **him** an e-mail. (indirect object)
Martha received messages from **them**. (object of a preposition)

Personal Pronouns

Personal pronouns change form depending on person and number. Third person singular pronouns change form to reflect gender.

	Singular	Plural
First Person	I, me	we, us
Second Person	you	you
Third Person	he, she, it, him, her	they, them

Personal pronouns also change form depending on whether they are used as subjects *(I, you, he, she, it, we, they)* or objects *(me, you, him, her, it, us, them)*.

Possessive Pronouns

A possessive pronoun shows possession or ownership. It takes the place of a possessive noun. Possessive pronouns must agree with their antecedents in person, number, and gender.

> The green bike is **mine**.
> Jill left **hers** near the fence.
> Joe, where is **yours**?

Possessive pronouns change form depending on person and number. Third person singular possessive pronouns change form to reflect gender.

	Singular	Plural
First Person	mine	ours
Second Person	yours	yours
Third Person	his, hers, its	theirs

Reflexive Pronouns

Reflexive pronouns end in *self* or *selves*. A reflexive pronoun can be the direct or indirect object of a verb or the object of a preposition. A reflexive pronoun generally refers to the subject of the sentence. Reflexive pronouns must agree with their antecedents in person, number, and gender.

> I consider **myself** lucky to have won. (direct object)
> He gave **himself** a pat on the back. (indirect object)
> They did it by **themselves**. (object of a preposition)

Reflexive pronouns change form depending on person and number. Third person singular reflexive pronouns change form depending on gender.

	Singular	Plural
First Person	myself	ourselves
Second Person	yourself	yourselves
Third Person	himself	themselves
	herself	
	itself	

Relative Pronouns

A relative pronoun connects an adjective clause to the noun it modifies. The relative pronouns are *who, whom, whose, which,* and *that.*

Who and *whom* refer to people. *Who* is used as the subject of an adjective clause. *Whom* is used as the object of an adjective clause.

> George Washington, **who** was a famous general, was the first president of the United States.
> George Washington, **whom** we call the father of our country, started out as a surveyor.

Which refers to animals, places, or things. *That* refers to people, animals, places, or things. *Whose* often refers to people but can also refer to animals, places, or things.

> Mount Vernon, **which** was Washington's home, is in Virginia.
> It's a place **that** many tourists visit.
> They learn about Washington, **whose** possessions are displayed in the house.

Subject Pronouns

A subject pronoun can be used as the subject or the subject complement in a sentence. The subject pronouns are *I, you, he, she, it, we,* and *they.*

> **We** went to the mall on Saturday. (subject)
> The clerk we talked to was **she**. (subject complement)

Sentences

A sentence is a group of words that expresses a complete thought.

Complex Sentences

A complex sentence has one independent clause and at least one dependent clause, which may function as a noun, an adjective, or an adverb.

He claimed that he was the fastest runner.
The race that would decide the championship began at noon.
Because he tripped and fell, he lost the race.

Compound Sentences

A compound sentence contains two or more independent clauses.

The boys ran a race, and Hassan won.
Chris was leading at the halfway mark, but he tripped and fell.
Will they run the race again, or will Hassan get the prize?

Declarative Sentences

A declarative sentence makes a statement. It ends with a period.

I have a new cell phone.

Exclamatory Sentences

An exclamatory sentence expresses a strong emotion. It ends with an exclamation point.

It's so cool!

Imperative Sentences

An imperative sentence gives a command. It usually ends with a period but may end with an exclamation point. In imperative sentences the subject *you* is understood.

Call me tomorrow.

Interrogative Sentences

An interrogative sentence asks a question. It ends with a question mark.

Will you take my picture?

Inverted Order in Sentences

A sentence is in inverted order when the main verb or an auxiliary verb comes before the subject.

> Around the chimney curled the wispy smoke.
> When did you light the fireplace?
> There were many birds atop the chimney.

Natural Order in Sentences

A sentence is in natural order when the verb follows the subject.

> The wispy smoke curled around the chimney.

Simple Sentences

A simple sentence is one independent clause. It has a subject and a predicate, either or both of which may be compound.

> Milwaukee is the largest city in Wisconsin.
> Milwaukee and Green Bay have professional sports teams.
> Many people in Wisconsin fish and boat in the summer.

Subject Complements

A subject complement follows a linking verb such as the forms of *be.* A noun or pronoun used as a subject complement renames the subject of the sentence; it refers to the same person, place, thing, or idea. An adjective used as a subject complement describes the subject of the sentence.

> My uncle is a **police officer**.
> The officer who won the medal was **he**.
> His job can be **dangerous**.

Subjects

The subject names the person, place, or thing a sentence is about.

Complete Subjects

The complete subject is the simple subject plus all the words that describe it.

> **The tiny lamb with the black face** trotted across the field.

Compound Subjects

A compound subject contains more than one noun or pronoun joined by a coordinating conjunction.

The *lamb* and its *mother* trotted across the field.

Simple Subjects

The simple subject is the noun or pronoun that a sentence is about.

The *lamb* trotted across the field.

Tenses

The tense of a verb expresses the time of the action or state of being.

Perfect Tenses

Perfect tenses consist of a form of the auxiliary verb *have* and the past participle of the main verb. The present perfect tense tells about an action that took place at an indefinite time in the past or that started in the past and continued into the present. The past perfect tense tells about an action that was completed before another action was begun or completed. The future perfect tense tells about an action that will be completed before a specific time in the future.

Present Perfect Active	He *has finished* his homework.
Past Perfect Active	He *had finished* it before dinner.
Future Perfect Active	He *will have finished* dinner by six o'clock.

The passive voice of perfect tenses is formed by inserting *been* between the auxiliary of a form of *have* and the main verb.

Present Perfect Passive	The car *has been washed*.
Past Perfect Passive	The car *had been washed* before it started to rain.
Future Perfect Passive	*The car will have been washed* by the time Dad gets home.

Progressive Tenses

Progressive tense consist of a form of the auxiliary verb *be* and the present participle of the main verb. These tenses show ongoing action.

Present Progressive	I *am reading* my math book now.
Past Progressive	I *was reading* my math book when the phone rang.
Future Progressive	I *will be reading* my math book until dinner time.

Simple Tenses

The simple present tense indicates an action that is repeated or always true. The simple past and future tenses indicate action in the past or in the future.

Simple Present	I *eat* a lot of fruit.
Simple Past	I *ate* some melon for lunch today.
Simple Future	I *am going to eat* some cherries as a snack.
	I *will eat* them after school.

Verbals

Verbals are words made from verbs. There are three kinds of verbals: participles, gerunds, and infinitives.

A participle is a verb form that is used as an adjective. A gerund is a verb form ending in *ing* that is used as a noun. An infinitive is a verb phrase, usually preceded by *to,* that is used as a noun, an adjective, or an adverb. See GERUNDS, INFINITIVES, PARTICIPLES.

The *frightened* cat ran and hid under the porch. (participle)
Getting the dog into the house was my priority. (gerund)
My hope is *to establish* a level of tolerance between Coco and Buster. (infinitive)

Verbs

A verb shows action or state of being. See MOOD, TENSES, VOICE.

Lupe *opened* her mailbox. (action)
She *was* excited to find an e-mail from Carla. (state of being)

Auxiliary Verbs

An auxiliary verb is a verb that combines with a main verb to form a verb phrase. Auxiliary verbs help show voice, mood, and tense. Some common auxiliary verbs are the forms of *be, have,* and *did.* Other auxiliary verbs are *can, could, may, might, should,* and *will.*

Intransitive Verbs

An intransitive verb does not have a receiver of its action. It does not have a direct object.

Danny **relaxed** under the big oak tree.

Some verbs can be transitive or intransitive, depending on their use in the sentence.

Danny **plays** baseball in the summer. (transitive)
He usually **plays** in Gresham Park. (intransitive)

Irregular Verbs

The past and past participle of irregular verbs are not formed by adding -*d* or -*ed*.

Present	Past	Past Participle
sing	sang	sung
write	wrote	written
put	put	put

Linking Verbs

A linking verb joins a subject with a subject complement (a noun, a pronoun, or an adjective). The subject complement renames or describes the subject.

Ms. Roberts **became** a newspaper reporter.
She **feels** proud of her work.
The author of that article **is** she.

Common linking verbs are *be, appear, become, feel, grow, look, remain, seem, smell, sound, stay, taste,* and *turn.* Some of these verbs can be transitive, intransitive, or linking verbs.

He **felt** the heat of the sun on his back. (transitive verb)
She **felt** strongly about winning the game. (intransitive)
Danny **felt** tired after the game. (linking verb)

Modal Auxiliaries

Modal auxiliaries are used to express permission, possibility, ability, necessity, obligation, and intention. They are followed by main verbs that are in the base form. The common modal auxiliaries are *may, might, can, could, must, should, will,* and *would.*

Any amateur chef **may join** the committee. (permission)
We **might assign** dishes at the meeting. (possibility)
Blanca **can bake** delicious cakes. (ability)
Everyone **must agree** on the menu. (necessity)
Cooks **should prepare** enough food for everyone. (obligation)
Marco **will act** as the contact person. (intention)

Phrasal Verbs

Some transitive and intransitive verbs are phrasal verbs. A phrasal verb is a combination of a main verb and a preposition or an adverb. The noun or pronoun that follows a phrasal verb is the direct object.

He **looks after** his little brother on weekends.
Yesterday he **set up** the croquet set.
He **wakes up** with a smile each morning.

Principal Parts

The four basic parts of all verbs are the present, or base form; the past; the past participle; and the present participle. The past and past participles of regular verbs are formed by adding *-d* or *-ed* to the base form. The present participle is formed by adding *-ing.*

Base	Past	Past Participle	Present Participle
sail	sailed	sailed	sailing

Regular Verbs

The past and the past participles of a regular verb are formed by adding *-d* or *-ed* to the base form.

Base	Past	Past Participle
walk	walked	walked
smile	smiled	smiled
try	tried	tried
hop	hopped	hopped

Transitive Verbs

A transitive verb expresses an action that passes from a doer to a receiver. Every transitive verb has a receiver of the action. That receiver is the direct object.

Sheila **kicked** the ball into the net.

Voice

Voice shows whether the subject of a transitive verb is the doer or the receiver of the action.

Active Voice

When a transitive verb is in the active voice, the subject is the doer of the action.

Sheila **kicked** the winning goal.

Passive Voice

When a transitive verb is in the passive voice, the subject is the receiver of the action. A verb in the passive voice is formed by combining some form of *be* with the past participle of the main verb.

The winning goal **was kicked** by Sheila.

Mechanics

Capitalization and Punctuation

Apostrophes

An apostrophe is used to show possession.

the man's coat   the boys' jackets

An apostrophe is used to show the omission of letters or numbers.

can't   we'll   the flood of '98

An apostrophe is used to show the plural of lowercase letters but not of capital letters unless the plural could be mistaken for a word.

a's   *u*'s   *P*s   *U*'s   *A*'s

Capital Letters

A capital letter is used for the first word in a sentence, the first word in a direct quotation, and the first word of most lines of poetry and songs.

My dad asked, "**W**ould you like to take a trip?"

My country, 'tis of thee,
Sweet land of liberty.

A capital letter is used for proper nouns and proper adjectives.

Abraham **L**incoln   the **G**ettysburg **A**ddress
the **L**incoln **M**emorial   **W**ashington, **D.C**.
American hero   **K**entucky rail-splitter

A capital letter is used for a title when it precedes a person's name.

President Lincoln

A capital letter is used for the directions *North, South, East,* and *West* when they refer to sections of the country.

We left the **S**outh and drove north toward home.

A capital letter is used for the names of deities and sacred books.

Holy **S**pirit   **B**ible   **K**oran   **O**ld **T**estament

A capital letter is used for the principal words in titles (but not the articles *a, an,* or *the;* coordinating conjunctions; or prepositions unless they are the first or last words).

To **K**ill a **M**ockingbird   "**T**he **W**illow and the **G**ingko"

Capital letters are used for abbreviations of words that are capitalized.

Mrs.   **D**r.   **J**an.   **A**ve.

Colons

A colon is used before a list when terms such as *the following* or *as follows* are used.

I'd like to visit the following cities: New Orleans, San Francisco, and Chicago.

A colon is used after the salutation of a business letter.

Dear Senator Smith:

Commas

Commas are used to separate words in a series of three or more.

My family has two dogs, a cat, and some fish.

Commas are used to separate adjectives of equal importance before a noun.

It's a little, white, fluffy kitten.

Commas are used to set off the parts of addresses, place names, and dates.

Abraham Lincoln was born on February 12, 1809, in Hardin County, Kentucky.

Commas are used to set off words in direct address and parenthetical expressions.

Did you know, Eleanor, that the ship really sank?
Titanic was, as you may know, a popular movie.

Commas are used to set off nonrestrictive phrases and clauses.

The *Titanic*, a famous ocean liner, hit an iceberg.
The ship, which everyone had thought was unsinkable, disappeared under the icy waters.

Commas are used to set off a direct quotation or the parts of a divided quotation.

"I hope," said Mrs. Litwac, "you have all finished your work."

A comma is used before a coordinating conjunction that is used to connect clauses in a sentence.

I read the directions, but Joey built the model.

A comma is used after a conjunctive adverb in a compound sentence.

I missed a step in the directions; consequently, the model fell down.

Dashes

A dash is used to indicate a sudden change of thought.

My uncle cooked the whole dinner—a surprise to us all.

A dash (or dashes) is used to set off a series of words, phrases, or clauses in apposition.

The dinner—chicken, greens, and mashed potatoes—was delicious.

Exclamation Points

An exclamation point is used after most interjections and to end an exclamatory sentence.

Help! The rope is breaking!
Wow, that was close!

Hyphens

A hyphen is used to divide words between syllables at the end of a line.

The intense winds from the hurricane horrified the inhabi-
	tants of the fishing village.

A hyphen is used in numbers from twenty-one to ninety-nine and to separate parts of some compound words.

drive-in	mother-in-law

A hyphen is used to form some temporary adjectives.

He completed the three-year project.

Italics

Italics are used to set off the titles of books, magazines, newspapers, movies, television series, ships, and works of art. If you are handwriting, use underlining for italics.

> I saw a picture of the ***Titanic*** in the ***Atlantic Monthly***.

Periods

A period is used to end a declarative or an imperative sentence.

> The dog is hungry. Please feed it.

A period is used after an abbreviation and after the initials in a name.

> Co.   Mrs.   mi.   R. L. Stevenson

Question Marks

A question mark is used to end an interrogative sentence.

> What do you feed your dog?

Quotation Marks

Quotation marks are used before and after direct quotations and around the parts of a divided quotation.

> "Why," asked my brother, "didn't you play the game?"

Quotation marks are used to set off the titles of stories, poems, songs, magazine and newspaper articles, television shows, and radio programs.

> They sang "Deep River" and "Amazing Grace."

Single quotation marks are used to set off quoted material within a quotation.

> "Did they sing 'America the Beautiful'?" Salma asked.

Semicolons

A semicolon is used to separate clauses in a compound sentence when they are not joined by a conjunction.

> It rained all afternoon; the game was cancelled.

A semicolon is used to separate clauses in a compound sentence that are connected by a conjunctive adverb.

> The water washed out the flowerbeds; furthermore, it flooded the basement.

Semicolons are used to separate phrases or clauses of the same type that include internal punctuation.

> There were also floods on July 8, 2001; October 22, 2003; and August 15, 2005.

A semicolon is used before expressions such as *for example* and *namely* when they are used to introduce examples.

> Many streets were under water; namely, Morris, Elm, Cornelia, and State.

Index

Acknowledgments

Literature

Excerpt from *Under the Royal Palms* by Alma Flor Ada. Text copyright © 1988 Alma Flor Ada. Reprinted with the permission of Atheneum Books for Young Readers, an imprint of Simon & Schuster Children's Publishing Division.

Excerpt from "Creating Resilient Habitats: Native Fish Recovery in a Time of Climate Change" by Mike Bader and Jack Tuholske. Copyright © 2008 Sierra Club. All rights reserved. www.sierraclub.org

Excerpt and cover from *The Daring Book for Girls* by Andrea J. Buchanan and Miriam Peskowitz. Copyright © 2007 by Andrea J. Buchanan and Miriam Peskowitz. Reprinted by permission of HarperCollins Publishers.

Excerpt from *Smoky Night* by Eve Bunting. Text copyright © 1994 by Eve Bunting. Reprinted by permission of Houghton Mifflin Harcourt Publishing Company.

Excerpt from *Dinosaur Detectives* by Peter Chrisp. Copyright © 2001 Dorling Kindersley Limited. Published in the United States by DK Publishers, Inc. All rights reserved.

Excerpt from "Gorilla Copycats" by Elizabeth Deffner. *National Geographic Kids.* November 2008: 26. Copyright © 2008 National Geographic Society. Used by permission.

Excerpt and cover image from *The Lion, the Witch and the Wardrobe* by C.S. Lewis. Copyright © 1950 by C.S. Lewis Pte. Ltd. Copyright renewed © 1978 by C.S. Lewis Pte. Ltd. Cover art by Pauline Baynes. Reprinted by permission of HarperCollins Publishers.

"Meeting Becca" provided by Teaching That Makes Sense. Copyright 1995-2008 by Teaching That Makes Sense, Inc. Used by permission. For more information, visit www.ttms.org.

Merriam-Webster Online copyright © 2008 by Merriam-Webster, Inc. Used by permission. www.merriam-webster.com

Excerpt from *How to Write a Letter* by Florence D. Mischel. Copyright © 1957, 1988 by Franklin Watts, Inc. All rights reserved.

Excerpt from "Pediatric Private Practice after Hurricane Katrina: Proposal for Recovery" by Scott Needle. Copyright © 2008 by the American Academy of Pediatrics. All rights reserved. www.pediatrics.org

Excerpts and cover from *The Land I Lost: Adventures of a Boy in Vietnam* by Huynh Quang Nhuong. Text copyright © 1982 by Huynh Quang Nhuong. Cover art copyright © 1982 by Vo-Dinh Mai. Used by permission of HarperCollins Publishers.

Review of *Because of Winn-Dixie* comes from Kirkus Reviews. Used by permission. www.kirkusreviews.com

Review of *Owl Moon* used by permission of Through the Looking Glass Children's Book Review. Marya Jansen-Gruber, editor. www .lookingglassreview.com

Review of *Palace of Mirrors* used by permission of *Chicago Parent.* December 2008: 63. Copyright © 2008 Wednesday Journal, Inc. All rights reserved.

Excerpt from "Dig In" from *Busy in the Garden* by George W.B. Shannon. Copyright © 2006 by HarperCollins Publishers. Used by permission of HarperCollins Publishers.

Excerpt and cover from *The Reptile Room* by Lemony Snicket. Text copyright © 1999 by Lemony Snicket. Illustrations copyright © 1999 by Brett Helquist. Published by HarperCollins Publishers.

Excerpt from *The Red Pony* by John Steinbeck, copyright 1933, 1937, 1938, renewed 1961, 1965, 1966 by John Steinbeck. Used by permission of Viking Penguin, a division of Penguin Group (USA) Inc.

"A talented sculptor I know" copyright © Joe Thompson. For more information, see www.imaginesongs.com.

Excerpt from *Janice VanCleave's 201 Awesome, Magical, Bizarre & Incredible Experiments* by Janice VanCleave. Copyright © 1994 by John Wiley & Sons, Inc. Reproduced with permission of John Wiley & Sons, Inc.

Excerpt from "Television Can Teach: Elements of Effective Educational Television" by Deborah K. Wainwright. Copyright © 2006. The Annenberg School for Communication, University of Pennsylvania. www.asc.upenn.edu

All other excerpts come from public-domain sources, including Project Gutenberg.

Loyola Press has made every effort to locate the copyright holders for the cited works used in this publication and to make full acknowledgment for their use. In the case of any omissions, the publisher will be pleased to make suitable acknowledgments in future editions.

Art and Photography

When there is more than one picture on a page, credits are supplied in sequence, left to right, top to bottom. Page positions are abbreviated as follows: **(t)** top, **(c)** center, **(b)** bottom, **(l)** left, **(r)** right.

Photos and illustrations not acknowledged are either owned by Loyola Press or from royalty-free sources including but not limited to Alamy, Art Resource, Big Stock, Bridgeman, Corbis/ Veer, Dreamstime, Fotosearch, Getty Images, Northwind Images, Photoedit, Smithsonian, Wikipedia. Loyola Press has made every effort to locate the copyright holders for the cited works used in this publication and to make full acknowledgment for their use. In the case of any omissions, the Publisher will be pleased to make suitable acknowledgments in future editions.

iStockphoto, Frontmatter: iii, v, vi, vii, vi **Section 1:** 4, 5, 6, 8 **Section 2:** 23, 30 **Section 3:** 34, 35, 46, 51, 56 **Section 4:** 61, 63, 64, 66, 68, 71, 73, 74, 75, 76, 77, 79 **Section 5:** 86, 89, 90, 91, 92, 93, 103, 104, 105 **Section 6:** 112, 114, 115, 116, 119, 122 **Section 7:** 124, 125, 127, 128, 129, 133, 135, 138 **Section 8:** 145, 153, 153, 156, 157 **Section 9:** 168, 171, 174, 175, 176 **Section 10:** 183, 184 **Section 11:** 197, 206, 215 **Chapter 1:** 222, 223, 232, 235, 238, 241, 246, 248, 253, 255, 259 **Chapter 2:** 260, 268, 274, 276, 277, 279, 281, 285, 287, 289, 290, 298 **Chapter 3:** 299, 303, 305, 307, 308, 309, 311, 312, 314, 317, 319, 320, 324, 325, 327, 329 **Chapter 4:** 336, 337, 338, 339, 342, 343, 348, 350, 351, 352, 354, 356, 358, 362, 363, 364, 365, 366, 367, 368, 371 **Chapter 5:** 374, 376, 377, 380, 384, 385, 386, 388, 389, 390, 391, 392, 393, 395, 396, 397, 401, 403, 405, 407, 411 **Chapter 6:** 412, 418, 420, 421, 422, 424 **Chapter 7:** 451, 452, 453, 454, 455, 462, 465, 468, 470, 471, 476, 477, 479, 487 **Chapter 8:** 494, 498, 501, 504, 505, 509

Jupiterimages Unlimited, Frontmatter: v, vi, vii, viii Section 1: 6, 8, 16 Section 2: 22, 27 Section 3: 36, 44, 48, 56 Section 4: 68, 72, 75 Section 5: 87, 88, 100, 102 Section 6: 110, 116, 118 Section 7: 124, 130, 133 Section 8: 143, 148, 149, 150, 151, 152, 155, 158 Section 9: 166, 167, 173, 177 Section 10: 182, 185, 188, 189, 190 Section 11: 196, 197, 202, 204, 206, 207, 209, 210, 215, 216, 218–219, 220 Chapter 1: 222, 223, 225, 230, 253 Chapter 2: 260, 264, 272, 279, 288, 298 Chapter 3: 304, 308, 317, 318, 323, 329 Chapter 4: 336, 337, 338, 349, 352, 353, 357, 359 Chapter 5: 374, 375, 381, 384, 385, 387, 398, 402 Chapter 6: 412, 413, 414, 417, 419, 422, 425, 426, 427, 428, 429, 430, 432, 434, 435, 437 Chapter 7: 451, 456, 461, 463, 465, 466, 470, 471, 472, 473, 474, 475, 477, 478, 481 Chapter 8: 488, 489, 491, 494, 496, 488–489, 500, 503, 506, 509, 510, 511, 515, 516, 519

Frontmatter: iv Clockwise from upper left (a) Mary Evans Picture Library/Alamy. (b) ilian car/Alamy. (c) Stock. (d) E.O Hoppé/Corbis. (e) Getty Images. (f) Big Stock. vi Clockwise from upper left (a) iStockphoto. (b) Stock. (c) Jupiterimages Unlimited. (d) Fotosearch. (e) iStockphoto. (f) Steven May/Alamy. viii (br) Phil Martin Photography. viii (bl) Lawrence Lucier/Getty Images.

Section 1: 9 Phil Martin Photography. 11(t) Pictorial Press Ltd/Alamy. 11(b) Neal Preston/Corbis. 13 Jason Lindsey/Alamy.

Section 2: 19 Alaska Stock LLC/Alamy. 20 Dorling Kindersley/Getty Images. 30(c) Buddy Mays/Corbis.

Section 3: 33(t) Wallace Kirkland/Getty Images. 33(b) Philip Gendreau/Corbis. 34(t) ilian car/Alamy. 37 The Bridgeman Art Library/Getty Images. 41 Feng Yu/Alamy. 43 Kay & Karl Ammann/© Bruce Coleman Inc./Alamy. 45(t) Time Life/Getty Images. 50(t) Bettmann/Corbis.

Section 4: 59 Popperfoto/Getty Images. 61(b) Reuters/Corbis. 69 © V&A Images/Alamy. 70 Stuart O'Sullivan/Getty Images. 72(b) Dorling Kindersley/Getty Images. 76(b) Phil Martin Photography.

Section 5: 85 E.O. Hoppé/Corbis. 89 Victor Watts/Alamy. 91(t) Paris Pierce/Alamy. 94 North Wind Picture Archives. 95(t) Chartres Cathedral, Chartres, France/Giraudon/The Bridgeman Art Library. 95(b) Elevation of Sainte-Chapelle, Paris (w/c on paper) by French School (20th century) Archives Larousse, Paris, France/Giraudon/The Bridgeman Art Library. 96 Mary Evans Picture Library/Alamy. 97(t) American Press Association/Corbis. 99 Walker Art Gallery, National Museums Liverpool/The Bridgeman Art Library.

Section 6: 110(t) Lewis Wickes Hine/Corbis. 111 Image Source Pink/Alamy. 116(t) Time & Life Pictures/Getty Images.

Section 7: 125(t) Smithsonian American Art Museum, Washington, DC/Art Resource, NY. 130(b) C. Wilhelm/Getty Images. 131 Wilhelm, C. (1858–1925)/Victoria & Albert Museum, London, UK/The Bridgeman Art Library. 132 Bettmann/Corbis. 133(t) North Wind Picture Archives/Alamy. 133(c) Mary Evans Picture Library/Alamy. 134 Pat & Chuck Blackley/Alamy.

Section 8: 140 Jerry Cooke/Corbis. 146 The Print Collector/Alamy. 147 Benque, Franz (Francisco) (1841–1921)/Archives Larousse, Paris, France/Giraudon/The Bridgeman Art Library. 149(b) James Balog/Getty Images. 152 North Wind Picture Archives. 154 Steve Schapiro/Corbis. 155(t) David J. & Janice L. Frent Collection/Corbis. 159 amandabike/Alamy. 160 Sandro Vannini/Corbis. 161(t) Bettmann/Corbis. 161(b) Look and Learn/The Bridgeman Art Library.

Section 9: 170 dmac/Alamy. 172 North Wind Picture Archives/Alamy. 177(b) Phil Martin Photography. 180 Lake County Museum/Corbis.

Section 10: 183(b) Michael Ochs Archives/Getty Images. 185(b) Jeff Greenberg/Alamy. 186 Bettmann/Corbis. 187 PoodlesRock/Corbis. Section 11: 199(t) CinemaPhoto/Corbis. 199(b) Bettmann/Corbis. 205 Look and Learn/The Bridgeman Art Library. 210(bl) Chuck Place/Alamy. 211 Pictorial Press Ltd/Alamy. 214 Underwood & Underwood/Corbis.

Chapter 1: 223(cr) Steve Gorton/Getty Images. 226 Jack Maguire/Alamy. 234 2004 Getty Images. 245 Phil Martin Photography. 248(br) Phil Martin Photography. 251 Phil Martin Photography. 259(br) Phil Martin Photography.

Chapter 2: 263 Don Smetzer/Getty Images. 265 North River/Alamy. 266 Paul Bricknell/dk Images. 270 Hulton Archive/Getty Images. 284 Erik Dreyer. 287(br) Phil Martin Photography. 291 Phil Martin Photography. 297 Phil Martin Photography.

Chapter 3: 299(cr) Phil Martin Photography. 299(br) Jan Cobb Photography Ltd/Getty Images. 300 Patrick Molnar/Getty Images. 303(t) Steven May/Alamy. 311(t) Hulton Archive/2007 Getty Images. 313 Hulton Archive/2003 Getty Images. 316 Hulton Archive/Getty Images. 318(bl) Phil Martin Photography. 319(t) Bruce Laurance. 322 Phil Martin Photography. 327(b) Copyright © Billy E. Barnes/PhotoEdit.

Chapter 4: 336(bl) Phil Martin Photography. 340 Juniors Bildarchiv/Alamy. 345(bl) Thomas Schweizer/Getty Images. 352(t) Cynthia Hart Designer/Corbis. 356(b) Mary Evans Picture Library/Alamy. 360(bl) Phil Martin Photography. 362(bl) Phil Martin Photography. 363(bl) Phil Martin Photography. 365(b) Phil Martin Photography. 369(b) Phil Martin Photography. 373(br) Phil Martin Photography.

Chapter 5: 375(c) Kathryn Seckman Kirsch. 382(b) Getty Images/Andres Hernandez. 388 Pictorial Press Ltd/Alamy. 389(bl) Mark Bolton Photography/Alamy. 392(t) Mary Evans Picture Library/Alamy. 394 Mary Evans Picture Library/Alamy. 401(b) Phil Martin Photography. 404 Phil Martin Photography. 411(br) Phil Martin Photography.

Chapter 6: 415 Blue Lantern Studio/Corbis. 430(t) Hulton-Deutsch Collection/Corbis. 431 Steve Gorton and Karl Shone/Getty Images. 433(t) Frances Broomfield/Portal Gallery, London/The Bridgeman Art Library. 440 Blue Lantern Studio/Corbis.

Chapter 7: 451(cr) NASA/Handout/CNP/Corbis. 456(bl) Bettmann/Corbis. 458(bl) Medical-on-Line/Alamy. 460 PoodlesRock/Corbis. 463(b) Bettmann/Corbis. 464 Pictorial Press Ltd/Alamy. 467 Blaine Harrington III/Alamy. 469 Tony Duffy/Getty Images. 481(t) Mary Evans Picture Library/Alamy. 483(bl) Mary Evans Picture Library/Alamy. 487(t) Sue Flood/Getty Images.

Chapter 8: 488(cl) INTERFOTO Pressebildagentur/Alamy. 488(br) Lawrence Lucier/Getty Images. 492(t) JoeTomelleri. 493 North Wind Picture Archives/Alamy. 497(t) Look and Learn/The Bridgeman Art Library. 497(c) For Wikipedia and Mamoon Mengal. 497(b) Borromeo/Art Resource, NY. 499(t) Gary Ombler/Getty Images. 506(bl) Popperfoto/Getty Images. 512 Dea Picture Library. 517 North Wind Picture Archives/Alamy. 519(br) Phil Martin Photography. 523 North Wind Picture Archives. 524 North Wind Picture Archives/Alamy.

Common Proofreading Marks

Use these proofreading marks to mark changes when you proofread.
Remember to use a colored pencil to make your changes.

Symbol	Meaning	Example
¶	begin new paragraph	over. ¶Begin a new
⌒	close up space	close u p space
∧	insert	students think *should*
℘	delete, omit	that the the book
/	make lowercase	Mathematics
∽	reverse letters	revesre letters
≡	capitalize	washington
⌄ ⌄	add quotation marks	I am, I said.
⊙	add period	Marta drank tea